Muslim-Christian Relations
and Inter-Christian Rivalries
in the Middle East

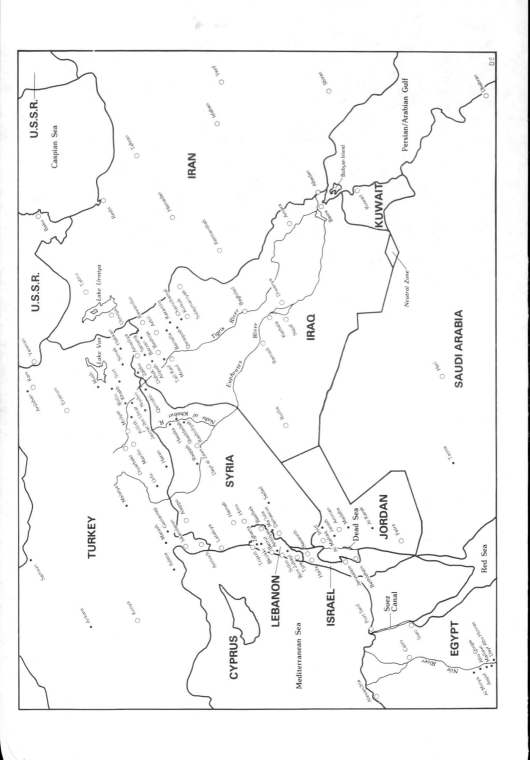

Muslim-Christian Relations and Inter-Christian Rivalries in the Middle East

THE CASE OF THE JACOBITES IN AN AGE OF TRANSITION

John Joseph

FRANKLIN AND MARSHALL COLLEGE

State University of New York Press   ALBANY

Published by
State University of New York Press, Albany

© 1983 State University of New York

Printed in the United States of America

For information, address State University of New York
Press, State University Plaza, Albany, N.Y. 12246

Library of Congress Cataloging in Publication Data

Joseph, John.
  Muslim-Christian Relations and inter-Christian
rivalries in the Middle East.

  Bibliography
  Includes index.
  1. Jacobites (Syrian Christians) I. Title.
DS59.J25J67   281'.63'0956   82-870
ISBN 0-87395-611-7   AACR2
ISBN 0-87395-612-5 (pbk.)

82-870
AACR2

10 9 8 7 6 5 4 3 2

To Betty, so genuine

Summary of Contents

Contents

Middle Eastern Christianity—Eastern Christians not united—Greek Orthodoxy versus Syrian Orthodoxy.

Christological controversies in brief—Edessa, Antioch, Alexandria, and Constantinople—Monophysites of Egypt and Syria—some Arab tribes Monophysite.

The "Jacobites"—patriarchs of Antioch—Antioch Christianity Jewish-flavored—decline of Antioch after Arab conquest.

Muslim rule assures Middle-Eastern Christians' survival—"heretical' Christians favored—Jacobite patriarch influential leader in Syria—Jacobites intellectually active—church leadership corrupted by power—Christians learn to endure discrimination.

Crusaders' legacy of mistrust—Michael the Syrian on Crusades—Armenians and Maronites and Crusaders—Mongol invasions and native Christians—Muslims alienated—Jacobites seek security in northern Iraq and south-central Anatolia.

Ṭur 'Abdin Jacobite stronghold—Syriac preserved as mother toṅgue—Mardin their capital city—Dayr Za'farān seat of

Trade routes threatened—"Russian agents and Jacobites"—British
military consuls—Islam disparaged—Muslims excluded from
Western reforms and benefits.

Kurds feel threatened—trade declines—commercial routes
diverted—famine leads to violence—Kurdish-Turkish alliance
formed.

Armenian massacres—attacks on Jacobite villages—Mardin a
"Noah's ark"—relative safety of Syrian Orthodox—conflicting accounts.

A brief honeymoon—prelude to World War I—Turkish
defeats—Armenian atrocities—"The flood that carried
everything."

Post-World-War-I period—Turkey dismembered, strikes back—all
Christians granted "permission" to leave country—Jacobite
delegation at Paris Peace Conference—Jacobites victims of suppression, deportation of Kurds—many stay in ancestral
strongholds.

Jacobites settle in Syria, strike roots in Jazirah—tensions and progress—normalization after independence—Damascus becomes
seat of Jacobite Patriarch (1957).

Lebanon and Jacobites—historical connections with
Maronites—Beirut seat of Syrian Catholic patriarch—patriarch
made cardinal of Roman church—civil war of 1970s and interfaith relations—Jacobites' uneasy neutrality.

Iraqi Christian population increases after World War I—Jacobites
Arabized, adjust politically, culturally—Iraq helps minorities
with no political ambitions—Jacobites, Kurdish neighbors, find
northern Iraq uncomfortable—Iraq accommodates Syriac-
speaking minorities under Ba'th.

Jacobite historic presence in Jerusalem and Holy Land—early status
under Mamluks and Ottomans—their niche at Church of Holy
Sepulchre—monastery of St. Mark—population of Jerusalem,
Bethlehem increased after World War I—establishment of Israel
and the Jacobites.

Middle Eastern Christians feel imperiled by tide of events: warfare in
Lebanon, antagonism toward West, rise in fundamentalist-
sectarian movements—post-World-War-I developments arouse
Arab, Muslim suspicion—Christian-Muslim cooperation increases as horrors of war recede into memory—Christians' new
image of themselves—try to achieve mutual understanding be-

tween Islam and the West—Arab grievances against West.
Palestinian problem symbolizes Arab powerlessness—helps pull two faiths apart—religion, idiom of political expression, used to express dissatisfaction with West—youth and educated classes join movement—shah's narrow base of support leads governments to join hands with "the people."
Position of ethnic and religious minorities untenable when state emphasizes religion—situation leads to tension, crisis of identity—emigration or coexistence two valid alternatives—oil wealth, free education, gainful employment entice many to adapt—others seek opportunities in Western lands that will accept them.

Preface

The purpose of this study is to write a modern history of the Syrian Orthodox (Jacobite) and Syrian Catholic (formerly Jacobite) Christians of the Middle East, using them as a case study in Christian—Muslim relations and inter-Christian rivalries in modern times. The study concentrates on developments since the early 1800s—earlier in the case of the Syrian Catholics—when the Eastern Christians emerged from their isolation of centuries, while the Islamic society around them was itself significantly affected by Western influences. The period covered is an important transitional one in the history of the Middle East, marked by the rise of movements and processes that have channelled Christian-Muslim relations in new directions, posing new questions for the indigenous Christians of the area.

Nestorians and Jacobites are well known in the West to students of Islamic and Christian history. In the case of Christianity, Rome and Constantinople viewed them as heretics, a subject that has generated a great deal of polemic writing. In Islam, Nestorians and Jacobites, representatives of Semitic-Syriac Christianity, flourished under the early caliphs; as their most loyal and learned subjects, these Christians introduced the Arabs to the mysteries of Greek science and learning and had a major role in guiding them to the greatness of medieval Islamic civilization. As a student of Middle Eastern history, I have used the terms Nestorian and Jacobite only because of their familiarity and the just fame that surrounds them. Certainly, no theological connotation is to be read into my usage.

After finishing my work on the Nestorians, I cherished the thought of writing a parallel volume on the Jacobites, whose post medieval history was even more neglected than that of the Nestorians. Since the eighteenth century, scholars have lamented this neglect, which, one suspects, stems generally from the political unimportance of Christian minorities. What has been written on the Syrian Orthodox in modern times continues to emphasize their past history, theology, and liturgy; the attention paid to their social and political conditions and to their relations with others has been insignificant.

A probable reason for overlooking this history is the scarcity of source material on the subject. Centuries of neglect meant a paucity of primary and, consequently, of scholarly secondary sources. The indigenous sources, the most important for a historical account, are scant and scattered. Most of the manuscripts that have come to us are of a religious nature, such as psalters and hymns, or, if "histories," the lives of saints and martyrs expounding their legends and miracles. Most of the historical records have perished by fire and pillage, inspired by fanaticism, Christian as well as Muslim. A Jacobite historian speaks of Kurds making moccasins out of the manuscripts written on gazelle skin; a European scholar notes the eagerness with which the Syrian Catholics (formerly Jacobite) and Chaldean Catholics (formerly Nestorian) have obliterated the memory of their "heterodoxy" by effacing all that they associated with their mother churches.

In my travels and researches in the Middle East, I found valuable secondary sources by Jacobite and Syrian Catholic writers, rare and out-of-print books and pamphlets, some of them eye-witness accounts by men with an intimate knowledge of their people's recent history. A few of these works, such as those by Ishāq Armalah, were based on extensive readings of works destroyed during World War I. My most important indigenous sources were the oral traditions and impressions received from the observations, daily contacts, and conversations that I had with both the ordinary and knowledgeable people whose history I was seeking to understand and record.

In American and European libraries and archives, however, I found most of my source material. Indeed, it would be practically impossible to write a history of any Middle Eastern Christian community, especially the history of the early modern period, without the writings of Westerners—travellers, government officials, members of the various religious orders, or, since the nineteenth century, American Protestant missionaries. But, as some Western writers themselves realized, many European or American writers were too callous, prejudiced, or ill informed to be of much value as witnesses. Nevertheless, there is a mass of material available there, on a great variety of topics. Many Catholic friars, Protestant preachers, and consular agents investigated the conditions of their region intelligently; they became well acquainted with the policies and practices of the government and with the laws of the land. Some stayed in one place long enough to develop an intimate knowledge of the people and their language. Many were articulate men who recorded their observations with accuracy and sound judgement. Without the invaluable depository of information that they have left us in the form of journals, letters, chronicles, and diaries, there would be periods of history of which we would be totally ignorant.

Thanks to a large number of persons and institutions whose generosity and cooperation I shall acknowledge elsewhere, I have had the time and opportunity to draw on a wide variety of this source material. But, treading on such virgin territory, I can claim only a beginning. There is no comprehensive material on the modern history of Christians in "Asiatic Turkey"; a comprehensive and accurate account of that history cannot yet be written. Many years of work and more source material are needed, from the uncollected, untranslated archives of Moscow, Rome, Istanbul, and Cairo. More data are needed; social scientists in the various disciplines have to tell us more about the character of the Middle Eastern society during the early modern period, its resources, stability, stratification, economy, and composition.

Writing on the Christians of the Muslim world, one becomes painfully aware of the complexities of the subject. How is one, for instance, to evaluate the condition of the Christian peasant in nineteenth century Muslim Turkey when the life of the peasant in Christian Ireland or Poland is just as heart-rending? What if some of the sources observe that the peasant of Gladstone's England was not as well fed, housed, or clothed as the peasant of Ottoman Bulgaria? Why, one wonders, was the good name of Christianity not tarnished in the West—as Islam's was—by the violent struggles of the Christian sects against each other, or by the religious wars of Europe, stained as they are by frequent massacres. And why the epithet "the terrible English" was not applied to the people of England, whose settlers in Tasmania engaged in a continuous massacre until they had exterminated the entire native population? In his excellent study of the Orthodox Patriarchate of Constantinople, *The Great Church in Captivity,* Sir Steven Runciman writes that we shall get nowhere if we denounce the Greeks as deceitful or the Turks as savage. Erudition, he wisely notes, will not produce understanding unless it is tempered with tolerance and freed from prejudice, no matter what the historian's personal tastes and sympathies. When a study involves, as my work does, Turks and Armenians, Jews and Arabs, Maronites and Muslims, Syrian Orthodox and Kurds, as well as Catholics and Protestants, the fair-mindedness of historians is subjected to the supreme test. We soon realize that we are working within the glass house of history, often tempted to throw stones, especially if we let ourselves be persuaded by partisan "documents" and "original sources." Fair-mindedness and thorough investigation finally convince us not to shatter our shelters of glass.

In recent times, especially, historians have learned from sociologists and psychologists, as well as from the members of our own discipline, that no race or religion has monopoly on violence or on compassion. We have found that it is always the members of "their" group who are the unbelievers, the gāvur (Kafir), the barbarians, and the uncircumcized; "our" group is made up of the faithful, the chosen, and the true believers. We know that conflicts arise whenever the terrritory inhabited by one ethnic group is conquered by the members of another group or the followers of another religion, especially when that religion is monotheistic, immediately identifying a person as either one of the faithful or not. The conquered people become a defined community, relegated to an inferior status unless they join the "true" faith of the conqueror. Because it possesses power, the dominating group becomes socially and economically superior and gradually develops notions of moral and intellectual superiority. Its members have all the opportunities for social and cultural development that are denied to those who have suffered defeat. Thus the former natives become aliens in their own homeland, their rights of residence, property, and legal redress restricted, because rights belong only to the in group and are extended only partially, if at all, to the outsider. The insiders and outsiders may be Christians and Muslims, Catholics and Protestants, Shiites and Sunnites, bedouins and city dwellers, tribe A and tribe B. And this tribalism is still with us, everywhere. Outside Europe and America, "most of the people of the world," writes Edward C. Banfield, "live and die without ever achieving membership in a community larger than the family or tribe."

My method of approach, guided by the above observations and hypotheses, may be best described as a combination of significant narrative and interpretation, an account of those forces and events that have helped shape the modern history of the Jacobites and intercommunal relations in their part of the world. As a historian, my investigations of the past have been guided, as were those of Benedetto Croce, by an interest in the present. I have selected those events and facts from the past that can and must answer to the interests of the present. This is an approach especially suited to the history of the Middle East, whose society, institutions, and way of life still have deep roots in the past and to a large extent have sanction in it. In the preparation of this work, therefore, I have gone beyond the goal of producing a monograph for a small circle of specialists, students of "Oriental Churches," and occasionally have not been reticent about making generalizations which, it is my belief, are nevertheless supported by the sources and data used.

John Joseph

Lancaster, Pennsylvania

Acknowledgments

The preparation of this monograph has been made possible by two major grants. A stipend from the Joint Committee on the Middle East of the Social Science Research Council and the American Council of Learned Societies made possible travel and research in Europe and the Middle East in 1966-67. A fellowship from the National Endowment for the Humanities enabled me to devote the year 1979 to the writing of this work. None of these donors, of course, are responsible for the opinions expressed herein; neither do their generous grants mean an endorsement of the positions that I have taken.

Franklin & Marshall College made available freed time through sabbatical leaves, and the college's Faculty Committee on Grants has generously helped my travels and research both here and abroad during the past few years.

This work could not have been written without the cooperation of scores of generous and dedicated people—librarians and archivists, scholars and laymen, Patriarchs and monks, Christians and Muslims—whose help I have sought and received. In my bibliography and notes I have acknowledged my debts to these institutions and people by name and they need not be repeated here, with one exception: to the monks of the Syrian Catholic monastery at al-Sharfah, I owe some of my most cherished memories. Not only did these friars open their library and archives for my use, but they also offered all they could, including their excellent local wine, good food at the seminary refectory, and even a bed for an after-meal nap, the only gracious offer that I could resist.

Among the many others who have kindly helped me, I am indebted to my colleague Dr. Robert J. Barnett, Jr., for the translation from Italian of the document that appears in Appendix A. My friend Roger Olden has aided in the translation of difficult passages in German. The Reverend Father John P. Meno, Archdiocesan General Secretary and Pastor of St. Mark's Syrian Orthodox Cathedral in Hackensack, New Jersey, has been graciously helpful whenever I have needed him. Professor Richard G. Hovannisian of the University of California at Los Angeles has kindly commented on the chapter "Russia, Rebellion, and Refuge." Professor John B. Payne of the Lancaster Theological Seminary, my colleagues Louis L. Athey, Solomon Wank, Sue Ellen Holbrook, and Norman W. Taylor, and my friend Dr. Muhammad K. Hamid of Millersville State College, have read parts of the manuscript. Through their suggestions and comments each one of these good people has helped enhance the quality of this work, whose imperfections remain, of course, wholly my own. Mrs. Linda Kissinger and Mrs. Betty M. Baker have been patient as well as efficient typists.

My wife Betty and daughter Deena have been a constant help through their love as well as their work: their many hours proofreading, and Deena's reading aloud made the work on the manuscript much less onerous.

1

The Background

1

Since the sixteenth century the Christian world has been divided into four major groups: Roman Catholic, Greek Orthodox, Protestant, and Middle Eastern. The sole tie that these divisions have in common is their belief, variously interpreted, in the divinity of Jesus Christ. They are independant of each other in their hierarchy, and theologically they disagree on a number of issues. Whereas the Protestants broke away from the Roman Catholic church during the sixteenth century, the Middle Eastern Christians had freed themselves from a church dominated by the Greeks and Romans over a thousand years earlier. The Greeks and Latins themselves finally parted ways in the eleventh century: the former, with Constantinople (Istanbul) as their base, spread Greek Orthodox Christianity in the Balkans and Russia,[1] while the Latins, with Rome as their See, spread their form of Christianity in, and dominated the religious life of, Central and Western Europe until the Protestant revolt challenged their supremacy there.

The Middle Eastern Christians, like the other groups, do not represent a united political and theological body; they were and are made up of a number of nationalities and theologies. They were often united in their opposition to the political and religious domination of the Greco-Romans, whose supremacy of almost a thousand years was brought to an end in the seventh century by the Muslim-Arab conquest. The "protesting" Middle Eastern Christians were the Aramaic-speaking natives of Syria and Iraq as well as the Armenians of Asia Minor and the

1

Egyptians and Abyssinians of Northeast Africa.

Not all Middle Eastern Christians "revolted" in the fifth century against the established church, which since the fall of Rome in that same century, and even earlier, was under the control of the Byzantine government of Constantinople. The East Roman Empire, of which the Middle East was a part until the advent of the Arabs, was Greek dominated. "Greek Orthodox" Christianity continued to be the faith of millions of Syrians and to this day their descendants are known as Rūm Orthodox, Rūm being the Arabic term for the Greek-dominated East Roman or Byzantine Empire. The churches of the various nationalities that remained in union with the Church of Constantinople, whether in Slavic Balkans or Arab Syria, were controlled by a Greek hierarchy until the last century. This link between the Greek and Middle Eastern Christians, weakened by the Arab victories, was again strengthened by the Turkish conquest of the Middle East in the sixteenth century. Under the Ottoman Turks, Greek Orthodox and Middle Eastern Christians were once again brought under the same political umbrella after a political separation of over eight hundred years.[2]

The Christians of Syria and Egypt who remained loyal to the Greek Patriarch of Constantinople before and after the Arab-Islamic conquests of the seventh century were called Malkites ("Royalists," also spelled "Melchites")—those who owed their existence to the support of the Byzantine emperor and who accepted a faith that was supported by him.[3] To add to the confusion of terms, "Malkites" today is not applied to the Syrian Christians who are still in communion with the Greek Orthodoxy, but to those of them who broke away from that church to become Catholics, forming since the eighteenth century a church in union with Rome: "Rūm Kathūlīk" (Greek Catholic).[4] The "Greek Orthodox of Syria", originally Malkites, are not to be confused with the "Syrian Orthodox," also known as Jacobites; the latter were among those who revolted against the Greek Orthodox Church, along with the Egyptians (Copts), Abyssinians, and Armenians.

The "Greek Orthodox" of the Middle East, together with their Catholic brethren—the present-day Malkites—were the earliest Christian sects to adopt the Arabic language, which, indeed, was the mother tongue of some of them.[5] Affiliated as they were with the Byzantines, with Greek and not Syriac as the language of their church, these Syrian Christians found the changeover from their vernacular Syriac to Arabic easier; their Arabization seems to have been complete within a century after the Arab conquest, even though isolated Malkite villages near Damascus still use Syriac in daily speech. Among the Syrian Orthodox (Jacobites), and the Nestorians, whose liturgical language has always been Syriac, the changeover would be gradual; in the case of the Nestorians, Syriac to this day is also the mother tongue of the whole community.[6]

The Middle Eastern Christians who broke away from the established church in the fifth century did so on theological grounds, just as the Lutheran revolt did. Political, social, and economic factors, however, lay behind the theological controversies, just as those same factors led to the success of the German reformer. The theological positions that were taken by the Middle Eastern Christians are confused and confusing, and need not long detain us. A brief attempt will be made to present these early doctrinal developments in order to differentiate more clearly one sect from another.

2

The question of the divinity of Jesus, whether he was God incarnate—God become man—gave rise to passionate controversies which often resulted in violence, persecution, and exile. Questions raised about the humanity and divinity of Jesus were debated and settled in church councils convened by the Byzantine emperor. Those who upheld a view that clashed with what was defined as orthodox by the Greeks and Latins were accused of heresy and were treated accordingly.[7] The first ecumenical church council that met to discuss a controversy took place in the fourth century (325) at Nicaea. The church fathers were convoked by the first emperor to become Christian, Constantine. They were to consider what has been called the Arian heresy or Arianism, after the Priest Arius of Alexandria, Egypt. Arius taught that in the Christian Trinity only the Father is true God. He asserted that the Son was a lesser diety not coeternal and equal to the Father ("There was when he (the Son) was not"). The Son was chosen to be divine intermediary in the salvation of the world, but his nature is not of the same substance as the Father in the Trinity. The Council of Nicaea condemned Arianism as blasphemous and maintained that the Son was of the very same substance as the Father.[8]

The second ecumenical church council was convened in Constantinople about sixty years after Nicaea (381); it reaffirmed the Nicene creed and clearly defined the divinity of the Holy Spirit, which some Arian bishops had continued to deny. The second council gave us the creed commonly called "Nicene," accepted by the church of both the East and the West.

It was in the fifth century, fifty years after the previous council, that a theological controversy, this time dealing with the issue of the relation of Christ's humanity to his divinity, led to the first schism between the East and the West. The question being asked, especially by the school of Antioch, revolved around the nature of the union between divine and human in the person of Jesus Christ. As early as the fourth century, Diodorus of Tarsus, head of a monastic establishment close to Antioch, had tried to emphasize the completeness of the human nature of Christ. He had emphasized the distinction between the divine and human natures of Christ to the point of undermining their unity. The most prominent exponent of these controversial views was the Patriarch of Constantinople, Nestorius. Following the teaching of the school of Antioch and the Christological studies started by Diodorus and Theodore of Mopsuestia,[9] Nestorius emphasized the completenesss of the human nature of Jesus. The "Nestorians" were interested in the earthly life of Christ and in his human relations as a model for Christian living. They objected to such phrases as "God dies," "God was born," and the "Mother of God"; they considered these terms blasphemous, confusing creator and creature. They preferred the formula "two natures of Christ after the union," whereas the Alexandria school under Cyril proposed the formula of one nature after the union, since there was no independent humanity after the incarnation.[10]

The Nestorian doctrine was condemned as heretical at the Third Ecumenical Council, convoked at Ephesus in 431. There the Alexandrian position won the day; the adherents of the condemned doctrine, most of them in the Patriarchate of Antioch, were forced to organize their own church. Establishing themselves first in Edessa, a city early evangelized by Christians from Palestine, the Nestorians were driven out of there in 457, forced to move farther east in the direction of northern Iraq and northwestern Persia, where Christianity had penetrated soon after the apostolic age. Alphonso Mingana's researches show that as early as 225 there were more than twenty bishoprics in northern Iraq and in Persia, one of them among the Dailams near the Caspian Sea. The large majority of the "Nestorian" Christians who lived in Sasanian territories were converts from Zoroastrianism and therefore of Persian and not Syrian or Semitic origin. The enmity of Byzantium toward them meant that the Persians trusted them more, whereas previously their doctrines were identified with the Byzantine enemy. They lived in our realm, Shapur Shah is reported to have said, "but share the view of Caesar our enemy."[11]

The Egyptian school of Alexandria emphasized the divinity of Christ at the expense of his humanity, a position which some church historians trace to Eutyches, the superior of a monastery of about three hundred monks near Constantinople, who was an extreme representative of that position. Eutyches had insisted that after the union of the human and the divine, the two natures so blended together in the one person of Christ as to have become one nature, divine. The human nature of Christ, these one-nature advocates taught, was absorbed by the omnipotent nature of God much as a drop of honey is vanished in the ocean, or like wine mixed with water.

The controversy continued and led to the Fourth General Council, convoked by the Emperor Marcian in 451 at Chalcedon, a town in Asia Minor across the straits from Constantinople, in the Church of St. Euphemia. More than six hundred bishops attended the council, the largest of the four ecumenical conferences. The emperor and his empress attended all the sessions, the Empress Pulcheria being given the honor of presiding in the sixth session, at which time the declaration of faith was solemnly proclaimed. The declaration repudiated the doctrines taught by both Nestorius and Eutyches. The Patriarch of Alexandria, Dioscorus, and his Monophysite followers were condemned as heretics. Like his opponent Nestorius before him, Dioscorus died in exile. The declaration of Chalcedon stressed that Christ, in order to be savior of humanity, had to be both man and God; he was "One person in Two Natures; he existed not only as One person resulting from two Natures, " but "in two Natures." The famous definition read that the two natures were unmixed and unchanged, undivided and unseparated, since the distinction of natures is by no means destroyed in the union; the quality of each nature is preserved and both are united in one person and one hypostasis.[12]

The theological disputes that followed the Council of Chalcedon led to uprisings in Egypt and Syria. Unlike the Nestorians, who had emigrated or fled out of the empire to join their coreligionists in Persian territories, the Monophysites remained, a nonconforming sect which became a thorn in the flesh of the Byzantine emperors until the coming of the Arabs, whom the Monophysites supported. The Monophysite quarrel, again unlike the Nestorian controversy, proved to be dangerous to the Byzantine Empire, since many Monophysite adherents in Syria and especially Egypt mixed national and anti-imperial tendencies with their religion. In the patriarchs of Alexandria and Antioch they found champions of their cause.[13]

The Monophysites of Syria and Egypt were so powerful at times that some Byzantine emperors found it politically expedient to side openly with them; it was not easy for an emperor in Constantinople to attack Egypt, a "hotbed of nationalistic monophysitism."[14] Early in the sixth century, Emperor Anastasius, in an effort to strengthen his eastern frontier, began to strengthen the Monophysites as an anti-Persian and anti-Nestorian party. Indeed, Persian partiality toward Nestorians meant that the Monophysites were not welcome there; we read of Monophysite refugees from Persia during the Byzantine-Persian wars, where they were persecuted by the Nestorians.[15] Other Byzantine emperors, in order to appease Rome and to strengthen their frontiers in Europe, took a firm policy against the Monophysites.

Emperor Zeno in the late fifth century tried to heal the divisions within his empire by backing a statement of faith that he hoped would be acceptable to both the supporters and the opponents of the Chalcedonian definition. The statement, published as a religious law, was prepared by the Patriarchs of Constantinople (Acacius) and Alexandria; it cited the first three ecumenical councils and affirmed the consubstantiality of Christ with God and with man. The decree skillfully avoided the Chalcedonian use of the terms "nature" and "persons."[16] Instead of bringing Constantinople close to Alexandria and Antioch, however, the Emperor's decree resulted in the first official estrangement between Rome and Constantinople. The Pope of Rome, Felix II, excommunicated and deposed Acasius for his role in drawing up the "Instrument of Union."[17] This caused a breach between the Roman and Greek churches that lasted thirty-five years, known as the Acacian Schism.

In an effort to heal this schism, Emperor Justin I convoked a synod at Constantinople soon after he assumed power in 518. He had more than fifty bishops with Monophysite tendencies excommunicated. This imperial move ended the Acacian Schism (484-519) but caused irreparable damage in the Middle East. The Patriarch of Antioch, Severus, an influential Monophysite considered by the Syrian Monophysites as the founder of their church, fled to Egypt carrying with him the apostolic succession.

The policy of suppression of the Monophysites was continued under Justinian I ("the Great"), whose schemes of reconquest in Italy, Spain, and North Africa depended on Western support. Fortunately for the Syrians, his Empress Theodora urged him to bring about a reconciliation of the moderate Monophysites and Chalcedonians. She is hailed by the Syrians as a champion of Monophysitism and as a Syrian patriot who favored their doctrine.[18] In her efforts to reconcile the Monophysites, she sheltered them at the capital and helped them establish churches and monasteries there. More important, she instigated, together with the Ghassanid Prince Harith,[19] a movement to have a Syrian-born Monophysite monk, James (Jacob) Baraddai, consecrated Bishop of Edessa by the Patriarch of Alexandria (Theodosius), then in exile in Constantinople. Baraddai, a moderate Monophysite, set out on extensive missionary journeys in Syria, Mesopotamia, and Egypt, often disguised as a beggar in order to avoid arrest. He is credited with the ordination of thirty Monophysite bishops and thousands of priests and deacons.[20]

While these politicoreligious controversies were raging, the Christian-Arab Ghassanids had established themselves as a pro-Byzantine and anti-Persian buffer state in Syria. A number of Arab tribes that had moved northward from the peninsula before the advent of Islam had become Christianized, the Banu Taghlib on the frontier of Iraq and Banu Ghassan on the border of Syria being the best known. Their Christian religion helped them assimilate with the Aramaic-speaking Syrian Monophysite population, just as their Arab blood was strengthened by large numbers of Arabs from the desert who settled among them and naturally adopted their religion. It is fair to assume that large numbers of present-day Christians of Syria, Palestine, and Iraq are descendants of these Arabians.[21] The Jacobite bishop in Hira, capital of the Lakhmid state, was called "bishop of Arabs," referring to those portions of the tribes, such as Tanūkh, Ṭayy, 'Aqūla, and Taghlib, who remained Christian. A number of these Arab Christians migrated up to Mosul and resided there.[22]

The Ghassanids are described by one scholar as "passionately attached to Monophysitism," remaining Arabs at heart, even though Romanized in many respects. As Monophysites, their mercenaries defected from the army of the hated Byzantine emperor during the first half of the seventh century and facilitated the Muslim victory at the decisive battle on the river Yarmuk in 636.[23]

3

The Monophysites of Syria became known as Jacobites, most probably after Jacob Baraddai, through whose efforts, as we have noted, the Monophysite church in Syria was restored.[24] Early in the nineteenth century, members of the Jacobite hierarchy had derived the appellation from the Biblical Patriarch Jacob. "We are the children of Israel," one of their deacons is quoted as explaining, descendants of Jewish converts to Christianity. Another derivation of their name is from Saint James, brother of Jesus and first bishop of Jerusalem.[25] Today the name is applied only to the Syriac-speaking Monophysites who hailed from the Patriarchate of Antioch and consolidated themselves there and in Mesopotamia as a specific community. There are times when the term "Jacobite" is applied to all Monophysites, whether Abyssinian, Armenian, Egyptian, or Syrian. Al-Birūni, writing in the eleventh century of the various Christian sects of the Muslim world, noted that "the Jacobites mostly live in Egypt and around it."[26]

Just as the Greek capital of Constantinople refused to submit to the Latin capital of Rome, so did the Syrian capital of Antioch refuse to surrender to the dictates of Constantinople. To this day, a number of patriarchs of the Middle Eastern churches, among them the Monophysite Jacobite prelate, call themselves patriarchs of Antioch. The titles of the Jacobite patriarchs have varied from time to time, but have always claimed Antioch as their capital even though they found it difficult to establish firm residence there after the Council of Chalcedon in the mid-fifth century.

Writing at the end of the nineteenth century, Parry wrote that the title most generally used by Jacobite prelates was "Exalted Patriarch of the Apostolic See of Antioch and of all the Jacobite Churches of Syria and of the East." Early in the twentieth century, Adrian Fortescue reported the title as "Patriarch of Antioch, the Divinely Protected City and of all the Domain of the Apostolic Throne." Early in the nineteenth century, Etheridge noted that the patriarchal dignity as proclaimed at his enthronement was "Patriarch of the city of Antioch and of the whole domain of the Apostolic See." Attwater translates the title as "Patriarch of the God-Protected city of Antioch and of all the Domain of the Apostolic Throne."

In the 1840s, Badger noted that the Jacobite patriarch styled himself "Patriarch of Antioch and Successor of Saint Peter." Southgate, who visited the patriarch at about the same time that Badger was there, has recorded that above the altar in the chapel of St. Peter at Dayr al-Za'farān is a stone set into the wall with the inscription: "Upon this rock will I build my church and the gates of hell shall not prevail against it."[27] The stone is reported to have been brought from the church in Antioch where St. Peter himself ministered. When Southgate had asked the patriarch for the whole number of patriarchs in the line which he represented, the prelate had sent for the annals and, turning to the list, had counted 141, including St. Peter at the beginning and himself at the end.[28] At the time of this writing (1981), the full title of the present Jacobite patriarch, Ignatius Zakka I Iwas, is "Patriarch of Antioch and all the East and the Supreme Head of the Universal Syrian Orthodox Church."[29]

The city of Antioch, claimed as their patriarchal capital by both the Syrian Orthodox (Jacobite) and the Greek Orthodox (Malkite) Christians, was the principal Christian city in the Fertile Crescent. It was from it that Christianity had spread to the confines of Syria and beyond. Founded in 300 B.C. by Seleucus, Antioch became the capital of Syria and one of the three chief cities of the Roman Empire. Before the schism of the fifth century it was recognized after Rome and Alexandria as one of the ancient apostolic patriarchates.[30] St. Peter, who taught and preached at Antioch, is considered by a tradition universally held by the early church to have been the first bishop of the city. According to all accounts, he was the first of the twelve to visit the city; this most probably is what gave rise to the inference that he officially "founded" the church there.[31] St. Paul, too, taught and helped to organize the Church of Antioch. We read in Acts (11:26) that Barnabas departed "to Tarsus...to see Paul; and when he found him he brought him unto Antioch. And it came to pass that a whole year they assembled themselves together with the Church and taught much people." Antioch, continues the verse, was the first place in which "the disciples were called Christian."

The new religion grew rapidly in Antioch, rivaling Jerusalem. Indeed, Jerusalem had been a minor bishopric until the fifth century, when it became a patriarchate, created at the council of Chalcedon in A.D. 451. At that time the patriarchate of Antioch lost fifty-eight bishoprics to Jerusalem.[32]

Jewish opposition to Christianity, combined with pagan resistance, and imperial persecution of both Jews and Christians, meant that Christianity was not going to flourish in the land of its birth until about the fourth century, when the first Roman emperor converted to it. After the Jewish revolt and the destruction of Jerusalem by Titus, the headquarters of the church were moved to the Roman capital of the province, Caesarea. It was not until the third century that the bishop of Jerusalem and his congregation, composed chiefly of non-Jewish converts, began to play an important role in the city. The church in Palestine continued to be Greek "Orthodox" unaffected by the Semitic Christianity of the Syro-Arameans, who under the banner of Nestorianism and Monophysitism had challenged the Greco-Roman church in Syria. The church of Jerusalem was ruled by a series of exceptionally able patriarchs, the last of whom was Sophronius, "the honey-tongued defender of the Faith," whose fate it was to surrender his city to the Muslims.[33]

The Christianity of Antioch was Jewish flavored, greatly influenced by the faith that Jesus and his disciples and their early followers preached and practiced. The public worship and devotions as formalized and practiced in Jerusalem were taken over by the Syrians of Antioch and modified. In the fourth century, when interest in Jerusalem was renewed, the old rite of Jerusalem, often referred to as the liturgy of St. James, the brother of Jesus, began to have strong and renewed impact on the development of the liturgy at Antioch.[34] The Monophysite Christians eventually alone inherited this ancient liturgy of Antioch which, since the schism, has been used only in its Syriac form. As Fortescue has put it, "the rite of Antioch, once so mighty in the East, became the specialty of one little sect only," the Jacobite.[35]

The Chalcedonian schism stimulated the production of Syriac literature—almost exclusively of a religious and ecclesiastical character—reaching its peak during the fifth and sixth centuries when the Monophysite rite, called Syrian, acquired a richness and variety rarely matched.[36] The Greek form of the Antioch liturgy, used by the Greek Orthodox Syrians, was gradually Byzantinized, especially after the Arab conquest of Antioch in the seventh century; it was abandoned altogether in the thirteenth century, when the Byzantine rite alone was used.[37] The same development took place in Egypt after the Chalcedonian schism. The Copts adopted the Jacobite rite, in Coptic, while the Greek Orthodox or Malkite group eventually joined the Byzantine rite.[38]

Under the Ottomans, who started ruling the Arab lands early in the sixteenth century, and had occupied Constantinople in the mid-fifteenth century, ties between the Greek Orthodox Syrians and the Byzantine Patriarchate of Constantinople were strengthened. The Greek Orthodox Syrians, weak under the Arab rule, were therefore, restored to power under the Turks. With both Greeks and Syrians (by now Arabized) under the same political umbrella, however, the Hellenic element became especially prominent; any transaction that the Syrians wanted to conduct with the Turkish government had to be done "through their brother of Constantinople." In Palestine, where the church had remained "Orthodox," the Greeks during the Ottoman period were able to Hellenize and control it even more than in the rest of geographical Syria. They felt more at home in the "Holy Land," to whose monasteries they loved to retire.[39] The Syrian and Palestinian "Greek Orthodox" hierarchy was almost completely Hellenic until the nineteenth and twentieth centuries.

The patriarchs of the Greek Orthodox Church in Syria, like their Monophysite rivals, continued to claim to be successors of the patriarchs of Antioch. Being of the dominant party, the patriarchs of the Greek Orthodox Syrians continued to reside in Antioch long after their Monophysite rivals had been banished from there. The last Monophysite patriarch of Antioch was forced to flee the city in 518 by Emperor Justin.[40] The last Greek Orthodox Syrian patriarch of Antioch transferred his residents in the fourteenth century (1366) to Damascus, where his wandering Monophysite coclaimant would eventually join him almost six hundred years later, after World War II.[41]

With the advent of Islam, Antioch declined in prominence and prosperity. "The queen city of the East" in the nineteenth century was the poor village of Anṭākiya. Toward the end of that century, Anṭākiya was reported to be somewhat reviving, with a "pushing, thriving, striving population; the manufacturers and mechanics of the place being mostly Muslims, and a fair portion of the trade in Christian hands of rather a low and degraded type.[42] The Greek Orthodox Patriarchate in Damascus has a vicar and a small community there now, centered about the Church of St. Paul, a structure built in the nineteenth century.[43]

4

The efforts made by the Byzantine emperors and the Greek Orthodox church to suppress Middle Eastern "heresies" ended when the area was conquered by the Muslims, thus assuring the survival of Monophysites and Nestorians all the way to the present. Muslim rulers, like the Persians before them, favored the Christians who were "heretical" in the eyes of the Roman emperors of Byzantium. The Arabs granted the Monophysites and the Nestorians civil recognition, which had been denied them under the Byzantines, thus paving the way for them to establish national churches in Armenia, Syria, Iraq, and Egypt. The new security that the Middle Eastern Christians would enjoy at the beginning of the Muslim rule was formally proclaimed by the Caliph Umar to the people of Jerusalem: "I grant them security for their lives, their possessions and their children, their churches, their crosses, and all that appertains to them in their integrity and their lands and to all of their religion."[44] Under the rule of Islam, these Christians developed

through the centuries a culture entirely foreign to the Hellenistic world
view that had dominated their lives earlier.

The Middle Eastern Christians helped the Arab conquerors and
welcomed them as liberators from persecution. "The hearts of the Christians rejoiced over the domination of the Arabs—may God strengthen it
and prosper it," wrote a Nestorian chronicler a few centuries after the
Arab invasion.[45] For the Monophysites of Egypt likewise, the Muslim
conquest was a relief from persecution. Writing during the crusading
period, Abu Ṣāliḥ the Armenian spoke of how the Arabs had humbled
the Romans and taken possession of the land of Egypt, thus freeing "the
Jacobite Christians" from Roman tyranny.[46] During the same period, a
Jacobite patriarch of Antioch, Michael the Syrian, saw the coming of the
Arabs as an act of "the God of vengeance" to "deliver us by them from
the hands of the Romans—from their wickedness, from their anger,
from their cruel zeal towards us, and to find ourselves at rest."[47] The
Jacobites of Edessa had welcomed the Muslims as deliverers from the active persecution that they suffered at the hands of the Malkites.[48]

Under the Umayyads, the patriarch of the Jacobite Syrians became
"one of the most influential leaders in Syria."[49] The reason for the
preferential treatment extended to the non-Chalcedonian Christians was
more than political; self-interest dictated it: these non-Muslim citizens
were useful to the new conquerors as artisians, merchants, tax collectors,
scholars, and physicians. A century later, under the Abbasids, it was the
more numerous Nestorians who were favored over all the other Christian
sects. The Nestorian patriarch had the right of residence in the capital
itself, a privilege denied even to the Jacobites during the early period. As
early as 676, the Nestorians were able through their cannon law to pro-
hibit Christian tax collectors from exacting the poll tax from a bishop.[50]

After the Nestorians, the Jacobites were preferred over those who
owed allegiance to Byzantium. We read that in the ninth century,
Dionysius of TellMahre, who became Jacobite patriarch in 818, often
visited the court of the Abbasid caliphs, and on a trip to Egypt he had
traveled in the company of Caliph al-Ma'mūn.[51]

Of the two preferred "heretical" Christian sects, the Jacobites seem
to have been more active intellectually than the Nestorians, probably
because of their closer contact with the old cultural centers of the
Hellenistic world. While both communities attained prominence in the
fields of medicine, science, and literature, it was the Jacobites who took
the leading place in translating masterpieces of Greek thought into
Syriac, even though the great philosophers and polemists of the tenth
and eleventh centuries, such as Yaḥya ibn 'Adi and his school, wrote exclusively in Arabic.

Whether Jacobite or Nestorian, Christian influences were not
limited to non-Islamic learning and disciplines. Some scholars have concluded that Islamic mysticism (Sufism) "is wholly based on the teachings

and practices of the Christian monks and ascetics," and that "there is hardly any point in Islamic Mysticism which has not been borrowed from the main body of earlier Christian mystical thought." Professor Philip K. Hitti has written that the introduction of neo-Platonic speculation and mysticism to the Arabic world was chiefly through the influence of Jacobite authors.[52] Some Orientalists, such as Louis Massignon, disagree. They argue that Sufism was a direct offshoot of the Muslims' own primitive asceticism, brought about by their intensive meditation on the Quran and on the Sunna of the Prophet; it owed little to Christian or other influences.[53]

While Muslim rulers favored some Christian sects over others, they did not try to distinguish between the different Christian sects on religious or theological grounds. They recognized the patriarchs of all denominations and granted them diplomas. The Syrians who remained loyal to "Greek Orthodoxy," and who were therefore politically suspect, received civil recognition from the caliph just as the others.[54] The religious ties of the Malkites with Byzantium were respected even though this relationship with the enemy encouraged a large number to join the "heretical" churches. The emperor at Constantinople, as God's viceroy on earth, was the head of the Greek Orthodox patriarchs of Alexandria, Antioch, and Jerusalem, all three of which had been under Muslim rule since the seventh century. At times the caliphs accepted the emperor's intervention in behalf of the Greek Orthodox Syrians.[55] With the rise of the Saljuks to power, and the beginning of the Crusades a few decades later, trade between the Arabs and the Greeks was interrupted and relations that had existed between the Byzantines and Muslims came to a close. Thereafter, no cultural intercourse would take place between the two worlds until the Ottoman takeover brought them together again.[56]

Under Islam, the persecution of the Greek Orthodox Syrians was often initiated by the non-Chalcedonian Christians within the Arab world; the rival churches often engaged in struggles against one another to the disgust and anger of their Muslim rulers. Under the Abbasids, we read that the Chalcedonian patriarch of Antioch had sent a bishop to Baghdad to administer to the needs of his flourishing community there. The Nestorian patriarch (Abraham III, A.D. 905–936) had objected to the wazir to the presence in the capital "of a foreigner and an enemy of the Arabs." The wazir had dismissed the case, telling the Nestorians that "you Christians all" hated the Muslims equally. The Nestorian prelate eventually had won his case when with a suitable bribe he had a fellow Christian court physician protest the putting of the Nestorians, "who have no other king than the Arabs, in the same place as the Greeks whose kings never cease to stir up war against the Arabs."[57]

The prestige and power associated with high religious office often led to rivalry and bickering within the same Christian community. The story of discord and depravity among the Jacobite leaders is astonishing, writes a student of eastern Christianity. A Jacobite contemporary himself accuses the bishops of his church of being "proud, overbearing, truculent, quarrelsome, and crafty. . . [and adds that they] did not set the law of God before their eyes." The leaders of the community, "particularly the members of the Church," writes a chronicler, "hated one another. . . and wronged each other, and oppressed and took by force." Bar Hebraeus records a "great disaster that befell the Christians" when the Jacobite monks of a monastery at Aleppo asked their patriarch to consecrate one of their number as a bishop. When the patriarch refused their candidate, they defamed their prelate to Hārūn al-Rashīd, accusing the patriarch of being a "spy of the Greeks in our land." The caliph's reaction, records the Jacobite historian, was to have all the new church buildings destroyed, in the process destroying many ancient ones.[58]

As an "out-group," the Christians learned to endure the discrimination that seems to be the lot of a minority anywhere, anytime. As a community of "believers," Islam did not consider the non-Muslims as an integral part of the Islamic *Umma* or nation. The "non-believers" shared neither the rights nor the responsibilities of the *Umma*. Moreover, because the state was built on Islamic foundations, Islamic law could not apply equally to both Muslims and non-Muslims; indeed, that might infringe on the latter's right to practise their own religion, since the laws of the Islamic state were religious laws. It was the duty of the state, however, to protect its non-Muslim subjects—their life, property, the freedom to worship their own religion and to govern themselves in accordance with their own laws. But they had to accept their status as a protected millet (*millah*: nationality, community). Otherwise they would lose the right of protection as well as their right both to "blood and property." They were separate but protected. The "their"–"our" relationship (see the Preface) was reinforced. As a conquering people, the Muslims automatically enjoyed the upper social status, their only merit being their demonstrated military prowess. By most counts, the Muslims were comparatively more humane and more tolerant than most conquerors. The Christians were sometimes oppressed by some fanatical local governor,[59] or had their homes sacked by a jealous Muslim rabble in moments of popular commotion when even their churches and monasteries were plundered. Non-Muslims were often subjected to annoying and humiliating restraints such as regulations concerning dress, housing, and property, but these were modified from time to time by well-meaning jurists or rulers, if observed in some places, they were neglected in others.[60]

In time the Christians accepted their lot, for they were not forced to give up what they held holy. Their religious leaders, recognized by the state as leaders of the community, preached the necessity of obedience and promised the consolation of a better world in the hereafter. Their efforts to rationalize or justify their second-class status led the majority to a theology and folklore that emphasized the superiority of their faith over Islam, and of Jesus Christ over Muhammad. Other members of the Christian community, usually in the urban centers, were more attracted by the prestige of the ruling religion and tried to imitate it and converted to it. Generally speaking, the Christians do not seem to have felt the humiliation and discomfort of their status, especially when the vast majority of their Muslim compatriots themselves did not seem to fare any better even in this world.

Wars with Christian states and princes were often the cause of attacks against native Christians. During the first half of the ninth century, when the Byzantine emperor Theophilus invaded Addasid territory, not only did the Byzantines massacre their Monophysite enemies but the Muslims too turned their hatred "against the rest of us who were Christian...because of the invasion of the Byzantine," wrote a Jacobite chronicler. The Christians of Edessa had especially suffered because one of them had "attached himself to the Byzantines and encouraged them to destroy the Moslems."[61] But as Guy Le Strange points out, during a crisis Shi'ah Muslims as well as the Sunnis alternately suffered a like experience.[62]

In general, the authorities behaved justly and without revenge toward their Christian subjects.[63] In the twelfth century, a metropolitan of Nisibis (Eliyya, A.D. 1008–49) favored the Muslims to peoples of other religions and persuasions "whether they treat us well or not." The reason he gave was that the Muslims regarded it as a "matter of religion and duty to protect us, to honor us, and to treat us well." Even when the Muslims have "oppressed us and done us wrong," they find out when they "have turned to their law" that "it does not approve of harming and oppressing us." The metropolitan concluded that the occasional harsh treatment at the hand of the Muslims coupled with "their confession that in treating us thus they are acting contrary to their law, is better for us than the good treatment of others who confess that it is contrary to their law to treat us well."[64]

It was certainly an indication of their good life that the cultural activity to which we have alluded above flourished among the Middle Eastern Christians. As for the group with which we are specifically concerned here, the Jacobites, we find them, after five hundred years of Muslim rule, faring well as a community of two million faithful, with 20 metropolitans, and 103 bishops in Iraq, Syria, and Cyprus.[65] Although they did not match the Nestorians in their missionary effort,[66] which covered Turkistan, China, and India, they compared favorably with them, as we have noted, in their intellectual and cultural life. Theology, philosophy, history, and the sciences flourished in their schools throughout the Middle Ages, bursting into a great revival of letters in the twelfth century.[67] After the twelfth century, however, relations between Christians and Muslims deteriorated; it was during that century that the lands of Eastern Christendom become a battleground of religious wars.

5

The Crusaders, whose presence lasted for two centuries, were to influence Christian–Muslim relations for centuries to come, leaving behind a legacy of mistrust and antagonism that would be revived in modern times. The Middle Eastern Christians were to pay a heavy penalty for the sympathy that some of them had toward their coreligionists from the West. The fear of a counteroffensive drove the Muslims against their Christian subjects, especially those who had spiritual and cultural connections with the Christian powers.

The crusading European kings and feudal lords realized very early in their conquests the importance of a native Christian population upon whose loyalty they could rely. King Baldwin I and his nobles soon discovered that they could not establish themselves without the native Christian population which had recently deserted the place, fleeing to Egypt before the Turkish armies.[68] The natives were especially needed for their services as traders and craftsmen. It was thus decided to invite the refugees back to settle in Jerusalem. Tempted by Baldwin's offers, large numbers of Orthodox and non-Orthodox Christians of Syria came back or emigrated for the first time to their holy city, where a number of concessions and privileges awaited them.[69]

In Crusader centers outside Jerusalem, such as Antioch and Edessa, where the native, Christian population was in the majority, Latin secular leaders were even more aware of their need for friends, no matter how "heretical" the views of those friends in the eyes of the Church. Early during their conquests in the East these leaders had notified Pope Urban II that while they had expelled "the Turks and pagans" from Antioch and Edessa, they could not do the same to the heretics such as "Greeks, Armenians, Syrians, and Jacobites."[70] Michael the Syrian, the Jacobite patriarch of Antioch from 1166-1199, perhaps exaggerates the tolerance of the Crusaders. The Franks, he wrote, "never raise any difficulty on the subject of faith, nor concerning the adoption of one sole formula among all Christian peoples and tongues...they consider as Christian anyone who adores the cross, without further inquiry or examination."[71]

Patriarch Michael spoke well of the Muslims too. He praised the relations that existed between the Muslims and members of his community, "The Turks," he wrote, "having no idea of the sacred mysteries—were in no way accustomed to inquire into professions of faith or to persecute anyone on their account." The patriarch personally maintained the closest relations with Qilij Arslan II, who visited him and discussed religion with his learned men.[72] When the Zangids reconquered Edessa they had spared the Jacobites, Armenians, and Malkites, although the Latins were plundered and killed. Zangi had ordered that two great bells be presented to the Jacobite churches which he had visited; he had taken the Gospel, and kissed it.[73]

The position of the Jacobites was different from that of the Armenians and the Maronites, whose relations with the Crusaders were cemented by military alliances. Renowned for their skill as archers, the Maronites were used in war against the Muslims, and formed a most useful part of the Latin infantry.[74] The Armenians of the barony of Cilicia often called upon the Latins to strengthen their political and military position. Throughout the crusading period, the Armenian rulers of Cilicia maintained friendly relations with the Franks, who in turn considered the Armenians as their natural ally against both the Muslims and the Byzantines.[75] The Armenians occasionally paid a price for the good will of the Franks. In the words of Matthew of Edessa, Armenian leaders received "terrible chastisement...on the part of the Turks and their brothers, the Byzantines."[76]

When the Mongols invaded the Middle East in the thirteenth century, the Christians of the area were again caught in the middle. Those of them who found it expedient to side with the Asian invaders were severely punished. Like the Latins, the Mongols at first favored the native Christians over their Muslim neighbors. A number of Mongol conquerors had Christian wives, converts of Nestorian missionaries to Central and Eastern Asia. Conscious of the good relations between the Mongols and his Christian subjects, the caliph al-Musta'sim sent the Nestorian patriarch of Baghdad along with his wazīr in order "to treat with Hulagu," whose queen Doquz Khātūn was a Nestorian Christian. Hulagu was not moved; according to Bar Hebraeus, he "continued the war with still greater ferocity."[77] Baghdad was sacked and the caliph murdered, but the Nestorian patriarch was rewarded;[78] he "was given rich endowments and a former royal palace as his residence and church."[79]

These pro-Christian policies of the Mongols gave rise to false hopes among the Christians. The news of the fall of Baghdad, capital of Islam for five hundred years, was a "ghastly shock" to the Muslims, but was received with jubilation by some of the Middle Eastern Christians. An Armenian writer hailed Hulagu and his Christian queen as "the new Constantine and Helena."[80] Reporting the death of the Mongol khan, Bar Hebraeus noted that nothing could compare to the "king of kings" in "wisdom, high-mindedness and splendid deeds."[81]

The Mongols not only had Christian wives but also Christian generals. The man who led Hulagu's forces into Syria after the fall of Baghdad was the Nestorian Kitbuga. With the fall of Damascus, the Arab historian Maqrīzi wrote that the Christians there began to be in the ascendancy, and started to act accordingly. "They drank wine freely in the month of Ramadan," he reports, "spilling it in the open streets on the clothes of the Muslims and the doors of the mosques." It was the turn of the Christians to treat the Muslims as second-class citizens. They traversed the street, writes Maqrīzi, "bearing the cross, [compelling] the merchants to rise and ill-treated those who refused." They preached sermons proclaiming their new-won liberty, saying that "the true faith, the faith of the Messiah, is today triumphant." When the Muslims complained of these indignities to Hulagu's governor, they were bastinadoed.[82]

While the Middle Eastern Christians welcomed the oriental invaders, the Latin Crusaders were alarmed by them. They not only feared the Mongols, but also preferred the Muslims to the native Christians.[83] With some hesitation, the Latin barons allowed Mamluk troops to pass through Crusader territory on their way to fight the Mongols.

After the Mamluks had defeated the Central Asian invaders, they turned their anger upon the native Christians. Many were massacred or sold into slavery; others were forcibly converted to Islam, their church and monastic property confiscated. The slaughter that followed the occupation of Antioch by the troops of Baybars shocked even the Muslim chroniclers who reported it.[84] The fate of the Christians of Damascus was determined by their behavior during the Mongol occupation of the city. Many of them were massacred along with the Jews and Muslims as collaborators with the enemy.[85] The Jacobite patriarch was told not to entertain foreigners and so were the other Christian leaders warned.[86]

The descendants of Hulagu had embraced Islam by the early fourteenth century and did not treat the Christians kindly. The devastation that the Middle East experienced under Taimur (Tamerlane), during the century that followed the sack of Baghdad, saw the destruction of such important Christian centers as Takrit, Amid, Mardin, Arbil, Mosul, and Tur Abdin. At Amid we are told that the inhabitants were burnt in a great fire. At Tur Abdin the Christians were hunted out; "those who took refuge in underground caves were suffocated with smoke."[87] In the words of a well-known Jacobite Church historian, only a fraction of the Jacobites survived these blood-soaked decades and their confession became everywhere, even in the densest areas between Mardin and Mosul, the religion of a minority.[88]

By the second half of the thirteenth century, Syria was desolate and unsafe for the Christians. The Jacobites found security in northern Iraq and in the territory north of it, in south-central Anatolia. Bar Hebraeus, writing toward the end of the thirteenth century, found in his diocese in Iraq "much quietness;" the Syrian diocese he described as "wasted."

2

Among Arabs, Kurds, and Turks

1

After the dust of Tamerlane's marches had settled, we find the Jacobites mostly in regions east of Aleppo and west and north of Mosul. From the fourteenth to the twentieth century their centers would be northern Iraq and the south-central Anatolian regions adjacent to it. Their neighbors would be Kurds, Arabs, and Turks, the three Muslim groups who meet and intermingle in this corner of the Middle East. This area, often referred to as northern Mesopotamia, was Arabized and Islamized soon after the conquests of the seventh century: it remained fundamentally Arab in spite of the fact that since Saljukid times Turkoman rule and influence were introduced and maintained there. The Arab population and language began to fade away as one moved north of Mardin, ceasing almost entirely upon reaching Diyarbakr. From Diyarbakr the Muslim population became chiefly Turkish and Kurdish. In these northern regions the Jacobite population adopted Turkish and Kurdish as vernacular languages in place of Arabic, their common medium of communication in Monsul and Mardin. By the nineteenth century their mother tongue, Syriac, was generally unknown to them in the urban areas; the only Jacobites who spoke it were the villagers of Tur Abdin.[1]

The center and stronghold of the Jacobites was the Tur Abdin region, just as the homegrounds of the Nestorians were the Hakkari Mountains farther east.[2] The convents and monasteries of the area and their ruins suggest that it was once entirely Christian, especially before Islam.[3] Most probably the persecuted Monophysites had flocked there because of the security that these rugged mountains afforded. Because of its isolated location, the region plays a more important part in the history of Christian churches and literature than in political history. Albert Socin has noted that Arab authors mention the Tur Abdin conspicuously seldom.[4]

Nineteenth-century travelers described these regions as "wild" with "an utter want of water."[5] The villagers depended upon the immense and numerous reservoirs that they cut into rocks to collect the winter rains and snows.

The mountainous character of the territory gave it its name, Jabal Ṭūr, or Ṭūr Dāgh, both names implying a tautology, since *Jabal* (Arabic), *Dāgh* (Turkish), and *Ṭūr* (Syriac) mean *mountain*. The old and proper name is Ṭūr 'Abidīn, Mountain of Worshippers.[6]

During the last century the population of the Tur Mountain was estimated by a Jacobite patriarch to be "about 6,000 families," inhabiting just over one hundred villages.[7] They lived in total isolation from the rest of the outside world. An American missionary who visited them in the mid-nineteenth century wrote that Mosul and Diyarbakr were more distant and unknown to them than Europe was to the American schoolboy. With the weakening of the central government in Istanbul after the seventeenth century, travel in these regions gradually became as dangerous as it was slow. As late as a hundred years ago, travellers from Diyarbakr to Mosul would make the journey on the Tigris by raft (*kalak*), the current moving them at the rate of three miles an hour, as in the days of King Sennacherib of ancient Assyria. A trip between the two cities took about five days in spring and from fifteen to twenty-five days after the snows had melted.[8] The river route was safer, though slow. Early in the nineteenth century Buckingham had found the road from Diyarbakr to Mosul so infested with robbers that caravans preferred to go by way of al-Jazirah on the Tigris.[9]

Mardin, situated at the western extremity of Tur Abdin, was the nearest point of communication with the inhabitants of the mountain; Midyat, the capital of the Tur, served as the residence of a Governor. In mid-nineteenth century its population, mostly Christian and Jacobite, was estimated at about "fifteen hundred" inhabitants.[10] As late as the mid-twentieth century and after two world wars, it was the only town in Turkey having the distinction of possessing a population made up mostly of Christians (Jacobites).[11]

The isolation of the Tur Abdin Jacobites had preserved Syriac as their mother tongue. They spoke a dialect distinctly their own, sometimes called "Turane" "mountains", also known as "Falehi," referring to the peasant (Fallāh) element that spoke it.

Mardin and the region surrounding it was the chief center of the "Syrian nation" and population. The city had a Jacobite bishop as early as the seventh century. He lived there in the environs of the city at the convent of Dayr al-Za'farān. It was in 1171 that the Jacobite patriarch Michael I moved to Mardin from Diyarbakr, where the patriarchs had been since 1034. Prior to that they had resided at Melitene (Malaṭiya) in Byzantine territory, where they had moved in 975 from Abbasid lands at the invitation of the Byzantine emperor. Owing to tension between the Syrian and Greek Orthodox, the former moved to Islamic territories once again, settling in Diyarbakr, farther east in Anatolia.[12] Early in the last century the city of Mardin had a Syrian Orthodox population of almost two thousand but served as the center of a circle that comprised some fifty-five thousand Jacobites, all within a few days' journey from the city.[13] Until the post-World-War-I period, the Muslim population of the city was a mixture of Arabs and Kurds, the latter forming the majority. The language of the city was Arabic, but Turkish, spoken by a few, served as the official language and was used in all transactions with the government.[14]

Situated on one of the outer peaks of the Jabal Tur range, Mardin overlooks the vast plains that stretch from Urfa to Jazirah and Mosul. The caravan road from it to Jazirah passed through these plains which for miles are level and were often dominated by Arab bedouin tribes.[15] Mardin is built on a height of 1600 feet above the plains to its south, southeast, and west. The declivity on the west side of the mountain is described by a mid-nineteenth century observer as covered with vineyards and orchards of fig, pear, apple, walnut, and other trees, planted wherever the rock afforded sufficient soil for their growth. The houses, built of stone, were for the most part built in terraces one above the other like steps; the roof of one formed the yard to that which was above it, and the windows of each house looked down on the flat roof on the house below it.[16]

The convent of Dayr Za'faran was located about five miles northeast of Mardin. The monastery was described by an Englishman who visited it in the mid-1800s as a plain, square, substantial building, outwardly devoid of any architectural ornament; it reminded him of the fort or stronghold of a band of robbers rather than the abode of a group of pious monks.[17] The original structure, which, according to Jacobite tradition, did serve as a Byzantine fortress, dates back to the fifth or sixth century, though the major part of the monastery is of more modern construction.[18] Jacobite historians tell us that the building was purchased in the ninth century by the bishop of Jazirah, who converted it into a monastery.[19]

Diyarbakr, to the north of Mardin, was another important and old Syrian center. It was a Monophysite center as early as the sixth century and, as already noted, the seat of the Jacobite patriarchate during eleventh and twelfth centuries. Known in Turkish as Qara-Amid, in

Latin, Amida, and in Arabic, Diyarbakr, the city continued through the centuries as a Christian (Armenian and Jacobite) stronghold, even though always decreasing in numbers because of conversions to Islam.[20]

From northern Mesopotamia, the Monophysite Jacobites spread eastward into Iran, whose Christian population was almost exclusively Dyophysite Nestorian.[21] From the sixth century on, Jacobites were occasionally able to send their missionaries eastward toward Iran even though with little success; Iranian Christianity would continue to be Nestorian until modern times.[22] The nucleus of the Jacobite communities in Iran was formed by the Syrian prisoners, most of them Monophysites, whom the Sasanian kings brought back from their campaigns against the Byzantines. Khusrau II is supposed to have brought an especially large number of these prisoners. Jacobite communities in Iran, small, and limited to a few urban centers, were under the jurisdiction of the Maphrian, the bishop of Takrit in Iraq.[23] Carmelite missionaries reporting from Iran in the seventeenth century found Jacobite communities in Shiraz and Isfahan, far removed from the Nestorian centers in the northwestern parts of the country. Those in Isfahan, numbering some "600 households," had become Catholics under the direction of the Latin Fathers.[24]

The Christian population of Iraq as a whole flourished in the regions north of the Zab river, Mosul having the largest concentration.[25] On the fertile plains of Mosul, Jacobite villages were interspersed among Arabs, Turkomans, and Kurds. Their most ancient settlements were those of (1) Qaraqūsh, which, as late as the nineteenth century, had nine churches, one of them in ruins, and the monastery of Mar Behnām; (2) Barṭalla, formerly a bishop's see, where Bar Hebracus had settled as a Maphrian;[26] (3) Ba'shiqa; (4) Bahzāni, at the foot of the mountain of Maqlūb on which stands the monastery of Mār Matta; and (5) Qūb, a small village on the other side of the mountain.[27]

In Syria, Aleppo had become an important center of anti-Chalcedonian Christians.[28] The city, known in ancient times as Beroea, had a Jacobite archbishop since 543. After the Arab conquest in the following century, Malkite, Jacobite, and Maronite Christians each had a bishop there. The Armenians established their bishopric in Aleppo around 1200.[29] In time, the city outstripped Damascus in commerce and trade and continued to have a sizable Christian population. A Jesuit missionary writing in the mid-seventeenth century estimated its population at 250,000, one-fifth of them Christian, and called the city "the Lyon of Syria" in terms of its size, beauty, and commerce, and the wealth of its population.[30] As one of the largest and richest cities of the empire, Aleppo attracted a large community of European merchants, especially French, English, Dutch, and Venetian, all referred to as "Franji" by the Syrians. By the 1600s, Aleppo, as we shall see, would become a Catholic stronghold, thanks largely to French influence. Gradually the Jacobite community there, known as Syrian Orthodox, would embrace Catholicism and establish a "Syrian Catholic" Church with its own "patriarch of Antioch."[31]

Arabic, which by the eleventh century had become the dominant language of Syria, Lebanon, Palestine, and Egypt, was early spoken by the Jacobites, a fact true also of the other Middle Eastern Christian sects of those countries. In the thirteenth century the Jacobite patriarch Ighnā-ṭīyūs (Ignatius) Dāwud II had found it necessary to write his profession of faith in Syriac and Arabic. The language of Islam had become the medium of Christian liturgy and thought and was soon to become the Christians' "mother tongue."[32]

The Jacobites adopted the Arabic language before its alphabet. As early as the fifteenth century they wrote Arabic in Syriac characters, called Garshūni. In the first half of the seventeenth century, when a Jacobite bishop wrote to Pope Urban VIII, he used Arabic words, rendered in Syriac script with only his signature in Arabic characters.[33] As late as the middle of the last century, the Reverend Horatio Southgate found that Arabic books written in Syriac script were the most easily read by the Jacobites. Jacobite prelates had asked an English missionary during the 1840s to send them "our Prayer Books in Arabic." The Arabic that these Christians spoke was naturally interlarded with Syriac vocabulary.[34]

Unlike the Nestorians, who in their more isolated geographical and social conditions chose their first names from the Bible, the Jacobites used more Arabic- and Muslim-sounding names, such as Fatḥ Allah, 'Abd al-Karīm, or Christian names patterned after Islamic names, such as 'Abd al-Masīḥ (Servant of Christ). Women frequently had Biblical names; no names were used that implied Muslim faith.[35]

2

In urban centers, where Jacobites formed an important element of the population in such places as Mosul, Mardin, Urfa, Diyarbakr, Aleppo and even Baghdad, the ethnic origin of the man on the street was often discernible from his dress, especially his turban.[36] Writing of Baghdad, which he visited in the 1870s, Max von Thielmann noted that "everybody's nationality and creed are easily distinguishable at a distance," the Jew always recognized by his blue and flowery headdress and the huge blue cotton tassel on the fez underneath. The Jacobites and Chaldeans wore a black silk turban, unless they had adopted the fez without any turban, "as worn by Turks and Armenians."[37] In some localities restrictions on dress and color were disregarded, but the freedom to ride a horse was denied to non-Muslims. Yet even this restriction was not uniformly applied. The Jacobite patriarch not only rode a horse but had a bridle and martingale that were green, the Prophet's color, and this gave no offense, while in Damascus at the same time such a disregard of custom, Buckingham noted, would probably have cost a Christian his life. Half a century after Buckingham, even in Damascus these restrictions and prejudices had passed away. The Christian, wrote a British consul in 1867, could wear any kind of dress and ride horses at his pleasure.[38]

Interfaith relations in towns were fairly cordial, "if an allowance be made," as an eighteenth-century Englishman observed, "for the superiority which the Mahometans assume over all who are of another faith."[39] In such Jacobite centers as Mosul and Mardin, intergroup relations were, on the whole, friendly. In Mosul, Southgate had observed an unusual degree of "familiarity and regard" toward the Christians by Muslims. He was struck by the cordial and respectful manner with which Christian priests were everywhere saluted by the Muslims. One of the reasons for these congenial relations in Mosul, he was told, was that in former times the Christians had rendered eminent service in defending the city in war as masons, carpenters, and blacksmiths.[40] Another reason for the good intergroup relations was the fact that some of the Muslims of the city, among them the most prominent, were descendants of former Christians, "as they themselves are often heard to acknowledge." The most important and popular governing family of Mosul, the Jalilis, was of Christian descent. Instead of becoming zealous converts, as renegades are apt to be, the family preserved the memory of their last Christian ancestor, a Nestorian, by visiting his tomb and keeping it in repair in a Christian cemetery.[41] Early in the nineteenth century, Buckingham wrote that the Christians of Mardin greeted Muslims with "Salem 'Alaykum" and received its answer, even from Sharifs, something which would be deemed "the highest possible outrage" in other places.[42]

The Episcopal missionary Horatio Southgate noted that Christian churches in Mardin were visited by Muslims who "sometimes join in the worship." At a church that he had attended he had seen Muslim women coming in, with their children in their arms, asking the priest to say prayers over them. Dr. Henri B. Haskill of the American Board mission wrote from Mosul just over a century ago that in cases where a sick child was not expected to recover, it was not uncommon to have it baptized and annointed with holy oil by a Christian priest.[43] Southgate was assured that Muslims visiting Christian churches went through all the acts of devotion with the same regularity as the Christians, kneeling, bowing, and prostrating themselves, but without making the sign of the cross, considered the distinctive and peculiar badge of a Christian.[44]

It was not uncommon for Muslims to visit the shrines of Christian saints. Their reverence for Christian monks and "holy men" may again be partly due to the Christian ancestry of the Muslims.[45] Indeed, the veneration of Christian monks and monasteries has an ancient tradition in folk Islam, its origin going all the way back to the Prophet Muhammad. The special privileges which he is said to have granted to Christian ascetics and convents were observed throughout the centuries. Exempted from taxes and allowed to receive revenues, some of these religious centers amassed great riches. Their privileges, as Southgate observed, were sometimes violated by "rapacious Pashas" and other enemies, but as a rule they were respected and revered. Moreover, superstition and belief in magic was rife among the Christians and Muslims on these humble levels. Some Jacobite priests, described by missionaries as sorcerers, wrote charms for both Muslims and Christians. They were believed to have the power to "make any woman love any man, or make a barren woman fruitful, or protect stray cattle . . . by shutting the mouths of wild animals."[46]

In rural areas, where the vast majority of the Jacobites lived as farmers, they were hardly distinguishable from their Muslim neighbors. A report of the American Board of Commissioners for Foreign Missions described the Syrian Orthodox as "Christians in name, but that alone." They did not differ "a whit" in character and conduct from the rest of the population around them.[47] The first few missionaries who visited the Jacobites and lived among them found them in "good temporal circumstances," in the words of George P. Badger.[48] Southgate, a contemporary of Badger, described them as a cheerful, frank, and naturally intelligent people. He attributed the reason for this circumstance to "the unusual terms of equality in which they stand with the Musselmans around them, and the semi-independent state of the government under which they have lived."[49] The majority of their Muslim neighbors were Kurds, a much maligned society.

3

The major source of our misunderstanding of the Kurdish tribal society has come from the fact that the sedentary among them have been grouped indiscriminately with their nomadic and semi-nomadic brothers even though the three groups are entirely different social classes. Indeed, the Kurdish people are divided into several large divisions "with countless subdivisions or tribes," each under its petty chief (*āgha*). The great majority of them live a relatively quiet life in their mountain villages, pursuing lawful occupations. Sedentary Kurds lived, as they now do, in villages on their own land, cultivating the soil, grazing their flocks on the surrounding hills, keeping their sheep and goats in their houses in winter.[50] They were, as they still are, industrious and ingenious agriculturalists, cultivating every available piece of ground in the vicinity of their villages. People who have lived among them often describe them as quick to make friends, for the most part warmhearted, and usually loyal in friendship.[51]

As in all relatively isolated societies,[52] Kurdish villagers, just as their Christian neighbors, tended to be self-sufficient, the family manufacturing much of its own goods. Nearly all the cloth they used, for instance, was of their own manufacture. The cold winters called for heavy clothing and quilts, which were usually made by men, whereas the shirts and skirts and men's cotton pants were made by the women.[53] The men and boys joined the womenfolk in preparing the yarn for the hand looms, the men specializing in weaving warm blankets in large plaids.[54]

The Kurds also wove carpets from the strong coarse wool of their large-tailed sheep, which, as all who are familiar with their handiwork know, are very durable, lasting from generation to generation.[55] An artistic people like their Persian cousins, the Kurds produced carpets with some of the most beautiful designs and finest weaving. They made their saddlebags the same way, together with shawls, socks, and warm gloves.[56] Not all carpets were made for one's own use. During the nineteenth century especially, carpet companies formed by exporters, established branches throughout Anatolia and gave out work to the villagers. In these cases the villagers did not have to fleece their own wool and prepare their own dye; the company provided a loom and pattern as well as all the material. They paid the family by the yard; an industrious household could finish a good-size rug in less than a year.

Where the Kurds were settled in fertile regions such as northwestern Iran or northeastern Iraq or south-central Anatolia, and enjoyed an abundance of better-quality food, varied with vegetables and fruits, this tempering influence of their settled existence meant harmonious intercommunication with the surrounding non-Kurdish communities as well as with the government.[57]

Many of the tribes had permanent villages as well as seasonal encampments. They attended to the production of flocks and herds, and provided the country with milk, butter and cheese, wool, meat, hides, and tallow, and supplied it with wheat, barley, and maize, as well as fruit from their orchards and vineyards. This was, as indeed it still is, a busy society, where the women were up before daybreak churning the previous day's milk to make butter, while the men and boys at the peak of the day brought out the flocks and herds, readied them for milking before sending them off to pasture where the younger boys would shepherd them. The day's work had just started; it would not end until sunset.[58]

The semi-sedentary Kurds did little cultivating, but they owned large flocks; they lived in tents on their own hills in the summer, and wintered in villages in the valleys. Their farming was limited to the cultivation of wheat, tobacco, and barley, both in their winter and summer homes. They excelled as smiths, weavers, and tentmakers.[59] The purely nomadic

Kurds, sometimes described as armed gypsies, lived in their tents throughout the year. They too owned large flocks of sheep, goats, mules, and horses, but no land. By ancient custom they had the right to graze their flocks in certain well-defined pastures, and ancient rights of way allowed them to get to them in their annual migrations. Oftentimes their rights were challenged by the powerful chief of a sedentary tribe, who imposed tolls on them, while they insisted on their rights and resisted. "The migration season," wrote an observer, "is an anxious time on the hills, leading as it often does, to much bloodshed."[60]

Even Kurdophiles testify that many of the nomadic tribes were "addicted to pillage and robbery."[61] Their victims were not only Christians but Turks and other fellow Kurds. Often an irritated Turkish governor would send a strong force into Kurdish villages that might have been innocent, the Turkish soldiers committing every kind of atrocity, burning the village and putting most of its inhabitants to the sword. Such treatment produced the conviction among the Kurds that they could rightfully plunder and oppose the Turkish government whenever they could with inpunity.[62] It should be pointed out, however, that while the Ottoman government tried to combat the evils of nomadism—yet it also took into account the useful economic and military functions that many of these nomads performed. The chief source of livelihood of many nomadic tribes was the extensive breeding of horses. Indeed, horsebreeding perpetuated nomadism since it compelled the breeders to seek low grounds in winter and cool regions in summer.[63] The government valued these nomads as breeders of a "hardy type of horses excellent for military purposes."[64]

Where Christian villages were not protected by a settled Kurdish tribe, they paid tribute to nomadic Kurds in order to restrain them from robbery and pillage.[65] Generally the unarmed Christians of the plain were a protected, "vassal" people. The exactions of the feudal chief were not so much arbitrary as customary, granted that the servile classes, Christians or Muslims, were at a disadvantage when their rights needed to be enforced. The peasants were compelled to perform serf-service, to cultivate their master's field without any compensation for their labor.[66]

In remote districts feudal rights continued to exist until the late nineteenth century, "rights" sometimes referred to by European consular agents as "blackmail." "In many cases," wrote consul Chermside, "the chief alone raises black-mail on Christians; in others it is a tribal right, which is asserted by periodical forays," the tax in some places amounting to as much as one-fourth the produce.[67] In most cases the *āghas* protected their serfs against anyone or any tribe—Christian or Muslim—that might molest them. "It is no small advantage," noted the British consul, "to be able to send for help to a powerful Kurdish village which can (and actually *will*) send a force of well-armed and war-like men to their assistance.⁶⁸ It should be pointed out here that "protection" did not mean that the Christians did not share or own lands on a footing of equality with the Muslim tribesmen. Sometimes, as in the case of the Mountain Nestorians, it was the Christians who protected the Muslims. Indeed, religious differences were not an important factor in everyday life.⁶⁹

Christian and Muslim tribes, as pointed out above, shared a good deal in common—in dress, usages, superstition, character, appearance, and custom, and, in some cases, they spoke the same language and enjoyed the same music and dance, which seem to be a special passion with the Kurds.⁷⁰ Differences in religion did mean some differences in customs and traditions: the different religious communities had distinctive ways of celebrating holidays; they conducted their marriage ceremonies and funeral services differently; they fasted and worshipped differently.

4

Because of the important role that religion played in the social and political life of the people, religious differences between the majority and minority set the various sectors of the population apart, widening social distance and strengthening ethnic identity. Indeed ethnic survival was made possible through the ideology that religion provided; it was a source of stability as well as a means of emotional expression and an area where concepts and fundamental beliefs could be expressed. It is not surprising, therefore, that religion played a major role in the life of the Jacobites. O. H. Parry, who lived among them at the end of the last century, described them as "intensely patriotic and tenacious of their creed."

As in the case of all other religious sects, the Jacobites were subject to their clergy in civil as well as in spiritual matters. The poor and the distressed often sought them for assistance, advice, and consolation. The poverty of the priests or their ignorance, so often stressed by Western missionaries, did not seem to imply their abasement and degradation. They were still the most "educated" in the community, rudimentary as their learning was. The respect with which their persons were held "fully compensated for any inconvenience which they might suffer," wrote a sympathetic Episcopal clergyman.⁷¹ He found among them an unusual degree of dignity and propriety of deportment. (The Jacobite priests were, as they still are, expected to marry before ordination, the people having "a strong feeling against an unmarried parish priest." But the canons of the church forbade the marriage of a widowed priest; he generally retired to a monastery if he did not become an *asquf*.)⁷²

The laity also found comfort and at times refuge in their monks and monasteries. Buckingham has recorded that on Sundays and holidays crowds of female visitors and their children came to Dayr al-Za'farān in order to "divert themselves, free from the more rigid observation of the town." The women visitors, all unveiled, were "as full of frolic and gaiety as young girls of fifteen." To these Christian women, the convent seemed to be what the bath was to their Turkish sisters—a place of recreation, free from the "fetters of their husbands."[73] But to the monks and priests who lived there the convent was a place mostly of prayer, where they performed their religious and devotional duties. Prayers were observed seven times during the day, namely Matins, at dawn; the Third Hour, three hours after sunrise; the Sixth Hour, at noon; the Ninth Hour, three hours before sunset; the Vespers, at sundown, the Compline, or Evening Service, three hours after sundown, and the Vigils, at midnight.[74] At the turn of the century Parry noted that worship "three times a day" occupied much of their time.

The monks must have enjoyed the diversion that came with every autumn when the patriarch sent them to collect tithes of corn and money throughout the villages, and to report on the state of the patriarchal property. The monasteries themselves received gifts and donations in the form of grain, rice, fruit, sheep, and money from Jacobite villages as well as from villages that the monastery owned in the form of fiefs. Southgate reported that a considerable revenue was acquired each year from the sale of the holy water (al-Mīrūn) used in baptism, which only the patriarch could prepare. All this revenue did not make the monastery rich but it sufficed for its support.[75] The resources of the monastery were pinched by the hospitality that the monks were expected to provide to every party of armed Kurds and Turks that passed their way; in return, they received an immunity that they could not otherwise have enjoyed in the might-is-right world in which they lived.

At the head of the hierarchy was the patriarch, who, once consecrated, acknowledged no control from any of his clergy, except in the case of heresy, when the bishops could depose him. He was elected, as he still is, by a synod of bishops who reach their decision after consulting the members of their congregation—at least those important among them.[76] During the Ottoman period the Sultan approved one of the three candidates who had received the highest vote of the electoral synod. After the election a synodical letter was sent to the Coptic patriarch of Alexandria even though this custom was not always observed.[77] The firman of confirmation was usually granted to the candidate who bore the richest gifts or belonged to the most influential faction in the community. Appropriate gifts also had to be presented to all other civil officials concerned, such as the pasha, who had to endorse the petition before it was forwarded to Istanbul for the imperial decree. Local *qādis* and governors were also concerned with the election of the high ecclesiastical officials in their region. The former had to ratify the election of any bishop in his district.[78]

The fact that the church leadership was granted duties that were temporal as well as spiritual—its temporal power always limited in the Muslim state—meant that the political, fiscal, and judicial burdens imposed on it distracted the leadership from matters spiritual. Thus we find the church hierarchy often involved in petty politics and intrigues that were as unbecoming as they were corrupting. Less and less time and energy were devoted to theology and education, in time leaving the leadership entirely impoverished in the realm of mind and spirit. Western visitors in the early nineteenth century were horrified at the church officals' ignorance.[79]

5

To complicate matters for the Jacobites, their official link with the Sublime Porte was through the Armenian patriarchate. By mid-nineteenth century, the Armenian patriarchs—one Catholic,[80] the other Gregorian—were two of the four prelates who resided in Istanbul, the others being the patriarchs of the Greek Orthodox and Greek Catholic churches, respectively. The "Patrak-Khanehs" (patriarchal residences) were large establishments responsible for all the official affairs of all the other Christian communities in the empire. It was not until 1873 that the Jacobites attempted to establish direct contact with the Porte even though some of their leaders did not wish to sever the traditional Armenian-Jacobite ties. It took ten years before the Jacobite millet, with the strenuous exertions of its patriarch and help from Great Britain, was finally recognized (1882) as a separate and distinct community.[81] When O. H. Parry visited the Jacobites on a special mission in 1892, the patriarch had a bishop at Istanbul "with the right of audience of the Sultan." At the primate's guest room at Mardin the English scholar had seen hanging upon the wall a framed "Nishan or Tughra," from the Sultan, "a visible token of the recognition of the Sublime Porte."[82]

The relations between the Armenian and Jacobite churches, both Monophysite, were at times marked by friction, starting from very early times when the Armenian Church was dominated by Syrian bishops and Syriac was the written language used in Armenia. In public worship the scriptures were read in the Syriac language and then translated orally into the Armenian vernacular. Sometimes Syrian bishops, who wrote and officiated in Syriac, aspired to the Armenian patriarchate, thus increasing the alienation between the two Monophysite communities.[83]

Theologically, the Jacobites have felt closer to the Coptic Christians and have normally been in communion with them in spite of occasional disputes. As a larger and wealthier community, the Copts have been looked upon as the leaders of Monophysite Christianity; the seat of their patriarchate, Alexandria, traditionally was given precedence over Antioch. In modern times, however, the Jacobites, far removed geographically from the Christians of Egypt, lived in the shadows of the Armenians. As we shall see in this study, Jacobite fate, for good or ill, was much influenced by the fortunes and misfortunes of their Armenian neighbors in Anatolia, who early in the nineteenth century had become close neighbors of Russia.

3

Catholics, Consuls,
and Conversion

1

Political persecution and insecurity often increased internal dissension within the Middle Eastern Christian communities. There were always personal rivalries between bishops; scandalous intrigues often led to bribing Muslim authorities into these internal quarrels. Litigations were frequently generated by the shameful bargaining for succession to the patriarchal throne or a contested bishoprical seat. Starting in the late thirteenth century and lasting with brief interludes of reconciliation into the nineteenth century, the patriarchal office was simultaneously occupied by two or three and sometimes four prelates who were often violently hostile toward one another, their relative legitimacy often in question.

By the mid-fifteenth century (1445), Patriarch Ignatius X of Mardin ended a schismatic patriarchate that had started a century and a half earlier (1293). In 1494 the rival patriarchate of Tur Abdin, which had existed since 1364, was temporarily removed by the death of its primate Ignatius Mas'ūd al-Zāzi. The Tur Abdin region often backed a patriarch opposed to the one who resided at Dayr al-Za'farān near Mardin, who was considered by the majority as legitimate.[1] As late as 1814 four men claimed the patriarchal throne.[2]

The consequence of these intracommunity rivalries was a deep-seated decay of the church which often led to the defection to Islam of many of the faithful, usually the most prominent among them. When the political situation allowed it, an unsuccessful candidate for an ecclesiastical office sometimes started negotiations with the Roman Catholic Church, sending a letter of "obedience" to the Pope of Rome.

There had always been sporadic movements to unite with Rome among the "separated churches" of the Middle East. As early as the beginning of the eighth century (A.D. 709), the Jacobite bishop of Myafarqin had made a profession of the Catholic faith, followed by the bishop of Harran and his successor. At the beginning of the eleventh century a group of Jacobite bishops made the move toward "reunion," including Isaac of Agra, secretary of the patriarch John bar Abdun.

During the first century of Crusader rule (1183), a rival of the Jacobite patriarch Michael the Syrian had succeeded in bringing the greater part of the community in Jerusalem over to the Catholic communion.[3] It was in the year previous to this event, 1182, that the Maronites were united with the Catholic church, the only union that would prove to be permanent (by the sixteenth century, the entire Maronite community had accepted the move).[4]

During the following century (1237) the Jacobite patriarch himself (Ignatius Dāwūd III, 1222-53) made his submission to Rome.[5] The union did not last long nor did it affect the rest of the community, for after his submission he resigned his office and entered the Order of the Friars Preachers in the Holy Land.[6] The prelate who succeeded him, Ignatius Dionysius, was consistently opposed to the Latins, and only a small portion of the Jacobite community, based in Tripoli, close to the Maronites, maintained the union.[7]

After the Crusades, Benedict XII called (1340) a provincial synod in Cyprus, where the Jacobite, Armenian, Georgian, and Nestorian bishops professed the Catholic faith, but this move too proved to be without any firm foundation.[8] A more formal contact was made between Rome and the various Middle Eastern churches at the Council of Florence (1438), about a hundred years later. After healing the schism with the Greek Orthodox Church of Constantinople, union with the Monophysite Armenians was effected in 1439,[9] followed by others: Egyptians and Ethiopians (1442); Syrian Jacobites (1444); and Nestorians (1445). The union with the Jacobites, which together with that of the Nestorians was negotiated in Rome, was signed in the name of the Patriarch Ignatius Behnām I "for all the Jacobite nation" by 'Abd-Allah of Edessa, the emissary of Ignatius.[10]

Not long after the conclusion of the negotiations of Florence and Rome, the Ottomans conquered Constantinople. One after another the newly converted Catholics of the Middle East found it politically expedient to repudiate their signed decrees of reunion. Indeed, most of the reconciliations with Rome cited above and others like them until the end of the seventeenth century remained personal unions, rejected by the majority of the faithful as actions of ambitious men, most of them rejected by their own church.[11] Nevertheless, the memory of these contacts with Rome and especially those of the ecumenical moves of the Council of Florence would make the reopening of similar negotiations easier, particularly when more than a century later Ottoman rule would make them possible.

The Roman Catholic Church suffered severe setbacks during the century that followed the Ottoman conquest of Constantinople. The Ottoman push through the Balkans, followed by the Protestant revolt from within the church, slowed down the missionary effort. But these setbacks were temporary; new opportunities soon presented themselves elsewhere during the Age of the Discoveries. There were new continents to conquer in order to make up for those lost to the faith in Europe.[12] Portuguese and Spanish ships sailing for the new world invariably carried the Catholic soldiers of the cross. The old religious orders of Benedictines, Carmelites, Dominicans, and Franciscans would now be reinforced with new missionary orders and societies, such as Jesuits, Capuchins, and Lazarists. According to agreements reached early during the Age of the Discoveries between the Church and the two Catholic governments, papal intervention in the missionary effort was neither permitted nor attempted. A papal grant to the monarchs of Portugal and Spain had given them the exclusive right and responsibility to carry on the missionary work of the church. As early as the year when Columbus returned from his first trip to "America," Ferdinand and Isabella had asked Pope Alexander VI (1492-1503) for the affirmation by the church of their right to the lands discovered in the Western Hemisphere. In 1493 Pope Alexander affirmed that right but on the condition that the royal Catholic couple assume the obligation of converting to Christianity the natives of the newly discovered areas.[13]

This royal patronage, giving the monarch the right to engage in the "spiritual conquest" of the Americas (and later of Asian and African colonies), meant that after the Protestant Reformation the Catholic governments, including France, would start competing with each other in their effort to spread the Gospel, while at the same time challenging the spiritual as well as the temporal power of the papacy.

In noncolonial areas, however, such as in the Ottoman empire, popes and Catholic monarchs collaborated in a common cause. Pope Pius V had been instrumental in organizing the Spanish-Venetian alliance against the Turks, which ended with the victory of Spain and Venice at Lepanto in 1570. The flagship of the Christian powers at Lepanto flew the pope's blue banner showing Christ crucified.[14] Their naval superiority over the Muslims seems to have "turned the mind of all lovers of the Cross towards the East." Churchmen at this time, as Peter Guilday has noted, were especially interested in following up their naval triumph at

Lepanto with a spiritual victory; they wanted the sultan's Christian subjects to unite with Rome.[15] But as the Jacobite patriarchs found out, union with Rome could prove to be a very hazardous move in the sixteenth century.

About twenty years before the battle of Lepanto, the Jacobite patriarch Ignatius 'Abd-Allah had sent one of his priests as his representative to Pope Paul III, and two years later (1551) to Pope Julius, with letters bearing the patriarch's profession of the primacy of the Roman church. Scholars who have studied the correspondence between Julius and 'Abd-Allah are of the opinion that even though it is not clear that the patriarch wholeheartedly subscribed to the Catholic profession of faith, Pope Julius seems to have considered the Jacobites as Catholic.[16] The two missions of Ignatius to Rome paved the way for further negotiations between the Holy See and 'Abd-Allah's two successors, Ni'mat-Allah and Dāwud Shah. Ni'mat-Allah was invited by Pope Pius IV (1559-65) to reestablish the union that had been reached by his predecessor. This Ni'mat-Allah did with enthusiasm and signed the profession of the faith.[17] But upon his return to his people, trying to convince them of the wisdom of his negotiations with the Roman church, he was met with opposition and was accused before the Turkish authorities of collaboration with the enemies of the sultan. Ni'mat-Allah denied not only these charges but also his Christian faith. He apostatized to Islam. Later he fled the country, finding refuge in Rome early in 1578. There he sought and received absolution from Gregory XIII (1572-85). He remained in Rome until his death, occupying himslef with scholarly pursuits and with composing "moving lamentations" for his mistakes.[18] He also helped Catholic scholars in compiling and translating Syriac liturgies, explaining to them Jacobite beliefs and usages.

It was largely through Ni'mat-Allah's efforts that his nephew Dāwud Shāh obtained a papal confirmation recognizing him as patriarch of Antioch. This recognition by Rome, however, was not accompanied by Dāwud Shāh's formal acceptance and signature. When the "Apostolic Nuncio to Syria, Assyria, Mesopotamia, Egypt, and other regions of the East" sought Dāwud Shāh to deliver to him the papal Bull and pallium, he was able to speak only to the patriarch's brother, Bishop Thomas. "Sinister rumors had circulated in Syria," writes Euw concerning the papal representative's mission. There was talk that he had come to ally the Christians of the Middle East with the European troops against the sultan. These rumors were not entirely sinister or misplaced, however, for Ottoman relations with Rome were especially suspect since Lepanto. Dāwud Shāh was afraid to meet the papal nuncio publicly lest he be accused as his uncle had been of plotting with the Pope against the Sublime Porte.[19] Jacobite union with Rome had to wait for better times, when better relations between Istanbul and Rome would make that union possible. Fortunately for Roman Catholicism, it was soon championed by a power friendly to the Turks: France.

2

Toward the end of the sixteenth century political rivalry among the three leading Catholic countries (Portugal, Spain, and France) forced the Church of Rome to take the side of France. In France, a Catholic country with anti-Habsburg (Spanish) policies, Rome found a friend with whom she could especially collaborate in its world missionary movement, and thereby strengthen its determination to take over the leadership of that movement. Pope Clement VIII (1592-1605) reversed the church's pro-Spanish policy, tolerated the Edict of Nantes (1598), and absolved Henry IV, recognizing him as the legitimate king of France. Early in the seventeenth century, the French government, led by Cardinal Richelieu, wooed the papacy to serve its own political ambitions, and succeeded in having Pope Urban VIII (1623-44) lean on the French side during the Thirty Years' War, 1618-48.[20] This reversal of policy led to the establishment at the beginning of 1622, by Pope Gregory XV, of the Congregation for the Propaganda of the Faith, a centralized organization within the Vatican with the responsibility of directing missionary work and gaining effective control over it. Exploiting the political situation in Europe to its own advantage, Rome preferred French missionaries and the Propaganda appointed them in Asian territories where Portuguese patronage had "historical" jurisdiction.[21]

These politico ecclesiastical developments encouraged missionary societies in France. It was not entirely a coincidence that the Society of Foreign Missions of Paris (Société des Missions Etrangeres de Paris; Latin: Societas Parisiensis Missionum) was established at this time. The society was approved by Louis XIV in 1663 and by the Vatican in 1664; its missionaries were assigned by the Congregation for the Propaganda of the Faith. In 1673, France renewed its capitulatory rights with the Ottoman government, first negotiated in 1535. Latin religious orders were recognized in the Middle East and were permitted the "undisturbed exercise" of religious functions.[22] In addition to their religious labor, some of the papal representatives, when French nationals, were appointed French consuls.[23]

Relations between France and Rome were not without their own strains and tensions. France's Protestant alliances and her plan to dominate the French clergy—a policy that reached its apogee under Louis XIV (1643-1715)—were among the causes of the friction.[24] However, the French national policies do not seem to have affected the missionary enterprise. French demands mainly concerned the internal situation, dealing with the historical question of *régale*, the right of the monarch to appoint clergy to benefices not included in his privileges.

This royal policy was backed by the French clergy, who resented the fact that so many Italians held important French benefices. In the Church's apostolic effort overseas, Paris and Rome continued to collaborate with each other. Indeed, even after the French Revolution, anticlericalism in France does not seem to have affected the zeal of the French government and its administrators overseas not only to Gallicanize but also to Christianize the non-Europeans. A British consul noted in the mid-nineteenth century that the French had an unmasked and exclusive sympathy for the Roman Catholics. In the Middle East this meant that the non-Catholic Christian communities, such as the Greek Orthodox, Armenians, and Jacobites, were often exposed to "all the overbearing arrogance of the French and of those whom they especially protected."[25]

Under the direction of the Sacred Congregation for the Propagation of the Faith, with France as an ally, the church was able to reorganize its missions. New religious orders joined the old as they spread in all directions in the Ottoman and Safavid empires and the lands beyond. The men who joined these apostolic movements were of diverse backgrounds. Frequently they had achieved merit and attainment; some of them were former holders of titles and great estates, others, relatives of kings and princes; some were aristocrats or noblemen who had renounced their worldly life in order to work for the church; yet others were well prepared for the task at the seminaries in Rome in Oriental languages and history.[26] There were, of course, those who were simple or pious priests who went to preach the Gospel in the manner of Raymond Lull, who sought to conquer the Holy Land after the manner of Christ and his apostles—"by love and prayer, by the shedding of tears and blood"—or after the example set by St. Francis, who believed that the Muslims would embrace Jesus and follow his Gospel if it were only presented to them in all its simplicity.[27]

When Gregory XV founded the Propaganda in 1622, the Capuchins—an offshoot of the Franciscan order,[28] recognized as a distinct group in 1619—were the first to place themselves under its direction. By 1626 seven Capuchin fathers had sailed for Constantinople and Aleppo, and during the succeeding decades they spread out to establish missions throughout the region, including Arabia and Persia. They began their work among the Maronites, the Greek Orthodox, the Armenians, and the Jacobites.[29]

3

The Discalced Carmelites—who in the late sixteenth century became a separate group from the original order, whose beginnings go back to the early thirteenth century[30]—arrived in the Middle East about a year after the Capuchins and founded their mission at Aleppo in 1627, the year when the Jesuits had also established a mission there.

United in their desire to bring the "heretical" churches of the Middle East back into the Catholic fold, the missionary friars arrived, it will be noted, within six years after the establishment of the Propaganda. In a few more years Jesuits, Carmelites, Capuchins, and Dominicans had spread through Syria, Iraq, and Anatolia, with "houses" in Mt. Lebanon, Tripoli, Saida, Damascus, Mosul, Diyarbakr, Baghdad, Mardin, and other cities. Aleppo, because of its large Christian population representing various Syrian churches, attracted more than its fair share of friars.

In 1583, an English traveler who passed through the city was impressed by Aleppo cosmopolitanism. He spoke of "Jewes, Tartarians, Persians, Armenians, Egyptians, Indians, and many sorts of Christians" as constituting its inhabitants. He noted that the non-Muslims "enjoy freedome of their consciences," and as traders they "bring thither many kinds of rich merchandises."[31] Aleppo's flourishing commerce extended in all directions: to Baghdad, Mosul, and Diyarbakr to the east, to Egypt and Istanbul as well as to India, France, and England in other directions. By the middle of the seventeenth century, Father Joseph of St. Mary, a Carmelite missionary, wrote that Aleppo "by common consensus . . . is among the first cities of all Asia, without exception." An eighteenth century report speaks of large caravans that frequently arrived "from Baghdad and Bassora, charged with coffee . . . with the tobacco and cherry tree pipes from Persia and muslins, shawls, and other products of India."[32]

The Christian population of Aleppo in the seventeenth century was sizable; it was estimated to be between twenty and fifty thousand. Friar Joseph referred to the city as "the flower of the missions" because of the variety and the great number of people found there. The largest two communities of the city in the mid-seventeenth century were the Greek Orthodox and the Armenians, numbering around twelve thousand people each. The Jacobites formed an important sector of the Christian population, estimated at almost five thousand people.[33]

The religious importance of Aleppo was heightened in the seventeenth and eighteenth centuries by the fact that often three patriarchs resided there: the Greek (Malkite) patriarch of Antioch, the Armenian patriarch of Sis, and the prelate of the Syrian Catholics (Catholic-Jacobite).[34]

The Jewish community of Aleppo formed another important non-Muslim community. According to one authority, there were about eight to ten thousand Jews in the city in the 1850s. They enjoyed "great privileges," mentions the source, "under the protection of the European Consuls, of whom some are of their own faith."[35]

Another important community in Aleppo was the colony of European merchants who were looked after by their respective consuls. The

Venetians were the earliest to establish themselves in this corner of Syria, having come as early as the fourteenth century. The French had arrived in 1568, followed by the English in 1583 and the Dutch in 1613. The Syrian middlemen were mostly the Christians. "Almost all of the traders in the town are Christians," according to the report of an English consul written in 1860. While "almost all" the cultivators "were Muslims," the majority of the "manufacturing population was Christian."[36]

The European traders favored their Middle Eastern coreligionists; in some cases Catholics were especially regarded. It became very clear to the prosperous trading community that to be a Catholic was to their advantage. But there were also stumbling blocks in the way of those who wanted to leave their community (millet) in order to join another sect. It was an act of provocation when someone publicly defected from his "nation," let alone joined a community considered alien and antagonistic by the Ottomans. The Ottoman authorities were usually ready and willing to take reprisals against anyone who dared to take this action. "If one of the sectarians or schismatics becomes a Catholic," wrote Friar Joseph in the mid-seventeenth century, "he loses all his property and in exacting this penalty," he emphasized, "the Turks are most assiduous."

The Catholic converts became suspect when they maintained close relations with the Frankish friars, especially when the latter served as consuls of their respective governments. These uneasy relations were exacerbated by the protective attitude the European friars held toward their converts; they watched over the conduct of their flock and tried to protect them against persecution from their own community's monks, priests, and laymen. The European Fathers did not hesitate to strike back at their "heretical" opponents. In the mid-seventeenth century the Carmelites proposed to the Propoganda Fide that action in Europe be taken against the Armenian merchants who enriched themselves in Catholic lands but were the "most opposed" to union with the Catholic church and "the most mordant in turning" away those who desired that union. The Carmelites suggested that the Sacred Congregation arrange with the duke of Florence, the signory at Venice, or even the king of France, "to appoint someone as their resident agent in Julfa and write to the king of Persia to assign a place there for the agent," who would most probably be one of the friars.[37]

At the end of the seventeenth century a nephew of Pope Innocent XII, Archbishop Peter Paul, was sent to Persia as ambassador on behalf of "His Holiness, his Majesty the Emperor, and Other European Princes." The archbishop wrote to Rome in 1700 that no Armenian should be allowed to enter the Papal States "unless he first make a profession of Catholic Faith," and suggested that the Holy See "propose to the Venetian Republic, to the Grand Duke (of Tuscany) and to the Emperor to have an order jointly issued . . . to the effect that if the

Armenians do not within a certain time find means of reuniting themselves to their Head of Olden time, all their goods in those states will be confiscated." Such severe measures were apparently not taken, for almost twelve years later we find a Carmelite informing the pope from Tabriz that "all Armenians coming to Italy, and particularly to Rome, deceive your Holiness and the Cardinals, *there* they give themselves out to be Catholics and *here* they are the greatest persecutors of the missionaries and of true Catholics."[38]

A number of Jacobite bishops professed the Catholic faith in the early seventeenth century, but they had done so as individuals and often secretly. Patriarch Ignatius Hudayn had admitted that it was fear lest a written profession of obedience to the Pope might fall into the hands of the Ottoman authorities which had kept him from uniting with the Roman church. The Turkish officials had imprisoned the Jacobite archbishop of Damascus Cyrill 'Aṭallah ('Ata-Allah) for becoming a Catholic; he was charged with plotting with the Italians against the sultan, and was released only when enough money was raised to set him free.[39]

The difficulty for an individual convert was that not only was he uprooted from his community but when he was forced to go back to it, he had difficulty becoming rehabilitated. To overcome these problems, the Roman Catholic church favored the idea of establishing a separate church, united with Rome but using its mother church's own rites and liturgy. To facilitate this procedure, the church deemed it desirable to win over the hierarchy of the church, preferably the patriarch himself; if unable to do so, then a rival claimant, of whom there were always a number, was to be wooed. But trying to win over a whole community to loyalty to the Roman church was especially unacceptable to the Ottomans. To a Muslim government, such an approach was repugnant not only on political grounds but also on religious and legal bases. The Muslims argued that if the patriarch became a Muslim, his followers would not be forced to follow the ideas of the apostasized prelate. It should be pointed out here that the Ottomans did not oppose union with the Catholic church for any religious reasons; in the eyes of Muslims, all Christian sects were equally wrong. To force a dissenter back into his original sect for reasons of faith would imply an approval of the doctrines of that sect, a grave sin.[40]

The Roman Catholic church, however, found it necessary to establish a separate church for theological reasons. According to the Catholic principle of "communicatio in sacris cum hereticis," a true Catholic could not participate in false or heretical worship; the converted or "true believers" had to leave their mother church.[41] In order to avoid the danger of "communicatio in sacris," the Catholic church tried to win over a patriarch together with his flock, in spite of the difficulties of the task. At the beginning, writes De Vries, the Catholic missionaries hoped to penetrate the non-Catholic communities more and more with Catholic elements and in this way "to capture them." When this had gone far enough, they hoped to place a Catholic patriarch at the head of the community and thus "to pull it over entirely."[42]

4

Thanks to their zeal and the propitious political conditions that prevailed in northern Syria, the apostolic friars achieved at least some of their goals. Among the Jacobites of Aleppo, where there had been no native Catholic priests by the mid-seventeenth century, there were nineteen out of a total of twenty-two only twelve years later. Of the five thousand Jacobites who lived in the city, about 75 percent had become Catholic in the early 60s of that century. Under these encouraging developments, steps were taken to back the election to the patriarchate of a man who could bring into the Catholic fold his entire community with him.

The man of the hour was Andrew Akhijan (Akhījān), eventually consecrated patriarch of the newly founded Syrian Catholic church. Akhijan, whose father, a Jacobite merchant of Mardin, had settled in Aleppo, spent most of his life there.[43] In the city's exciting international environment, young Andrew was attracted to the religion preached by European missionaries. He studied its doctrine and practice and was received into the Maronite church, since no Catholic or uniate branch existed within his own Jacobite congregation.[44] From Syria, Andrew, an impressive young man of great piety and "thirst for knowledge," was sent by the Maronite patriarch to the Maronite college in Rome.

When the time came for the Catholic missionaries to consecrate a Catholic bishop for the Jacobites of Aleppo, the French consul in the city, Francois Picquet, had "promised to do everything in his power to persuade the Jacobite patriarch to agree."[45] The patriarch was invited twice to dinner by the representative of Louis XIV, and eventually was convinced to accept a former Jacobite, Andrew Akhijan, a Catholic, as the new bishop of Aleppo.[46] When the time for his consecration came, it was considered "illicit" to have the ceremony conducted by the Jacobite patriarch.[47] The problem was "resolved" in 1656 by having the Maronite patriarch, Ḥanna al-Ṣafrāwi, consecrate Akhijan a Maronite bishop first and then to have the patriarch of the Jacobite church install him as a Jacobite bishop. The "Maronite" bishop, now known as Mar Denis Akhijan, was instructed to work in Aleppo "for the conversion of the Jacobites," and was notified "not to interfere among the Maronites of Aleppo."[48] When the Jacobite community heard that Andrew had "defected" to the Maronites and was now supposedly one of their bishops, they refused to have him installed as one of their own. The

Jacobite patriarch, who had originally been willing to consecrate him and present him to his people, not only resented the high-handed manner with which Andrew's induction was conducted, but was insulted that another patriarch was asked to consecrate his bishop.

The Jacobite prelate was again invited to dinner at the residence of the French consul. When Picquet found the patriarch unwilling to accept Andrew, he took the matter into his own hands. Without consulting the patriarch, he had some leading "Catholic Jacobites" write and sign a testimonial petitioning that Andrew Akhijan be appointed their archbishop. The petition was forwarded to the French ambassador in Istanbul with a personal letter from Picquet, asking the ambassador to use his influence in getting a "command" from the sultan (Muhammad IV) recognizing Andrew as the legitimately elected pastor of the Jacobite community in Aleppo. The "command" duly arrived.[49] The French consul showed the decree to "his great friend" the pasha of Aleppo, who had "at once commissioned his chief subordinates to officially accompany Andrew into the Syrian cathedral of St. Mary." The pasha's officials were instructed to inform the Syrian Orthodox (Jacobites) that "the Sultan had consented to their request, that Bishop Andrew was their bishop"! The Jacobites were warned in the sultan's order of investiture that "anyone not recognizing Andrew Akhijan Bishop will be considered an enemy of the Empire."[50] According to the reports of the Propaganda Fide, the French consul had Akhijan maintained for eight months in his own house with two servants, provided him with sacred vestments, and gave gifts to the pasha and other ministers and priests "to attract them to the side of the bishop."[51]

In spite of the imperial warning and gifts to the priests, there continued to be frequent conflicts and violent arguments between the Catholic and Orthodox Jacobites. Jacobite priests refused to obey the instructions of Mar Denis and noisily interrupted the liturgy when the names of their Monophysite churchmen were passed over. Catholic deacons, on the other hand, refused to serve under "Orthodox" priests because the latter would insist on the commemoration of Dioscorus and others.[52]

The Jacobite leaders of Aleppo who were opposed to their new bishop were headed by Mar Denis's own brother Aslān.[53] But Aslān, in the words of Picquet, was "chased from the Church by the authority of the cadi." The French consul had Aslān summoned before the pasha; the Qāḍi had officially declared him mad and ordered that he was not to enter the Syrian church. In order to escape a similar treatment, the Jacobite patriarch had fled Aleppo to Damascus soon after he had heard of the sultan's firman.

Akhijan, unable to reconcile the opposition and perhaps repelled by the tactics used by the French consul to thwart it, decided to withdraw to

Lebanon. He was unhappy heading "a heretical sect." In a letter to Pope Alexander VII, Andrew "reveals his bewilderment and anxieties over the rites, customs and beliefs of the Jacobites, and reveals his doubt of the validity of so many of them." A well-trained Catholic, he questioned the Jacobite form of baptism and eucharist and the validity of their sacred orders and "worried at the custom of mixing 'pepper, cinnamon and other spices in the chrism';" questioned the fact that altars were made of wood rather than stone as well as the manner in which they made the sign of the cross with one finger signifying the single nature of Christ. He also had doubts about his own juridical status since he was consecrated archbishop of Aleppo as a Maronite but was serving as bishop of the Jacobites.[54] His participation in Jacobite rite and liturgy was to be avoided in accordance with the principle of "communicatio in sacris."

In order to solve the problem of Andrew's legitimacy, "the Supreme Pontiff, who held the keys, supplied the jurisdiction which was lacking." Andrew was granted a dispensation to follow a rite diverse from that of the Maronites. He was recognized by the pope as legitimate archbishop of Aleppo with the power and permission to perform all juridical acts incumbent in that office. While Akhijan's juridical status was legitimized in the eyes of the church, the situation in Aleppo did not bring him the "security of a good conscience." He was determined to withdraw to Lebanon and he did. Francois Picquet was equally determined to bring him back to Aleppo and to have the Jacobite priests go to him and beg him to return and at the same time promise that they would never again oppose him.

Picquet wrote the French ambassador in Istanbul and asked him to obtain a firman that would address itself to the Jacobite priests who had opposed their legitimately elected leader. The firman arrived but it was much stronger than had been expected: it asked for the execution of the Jacobite priests who had been responsible for Akhijan's departure to Lebanon. When the pasha of Aleppo, a new official, had asked Picquet what course of action he recommended, the consul had asked that the two most troublesome priests be summoned before him to be a little frightened. The priests, thoroughly frightened, had promised that they would do anything that the French consul wished. The consul ordered them to go and persuade Akhijan to return and to promise him total obedience. Before setting out on their journey, the two "ringleaders" had all the other priests meet together with them at the consul's residence and there all signed a statement confessing that they had been responsible for the flight of their archbishop, promising that two of them would go and persuade him to return. Their statement also noted that if he were again obliged to leave his see, they would forfeit three thousand scudi to the pasha. In order to put more teeth into the plan, the pasha himself decreed that if the priests failed to bring their bishop back, five Jacobite priests would be executed. The Catholic friars had no doubt about the result of the priestly mission to Lebanon. One of them is quoted seeing the "gain of 5,000 souls for . . . the holy Roman Church."[55]

Unfortunately for the missionaries, Andrew could not be persuaded to return. The priests returned empty-handed, their lives spared by assurances from Andrew to Picquet that they were not to be blamed.[56] The Catholic missionaries had to use another approach to have Andrew return: convince him that it was the will of God that he come back; that "it would be sinful to abandon such a wonderful project and that it was for the glory of God that he battles."[57] Andrew was eventually persuaded that his return was for his own salvation and for the salvation of his own people. He was received, according to a contemporary (1658) report, "with applause by the few Catholic Syrians, with disappointment by the heretics." The pasha's order warned that the Jacobites of Aleppo who did not obey Akhijan would be treated as rebels.[58]

The Jacobites were not easily intimidated. They even took the offensive and reinforced their campaign with the old familiar charge that the bishop was conspiring with the Franks to plot the overthrow of the Ottoman Empire.[59] Thanks to the bishop's policy of passive resistance, the situation did not erupt in any violence. Akhijan subjected himself to his foe's abusive treatment lest the Turks step in to arbitrate. He knew that fines and penalties would be ruinous to all concerned.

In time, opposition began to wane; by 1660 several of the priests and many of their congregations followed Andrew into union and professed the Catholic faith. Historian of the Syrian Catholic church Wilhelm De Vries is of the opinion that "a miracle" which occurred in Aleppo early in 1660 had contributed to Akhijan's success. The miracle concerned a young Polish slave who had killed his Muslim master, who had tried to force him to commit sodomy. The slave was then condemned to death and executed, and his body, together with the bodies of other executed men, was thrown to the dogs. The dogs, however, left the corpses of the Christian slave untouched and, what is more, his dead body lay there for ten days with a smile on his face. Indeed, a sweet odor emanated from him. This made a deep impression on everybody and was taken as a heavenly confirmation of the Catholic faith.

Also in 1660, Consul François Picquet, who had decided to return to France to prepare himself for the priesthood, was tonsured by Mar Denis Akhijan. He was ordained a priest in 1664. The secretary of the Propaganda had encouraged Picquet to enter into the clerical state, "although it was generally felt that he could do more apostolic work in his consular position than as a priest in France."[60] After his ordination, the Propaganda Fide named him vicar apostolic of Babylon and also apostolic visitator to Cyprus, Aleppo, Tripoli of Syria, Lebanon, and

Nakhichevan. In 1681 he was named by Louis XIV ambassador extraordinary to Shah Abbas. He died in Hamadan four years later.

With their great friend gone, the Catholic missionaries began to wonder how permanent their efforts would prove to be. What would happen if Bishop Akhijan died? Wouldn't the Jacobites replace him with a "heretic"? The decision was made to consecrate Andrew Akhijan's successor while the bishop was still living. In order to avoid the complications that had surrounded Akhijan's consecration, they decided that he himself should consecrate his successor, whom they suggested should be his brother Paul. The Propaganda gave its approval that Paul be constituted coadjutor, an assistant with the right of future succession. But how could a bishop consecrate another bishop? The laws of the Jacobite church reserved the right of episcopal consecrations to the patriarch of the church. The decision was therefore made that Akhijan first be consecrated patriarch and then have him ordain his brother bishop-successor.

The situation acquired great urgency in the summer of 1662 when the Jacobite patriarch died. The missionaries and the new French consul, Francois Baron, were "feverishly working" to have Akhijan nominated patriarch.[61] The only way that this could be done was to have a firman issued from "on high." Picquet, still interested and in touch with the Aleppo situation, wrote the secretary of the Sacred Congregation for the Propagation of the Faith that they should send "a courier to Constantinople to obtain the nomination from the Great Lord [Sultan] and by this means to close the door" to the Jacobite pretender, "the enemy of our faith."

The sultan's nomination could not be procured without spending "hundreds of Scudi;" Picquet suggested that the Holy Father be requested to make provisions for this. In Aleppo, Consul Baron and the missionaries had already borrowed "800 pieces of gold and had written Picquet to beg the Sacred Propaganda to aid them in this urgent situation." Always mindful of "his" bishop, Picquet also suggested that a "yearly subsidy of 1000 Scudi be paid Andrew so that the Catholics can take quick advantage in the future of opportunities similar to the present one." The Propaganda would not collaborate in these schemes and wanted the exconsul, his successor in Aleppo, and the missionaries to be "advised that this means of promoting the Catholic religion is altogether disapproved by this Sacred Congregation." Indeed, the Sacred Congregation had "no intention of promoting Andrew to Patriarch."[62]

In those days of slow communication the Sacred Congregation was discussing (on 11 September, 1662) the question of Andrew Akhijan's elevation to the patriarchate more than a month after Akhijan had already been elected patriarch, his election confirmed by the sultan. Akhijan was enthroned on 20 August, 1662 with great fanfare. He received a gold lettered *barā'ah* from Sultan Muḥammad IV confirming him the head of all the Jacobite millet.[63] The pasha of Aleppo had his guards salute the new patriarch, who at his enthronement chose the name *"Ignatius Andreas,* Patriarch of Aleppo.*"*[64] The captain of the guards presented him with a bouquet of flowers, and the crowds cheered and saluted him with the accompaniment of trumpets and drums. The pasha informed Akhijan that he had only to report those who would disobey him; the pasha would know how to enforce obedience.[65]

The missionaries had informed the Propaganda that Andrew would "not perform any patriarchal function until he had obtained the confirmation of the Holy Apostolic See." Faced with a *fait accompli,* the Congregation at a meeting held in audience with Pope Alexander VII voted for the confirmation of the first patriarch of the "Syrian Catholics." A letter bearing the pontiff's name and blessings was sent to Andrew Akhijan. The secretary of the Propaganda expressed "the joys which his assumption to the patriarchate has brought to the Cardinals of the Sacred Congregation," and advised Akhijan to use moderation so that "by pastoral affection, the aversion of the dissidents might be mitigated."

The warm congratulations of the cardinals were also sent to the French consul Baron for his "zealous work in effecting the election," expressing appreciation for the difficulties and expenses that he had faced. The Congregation realized, wrote the secretary, that it "can never repay the consul for what he has done on behalf of the Catholic Faith." the missionary fathers were commended for their industry in cooperating with the French consul in effecting the election, but they were also cautioned to use the favorable dispositions of the patriarch's authority with moderation so that they might render the persons of the patriarch and the missionaries less odious.[66]

Akhijan's reign of almost fifteen years was marked by many tribulations. At the very outset of his patriarchate, two Jacobite bishops, Shukr-Allah and 'Abd al-Masih, attempted to destroy the union and the man who headed it. The year following the enthronization of Andrew, 'Abd al-Masih, backed by the qāḍi of Diyarbakr, came to Aleppo claiming the right of the patriarchate, showing a forged *barā'ah* of recognition from the Sultan. He was able to influence both the pasha and the qāḍi of Aleppo, and was able to occupy the Jacobite church, forcing Andrew to take refuge with the European missionaries. 'Abd al-Masih's victory, however, was shortlived; the French consul and the missionaries rallied to the side of Akhijan and had Sultan Muḥammad IV issue a new *barā'ah* in behalf of the Syrian Catholic patriarch. The imperial decree, dated 21 January, 1664, declared that the monk Andrew, "to whom the patriarchate has been granted by my Imperial Firman . . . has had his rights violated . . . by the monk Shukr-Allah with the complicity of the

monk 'Abd al-Masīh. Notwithstanding the request of the qādi of Diyarbakr who recommends this dignity for the monk Shukr-Allāh, my Firman has been given, confirming the monk Andrew . . . and the two
monks . . . or any other cannot oppose him"[67]

According to a communication sent by the French consul Baron to
Rome from Aleppo at this time, dated 10 April, 1664, the sultan had sent
an official delegate to see to it that Andrew would be not only reinstated
but also accepted by his millet as the true and legitimate patriarch, not
only in Aleppo but everywhere. To this end it was arranged that the
sultan's representative, accompanied by an impressive retinue, would
conduct Andrew Akhijan "to Diyarbekir, Mardin and other cities, to
have him recognized also in these places." Consul Baron assured the
Sacred Congregation that "Monsignor Andrew has already been reestablished . . . with the applause of all nations," and boasted that "for a
thousand years, such things have never been seen nor heard here."[68]

5

When Andrew Akhijan died on 24 July, 1677, he was succeeded by
the Jacobite Patriarch 'Abd al-Masīh. Until he was fully recognized, the
new prelate was very cautious not to alienate the strong Catholic party in
Aleppo. Until then he pretended to be a Catholic in union with Rome
and anathemized those who opposed the decision of the Council of
Chalcedon.[69] His pretensions ended when his order of investiture arrived
from Istanbul. He then became a zealous partisan of the Jacobite
church.[70] The strong congregation of Catholic Syrians of Aleppo rejected him and chose as his successor his 37-year old nephew, Gregory
Peter Shahbaddīn, the bishop of Jerusalem, whom Andrew Akhijan had
won over to the Catholic church and had designated as his successor.
Another battle raged between the two parties, this time headed by an uncle and his nephew. Litigations, court cases, and intrigues on both sides
were so strong that five times the young patriarch was able to get an
order of investiture from the sultan and took possession of the Jacobite
cathedral and its dependencies by military force, and five times he was
expelled by his uncle or his uncle's successor, who got their *barā'ah* post
dating that of the nephew. In 1700 the nephew was reinstalled into the
patriarchate through the intervention of the Austrian emperor Leopold I
and the intercession of Pope Innocent XII with the Sublime Porte.[71] Ignatius Peter VI (Shahbaddīn) received also the support of Louis XIV,
who had assured him an annual stipend which Colbert had made the
monarch promise "will be given every year."[72] The final battle, however,
was won by the Jacobites. The nephew, who was named Mār Ignatius
Peter VI, and one of his Catholic bishops were at first imprisoned and
then sent into exile at Adana. The bishop died on his first day there; Ignatius Peter passed away three months later,[73] early in 1702.

After 1702 the Syrian Catholic patriarchal throne remained unoccupied for eighty years.[74] Gibb and Bowen, most probably following Graf, mistakenly count a third patriarch in the Akhijan line, referring to Ishāq Ibn Jubayr, whom Innocent XIII wanted consecrated. But Ishāq had "for reasons of prudence, thought he should not accept the dignity" and decided to go to Rome, where he spent the rest of his life. The French ambassador informed the Propaganda that he "would like to hold him (Ibn Jubayr) here until a favorable occasion will be at hand to make him the Patriarch of the Syrians, but I know not for what reason he decided to go to Rome."[75] In Rome he was surnamed Vicar Patriarchal. In the words of the French consul in Aleppo, "the Syrian Jacobites will never become Catholics except to the extent to which one gives them money. . . Even the bishops who were considered the most faithful Catholics, signed up with the other people [who] are yelling that the missionaries wanted them to refuse obedience to the sultan and to make them subjects of his enemy the Pope."[76]

For almost the next eighty years the "Catholic Jacobites" remained deprived of a patriarch, dispossessed of their churches. The majority of the Orthodox who had followed Akhijan in Aleppo returned to the Monophysite patriarch 'Abd al-Masih. The welfare and affairs of the officially unrecognized Syrian Catholics were attended to by Rome through Syrian Catholic bishops, some of them designated vicars patriarchal; they resided either in Rome or Jerusalem, or at the monastery of Mār Afrām Rughm in Lebanon.[77]

The Orthodox church was further strengthened at this time when a considerable portion of the Nestorian church membership in Malabar, India, which had joined the Catholic church at the very end of the sixteenth century, left it again. Instead of returning to its mother church, it joined the Jacobite communion (1665).[78]

Unfortunately for the Catholic church, Aleppo was not a major Jacobite city; the homegrounds of the community in mid-seventeenth century were still in northern Iraq and the lands to the north of it.[79] Although Mosul had been assigned to the French Capuchins in 1665, followed by Diyarbakr in 1667, and by Mardin in 1691, not much was accomplished in these Jacobite strongholds until the eighteenth century, when a special mission was sent to "Upper Mesopotamia."[80]

It was not until the second half of the eighteenth century that Catholic Jacobites began their struggle again. This time they were successful in establishing a line of patriarchs, which has continued uninterrupted to this day.[81] Their candidate for the office was Mikhā'il (Michael) Jarwah, who, like Akhijan, was a native of Aleppo. Jarwah had been consecrated bishop of that city just over a hundred years after Andrew Akhijan had been that city's primate. But Jarwah was a Jacobite, and his consecration at the age of 35 had been by the hands of the Jacobite patriarch at Mardin.[82]

6

Growing up in Aleppo, Michael Jarwah was much influenced and impressed by the Catholic organization and education there; he had become a "Catholic at heart," if not secretly converted to Catholicism.[83] As bishop of Aleppo he had introduced in the liturgy of his church Catholic rites, which his Orthodox clergy objected to. Michael had defended his innovations, pointing out their popularity with the people. The patriarch, suspicious of Michael's motives, decided to retain the bishop in custody at the Dayr al-Za'farān, where he remained for almost three years. In late 1774 he fled from the cloister and early in 1775 formally joined the Roman Catholic church, followed by almost the entire Jacobite community of Aleppo.

After the death of the Jacobite patriarch Ignatius Jurjus IV in 1781, Michael Jarwah was invited by a faction of the Jacobite community to go to Mardin and accept the patriarchate of their church. A large number of those who asked him had Catholic leanings even though officially still under the jurisdiction of the Jacobite patriarchate.[84]

The researches of William De Vries show that Michael accepted the invitation only when the Syrians promised to convert to the Catholic church. This they did by accepting the articles of faith demanded from Eastern Christians by the Pope.[85] At the end of 1781 Jarwah arrived at Mardin, where four out of the six bishops convened, converted to Catholicism, elected him patriarch, consecrated him, and enthroned him early in 1783[86] at Dayr al-Za'farān as Ignatius Michael III. That same year he received papal confirmaton but, unfortunately for him and his followers, he could not get the confirmation of the sultan in time.[87] The two rival bishops ordained four other bishops in place of those who had converted and soon a "Jacobite" patriarch was elected, Matta (Matthew), the bishop of Mardin.[88] While Ignatius Michael Jarwah waited for his *barā'ah*, the rival party was able to obtain theirs. When Michael's *barā'ah* arrived the Jacobites voided it by another decree of investiture dispossessing Michael of his office, churches, monasteries, and personal property.[89] His reign became one of flights, exiles, imprisonment, and attacks. Like Akhijan and others before him, Michael Jarwah sought refuge with the Maronites in Lebanon.[90] In Lebanon, war-torn at the time by conflict between Jazzār and Amīr Yūsuf Shihāb, Jarwah was housed in an old Maronite convent for four months and then for another four months subsisted on the charity of a Maronite village. After the conflict the Maronite hierarchy helped him to obtain an old schoolhouse in the mountains at al-Sharfah.[91] Unlike Patriarch Andrew Akhijan, Michael Jarwah did not have the strong backing of a Louis XIV and his ambassadors in the Ottoman Empire. France was at war with herself.

The anti-clericalism of the French Revolution meant a decline in French missionary activity. The revolution and the political upheavals that followed it had exhausted the resources of the various congregations and associations that had supported the apostolic movement.[92] By the time Michael Jarwah died, only a skeleton remained of the religious orders and missionary organizations once active throughout Asia and Africa. But from the relatively secure mountain fastness of al-Sharfah in Lebanon his successors followed him with no serious interruptions.

Because he had at least started as a patriarch of all the Jacobites, Michael was confirmed by the pope as "patriarch of Antioch," a title with which Akhijan and his successor has not been honored.[93] The line of prelates that Jarwah started is considered by the Catholic church as a continuation of the old "schismatic" Jacobite church; the old church was brought to "new life" by its union with Rome.[94]

Jarwah died in 1800; two years later he was succeeded by Ignatius Michael IV Daher, who, for personal reasons, resigned from the office in 1810, after eight years of undistinguished reign. His successor, elected in 1811, was Ignatius Sim'ān Zūrah, who also resigned, retiring in 1818 to the monastery of Mar Afrām in Lebanon. After a brief interregnum,[95] the Syrian Catholic bishops elected in 1820 a nephew of Mikhāi'l Jarwah, Butrus (Peter), as patriarch. Ignatius VII Butrus had a long reign of thirty-one years. Under him the fratricidal struggles between the Jacobites and their Catholic brethren ceased, and fortunately for the Catholic branch, the violent storms unleashed against the church by the French Revolution began to recede very early during the nineteenth century. By 1830 France was ready to come to the aid of the persecuted Catholics of the Ottoman Empire.

7

The missionary cause became a popular French as well as Catholic one soon after Napoleon came to power. The year after Napoleon signed his concordat with the Roman Catholic church, he asked for and received a report on the Catholic missions. The document, submitted to him in 1802, proposed that the first consul sustain and encourage the foreign missions, described as one of the most effective means of serving the interests and glory of the French nation.[96] Lay circles soon joined the religious in the task of reviving missions. The Society for the Propagation of the Faith, founded in 1822,[97] was the first nationwide organization to participate in the missionary effort, a task undertaken by numerous congregations, mission societies, institutes, and seminaries throughout France.[98]

French colonial interests, revived under Napoleon and expanded after him, brought the throne and the altar closer together. In the Ottoman Empire, however, friction between France and the Sublime Porte, begun under Napoleon, continued after him. In 1817 Sultan Mahmūd had prohibited all Catholic missionary activity; his Catholic subjects were forbidden to visit Latin missionaries; Malkite Catholics (Rūm Kāthūlīk) were ordered to return to their own Greek Orthodox mother church. During the Greek revolution the sultan, fearing Catholic relations with European powers, had the Armenian and Greek Orthodox patriarchs banish their own community Catholics from the empire. The active role that France played during the Greek revolution against the Turkish government exacerbated the situation. At the Battle of Navarino in the fall of 1827 the French fleet had helped in the complete destruction of the Ottoman Egyptian navy." Once again the Catholic proteges of France were exiled; many from Aleppo fled and found refuge in Lebanon.

Defeated on the Greek front the Ottoman Empire was faced with yet another war with Russia in 1828-29, which Turkey also lost.[100] After the war, exiled Catholics were allowed to return to their homes and property. In 1830 the Roman Catholic church and the Sublime Porte began negotiations which in the summer of that year transferred the charge of the Armenian Catholics from the Latin vicar apostolic to an archbishop-primate of their own. On 5 January, 1831 an Armenian patriarch was elected as the head of the newly created Armenian Catholic millet, setting the precedent for other Catholic communities.[101] A Catholic community was now represented before the Sublime Porte by its own spiritual and temporal head, freed from the jurisdiction of the patriarch of its own mother church.

From the Turkish government's point of view, the sultan's Catholic subjects would now no longer find it necessary to attend Latin churches or be protected by a vicar delegate from Rome. A sensitive issue between the Ottoman government and the Roman Catholic church, the question of "Latinization" of the Middle Eastern Catholics was regularized by the Congregation of the Propaganda of the Faith by a decree issued on 20 November, 1838. The decreee permitted the sultan's Christian subjects to choose any Middle Eastern rite upon entering the Catholic church; the Latin rite was closed to them.[102] This paved the way in 1839 for all the Ottoman subjects who had embraced Catholicism to be formally granted legal status, the division between them and their non-Catholic brethren confirmed and made permanent. They also objected to being under the jurisdiction of the newly created Armenian Catholic patriarchate. One after another, the different Uniat churches were formally recognized. The "Jacobite" Catholics were formally recognized as a separate and distinct community when Peter Jarwah was granted civil as well as spiritual jurisdiction over his flock in 1843.[103]

Sultan Mahmūd's son and successor, Abdul Majid ('Abd al-Majīd), entered into diplomatic relations with the Roman Catholic church. In 1847 his ambassador at Vienna requested an audience with the newly elected Pope Pius IX, the first request of its kind from an Ottoman diplomat.[104] A few months after the Turkish ambassador's visit Pope Pius announced the reestablishment of the ancient Latin patriarchate of Jerusalem and soon addressed a letter to all the Middle Eastern Christians letting them know that he was sending an ambassador to Istanbul; he invited these "separated" brethren into Catholic unity.[105]

The road to large-scale "conversions" from the Jacobite as well as other churches was wide open, well guarded legally and politically. "The movement towards Rome," wrote a British consular official, "took place not only in Aleppo and Damascus but in Rasheya, a small town lying at the foot of the northern slopes of Mount Hermon, and spread to places such as Nabak and Qaryatayn, to the north, and Qal'at Jandal where the Jacobites had a convent, to the southwest of Damascus."[106] In 1854 the Syrian Catholic patriarch dared to establish his residence in the midst of Jacobite heartlands, in Mardin,[107] where the patriarchs of the Syrian Catholic church would remain until the post-World-War-I period.[108]

After 1830 the Roman Catholic church was headed by Gregory XVI, a missionary pope who as cardinal had served as a prefect of the Propaganda Fide,[109] and had represented Pope Pius in negotiations with the Ottoman government.[110] Gregory started widespread reorganization of mission territories. Apostolic labors developed especially rapidly after the French colonial expansion started in earnest after 1860. The opening up of Africa, especially, stirred up the imagination for new spiritual as well as geographical conquests. In faraway regions of the globe such as Indo-China, "missionaries frequently arrived before the soldiers," according to a Catholic encyclopedia.[111] In the Ottoman Empire French aid against Russia during the Crimean War further facilitated the work of the Catholic religious establishments, many of them French.

Catholic gains spread eastward into Iraq, where the Roman Catholic church had established missions as early as the seventeenth century; this was after the fall of 1627, when the Propaganda Fide had given permission to enlarge the Capuchin mission area into both Iraq and Iran. The friendly relations that existed between the papacy and Shah 'Abbās the Great, whose realm then covered Baghdad, had a great deal to do with the decision of the Propaganda. The presence of the Roman Church in Baghdad was deemed important because it would strengthen the union of the Chaldean Catholic church (originally Nestorian), which had already taken place during the previous century.[112] The Baghdad mission was manned by the French Capuchins who very early gained a firm foothold there, thanks to the combined recommendations of King Louis XIII and Shah 'Abbās and the fact that the Propaganda had given the friars permission to practice the medical arts gratis.[113]

To the native Christians the political support that the fathers afforded was even more appreciated than the medicines. In less than ten years after their arrival the Capuchin fathers were able to repeal the Persian law in Baghdad which robbed children of Christian parents of their inheritance, bestowing it to those members of the family who apostatized to Islam.[114] Reporting to the Propaganda in 1665, the superior of the Carmelite mission in Aleppo noted that a large community of Jacobites in Baghdad had made a solemn profession of faith and had pledged obedience to Andrew Akhijan.[115]

The Discalced Carmelites established a mission in Baghdad soon after the Capuchins,[116] their mission created by Mme. Elisabeth de Ricouart, widow of a councillor in the Parlement of Paris. She offered the Propaganda Fide funds to set up and found a bishopric in the Middle East with the condition that she be allowed to nominate the first bishop and all his successors be Frenchmen. Her candidate was her confessor, Fr. Bernard of St. Teresa, who was appointed "Bishop of Baghdad." Unfortunately for Father Bernard, Baghdad was recaptured by the Turks in 1638 and he was forced to proceed to Isfahan without residing in his See in Iraq. Writing from Baghdad in a letter of 11 December, 1639, a few months after the capture of the city, a Portuguese priest noted that Turks had banned the building of new churches or the rebuilding of old ones.[117]

The mission, now serving two enemy territories, was suspect in the eyes of the Turks and, it would seem, for good reason. It was becoming clear to the Ottomans that the "Christian" embassies of Europe in Istanbul were trying to gain the sympathy and support of the sultan's Christian subjects in order to enhance their own influence within the empire.[118] The Roman Catholic hierarchy was often a willing participant in these political intrigues. An authority on the Carmelite missions emphasized that Pope Clement VIII in placing a mission in Persia was primarily using the friars "as legates to forward his policy, which was to protect Christendom against the Turks by developing friendly relations and ensuring direct and reliable communications and negotiations with the ruler of Persia."[119]

Intermittent wars with Safavid Persia in the 1730s and 1740s turned the Ottomans against the "diocese of Baghdad." Writing from Aleppo in 1742, the pro-vicar apostolic of Baghdad noted that, by an imperial decree, "It was forbidden to any Christian to profess the religion of the 'Franks' whether secretly or publicly, or to enter their churches, and all that under pain of confiscation of property and the most grievous punishment."[120]

During this period the non-Catholic Middle Eastern Christians were able to seize churches that the Catholic converts had taken over in years past. It was now easy for the "Orthodox" to present orders from the grand vizier or their local pashas to have Catholics exiled and suppressed and to hurl insults and anathemas against "our holy Father . . . and the

Council of Chalcedon."[121] But the Catholic fathers were not discouraged. By mid-eighteenth century Carmelite reports to the Propaganda Fide noted that the "greater part" of the Christians in Baghdad, some 150 families of Jacobites, Nestorians, and Armenians, had embraced the Catholic faith . . ."[122]

It was after the French Revolution, however, that the Roman Catholic church was able to establish a strong foothold among the Christians of Iraq. Its mission would especially prosper during the second half of the nineteenth century, under the leadership of Marie-Joseph de Jesus who headed the apostolate for forty years (1858-98).[123] In 1842 Catholic Jacobites (Syrian Catholics) were able to establish a school of their own. But as late as 1863 they had no church in Baghdad; together with other sects united with Rome, they worshipped in a small Carmelite chapel. Under their first bishop, their first church was built in 1863, called Kanīsat al-'Adhrā' (Church of the Virgin).[124] In 1894 they built a school whose eightieth anniversary was celebrated in 1974.[125] By the end of the nineteenth century the majority of the Jacobites of Baghdad had joined the Roman Catholic church. H. Swainson Cowper, writing in the early 1890s on the Christian population of Baghdad, mentioned no Jacobites or Nestorians but only their Catholic brethren, 130 Syrian Catholic families.[126]

Soon after the Syrian Catholics were recognized as a separate body from their ancestral church, they demanded that outside Syria too, the churches of the community be divided between the two parties since they could no longer worship together. Because the churches had been built and consecrated as Syrian Orthodox edifices, the Jacobites resisted any division. The problem was first solved by having the two groups worship in the same churches but at different hours, alternating as to the precedency in time, but the solution proved to be short-lived.[127] On one occasion when the Catholics had the precedence, the worshippers were detained beyond the hour "by the harrangue of a celebrated priest" from Aleppo; the Jacobites had entered the church and demanded that their "hour of prayers had come," a demand which resulted in "a violent combat." When the pasha heard of the incident he had "all the priests in the city indiscriminately," including the non Jacobites, seized and thrust into jail, on the ground that "they all belonged to the same unbelieving race."[128] The disputes between the Catholic and non-Catholic worshippers were eventually settled by an extraordinary Solomonic solution—a firman from Istanbul directed that disputed churches should be divided in the middle by a wall and that each party should take a half.

In 1837 a directive ordered that two of the churches of Mosul be partitioned by a wall. The wall was torn down the following year only to be raised again a few months later by yet another royal decree. Horatio Southgate had seen these partitions and had attended service on one side, overhearing the worshippers on the other, both parties praying "as enemies under the same roof."[129] "Ultimately," wrote Rassam, "the Catholics were permitted to appropriate the principal church" thanks to the interference of the French embassy at Constantinople."[130] Eventually three of the oldest Jacobite monasteries were allotted to the Catholic branch, the most famous of them being Dayr Mār Bahnām, near Mosul.[131] One of the most interesting Christian monuments in Iraq, its foundations were laid in the fourth century. Its patron saint according to Jacobite tradition[132] was son of the Assyrian king Sennacherib. Abandoned by the Jacobites in the 1840s, when it was occupied by a few Kurds, the convent was recovered in the 1850s and repaired by the Syrian Catholics.[133]

The establishment of the Syrian Catholic patriarchal residence in Mardin in 1854 led to greater expansion of Catholicism.[134] As early as the late 1850s the American missionaries in Anatolia were referring to Mardin as "the headquarters of the papacy in Assyria."[135] These Catholic advances were in a large measure due to the official recognition of their church by the Ottoman government referred to above. Only six years before that recognition, the Reverend Joseph Wolff had written that the Syrian Catholics had neither church nor priests in these remote Jacobite regions. "They were compelled," he wrote, "to have their children baptized by the Syrian (Jacobite) Bishop, and be married by him." The hundred Syrian Catholic families that he reported were called "Maklubin" (Maqlūbīn). He quoted a Jacobite bishop whom he had interviewed in the early 1820s as saying that "no Catholic missionary ever dared to go" to Jabal Tur, where even the Turks, according to the bishop, felt insecure.[136]

While Jabal Tur would continue to remain a Jacobite stronghold—because of its isolated and mountainous terrain—throughout the nineteenth century, this would not be true of the rest of the Jacobite homegrounds. As early as the 1840s Episcopalian Southgate found Jacobites turned Catholics to be more attached to their new faith than the Chaldeans (Nestorians turned Catholics).[137] Syrian Catholics were well-informed and persuasive missionaries of their new faith. Some of them were learned scholars educated in Rome, and familiar with the European currents of thought.[138] Their educated and disciplined priests, let alone the impressive Latin clergy, were ever ready to give religious instructions, which the Jacobite priests, like their other non-Catholic brethren, were not in a position to offer.[139]

The Middle Eastern Christians admired not only the instruction of Roman Catholic Christian doctrine and piety and the elementary truths of the catechism which they received from the seminary-educated priests of their own community, but they were also impressed by the schools and churches that their European coreligionists built. The Protestant missionaries wrote in 1874 that the Roman Catholics of Mosul had "the finest church edifice this side of Constantinople," in addition to five schools there, and a well-conducted press establishment.[140] In 1878 the Dominican fathers established the "Syro-Chaldean" seminary of Saint John, so called because it served the Syrian and Chaldean Catholics, both of whom had Syriac as the language of their rite and liturgy—which would serve the Uniat churches long and well.[141] At the turn of the century the papal representative in Mesopotamia resided in Mosul, his delegation supported "with considerable state" from funds bequeathed by a French woman. The "papists," noted an American missionary report, "have an overpowering influence in the Government and a large and valuable property in the midst of the city . . . ; nearly every Christian village [of the province of Mosul] is in name ruled by them."[142] It was a powerful incentive to become associated with the Catholic establishment. Its social and economic rewards were as significant in this world as its spiritual compensation was promised to be in the hereafter. The majority of the Jacobites in and around Mosul, predicted a report to the American Board of Commissioners in 1880, "in sheer despair will surrender to the Papal Bull and to the results of papal intrigue." A respectable minority, it hoped, "will fall to the side of Protestantism and progress."[143]

The Jacobite and other orthodox establishments were clearly threatened by the progress that the Roman Catholic church was steadily able to make during the post-Napoleonic period. In their desperation, they turned their attention to Russia, whose presence in Ottoman territories was especially felt after Russia's successful war with Turkey in 1878. But the grievances of the Jacobite ecclesiastical hierarchy were not so much anti-Ottoman as anti-Roman Catholic.

4

Protestants, Piety, and Politics

When the English Wesleyan minister-scholar John W. Etheridge wrote his well-known volume *The Syrian Churches* in the 1830s,[1] he wondered when the Protestant missionary societies would labor for the true evangelization of the venerable Jacobite church.[2] He did not know at the time of his writing that what he was espousing was being undertaken by the Episcopal church of the United States. In 1835 that church's board of foreign missions appointed Mr. Horatio Southgate to visit the Near East and to study missionary possibilities in Persia and Turkey, especially the Arab provinces of the Ottoman Empire, including Egypt. Mr. Southgate left for the Near East in 1836 and spent two years there. During his visit he became interested in missions among the Eastern Christians. He believed that the "native" and ancient followers of Christ offered great encouragement for the eventual conversion of their Muslim neighbors. The Eastern Christians, he wrote, had intimate connections with the "advancement of the Redeemer's kingdom among the Mohammedans."[3]

Mr. Southgate recommended to the Episcopal Society the founding of a mission to the Jacobites, basing his choice on the opinion that their Syrian church was free from "corruption" and was, like his own church, episcopal in its organization. Moreover, the Jacobites themselves were eager for instruction, and now that the second war between the sultan and Muḥammad 'Ali of Egypt had ended with the defeat of the latter, the settled condition of the country made the missionary effort possible.[4]

The fact that Turkish rule over Syria was reestablished, with the help of "Christian" England and Austria, gradually caused opposition to all Europeans to subside. Southgate saw a divine hand at work in these events. To him these developments were "one of the great links in the chain of Providence" which he hoped would lead "to the freedom, purity and renovated life of the long-afflicted Church in the East."[5] It is interesting to note that when Southgate first left for the Near East in 1836, Muḥammad 'Ali was in control of Syria. In a sermon that the evangelist delivered in New York on the eve of his departure, he spoke of mighty changes that had been taking place in the Ottoman Empire. He referred to Muḥammad 'Ali as a liberal and comparatively enlightened man, who afforded protection to foreigners and permitted freedom of opinion in matters of religion. To the young Episcopalian these events too were providential signs: "God is plainly calling to the Church, to enter in and possess the land."[6] He spoke of the necessity of preparing the way of the Lord, "even in the seat of the Empire," where the Turks, defeated by Muḥammad 'Ali, "have learned their weakness as a nation."

The Episcopal board of missions acted favorably and established the mission to the Near East in 1839, the year Southgate was ordained to the priesthood. The mission left for Istanbul in 1840, made up of two priests: Horatio Southgate, who after a brief stay in Istanbul was expected to take up residence at Mardin, where the Jacobite patriarch lived, and the Reverend John J. Robertson, who would labor among the Greek Orthodox Christians in the Ottoman capital.

The Episcopal mission was not the first American religious enterprise in Eastern Turkey and Mesopotamia. Also in the 1830s the Congregational church of New England has started its apostolic work among the Nestorian Christians in nearby Persian Azerbayjan.[7] In order to avoid interference with the work of this sister Protestant organization, the instructions to the Southgate mission explicitly stated that the Episcopal church intended no encroachment upon the Congregational board's mission field, which included the Armenians as well as the Nestorians of Turkey and Iran. But the Episcopal mission was instructed to point out to the Eastern churches the important differences that existed between the Episcopalians and the other Protestants. In a letter to the Jacobite patriarch from seven of the American Episcopal bishops, the Syrian prelate was informed that Mr. Southgate would make it clearly understood that the American Episcopal church "has no ecclesiastical connection with the followers of Luther and Calvin, and takes no part in their plans or operations to diffuse the principles of these sects."[8]

While emphasizing that they had very little in common with their fellow American Protestants, the Episcopalians stressed the similarities that existed between themselves and the Jacobites. Southgate was especially enthusiastic in emphasizing the beliefs and practices that the two churches had in common. He wrote of the "minute resemblances" that existed between the Episcopal church and the churches of the East, stressing the form of government and the prominence of traditional usage. Like the Jacobites, he liked to point out, he "belonged to a church governed by Bishops."[9] A "high" churchman, he thought that in some respects the Eastern Churches were ahead of those of the West, especially in the fullness with which their church services were carried out.[10] He found no real theological difference between the Monophysite Jacobites and the Episcopalians. "They attach," he explained, "to the one nature precisely the same idea that we attach to the one person, the difference is only in the word."[11]

However much the Episcopalians had in common with the Roman Catholic church in their sense of liturgy and tradition, they shared with the Reformation Protestants their opposition to Roman Catholicism. The Episcopalians, together with the other Protestants, often referred to the Roman Catholics as "our papal enemies,"[12] and the latter in turn treated the Protestants as adversaries and often tried to have them banished from the Ottoman Empire.[13] In its efforts to help the Jacobite church, the one-man Episcopal mission from the United States tried to save that church from the greatest threat that it thought the Jacobites faced—absorption within the Roman Catholic church, whose gains in popularity and influence in northern Mesopotamia we have already noted.[14] Early during his stay in Turkey, Horatio Southgate did all he could to resist the "torrent of Romanism" which had not only corrupted the literature of the Eastern churches by its "flood of Popish superstition," but was now forming alliances with the Sultan, which, however purely political on the one side, will be turned, on the other, to the advantage of Papal error."[15] As the lone member of his mission, Southgate was impressed, although undaunted, by the great number of Roman Catholic missionaries and the host of friars and sisters of charity who, in his opinion, were out to complete the work which political intrigues had begun.

2

The longer Mr. Southgate stayed in Istanbul, the more interested he became in the ecclesiastical intrigues which abounded in the sultan's capital, losing sight of the fact that the major function of his mission was to serve the Jacobite community in and around far-away Mardin. Soon after his arrival he had left Istanbul for a brief visit to the Jacobites in the spring of 1841, the only visit that he was to make with them during his decade as a "missionary to the Jacobites." In 1841, he had found the interior in "a sadly unsettled state, exposed to the depredations of the Kurds, badly governed and depopulated by famine."[16] The Jacobites, he wrote, had suffered dreadfully since his exploratory visit in 1838. His tour has lasted three months and was highlighted by a two-week stay with their patriarch at Dayr al-Za'farān.[17]

Southgate had returned sick from his tour, happy to be back in Istanbul to the refinement, social pleasures, and "holy delights of a Christian home." He had come back, he reported, from "a society of barbarous men, among whom one seldom meets with disinterested kindness but constantly with insult, churlishness or stupid indifference." He spoke of weary traveling day after day, over bad roads, on bad horses, under a burning sun; of lodging in stables thronging with fleas and lice.[18]

While still interested in establishing a station at Mardin, Southgate first wanted "to make all the necessary arrangements"—a task that would last ten years—in Instanbul before commencing his mission proper with vigor. He wrote the foreign committee of his church in New York that there was more to do in Istanbul than he could well accomplish. He hoped that "others" would eventually be sent to work among the Jacobites "for a more promising field I do not believe can be found in the world."[19]

The members of the foreign committee, who had expected him to stay in Mardin and to prepare the way for the mission to the Syrians, which he had advocated for so long and so ardently, were disappointed but patient. After his brief visit to inner Anatolia, Southgate started writing more and more of the importance of Istanbul as a "high post of observation" from which he could keep "all the Eastern Churches under survey and to act upon each part as we find opportunity."[20] In order to influence these churches, he explained, the Western church had first to gain for herself an influence such as she could never exert without establishing herself at the center. "Abandon Istanbul and the East is abandoned;" for the city "is the seat of some of the chief ecclesiastical powers of the East...the centre of life and action to the largest bodies of oriental Christians." If the mission at Istanbul were given up, he warned the foreign committee, he would not go to Mesopotamia or advise anyone else to do so.

After the spring of the following year (1842), it became more difficult for Southgate to exert "any further personal effort beyond Constantinople."[21] He started to write of his health, which had suffered severely through "multiplied labors," and complained that he could not sustain both the Constantinople and the Mesopotamia missions alone.

The foreign committee did not want Mr. Southgate to undertake any responsibilities in Istanbul. It had always regarded his presence in the capital as preparatory to his work among the Jacobites.[22] After prolonged deliberations, the committee decided to discontinue the Istanbul mission. It reminded the young priest that the instructions under which he had been sent out contemplated "at least a temporary residence" in northern Mesopotamia, where he would be joined by others in order to establish a more permanent station there.[23] He was instructed "to remove as soon as practicable, either to Mardin or Mossul'' for the direct accomplishment of the original objects of the mission to the Syrians.[24]

In order to help Southgate start the mission among the Jacobites, the committee sent two missionaries, the Reverend J. W. Miles and the Reverend Samuel A. Taylor. The two helpers arrived in Istanbul early in 1844 after a rough passage of fifty days from Boston.[25] Southgate was happy to receive them and was confident that the mission would be "hailed with joy and trust" by the Jacobites.

To the embarrassment of the foreign committee, it soon became clear that the two Episcopalian priests also wanted to remain in Istanbul rather than go to Mosul or Mardin. Moreover, they wished to work among the Armenians and not the Jacobites. Mr. Miles tried to convince the committee to direct its missionary energy toward the Armenians, "the most important and interesting clan of Christians in Turkey." It would take a long time before missionary effort among the poor, ignorant, and comparatively unimportant Jacobites would even begin to be felt beyond their own "little isolated nation." Among the Armenians, on the other hand, the same missionary labor would be directly influencing every other branch of the church in the East.[26] Then Mr. Miles began to stress the importance of Istanbul as a center. The capital afforded the church such facilities for operations even upon the interior that if a mission were maintained at all in Turkey, its principal force had to be concentrated in Istanbul.[27] He was sure that work among the Jacobites could be directed from the capital through the Jacobite patriarchal representative and agent then residing in Istanbul with the mission.

Needless to say, the foreign committee was disappointed at this material change of views—"in direct contrariety to those of the Foreign Committee as well as to the instructions given (the two missionaries) at their departure."[28] To complicate matters, Southgate himself wrote that he could not forbear to speak of the Armenians to whom circumstances had very much led him to direct his labors.[29] He went even further and threatened to resign if the mission were not given authority to commence labor among the Armenians.[30] The "hearty interest" of the Armenians in the Episcopal church, he wrote, had inevitably drawn him to them.

3

The interest of the Armenians in the Episcopal mission was most probably motivated by the association that young Southgate had cultivated in Istanbul with the missionaries and clergy of the Church of England. The Armenians must have been impressed by the fact that the American Episcopalian officiated at the chapel of the British embassy.[31] It is not surprising that the Armenians had a "decided preference [for the Episcopal Church] above all other foreign communions" and had told Southgate that his church, "with that of England," is best fitted for work among the Armenians and they desired it most.[32]

By the time he was serving at the chapel of the British embassy, Southgate had spent about eight years in the Middle East. He was not unaware of the political motivations of the Middle Eastern Christians when they left their mother church to join a communion from the West. "One never hears," he wrote in 1841, "of the Oriental Christians changing among themselves; there was no temporal advantage in it. An Armenian never transfers himself to the Greek communion, nor a Jacobite to that of the Nestorians." When they change, "it is to form a connexion with some Western body of Christians." Southgate correctly explained the reason why so many Eastern Christians had embraced Catholicism: as members of the church of Rome they "become, in a manner, Franks, and their temporal condition is often changed for the better."[33] He lamented the fact that, from the West, the Roman Catholic church was "the only one which is willing to receive such proselytes." The American cleric did not want his own church to harbor such religious refugees; nevertheless, he wished the British government to extend "its protection to the Christians of the East universally," permitting them to look "to the British Ambassador and, under him, to the British consuls for protection from civil injury, or reparation in the case of it."[34] If only the patronage of England were secured for the Eastern Christians, there would be nothing that could not be done for them, including the restoration of many of their churches which through the years, Southgate's investigations showed, had been converted into mosques.[35]

Partly because he wanted to discourage Eastern Christians from becoming Catholic, Southgate personally used his influence in Istanbul to redress the injury that the native Christians brought to his attention.[36] Fortunately for him, the Church of England had sent its own representatives and clerics to investigate the condition of the Eastern Christians at about the same time he was sent there for his exploratory tour. The English mission, supported by the Society for Promoting Christian Knowledge, with the encouragement of the archbishop of Canterbury, was to work among the Nestorians of Turkey.[37] Southgate looked forward to close cooperation between the two "Anglican" branches of the Church. "Our mother Church of England," he wrote, in 1842, "looks to us to take [the Jacobite mission] for our share of what is to be done in these lands. She will labor with us side by side....*She* will go to the [Nestorians], *we* to the [Jacobites]."[38]

Conscious of "the present preponderating influence of Great Britain in the East,"[39] Southgate cultivated close relations with the various missionary bodies and members of the hierarchy of the Church of England. "In setting forth our own Church [in the Ottoman Empire]," he wrote in 1844, "I have never forgotten the mother Church of England. Indeed, it is only by her that we trace our apostolic descent, and the primitive character of our formularies.'' He wanted to refer to her constantly ''from my desire to present to our Eastern brethren the substantial unity of the Reformed Episcopal Communions of the West.''[40] Aware of the great importance of this British connection, Southgate spoke of its ''healthy influence'' upon the Eastern churches, and entertained the expectation that good relations ''between [his] Mission and the British Embassy would have a favorable influence upon his plans in reference to the Oriental Churches.''[41] The tracts and treatises that he wrote and translated for the Jacobites, Greeks, and Armenians usually bore the name of the ''Anglican'' church in their title, a term not commonly used in the 1840s.[42]

The foreign committee in New York, unaware of the politics of missions, refused to lose sight of the fact that the major purpose of Southgate's presence in the Ottoman Empire was to serve the Jacobites of south-central Anatolia and ''Upper Mesopotamia.'' The committee was therefore determined to abolish the mission in Istanbul. Southgate, equally determined to stay in the capital, brought his case before the Episcopal church's board of missions, bypassing its foreign committee. The board was convinced by Southgate; it overruled its committee and voted for the continuance of the mission in Istanbul.[43] The foreign committee concurred but with the understanding that only Southgate would be stationed in Istanbul and that his duties would not be extended to the Armenians but to the Greeks and Jacobites as originally intended. The committee deliberately wanted to avoid work among the Armenians because of the Congregational church's connection with them. The committee, therefore, instructed missionaries Miles and Taylor to proceed to Mesopotamia to prosecute their appointed work among the Jacobites, after a temporary residence at Istanbul. The Committee realized that little had been or could be accomplished in Mesopotamia from distant Istanbul.

4

Before discussing the inevitable confrontation between Southgate and the foreign committee, let us pause briefly and turn our attention to what the Episcopal mission had done for the Jacobites spiritually and materially.

Not long after Horatio Southgate had established himself in the Ottoman capital, the Jacobite patriarch had sent one of his bishops to reside there and act as his representative.[44] Southgate's closest contact with the Jacobites was through this bishop. Muṭrān Bahnām had spent several months at the residence of the American missionary when he had first arrived in Turkey, the two clerics being ''on the most intimate terms of friendship.''

Muṭrān Bahnām was the only one among the Jacobites whom

Southgate had helped train theologically. The Muṭrān was taught such themes as might strike a Jacobite audience as very strange, but which Southgate thought were essential if the whole man were to grow up "towards a perfect stature of Christ." The Jacobite bishop was taught to emphasize "man's ruin and the Saviour's love, purity of heart and growth in grace, sorrow for sin and repentance before God, devotion to his service and an entire surrender to his will, the joys of heaven and the miseries of hell, the deep depravity and deceit of the human heart, the works of the spirit and faith in Christ working by love..."[45]

The Muṭrān proved to be an apt pupil, at least as long as Southgate remained in Istanbul. After returning to Mosul, the Jacobite clergyman wrote very frequently to his Episcopal mentor, his letters all breathing "the same tone of earnest devotedness to the spiritual welfare of his Diocese." He wrote that he wanted to establish schools in order that the youth "may know the will of God, according to the sense of the Holy Scriptures, and increase in that spiritual learning which conducts to the kingdom of Heaven." All this, "if it please the Most High," would mean that "the Church of Christ will increase in spiritual doctrine, and the Church of the Papists will be ruined."[46]

From Istanbul, Southgate encouraged the bishop of Mosul in his efforts to open schools.[47] The American missionary was able to procure books and scriptures in Arabic from the church missionary society press in Malta. Soon after his arrival in Turkey, while still thinking of the major purpose of his mission—to serve the Jacobites—Southgate had discussed with Bishop Bahnām the great objects he had in mind for his people. While the bishop was with him in the capital, Southgate informed the board of missions in New York that arrangements were being made for supplying "several important schools" with the means of instruction. He wrote that plans of labor had been formed and minute inquiries made with regard to expenses and other matters of importance.[48] Reporting on his visit to the patriarch in 1841, he spoke of the strong hopes that were "entertained of the happiest results," by the Jacobite community, which as a whole had given him a strong impression of gratitude.[49] The Jacobites must have come to the conclusion that they had at last found the support they needed if the Catholic dissidents were not to overtake the Syrian church.

The only representative that the Episcopal mission had among the Jacobites was a pious and trusted priest from the community itself, Qass Mīkhā'īl Jamāla. He acted as the sole agent of the American Episcopal mission in Mosul.[50] Through him and Bishop Bahnām, Southgate tried to invigorate the Jacobites by letters, maintaining correspondence with a "considerable number of their bishops, clergy, and laity."[51]

5

The foreign committee was not impressed by mission-through-correspondence and wanted at least missionaries Miles and Taylor to labor among the people they were supposed to serve. Faced with this problem, Southgate again sought support from the board. He now recommended that the Mesopotamia mission be abandoned, that the work of his church be concentrated at Istanbul, and that Messrs. Miles and Taylor be assigned to the mission there.[52]

The board again backed Southgate by overruling the foreign committee, whose objectives were to limit the efforts of the Constantinople mission to the Greeks and the Jacobites. The committee was requested to establish a mission to the Armenians—contrary to the original instructions—as soon as the funds were raised for the purpose, and to have Miles and Taylor transferred to the capital. Moreover, Southgate, who had recommended that the board appoint a bishop to Turkey, was himself consecrated bishop "to the dominions and dependencies of the Sultan of Turkey."[53] After a brief visit to the United States, Bishop Southgate returned to his see in Istanbul in 1845.

The foreign committee was in no mood to raise funds for the establishment of a mission to the Armenians. They were convinced, they emphasized a few months after Southgate was consecrated bishop, of the correctness of their view to discontinue the mission in Istanbul. The mission, pointed out the committee, "ought not to go any further than the will of the Church may be clearly manifested." The members of the committee were convinced that the plans suggested by the bishop of Constantinople were "on too extensive a scale" and that "no proportionate amount of good can be reasonably expected from any expenditure bestowed upon them."[54]

Self-respect and a sense of responsibility demanded that the committee members take a strong stand. In the summer of 1847 they decided to ask the mission some pointed questions.[55] "As the Mission towards the Syrian [Jacobite] Church was . . . established at the earnest insistence of the Missionary Bishop," the committee wrote, "why was that Mission considered as no longer to be prosecuted?" The committee wanted to know whether there were any efforts made towards the improvement of the Syrian Christians and "if any, what?"[56] Forty-two questions in all were addressed to the bishop and the two priests under him.

The foreign committee was not impressed by the answers it received. The report of Mr. Miles, who by then had decided to return to his home in South Carolina,[57] showed how feeble the efforts of the mission for the improvement of the Syrian church had been.[58] He mentioned "a Priest in the employment of the Missionary Bishop," at Mosul, referring to Qass Mīkhā'īl, and spoke of the "most friendly" relations that existed between the missionaries and the Syrian bishop resident in Constantinople. Southgate too could only emphasize the friendly relations that he enjoyed with the Jacobite hierarchy.[59] He hoped, however, that "the Mission to the Syrian Church will be duly prosecuted, according to our means," adding that at least this was his intention "from which I have never departed."[60]

The committee did not remind the missionary bishop that he had recently recommended the abolition of the mission to the Jacobites, but decided to fight him with the most effective weapon it had: to cut off funds. In 1848 a special resolution of the committee provided that "none but monies specially contributed to it should at present be sent . . . to the Athens or Constantinople Mission."[61] This meant, in Southgate's words, that the regular payment of the appropriations to the mission was stopped and in its place was substituted a plan of irregular payment, at uncertain intervals, and of uncertain amounts.[62]

The mission soon felt the impact of the committee's displeasure. "My family," wrote the bishop to the dominions and dependencies of the sultan of Turkey, "began to suffer for the very necessaries of life." He found himself compelled, "in order to save the Mission from destruction and my family from starvation," to resort to a loan and even to sell some of his furniture. His agent in Mosul, he reported, was in dire need of the funds that had been promised him. Qass Mīkhā'īl wrote that the schools had been opened for several months but he had not received even a piaster from Istanbul. He thought that an appropriation of 500 piasters (about $21)a month would support seven schools and that one of his able teachers would be content with $3 a month (80 piasters).[63]

The situation became worse in 1848, leaving the American bishop "almost utterly destitute." He was compelled to neglect Mosul, he wrote, and this had "offended the people there, who regard it as a violation of promise, as, *literally,* it was." Bishop Bahnām had become alienated and "ceased to correspond with me." Southgate wrote that "it was wholly out of my power to make (Mutrān Bahnām) understand the changes and crises in our financial arrangements at home. . .Both he and his people seem to be vexed, and I know not whether we can regain the confidence that we have lost."[64]

Once more Southgate tried to bypass the foreign committee and this time, if possible, to circumvent it permanently. He requested that the mission be separated from the foreign committee and be attached directly to the board. In 1848 he brought to the attention of the board that in 1838 he had been "the first Protestant Missionary" who explored Jacobite homegrounds. Ignoring the fact that he had recommended the abandonment of the field in favor of the Armenians in 1844, he wrote that the Jacobite "field is riper, richer, more abundant in its development." At this late date, more than ten years after he had first visited the Jacobites,[65] we find Horatio Southgate "heartily" recommending to the board "this interesting and important field in Mesopotamia."[66]

The elders in New York were not impressed. The bishop had finally to concede defeat. "All out attempts to bring about a change have failed," he wrote in 1849. In the spring of that year he felt that no course was left to him but to retire.[67]

His resignation was accepted in 1850; the foreign committee had unanimously come to the conclusion that "the removal of the Missionary Bishop with his family had closed the Mission in Turkey." This writer has not found any communication after 1850 between Southgate or the Episcopal church and the Jacobite hierarchy.[68] There was a move that year to renew the mission to the "decayed churches in Asia Minor," and Mr. Southgate supported the idea since Turkey was "a missionary station of the Church," but the foreign committee was not ready to take any further action on this matter. No sooner had the Episcopalians abandoned the Jacobites than the Congregationalists of New England came to labor among them.

6

While the Episcopalians were the first Protestants formally to organize a mission to the Jacobites, they were not the only Protestants to show interest in these Syrian Christian communities. We have already noted that the Congregational church of New England—interested mainly in the Nestorians[69] and Armenians—had sent its missions to the Middle East before Horatio Southgate had started his exploratory mission there. Their mission physician-explorer, Dr. Asahel Grant[70] of the Nestorian mission, had journeyed in 1839—the year when the Reverend Horatio Southgate's mission to the Jacobites was established[71]—to Diyarbakr, Mardin, and Mosul. Grant found that there were "no Nestorians remaining on the western side of the Koordish mountains," all having embraced Catholicism there and being known as Chaldeans.[72] His explorations had led him to the conclusion that although Mosul and its surrounding plains had no Nestorian population, the city itself had to be "occupied as soon as practicable" as a permanent way station to the Nestorians of Ḥakkāri.[73] The Christian mountaineers could be more easily approached from the Turkish than from the Persian territory. What is more, the Nestorians of Anatolia had recently been placed under the jurisdiction of the pasha of Mosul; his efficient measures had made Grant's visit to that hitherto inaccessible region very safe. Under Turkish rule, the Nestorians traded with other Turkish parts; it was therefore important for the mission to have a responsible agency on the Turkish side. The occupation of Mosul was important for yet another reason: the Congregational mission there could expect "efficient protection" from the British consul resident at nearby Baghdad. The British representative there had already assured Dr. Grant of his readiness "to aid our operations in every proper means in his power." Moreover, much good might result, it was thought, from labors in Mosul among the various sects there such as "Jacobite Syrians, Chaldean and Syrian Catholics, Yesidees, Jews, and Mahommedans."[74]

Mosul seems to have attracted Christian missionaries like a magnet. As a secretary of the Presbyterian board of missions would later put it, the missionaries seemed to hear a voice speaking to their evangelical conscience as they mingled with the varied sects of that city. The call they heard came "as clearly as that voice spoke to Jonah 'arise and go to Nineveh, that great city, and preach unto it the preaching that I bid thee.'" Not only was Mosul the site of ancient Nineveh,[75] but also the region of "the Fall," as well as a part of the Old Testament country from which Abraham went out. All this fired the imagination of the evangelicals and inspired the hope that "the hero of the Old Testament might soon be claimed for Him who is the Hero of the New."[76]

Unfortunately for the Protestant missionaries, more than one of them had come to this corner of the Ottoman Empire wanting to work in the same field, serving the same people at the same time. Competition among them became bitter at times and this was reflected in violent divisions among the native Christians.

As pointed out above, the Church of England had delegated a mission to investigate the condition of the Eastern Christians at about the same time that Southgate was asked to undertake his exploratory tour. The first representative of the Church of England was in Mosul when Dr. Grant was there. Writing in November 1842, Dr. Grant informed the American board of commissioners of his church that "Mr. Badger is here, and has commenced operations by assailing us." The Englishman had been telling the Jacobites that the Syrian Bibles being distributed to them were defective and "did not contain the Apocrypha." He had brought letters from the Jacobite patriarch against any Congregationalist activities among his people.[77] To complicate matters, a Congregational mission in Mosul—an important Jacobite center—was an infringement on the territory that Southgate hoped would be under his jurisdiction. Indeed, Dr. Grant had come into possession at this time of a letter that the Reverend Horatio Southgate had from seven of the American Episcopal bishops to the Jacobite patriarch informing him that their church had no ecclesiastical connections with the Congregationalists.[78] The *New York Observer* of 18 November, 1843 quoted the secretary of the American board of commissioners as saying that Mr. Southgate had cooperated with Mr. Badger in his opposition to the Congregationalist missionary operations and his influence against them had coincided with that of the papal missionaries.[79]

Faced with this kind of competition from the "Protestant" camp, not to mention the Catholic opposition to all Protestants,[80] Dr Grant's recommendation to establish a "way station" in Mosul was agreed upon by the American board but on condition that it be used only to reach the mountain Nestorians from that point.[81]

Horatio Southgate was certainly not happy with any Congregational presence in Mosul, especially when he preferred to serve the Jacobites from faraway Istanbul.[82] He resented also the determination of the Congregationalists to labor among the Nestorians of Ḥakkāri; that was a field coveted by his fellow missionaries from his "mother church." He wanted the Congregationalists to limit their efforts to the Nestorians of Persia; he had long cherished the hope that the Nestorians of Turkey would be under an efficient mission under the direction of the archbishop of Canterbury.[83]

We know that Dr. Grant's work among the Patriarchal Nestorians ended in a tragic massacre of that community in 1843 and that Dr. Grant's work among them contributed to that tragedy.[84] Indeed, the Reverend Mr. Southgate pointed an accusing finger at the Congregationalists for their part in the calamities and was particularly unhappy when Dr. Grant, forced to give up his work in the Ḥakkāri, returned to Mosul confident that the Lord had an important assignment for him among the Jacobites there.[85] Southgate's fears were alleviated when the prudential committee of the Congregational church decided to withdraw the mission entirely because of the Episcopal mission's avowed object among the Jacobites of Mesopotamia."[86]

It was not long after their decision to withdraw from Mosul that the Congregationalists decided to come back to it, their way paved by the withdrawal of the Southgate mission.[87] Their return this time was "irrespective of the Nestorians in the mountains."[88] Within a few weeks after the resignation of the Episcopal bishop,[89] we find the Congregational missionaries in Aleppo calling for "the occupation of Mosul."[90] Without the possession of that city, we are told, there would be "a great gap in the line of the invading army," which, it would seem, Horatio Southgate from distant Istanbul had for the past several years been able to repulse. The seizure of the city was made even more effortless now with the closing down of the French consulate in Mosul in the late 1840s.[91] The "poor, needy and ignorant" Jacobites to the north of Mosul, the American board was informed, would receive the Congregational mission favorably. Of all the Christians of the Middle East, besides the Nestorians, these Jacobite communities were the most untouched by the spirit and influence of "popery."[92]

The head of the Congregational mission to the Nestorians of Persia confirmed this new optimism. Visiting Mosul in the spring of 1849, the Reverand Justin Perkins[93] noted that there was a religious interest in Mosul, "mostly limited to the Jacobites." They, together with "papal Nestorians" (Chaldeans) there, were "heartily tired of the superstitions and follies of their churches, and anxious for something better."[94]

7

The first Congregational missionary to Mosul, the Reverend Dwight W. Marsh, a graduate of Williams College and the Union Theological Seminary of New York, was convinced soon after his arrival that as a missionary post his city was "far better than Baghdad."[95] One of his colleagues thought that there was no better spot "whereon to build a structure to the glory of God, and fulfill the mission of the Christians" than his newly adopted home.[96]

The Jacobites of Mosul, and especially those among them who had come in contact with Mr. Southgate, approached the Congregationalists soon after it was realized that the Southgate mission was too far away and too weak to be of any help to them. Their fears were confirmed when they found out that the Episcopal mission was actually closed. In 1849 we find none other than Mr. Southgate's protegé, Presbyter Mīkhā'ī; Jamāla,[97] together with another "evangelical" Jacobite, Mīkha al-Naqqūr, corresponding with the Urumiya mission, inviting its Congregationalists to visit Mosul. The Persia missionaries came and found "more than a hundred individuals, including their families, . . . under evangelical influences." The New England preachers reported that these "enlightened" persons were favorably disposed to receive religious instruction. Mr. Perkins was especially impressed by Brother Mīkha's leadership and piety "based on profound views of man's natural depravity" and the necessity of "a thorough work of the Spirit to regenerate the soul."[98]

The bishop of Mosul and once-close friend of Southgate, Bahnām, also wrote to the formerly suspected Congregationalists requesting their aid in forming schools, and their instructions and prayers for himself. "He has repeatedly urged us to come to Mosul, and preach the Gospel to him and his people," wrote one of the missionaries from Aleppo.[99] Mr. Perkins found Mutrān Bahnām "much enlightened," preaching the Gospel in his church regularly on the Sabbath "though not of course with the zeal and efficiency of a pious man." Noting that the bishop had spent two years at Constantinople with the Episcopalian Southgate, Congregationalist Perkins suspected the Jacobite's motives for preaching the Gospel. "We have reason to apprehend," he wrote, that the bishop's motives were "not always the most pure."[100] Nevertheless, Perkins rejoiced in the fact that the truth of God was preached, even thus imperfectly, "in this dark city."[101]

Hardly a year had passed when the missionaries from Aleppo concluded that all the hopes which had been entertained respecting the cooperation of the Jacobite bishop of Mosul were at an end. Bishop Bahnām, they wrote, had shown himself to be "utterly unprincipled, selfish, and hypocritical." They ascribed his attitude toward them to "his besetting sin [and] self-esteem . . . , held in bondage of that odious monster, pride."[102]

Bishop Bahnām had wanted the Congregationalists to open schools for his people; he told them he was willing to preach "from the Scripture," and would say in his sermons "whatever the missionary might wish him to preach," but he was opposed to having them "Americanize" his church or to preach in it.[103] The evangelists informed him that no schools would be supported by them if the children were instructed "in the forms and ceremonies of the [Jacobite] Church," The Muṭrān refused to comply with these restrictions. He considered himself "the Luther of the Jacobite Church," and insisted that he was "fully capable of preaching the Gospel." The apostles from New England disagreed; they told him that "his heart was still unrenewed, and that he was consequently unfit to preach the Gospel."[104]

Under these circumstances it was not easy for the Jacobite hierarchy to associate with the new Protestants. The relations of the Jacobite clergy with Protestants for the past decade had been with the Episcopal mission. Bishop Southgate had constantly emphasized working with the leadership of the Eastern churches and not against them. He had praised Jacobite church episcopacy, as well as the great antiquity and purity of its liturgy. It is true that Southgate too had thought that the church, as he found it, was deeply corrupt and spiritually dead in practice, but he emphasized its reformation from within, holding before the eyes of these Syrian Christians "a standard of their own"; he had gone to them "only to bring them back to what they once were."[105] At the same time he had at every opportunity warned the Jacobite hierarchy against the non-Episcopal missions from America, pointing out that they lacked the fasts, feasts, and observances that the Syrian churches, together with the Episcopal church, considered essential. (The head of the Congregational mission in Persia once wrote that he did not know "what more artful contrivance Satan could have invented, as a substitute for the pure religion of the Gospel, than he had furnished in the fasts of the Oriental Churches.")[106] It is not surprising, therefore, that the leaders of the Jacobite church trusted the Anglicans for their conservatism and affirmation of traditional institutions. Even the lower classes felt safe with them because of their paternalistic sense of responsibility.

It should be pointed out here that the evangelists of all the Protestant churches were at first instructed to help strengthen the Eastern churches from within and not to remake them in their own reformist image. The home missionary boards stressed upon them that the object of Western missions was not to introduce Protestanism among the Christians of the East. "The Oriental Christians," emphasized the instructions to the Reverend Cyrus Hamlin on his mission to the Ottoman Empire, "are probably no better fitted for [Congregationalism or Presbyterianism] than they would be for a republican form of civil

government." The missionary was instructed that he had two major points to bear in mind: to revive the knowledge and spirit of the Gospel among the Easterners and then to "operate upon the Mohammedans" through the revived churches. "You can never find the avenues to [Muslim] hearts like a native," the missionary pioneer was informed.

The fact that throughout the Muslim Middle East there were numerous bodies of Christians was seen as providential. If only the mighty power of God were to revive the spirit of the Gospel in these Christians, "a flood of light would burst upon almost the whole Turkish empire, and would shine far upon the great central high lands of Asia. The followers of the false prophet would look with wonder—perhaps with hatred and persecution; but new ideas of the Gospel would be forced upon them, and no longer could they boast of the more excellent nature and influence of their own religion."[107] The Christian conquests were to take place through the native Christians, the way England had conquered India. ("The great body of [British] conquering armies were natives of the country.") Indeed, Christ's apostles themselves had subdued the world in a similar manner; they were only a handful but assisted by a much greater number of native helpers.[108]

The early missionaries were also cautioned not to attack the rites and ceremonies of the native Christians lest they awaken alarm and hostility. The rites and ceremonies did not represent "the citadel," which was the object of their attack. "Direct your whole force to the principal post, and when that is taken, the others will fall at once."[109]

With this zeal and self-righteousness, it was inevitable that disputation and controversy would arise between the leaders of the Jacobite church and the new Protestants. Zealous evangelists, the latter were interested in "spiritual revival" and not much else, as if a revival of the spirit, or the lack of it, had nothing to do with the miserable existence of the people whom they wished to serve. The Reverend Mr. March commented in 1852 on a frank discussion that he had with the Jacobite patriarch. The latter had admitted that probably most of the Jacobites would not go to Heaven but he had wisely put the blame for their difficulty "upon the times" and upon the government, referring to its weakness and corruption.)[110]

Referring to this crusading spirit of the American missionaries and their frontal attack on others' faith and practice, Englishman O. H. Parry wrote at the turn of this century that "nothing strikes a stranger visiting the American stations so much as the apparent disregard fo native habits and customs."[111] While the Catholic friars and pries stressed the similarities that their church and the eastern churches had common, the non-Episcopal Protestants were always pointing out differences that separated them from others, speaking of the "emptir and the folly of [Jacobite] vain rites and ceremonies."[112] Protes

deliberations with the Jacobites during this period often had, in the words of the missionary-physician Dr. Henry Lobdell, "almost as formal a character as the disputes in the days of the Reformation."[113] The missionary-doctor would ask these "nominal Christians" if they ever lied, and was shocked to hear the answer invariably, "Is there a man living who does not lie?" Perhaps they would not be obliged to lie, they had explained, if the Kurds "could not swear falsely against us, not beat us to get our money." In vain, wrote the 26-year-old Dr. Lobdell, did he try "to demonstrate to them that God ranks liars with murderers," utterly oblivious to what he had been told.[114]

Theological controversy seems always to have been the main topic of conversation. At a Jacobite wedding party the two missionary guests present, one of them reported, had "spent nearly the whole of one forenoon debating with their Archbishop the points of difference between us."[115] It is not surprising therefore to read only two years after the American board's mission to Mosul was established, that the various sects of the city, "especially the Jacobites," were "industriously and laboriously" accusing the evangelists of "infidelity and other evil."[116] The Jacobite patriarch, once a close associate of the Reverend Horatio Southgate,[117] had explained to Mr. Marsh why "we like the Papists better than Protestants . . . —we are more like them."[118] (It should be pointed out here that among the beliefs and practices that the Roman Catholics and the Syrian Orthodox had in common were: prayers to the Virgin Mary and the saints, prayers for the dead, abstention from eating meat, fasting, celibacy for monks and bishops, and, in the case of the Jacobites, celibacy of widowed priests. And they both "loved churches and richly clad priests.")[119]

8

In spite of all these controversies, the Congregationalists were still able to attract a number of the Jacobite laity. Some were attracted by the sincerity of the missionaries' motives and by the simplicity of their faith. They were also impressed by the superior learning of the American clergy and especially by their medical knowledge and the medicines that they provided.

Missionary Marsh wrote that in their conversations in the villages, "our first object is to enlist the sympathy of the people by telling or showing them some novelty from Frangistan." The villagers, he observed, would stare at the compass "as did the savages in the day of Captain Smith," and an ignited match excited "universal enthusiasm."[120] The Congregationalists, unlike the Episcopalians, emphasized medical work as an important part of their apostolic effort. Soon after his arrival in Mosul, Mr. Marsh wrote that the mission needed a physician "to heal the sick and increase our influence with Moslems and with all classes."[121]

In one of his reports Dr. Lobdell wrote that "Bayeez Bey, the chief of the place, said he would receive us, not because of the *'bouyouruldu'* of the Pasha of Mosul, or the letter of 'Ali Bey, but because I brought medicines."[122] Very often a grateful pasha was found to be more helpful than all the firmans extracted from the sultan by a European ambassador. Because of the professional services to the dangerously ill pasha of Diyarbakr, wrote the secretary of the American board, the latter had given the preaching physician "an introduction to almost all the officers of the government and influential Moslems in the city, and obtained for him a public expression of the Pasha's gratitude." Instead of stoning the missionaries in the streets without redress, as had been done earlier, the missionaries by the mid-1850s "received respectful treatment and had free access to all classes."[123]

The Congregationalists exploited their medical contribution, subordinating "pills and plasters" to the preaching of the Gospel. The crowd of patients had to listen to a faithful expository discourse before receiving their medicines. Without the dispensary practice, admitted a missionary in 1857, a very large number of the Muslims could not be reached by any other means.[124] But while the patients listened, there were times when the Muslim clergy outside the mission compound were roused, denouncing "the American pills as well as the American Gospel." The situation became serious when the "congregation"—all there for medical aid—became almost entirely Muslim.

The native Christians were afraid and embarrassed by the preaching of the Gospel to the Muslims and most of them declined to proselytize. In order to lessen the tension, the week was divided between the sects and sexes; the doctors would see the Christians on Mondays, Tuesdays, and Wednesdays, the Muslim women on Thursdays and Saturdays, and the Muslim men on Fridays. Changes were also made "in the administration of the Word." Preaching to the Christians was from the Epistles; to the Muslims from the teachings of Jesus, "because all Moslems profess to acknowledge Jesus, and to receive as gospel whatever he taught."

The attending missionary-doctor was surprised one day by a police officer at his door with an order summoning him before the qādi. He was taken to "a room filled with grave Moolahs in the midst of whom sat a Kadi." Complaint had been made, the doctor was informed by the qādi, for preaching Jesus and the Gospel to Muslims; many were fearing a disturbance.

"All Muslims profess to receive the words of Jesus," the missionary had replied in self-defense.

"Jesus and the gospel we do receive," the qādi had rejoined, "but we are not under his law . . . ; to Christians you may preach what you please, and we will not interfere; but you must preach no more to Moslems."

"We will discontinue that and also the medicine, and confine ourselves exclusively to those who are not Moslems," the missionary-doctor had then threatened.

The qādi: "I do not forbid medicine, only preaching."

The missionary: "Our Master commanded us to heal the sick and preach the gospel. What he has united in one command we will not separate. And since you so order, we will hereafter, if a Moslem calls for medicine, tell him that the Kadi forbids us to attend to him."

The qādi: "No, I do not forbid medicine. Give as much as you please."

"Jesus put the two together," Dr. Lobdell insisted; "we shall consider a prohibition of the one a prohibition of the other." The missionaries thereafter informed the Muslims who had come for medicine that they had to bring "a permit to preach from the Kadi" if they were to get their medicine.[125]

9

The Jacobite hierarchy was also roused—by fear of the defection of the faithful to Protestantism. The missionaries reported that Jacobite bishops made every effort to induce "our Protestants by flattery and bribes, to return to their old communions." If flattery did not work, then more stringent measures were taken, including beating and persecution. Three years after the establishment of the mission, Dr. Lobdell wrote that native Christians were "deterred from leaving their old communities by the fear of increased taxation or of making their relatives their enemies." It is difficult, he explained, "to induce them to take up their cross and follow Christ."[126]

The most effective weapon in the hands of the church hierarchy was the imposition of taxes. Every sect paid taxes through its agent responsible to the government, the religious head of the community. By mid-nineteenth century, the total annual amount collected from each sect was estimated at the rate of fifty piasters per household. The tax was collected by the agents of the patriarch and paid in half-yearly installments. The aggregate of the tax was distributed among the members of each community as agreed by its leaders. Instead of paying fifty piasters a year, the very poor paid nothing, while some of the wealthy gave as much as six hundred piasters annually. What the Ottoman income tax officer (the daftardār) needed to know was the number of houses under the patriarch's jurisdiction; this they multiplied by 50 to reach the number of piasters due the state.

Two years after the arrival of the Congregational missionaries in Mosul, seven Jacobite "Protestant" families were assessed 602 piasters instead of the 290 piasters that they had paid prior to the arrival of the mission. The amount was deducted from the total revenue that the government demanded from the Jacobite community of the city of Mosul, thus granting those who remained loyal to the hierarchy some sort of tax reduction.[127] The Protestants who refused to pay the tax were reported by the Jacobite patriarch and jailed by the Ottoman authorities.

The Syrian Orthodox leadership had welcomed the mission of the Protestant Episcopal church in the United States because of the encroachments of the Roman Catholic missions, which in the 1840s saw the formal secession of Catholic ex-Jacobites, officially recognized by the Ottoman government under the leadership of their own patriarch.[128] Now the Congregational Protestants were posing the same threat. The Jacobite hierarchy was in a panic; reports of the early missionaries often speak of false imprisonment, excommunication, and increased rent demanded months in advance; and all this in addition to stoning and beating on the streets.[129]

The persecution and excommunication of the Protestant Jacobites (and this applied to the "evangelicals" of other sects) backfired and eventually gave rise to their secession and then official recognition as yet another millet. The native Protestants, often described as enduring persecution manfully and with good cheer, wanted to be fully recognized by the Ottoman state as a community on a basis of equality with other Christian bodies. Until then they were regarded as individual followers of foreign missionaries, who had betrayed their own community. Now they wanted the same privilege that had been granted to their brethren who had joined the Catholic church.[130]

Fortunately for the Protestants, the British ambassador in Istanbul was willing to intervene in their behalf. Through the efforts of Lord Cowley an order in favor of all of the sultan's Protestant subjects was obtained in November 1847 from the Sublime Porte. A vizirial order, addressed "To His Excellency, the Pasha Comptroller of the City Revenue," spoke of the difficulty and embarrassment experienced by the Christian subjects of the Ottoman government who professed Protestantism. Since they were not under a special and separate jurisdiction, explained the order, signed "Reshid, Grand Vizier," the patriarch and the heads of the sects from which these Christians have separated naturally were not "able to superintend their affairs." The pasha comptroller was notified that it was his imperial majesty's supreme will and command that the administration of the affairs of these Protestants would be thenceforward confided to him, "together with the allotment of the taxes to which they are subjected by law." The pasha was instructed to keep a separate register of their births and deaths "in the Bureau of your Department, according to the system observed with regard to the Latin subjects." In order to remove the proselytes from the jurisdiction of their former patriarch, the pasha was asked to appoint "as their agent at the Porte for the transaction and settlement of their current affairs" any person of "established character and good conduct chosen by them."[131]

The Reverend Mr. Marsh, the first Congregational missionary in Mosul, wrote that the 1847 proclamation had strengthened the resolve of the Protestants. "Our enemies at last realize that we are fully resolved to take possession, and my coming has stirred them up to let fall the long-impending anathemas. The blow is struck!" Bonds long mighty, he reported, "have melted like tow in the flame. The Protestants are free. They stand erect like men and give glory to God"[132] Steps were taken to lay the foundation in Mosul of a separate Protestant community. A petition for the recognition of these "friends of evangelical truth"—already excommunicated from their own sect—as a separate millet was forwarded to Istanbul as early as 1850, the year Mr. Marsh had arrived in Mosul. The mid-century saw the formal issuance of the Imperial Protestant Charter of 1850, officially recognizing the Protestants as a millet.[133]

It took a few years before the decrees issued in Istanbul were obeyed in Mosul and Diyarbakr. As late as the spring of 1853 the missionaries on the spot reported that the taxes of some native Protestants had been increased twofold. In January 1854, a firman was addressed to the pasha of Mosul calling his attention to the protection of the Protestants, most of them former Jacobites. By the mid-1850s the position of the Protestants had been strengthened; the Crimean War, 1854-56, which saw France and England cooperating with Turkey against Russia, resulted in liberal policies toward the French-protected Catholics and British-supported Protestants. Even the traditional death penalty for conversion for Islam to Christianity was abrogated at this time "and Muslims were legally permitted to receive baptism,"[134] even though only an occasional Muslim would take "advantage" of that right.

By 1855 the Jacobite patriarch's taxation weapon was being used against him. His own people refused to give him his accustomed annual donation. He was notified by his congregation in Diyarbakr that they would give nothing; "if he attempted to compel them, they as a body would become Protestants, and renounce all subserviency to him."[135] By the end of the decade the *Missionary Herald,* journal of the American Board of Commissioners for Foreign Missions, was confident enough to write in an editorial that "the steady, quiet light of Protestantism has shaken the Jacobite church to its foundations."[136] To missionary Marsh it was apparent that "before many years" Protestants and Papists would be the sole claimants of the Christian name in this part of the Turkish empire.[137]

This optimism soon proved to be premature, right only in its prediction that "the Papists" were, and would continue to be, strong. Indeed, by the end of the 1850s, the missionaries of the American board had almost abandoned Mosul, concentrating their efforts in Turkey on Diyarbakr and Mardin, where they had developed a strong interest in the

the various missionary stations of the American
such Armenian centers as Sivas, Bitlis, and Van,
the "Mission in Eastern Turkey." The cities of
, and Mosul were administered separately as "the
until 1860, when the name was dropped from the list,
bakr and Mardin with the "Mission in Eastern

all but abandoned, was kept as a mission station "in name
" and largely in order to prevent the entrance of other mis-
here.[140] For a while it was kept as a winter outstation served
in, its hot summers made even more uncomfortable by the
and active presence there of the Dominican fathers. At
the nineteenth century the American board decided to give up
togeer; it was turned over to the Board of Foreign Missions
byteria Church in the U.S.A., which had been active in the
king provinces of the Ottoman Empire.[141] By the beginning
ieth century the American Presbyterians also decided against
sul and handed it over to the British Church Missionary
had come to the Middle East in 1875, to establish a mis-
, Iran.[142] Interest in Shi'ah Iranians had eventually led the
ries to Baghdad where they established an outpost from
nd serve Iranian pilgrims on their way to nearby Karbala
lad was "occupied" by the society in 1882; after fifteen
there, the Iraq mission was separated from its Iran
the "Turkish Arabia Mission" in 1898. It was this mis-
Christians of northern Iraq until World War I, the
ecially happy with their renewed contact with

m to have posed special problems to the mission of
Anatolia. They were Monophysites like the Arme-
l language was Syriac and the language that they
is meant that missionary work among them re-
lin being the only station of the American board in
le East where evangelical work was carried on in
two major languages of the mission: Armenian and
of the nineteenth century, the Jacobites were dif-
two client communities of the American board in
hey had by then come under the strong influence of
church. Indeed, the major reason for the relatively
effort among the Armenians of Anatolia and the
ayjan was the fact that these two communities were
Catholic influence. The Mosul-Mardin-Diyarbakr
hand, was the ecclesiastical center and the residence
Catholic as well as Orthodox Syrian (Jacobite)—and

the seat of two Catholic bishops—Chaldean and Cathol
Jacobite Protestant congregations were usually a part of
Protestant churches. They benefited from the schools and
that were established to serve the Armenian Christians,
Monophysite neighbors. Only once during the second half
teenth century do we find missionary interest intensified in
clusively Jacobite. The defeat of Turkey by Russia in 187
subsequent British intervention in the affairs of the Chr
Anatolia, gave rise to high hopes within missionary circles and
establishment of a number of American institutions of higher
throughout "Turkey in Asia" where there were Armenians. A
thusiasm led also to a renewed interest in the Jacobites. Engla
board hoped to have a "footing in Jebel Toor' now their Asia
"just guaranteed Turkey against any further invasion
vinces." These political changes raised the Protest s in the esti
of the Jacobites, whose conflicts and grievances this time were
more against the French-supported Cath proselytization tha
were against the Ottoman government

The predominantly Jacobite town of Midyat, a flourishing
center of the Jabal Tur region, became in the 1880s the center of
sionary substation from which the nearby villages of the distric
served through the establishment of schools and evangelical con
tions.[148] Toward the end of the century, prayer meetings in Midya
described as well attended, amounting almost to a revival. The
was "blessed spiritually," and the community boasted a boys'
girls' school.[149] The "Protestant Jacobites" of Midyat and the Tu
din villages were reported as having a clearer apprehension of the
duties and rights, contributing to the relative prosperity of the villa
which they resided.

The Times of London found the native Christians especiall
timistic after the war of 1878. "Their hopes are reviving," wro
British correspondent, "and they are looking in all directions to see
they can do to prepare themselves and their children for the new er
seems to be dawning upon them." Unfortunately for the Christian
their Western mentors, they were not always aware of the realities
governed their condition.

5

Russia, Rebellion, and Refuge

1

Russian expansion southward through Transcaucasia was mainly at the expense of Iran and Turkey and involved territory inhabited by native Christians. The remote roots of Russian presence in the Caucasus go back to the early eighteenth century when Peter the Great, having got most of what he could in Europe, turned his attention in 1722 to the lands of the eastern Black Sea and those to the south of them. The state of anarchy there meant that with practically no resistance the Russian troops occupied, even though temporarily, such cities as Baku, Gilan, Darband, and Mazandaran. Russian hold on these territories, however, did not last long; it was not until the end of the eighteenth century—when, under Catherine the Great, the Crimea was annexed—that the way was paved for Russian expansion through the Caucasus, threatening eastern Turkey as well as northwestern Iran.[1]

The first year of the nineteenth century saw the Russians unilaterally declare Georgia a part of their empire. Iran, which had ruled parts of Georgia, went to war but was badly defeated; she signed most of her Caucasian possessions away in 1813 in the Treaty of Gulistan. Iran's desire to regain her territory and Russian provocations along the newly established boundary led to another war and another Russian victory. The tsar's troops captured Erevan and Tabriz and threatened Tehran. By the Treaty of Turkmanchai in 1828 the Russo-Iranian frontier was drawn up along the Araxes River, substantially as we know it today. During the war Armenian volunteers joined the Russian troops, lending them invaluable assistance. From then on most of the Persian Armenians would be under Russian rule and would attract thousands of their brethren from Eastern Turkey, a new battleground between Russia and the Ottoman Empire.

The war with Iran had hardly ended when the Russians overran Turkish territory; in the summer of 1828, Russian armies advanced westward as far as the citadel city of Erzerum, taking Kars along the way. "Along the entire route, Armenians welcomed the Russian troops as liberators and rejoiced that the day of deliverance was at hand."[2] Their joy, unfortunately for them, did not last long. The Treaty of Adrianople ended the war the following year. The Russian troops began to withdraw from the Turkish territory, followed by a stream of Armenian refugees fleeing their homeland, most probably afraid of reprisals that they expected.[3]

The die was cast. Russian conquest of Muslim-inhabited territories would often lead to Muslim migrations into Anatolia. The 1860s saw the wholesale immigration of Circassians seeking asylum in Ottoman territory, leaving their native regions in the Caucasus uninhabited and desolate. Almost the entire region from the Caspian Sea to the Black Sea, and from the Caucasus mountains in the north to the Turko-Persian frontier in the south, was embroiled in a civil war of the most bloody and ruthless character, inflaming age-old ethnic animosities by religious passions and fanaticism. With Russian advances, the flow of Muslim refugees increased, starting a movement, writes Stanford J. Shaw, "that was to mount into the millions in the 19th century, creating major social and economic problems that the empire was ill-equipped to handle."[4] In less than a hundred years after the coming of the Russians the events that would flow from their presence in this corner of the globe would completely transform its human ecology. The social, cultural, political and military developments of the next few decades would by the early twentieth century see the cessation of Christian existence in Eastern Anatolia, where Eastern Christians had lived for centuries.

With Russia established as an unwelcome neighbor on her eastern borders, Turkey began to suspect Christian loyalties there. After the mid-nineteenth century the sultan's government was certain that in the course of future events, the most serious attacks of the Russians against the Turks would be directed against the eastern provinces of Asia Minor.[5] The Turks suspected that in a future war, as in the past two conflicts, the Ottoman Christians would most probably side with their coreligionists from the north. They especially suspected the Armenians, the leading millet among the non-European Christians of the empire.

2

It was during the tumultuous decades described above that the

Armenians of the Ottoman Empire were experiencing a literary and national renaissance. Not only was their patriarch recognized by the Ottoman government, even having direct audience with the Sultan, but he also represented other non-European Christians in Istanbul, such as the Nestorians and Jacobites.[6] Besides the ecclesiastical establishment in the capital, there were a number of wealthy and educated Armenians there as well as in the other major cities of the realm.[7]

Armenian leaders were well aware of the events that were transpiring in Europe and were especially familiar with the developments taking place in the sultan's Christian provinces in the Balkans. They were among the first non-European subjects of the sultan to experience a literary renaissance and a national awakening during the post-Napoleonic era. By 1860, a veritable literary revival had swept over the Armenians in all branches of literature, adding momentum to their national rebirth. "They pictured in colorful words," writes Sarkiss, "the dignity of their ancestral past and the servility of their present state." Armenian intellectuals returned from Europe and began translating into their language the literature of the French Revolution. Victor Hugo's *Les Misérables* was translated in 1868, only six years after its publication in French. Before that, in the late 1860s, some of the works of Lamartine and Chateaubriand were made available to the Armenian reader.[8]

The national constitution of the Armenian community (millet) was the handiwork of these Western-educated Armenians. Soon after the issuance of the hatti humayun in 1856, which provided that the temporal affairs of each community were to be placed under the control of a council to be chosen by the community, the Armenians "immediately compiled a document" which they presented to the Ottoman government, asking for their rights and freedoms.[9] The document was rejected with the objection that it sought a state within a state. A new constitution was prepared in 1860; on the suggestions of the Porte, it was revised and eventually ratified (1863) as the new "Regulation of the Armenian Patrlarchate," which the Patriarchate preferred to call "National Constitution of the Armenians."[10]

These reforms would remain ink on paper as far as Armenian aspirations were concerned, but the regulation did reform and strengthen the community internally. The constitution limited the power of the patriarch and democratized the governing body, the general assembly, which was called to meet twice a year. The assembly, made up of 140 representatives, elected two bodies, known respectively as the ecclesiastical and lay councils; these, through several committees, had full charge of all matters relating to the community. The chief executive of the nation, under the sultan, was the patriarch in Istanbul; he was elected from among the bishops of the Armenian church and had to be an Ottoman subject by birth.[11] The Armenian people looked forward to a future of internal autonomy and security. In addition to their contacts with Western Europe and with Russia to the East, they began to establish within Turkey itself close contacts with the representatives of the "New World," the American missionaries, to whose activities we shall briefly turn our attention again.

Soon after they arrived in the Ottoman Empire, the American evangelists, as we shall see, became very attracted to the Armenian church and people. In a few decades mission schools and colleges in Anatolia would be almost exclusively serving these Eastern Christians. Indeed, the first missionary effort from the United States to the Jacobite Christians, as we have seen, came to an end when the head of the mission abandoned the Jacobites in favor of the Armenians.[12]

By the second half of the nineteenth century missionary institutions—churches, hospitals, dispensaries, and schools of all grades—were planted and sustained all over Anatolia in such centers as Smyrna, Istanbul, Marsovan, Sivas, Kharput, Erzerum, Bitlis, Van, Mardin, Aintab, Marash, Adana, Tarsus, and Kayseri (Caesarea), and in may smaller localities. In the words of a contemporary observer, the Armenians had at their disposal "some of the best equipped and most efficient institutions in Asia." There gradually emerged as the direct result of this evangelical work a large number of institutions of higher learning outside Istanbul, among them Centrl Turkey College at Aintab, established in 1874, Euphrates College at Kharput (1876), Anatolia College at Marsovan (1886), College for Girls at Marash (1886), St. Paul's Institute at Tarsus (1889), American College for Girls at Constantinople (1890), and International College at Smyrna (1902).[13]

The graduates of these colleges and seminaries engaged in professional life as physicians, teachers, and clergymen in the scattered towns and villages of Asia Minor. The medical program of the college at 'Ayntab prepared its graduates for the examination at Istanbul's Imperial Medical School, which they "easily passed," enabling them to practice medicine throughout the Ottoman Empire.[14] The Armenians had caught "the American fever," wrote Dr. George C. Reynolds, a missionary resident of Van, "longing for American ideas, products and methods."

With this awakening came the revolution of rising expectations well observed by one of the British consuls: "the Armenians have learned to realize," he noted, "what is their position compared with that of subjects in more civilized countries; discontentment has spread with the growth of this knowledge and, as a consequence, the demands and ideas of the Christian subjects of His Imperial Majesty, just and moderate enough in most cases, have outstripped the slow changes toward their accomplishment which can be noted in the acts of the Government."[15] An Armenian scholar has put it more succinctly: "Knowledge and learning and the dawn of self-consciousness," writes A. O. Sarkissian, had taken the Armenians to an impasse; "the more they advanced on the road of enlightenment the more they became conscious of their almost hopeless situation."[16]

The eagerness of the Armenians to patronize the mission schools, and their readiness to accept evangelical ideas, wrote a secretary of the American board, "led the missionaries to move along the lines of least resistance and devote themselves to building up among the Armenians, and to a less degree among the Greeks, a strong, educated, evangelical community. The responsiveness of the Armenians, and their liberality in supporting their own institutions of education and religion, made the work most attractive and rewarding."[17]

3

Events came to a head in 1875-76 when the Porte suppressed an uprising in Serbia and Bulgaria. Representatives of European governments convened in Istanbul in 1876 in order to avert another war between Russia and Turkey and to discuss peace terms between Turkey and her Balkan provinces. The Armenians wanted to be included in these deliberations; their patriarch in Istanbul brought to the attention of the conference the suffering of his people in a document entitled "Report on the outrages which occurred in the Provinces."[18] The Armenians had not rebelled against the Porte as the Bosnians and the Bulgarians had done, "but that did not mean that the grounds and justifications to rebel were wanting." If the sympathy of the European powers could be won only after an insurrection, the Armenian patriarch had told Salisbury, "then there would be no difficulty to start such a movement."[19] The European conference, however, was unwilling to deal with the Armenian question, just as the Turkish government rejected European interference in its affairs whether in behalf of the Armenians or the Balkan Christians.

Before the European recommendations could be formally presented to the Porte, the sultan promulgated the ill-fated 1876 constitution. Russia, unhappy with her relations with Turkey since the defeat of 1856, started war in 1877, involving the Balkan as well as the Armenian Christians in her battles. The Russian invasion of eastern Anatolia was spearheaded by Russian Armenian officers and administrators, who had risen in the tsar's service since his annexation of Eastern Armenia earlier in the century.[20] Armenians contacted their brethren in the Ottoman Empire, wrote the Shaws, in order to secure their help. Even though the of Armenians remained loyal subjects, "the deeds of the few who did not, left a feeling of mistrust."

The Ottoman government had her own helpers; the Circassians and other Caucasian mountaineers, supported by a force of 14,000 Turks, made a determined attempt to regain their native lands from Russian control. The result, unfortunately for the Turks, was a severe defeat.

They were forced to withdraw, accompanied by some 30,000 Abkhasian Muslim refugees who were also to settle in Anatolia. The advancing Russian troops used Turkish rifles that they had captured, to arm the local Christians, and stimulated, write the Shaws, "massacres of the Muslim villagers to thwart local resistance," something the Russians had done on the Balkan front in Bulgaria, where Russian moves were "accompanied by large-scale massacres of Turkish peasants to make certain that they would not disrupt troop and supply movements."[21]

During the armistice Armenian grievances were presented by an Armenian delegation to the Russians. The Armenian patriarch wanted the Russians to help introduce reforms in eastern Anatolia with a view to protecting the Armenian population from the exactions of nomadic Kurds.[22] The Russians promised that a favorable reference would be made to the Armenians in the projected treaty. At San Stefano, they secured from the Ottoman government the promise that in the provinces inhabited by Armenians, their security would be guaranteed against the Kurds and Circassians.[23] The sultan also agreed to surrender East Anatolia districts including Kars, Ardahan, and Batum, in return for part of the indemnity that the Russians were imposing upon him. It was further agreed that in these territories surrendered to Russia, the Muslim population was free to leave, allowed three years within which to sell their properties. This would mean a stream of more embittered anti-Christian refugees in Turkish Anatolia, a source of great hostility there for years to come.

When the Treaty of San Stefano was revised later (1878) at the Congress of Berlin, article 61 of the new treaty provided that the Porte would undertake to carry out "without delay, the improvements and reforms demanded by local requirements in the provinces inhabited by the Armenians."[24] The Armenians hoped that with the help of Russian and other "Christian" powers such as England, they could at last enjoy at least a semi-independence or a local Christian administration like the Christians of the Lebanon. Unfortunately for them and other Ottoman Christians, the realities of geography, history, and power politics dictated otherwise.

There were those in England who thought that because of England's own self-interest she should encourage the establishment of an autonomous Armenia under her influence, thus giving England an advantage in her effort to observe and control Russian intrigues and movements in eastern Anatolia. An Armenia in Turkey, dependent on Russia, would eventually be annexed to the Russian Empire, leading to the virtual conquest of those parts of Asia Minor which according to some strategists of the day had to be "regarded as one of the central positions of the globe."[25]

4

Military observers considered the Caucasus as Russian's best base of operations for future designs even against the Far East. Since the 1860s, the Caucasus had about 150,000 men constantly massed in the highest state of efficiency. To some this constituted "a tremendous engine of war, at all times ready either to overthrow Asia Minor...or to threaten Persia...,"[26] a country of growing economic importance to England.

Some of the major trade routes of the day used by British merchants, whether from Istanbul to Erzerum, or from Diyarbakr to Mosul, Aleppo, or Baghdad to the south, or to Trebizond and Batum to the north, crossed this tableland now threatened by Russian annexation.[27] Turkish imports to Diyarbakr and the surrounding regions amounted to L115 thousand a year in the late 1870s; more than 75 perent of the goods came from England, the remainder from Russia, France, and Persia. The trade routes between the ports of the Black Sea and the interior of Iran also passed through these parts. The possession of Erzerum by Russia would, therefore, not only strike at the heart of Turkey but would sever Persia from the Black Sea.[28] Moreover, with the introduction of railway communication and better irrigation, these regions, under British supervision, might become the granary of both Europe and India, and this in spite of the fact that the overland route from the Mediterranean to India had of late suffered due to the opening of the Suez Canal in 1869.[29]

Thus we find England making a vigorous effort after 1878 to ameliorate the unhappy condition of the Christians of Turkey. British intervention in their behalf—whether Armenians, Nestorians, or Jacobites—was motivated by the desire to keep them loyal to the Turkish government in the event of a future Turko-Russian war, which could involve Great Britain.[30] "It is well known," wrote an informed observer of the day, "that the Russians have agents constantly at work among the Nestorians and Jacobites; and there is some likelihood of these sects being induced to declare themselves Orthodox Greeks, in order to acquire a title to the active sympathy and support of Russia." When these Chris tian groups find themselves properly protected, wrote Grattan Geary, "they would soon learn to have confidence in their government and would cease to cast their eyes toward Russia.[31] In the case of the Jacobites, our evidence shows, their overtures to Russia were motivated more by their fear and helplessness in the face of aggressive Catholic and Protestant proselytism among them, than by political incentives aimed against Ottoman mismanagement.

While the powers were in the midst of their deliberations at the Congress of Berlin, Great Britain and Turkey signed a "Convention of Defensive Alliance" with respect to the Asiatic provinces of Turkey. Commonly known as the Cyprus Convention, the treaty, signed as a result of an ultimatum from Great Britain, provided for British armed support in the event of Russian aggression in Asiatic Turkey. In return, the sultan consented to place the island of Cyprus under British administration.[32] Toward the end of 1878, it was also proposed that the major cities of eastern Anatolia be served by consuls or vice-consuls. Layard, England's ambassador at the Porte, thought that the presence of these representatives of the British government would be the most effective way of checking corruption and misconduct and of guaranteeing the rights of the Christians and seeing that the proposed reforms were executed.

The consuls started their work in earnest early in 1879. The reports that they "showered" upon the Porte seem to have alarmed not only Turkey but the European powers as well. The enforcement of the proposed reforms through European supervision was tantamount to taking the whole of Turkey under European tutelage.[33] The cession of Cyprus to England and the Anglo-Turkish convention were seen as bringing most of the Middle East within the British political system. A book published during this period bore the title *Our New Protectorate—Turkey in Asia*.[34] Among the Turkish population itself there was a widespread impression, according to a reporter of *The Times* of London, that their political supremacy in their own lands was coming to an end.[35] There was disquiet in the land; reports of the plight of the Muslim populations, of both Anatolia and the lands beyond, graphically describing their massacre and suffering, were beginning to stir public sympathy in Turkey, which the Muslim establishment, led by the theologians and the clergy, utilized to fight back.

Their power already threatened by the secularist policies of the reform movement (Tanzimat), the theologians were able in the difficult decade of the 1870s—just as the Ayatollah Khomeini and the clergy were able to do in Iran in the 1970s—"to build mass support for the idea that it was secularization imposed by the Tanzimat, the influence of foreigners, the intrusion of the foreign representatives—that had caused the empire's difficult situation."[36]

Unaware of these unfolding realities that surrounded them, the Ottoman Christians, encouraged by their mentors from the West, were convinced that a happier destiny awaited them as they entered the decade of the 1880s. The defeat of Turkey at the hand of the Russians in 1878 was interpreted by the missions as the waning of the political as well as the religious power of Islam. Admittedly, few Muslims had as yet converted to Christianity, but "a great and speedy turning on their part may be looked for with hope." In the midst of the Islamic stirrings that we have noted, the missionary establishment was engaging in the delusion that Islam was losing its hold "on the popular mind." The American evangelists saw the changes then taking place in the Middle East as "breaking down the pride of the adherents of Islam, and thus leading them to distrust the worth of their system of faith." Some of the leading newspapers and scholars of the day supported the Americans in their views of Islam.[37]

There were individual missionaries in the field who were not unaware of conflicts that their enterprise was creating, but they were incorrigibly optimistic. The Reverend Alpheus N. Andrus, who long served the Jacobites of Midyat and Tur Abdin from his headquarters in Mardin, blamed Muslim grievances on Islam's being "envious of the progress of her [Christian] neighbors." This envy had accentuated the pan-Islamic movement, he noted, and had led to a separation from the more intimate contact with the Christian population that had prevailed before. The missionary leadership was aware also of the fact that the scheme of reforms urged by the West in behalf of the Ottoman Christians was resented by both the government and the dominant Muslim population, but this was a bitter pill that the Muslims had to swallow.[38]

Many on the Muslim side interpreted the concessions of reform as amounting to autonomy for the Christians, from the benefits of which the Muslims alone were to be excluded. Some contemporary Western observers empathized with the Muslims; the whole reform movement urged by the signatories of the Congress of Berlin, they argued, would have had far better chances of success had the architects of the treaty pressed for reasonable reforms which would apply to all classes and creeds of the empire, "instead of making desultory protests at long intervals, in favour of a small and hated [Christian] minority." Had European diplomats emphasized reforms for the equally hard-pressed and exploited Muslim population, "they might have gradually created a popular sentiment, of which both the civil and ecclesiastical authorities would have been obliged to take account."[39] In his book *Armenia and the Campaign of 1877,* published in 1880, C.B. Norman asked for the obliteration of the word "Christian" from the literature of certain groups in England, where "the fanatical hatred towards the Moslem shown by a large section of the Christian community...has done more harm to bring about the present crisis than we dream of." Europeans who had lived in Turkey often pointed out the injustice of not taking the unhappy Muslim population into consideration, the vast majority of whom were not only the victims of their own weak and corrupt government but were now also made the scapegoat of its crimes by Europeans who lavished all their sympathy on the Christian, especially the Balkan Christian.

Enlightened Muslim leaders were also conscious of the plight of their Muslim brethren. In a letter to Sultan Abdul Aziz, Mustafa Fazil Pasha from Egypt spoke of backwardness and bad government "that afflicted the uncomplaining Muslims even more than the Christians;"

these, he said, were the real reasons for the Christian revolts in the empire.[40]

During the early 1880s the Sublime Porte was itself well aware that the Muslim population was far behind the Christians in education. The schools in Mardin, the majority of whose pupils were Jacobites and Armenians, were inspected in 1884 by a delegation from Istanbul with the intention of securing "equalization between the different communities in educational progress." This was to be effected by stimulating the communities that were backward to greater zeal, and "by checking those that are in advance." The Constantinople branch of the Evangelical Alliance mentioned in 1884 a recent law which claimed for the Turkish authorities the right to decide whether or not Christians should be allowed to have schools at all. Christians, even in the remotest parts of the empire, complained the evangelical body, are required to send to the capital for a permit "before they can open the most elementary school in the most insignificant village."[41]

The alliance presented a memorandum to both the Turkish authorities and the foreign embassies at the capital, complaining of the restrictions that were being put upon the Protestant community. As a result of these pressures the Porte had temporarily moderated its policies; a vezierial circular dated 16 May, 1899 declared that American schools should not be closed for the lack of official permits, required that complaints against schools to be sent to the capital, and forbade the closing of schools by local officials.[42] Yet three years later a government order was sent to the provinces announcing that all schools and places of worship must be provided at once with government firmans "or else closed."[43]

5

The Muslim population in Eastern Anatolia, predominantly Kurdish, felt especially threatened. The British consular agents' reforms in inner Anatolia were largely directed against the Kurdish tribesmen who were occasionally punished at the instigation of the consuls. But while the Kurds bitterly resented British interference in their affairs and often revenged their punishment,[44] they also mistrusted their Turkish overlords. Some Kurdish leaders wished to improve their relations with the British government and hoped that the terms of the Treaty of Berlin would improve the condition of their people as well as those of their Christian neighbors. The oldest son of Badr Khan, Mustafa Aali, was of the opinion that the fulfillment of the conditions of the Treaty of Berlin would mean semi-independence and autonomy for Kurdistan. He emphasized Kurdish allegiance to the Ottoman government as well as England. The Kurds would be ready to pay "a certain tribute, and furnish troops to the Porte as their Suzerain," while at the same time they would provide Britain, with the Porte's consent, with "100,000 troops, horse and foot, in case of any war with Russia which should imperil [the British] position in India."

Missionary reports from eastern Anatolia spoke of the desire of some Kurds to convert to Christianity. "We know," wrote some Kurdish petitioners who claimed to represent more than 21,000 families, that "the way preached by our Lord Jesus is right and we have accepted it in our inward hearts." They were anxious to know, however, if upon conversion, the American missionaries would protect them and whether "like other Christians, we may be freed from the necessity of furnishing soldiers." The missionaries wondered whether "political protection" was not what the Kurds had "in their mind."[45] As Muslims, of course, the Kurds were beyond the limits of missionary proselytization; as free-spirited and armed mountaineers, they were feared, suspected, and, consequently, much maligned. As late as the opening of this century, a church missionary society report referred to the Kurds as "the cruelest of savages."[46]

Robbery and pillage were often resorted to during periods of famine. Conditions worsened toward the end of the nineteenth century, especially after the Turko-Russian War of 1877-78, whose demands had stripped the triangle between Van, Diyarbakr, and Mosul, of Turkish troops, paving the way for nomadic forays which until then had been drastically reduced. When it was over, the war of 1878 left its impact everywhere, on faraway Damascus as well as on Diyarbakr,[47] even though it was inland Asia Minor that was affected most.

Trade routes in Asia Minor has suffered for a long time due to the introduction of steam navigation and the discovery of the routes around the Cape of Good Hope long before that.[48] The difficulty of transportation to a maritime outlet further crippled both trade and industry. As late as the 1880s the British consul at Diyarbakr observed that while the markets of the world had been revolutionized, Asia Minor and Kurdistan remained at the same distance as before. What little trade remained in these regions was diverted eastward between Persia and Russia. These factors, compounded always by the general rise in prices, left no incentive to the producer and merchant who in days past had engaged in the exportation of a number of raw products such as gallnuts, linseed, gum, dried fruit, wool, silk, shawls, carpets, skins, copper, bitumen, and saltpetre in addition to butter, cheese, and honey, and in certain areas, tobacco and opium. While some of these products were exported from Diyarbakr to foreign countries, especially to Austria, France, England, and Russia, a considerable home business in them was done, sent to Van, Erzerum, Mosul, Baghdad, and Aleppo.[49]

The missionaries stationed all over "Eastern Turkey" wrote voluminously during the 1880s and 1890s on the want and violence that the country was going through. They often wrote of famine, locusts, and epidemics, occasionally of earthquakes, and always of a weak and corrupt government. The *Missionary Herald* of the summer of 1880 spoke of famine "extending from Diarbakir to the Persian Gulf," when wheat was selling at "fifteen times the usual price." There had been scanty rainfall the previous winter and this was followed by a winter of almost unexampled severity from cold and snow, causing food and fuel to vanish and thousands of cattle and sheep to perish.[50] Half a dozen years later we read of the region desolated by locusts. "The wheat, barley, cotton, tobacco, lentiles," wrote the American evangelists, "were almost entirely destroyed." This was the third year "that the locusts have worked desolation." The report spoke of the resulting stagnation of trade and employment.[51]

It is not surprising therefore that a caravan of goods and foodstuff would be the object of attack. The robbers did not steal from the peasants, especially those who were friendly. Indeed, the brigand bands were made up of former peasants; their enemies were the local government officials and tax collectors, the rich landowners and the military. More than one writer has likened the brigand's relation to the peasant to that of Robin Hood and "the villagers of England centuries ago."[52] No matter what the way of life, it was further impeded by lack of an efficient government. "At bottom," writes Leon Dominian, the vices of the Kurds were chiefly "those of the restless life they lead in a land in which organized government has been unknown for the past several centuries."[53]

By 1883 even England had given up on reforms in Asiatic Turkey. Her withdrawal paved the way for a Kurdish-Turkish alliance. As fellow Muslims, close to the Russian Caucasus on the eastern borders of the Octoman Empire, the Kurds were the only large sector of the population that the Ottoman government could trust. It was therefore of the utmost importance for the Porte to win them over. By the early 1890s Kurdish men were officially conscripted and armed into an elite group bearing the name of the sultan, and throughout Abdul Hamid's reign, the Hamidiyah cavalry regiments, and through them implicitly the Kurds of eastern Turkey, were given favorable treatment.[54]

Not all the Kurds, let alone the Ottoman government itself, were happy with the Hamidiyah. Many of the Hamidiyah soldiers were from Kurdish tribes who were Shi'ites (Qizilbāsh) and as such they "did not spare the Sunni Kurds," wrote Mark Sykes.[55] Only two years after the Hamidiyah's organization, a British government "confidential" reported that the situation in eastern Turkey "was so bad" that the Muslim merchants of Erzerum had addressed a strongly worded telegram to the imperial palace at Constantinople complaining that the state of insecurity in their province was rapidly bringing all business to a standstill, "ruining the population."[56] Arshak Safrastian, who served as a British vice-consul at Bitlis, wrote that the Kurdish cavalry divisions became a scourge to all indiscriminately, and produced hostile feelings between the Kurds and Armenians who had an "unwritten pact of friendship" between them.[57]

6

This is not the place to discuss the tragedies that befell the Armenians in 1895-96; a great deal has already been written on the subject, most of it partisan.[58] It can be stated with certainty, however, that originally the conflict was not religious but political. Contemporary sources have recorded that the vast majority of the Christian victims were Armenians.[59] The correspondent of the *Daily News* of London has noted that in Trabizund there was a large Greek population but that neither there nor elsewhere, with possibly one or two exceptions, had the Greeks been molested.[60] Our sources conflict on the involvement of the Syrian Orthodox and Catholic Christians in these atrocities. The violence was not directed against these non-Armenian Christians even though they were not spared in a number of places. Syrian Christians lived as neighbors of the Armenians in a number of towns such as Diyarbakr, Mardin, Kharput, and Urfa, and naturally were panic-stricken, alarmed that they might share in the fate of their coreligionists. To them this was a persecution declared on the Christians generally and on the Armenians particularly. According to a Jacobite historian, the "rumor" was that the Armenians had rebelled; in reality the mobs were calling for extermination of "all the Christians."[61]

Brigands and outlaws had joined in the melee and did not discriminate between a Syrian or an Armenian—indeed the innocent Armenians who were in the vast majority, and the guilty few, were alike victims in that marked community. There were Kurdish attacks on the villages of Tur Abdin, many of them burned and looted, large numbers of the men killed and mutilated, their women carried away. Jacobite villages outside Mardin, helpless, were devastated in 1896, most of their inhabitants escaping to safety in Mardin. In Mardin, the ordinary Muslim citizens, repelled by what was taking place, had defended the city together with the Christians, the municipal government providing them with ammunition. Criers in the city had exhorted all lovers of the Prophet Muhammad and of Islam to resist the Kurdish attackers.[62]

When the atrocities by the Turks against the Armenians started in Diyarbakr in December 1895, the Jacobite patriarch Ignatius 'Abd al-Masih II had sent a telegram to Sultan Abdul Hamid and had received a royal proclamation emphasizing the protection of the Syrians.[63] The vali of Diyarbakr, in a telegram to the governors of Mardin, Midyat, and the Jazirah, had ordered them that "no one harm any Syrian." For a while the Jacobite Church of the Mother of God in Mardin became "like a Noah's Ark for all." In other Jacobite regions, Turkish commanders had toured Jacobite areas to lend their help. Yet "in spite of all that, thousands" were killed and their homes looted, others were left naked and hungry.[64]

Some Western observers have noted that because the Jacobites had never preached revolution, they "escaped unscathed through the horrors of the last few years."[65] In Urfa, writes Lord Warkworth, "not a hair of their head was touched." The Syrian Orthodox and Catholics were as defenseless in Urfa as the Armenians, "yet care was expressly taken beforehand to warn them to shelter themselves in their churches, and not to stir out until the riots were over."[66]

Other contemporaries have attributed the relative safety of the Syrians to their exclusion from the stipulations of the Treaty of Berlin in 1878. "One cannot help thinking," wrote J. Aston Campbell, "that but for this Treaty, the Armenians might have been equally prosperous" as the Jacobites.[67] Parry, who lived among the Jacobites for half a dozen years, attributed their comparative security to the fact that they cherished no idea of rebellion, "even were it practicable." Unlike the Armenians, of course, the Jacobite Syrians had not experienced a renaissance and a national awakening; they do not "seem to realize any other position for themselves than that of dependents," wrote Parry. "They are not powerful or ambitious enough to have any desire to shake off the rule under which they live, like the Armenians."

It should be pointed out here that the Jacobites were unlike a number of other fellow Christians in the Ottoman Empire: unlike the Maronites of Mount Lebanon "consumed by a hereditary feud with a neighbor," and unlike other "Papal Christians" who were "objects of suspicion, as dependents and spies of a foreign power." They were unlike the Nestorians, for the Jacobites were strong enough, and lived in civilized places enough not to be a prey to mountain robbers. Their homegrounds, unlike those of the Nestorians, were accessible and close to the seats of government. Their Turkish rulers, therefore, had never "regarded them, nor do now regard them, with anything but friendliness and toleration."[68] Another student of the Syriac churches of Anatolia, W.A. Wigram, emphasized at the time that the massacre of the 1890s "was political and not religious," and gave as proof the fact that "the Syrian Christians (who are also numerous in Diarbekr) did not suffer to anything like the same extent as their Armenian co-religionists...only isolated individuals fell victims to the fury of the mob."[69]

The Jacobite patriarch of the day wrote the grand vizier a letter, dated 27 April 1896, complaining of the Armenians.

My nation is most grateful to his Majesty for the protection
he has ever accorded to it, as also to our Mussulman com-

patriots, but the Armenians have for some time past endeavored to Armenianize our language and religion, so long preserved thanks to the Mussulman law....Letters from our spiritual Chiefs at Ourfa and Bitlis, amongst other places, signed by many respectable persons, have reached us which prove that the Armenians have slain and plundered many of our community, and that their design is to completely annihilate it by famine and by other means. Under these circumstances we can but appeal to the Sovereign, our sole refuge to protect us in his clemency.[70]

In the summer of 1896 the Jacobite prelate also wrote to Queen Victoria, expressing "his satisfaction with the Turkish authorities, and stated that the Armenians were responsible for the disturbances." The patriarchs of the Syrian Orthodox, Syrian Catholic, and Chaldean communities sent telegrams in 1895 to the vali of Mosul expressing their thanks, noting that "through measures adopted by his Excellency, they, with all their communities are enjoying perfect safety" in Mosul, where "tranquility prevails throughout the vilayet."[71]

The British consul at Diyarbakr informed his embassy in Istanbul that these telegrams were sent "at the instigation of the Vali Saleh Pasha."[72] The British consul wrote that the Jacobite patriarch was "a man of bad character" who was recently elected contrary to the wish of the majority of his people, partly by the influence of the vali and partly by bribery.[73] The consul contradicted the patriarch, noting that the Syrians had "suffered as much as the Armenians in this district."[74] The mission of the Presbyterian church in the United States, however, writing from Mosul in the spring of 1896, supported some of the statements contradicted by the British representative. The annual report of the mission for the year 1896 speaks of the Turkish government as "anxious to suppress any outbreak upon the Syrians from the Mohammedan population." By command of the governor of Mosul, a city with practically no Armenian inhabitants, the chief mullah had in a sermon enjoined the populace "to refrain from all demonstrations against the Christians." The sermon is reported to have closed with this alarming note, however: "When the Sultan bids us rise against the Christians we will rise, but until he does we must remain quiet."[75] In general, wrote the Reverend Edwin M. Bliss, there was "considerable effort on the part of the government to protect [the] Jacobite Christians..., in numerous villages the soldiers not merely drove off the Kurds, but escorted the villagers to places of safety."[76]

7

After years of bloodshed and famine, reports from eastern Anatolia spoke of abundant crops.[77] A few months after the upheavals of 1895-96, the Porte issued an imperial decree which sanctioned some of the reforms concerning the administration of eastern Anatolia suggested by the European Commission.[78]

The part which Armenians played in the government of the provinces where they lived in substantial numbers, gradually began to increase. Apart from the official services that they performed they once more started to contribute to the economic and general development of the country through trade, agriculture, handicrafts, and the professions.[79] The twentieth century opened with optimistic reports on railroad construction in Asia Minor, which proposed to open wide districts in central and eastern Anatolia, connecting them with Istanbul, Baghdad, and the Persian Gulf.[80]

But the Christians were intimidated, their "eye broken." The reality of the situation was different from what the government and the European entrepreneurs envisioned. Local reports during the opening years of the twentieth century once again began to tell their tales of woe; they spoke of the Diyarbakr-Mardin region as exposed to constant robbery and oppression at the hands of some Kurdish tribes, the Christian population kept in a continual state of panic by the threats of some of the leading men of that region. In 1904 *the Times* of London reported that no fewer than three thousand Armenians, men, women, and children, had been killed in the district of Sassoun.[81] A British consular report from Diyarbakr dated 4 December 1905 had come to the conclusion that the Turkish government, working through the Kurds, wished the Christian inhabitants of the region either to become Muslims or to leave the country for the towns. To the missionaries on the spot, too, it looked "as if the policy were to extinguish the Armenians, or at least drive them from the villages." They reported Armenian villages practically depopulated, their property passed over to the Kurds.[82] On the eve of the First World War we read of an Armenian village all of whose inhabitants had turned Muslim. The only thing the villagers knew of Christianity, they are reported saying, was "that we have to fast, and we don't care to be robbed because of that." As Muslims they could "rob others instead."[83]

The missionaries blamed also the Armenian revolutionaries in 1904. To the Americans it seemed that these revolutionaries, too, "were determined not to leave anything of their people here." Many of them "from across the Russian border, with a number of natives of the district, have sought to incite insurrection, and the Turkish authorities [are] determined to wipe out these offenders." Some Armenians dreaded the revolutionists as much as the Turks.[84]

Then came the brief honeymoon that started with the Young Turk revolution. The news that the sultan has been overthrown was greeted with disbelief at first but then with great expression of joy, even though not in all Muslim quarters. Turkish officials and Armenian ecclesiastics were seen publicly embracing one another, exchanging congratulations and pledging themselves to mutual brotherhood. Muslims paid honors at the graves of massacred Armenians as well as to martyrs who had died for their country. "Oaths were sworn," wrote a missionary eyewitness, "that all partisan differences of blood and creed should be merged and forgotten in a brotherhood of a common freedom and one Fatherland." A Turkish newspaper in the capital printed a statement that those who shared in the oppression of the Armenians and in the massacres belonged outside the pale of Islam and even of humanity. "The Sultan," wrote an American, "has received personally at his palace the Armenian patriarch, Msgr. Izmirlian, in great state, and has expressed his sorrow at the past sad events."[85]

The Shaykh al-Islam and other religious leaders invoked the Koran, which, they said, commands friendship toward Christians; there was no justification in it, they added, for calling the Christians 'unbelievers.' A sermon widely distributed throughout the empire emphasized that the Christians constitute a trust given to the Muslims by God; "Moslems should guard the rights of Christians more jealously than their own."[86]

Some important changes were beginning to take place in inland Anatolia. The city of Diyarbakr had its first Christian mayor after the 1908 revolution and "what is more," reported the *Missionary Herald* with pride, "he is a leading Protestant Armenian and the son of a Protestant." On the eve of the First World War the Jacobites of Mosul were described as a "well-to-do community."[87]

Unfortunately for the missionaries and their coreligionists the Young Turk "democracy" was soon replaced by a military dictatorship, as the new regime was faced with one crisis after another.[88] When the news reached Cilicia in the spring of 1909 that Sultan Abdul Hamid had tried to regain power through a military coup, his loyal followers fell upon the Armenians who had shown elation over his overthrow in most of the towns and villages of the region.[89] The conflict started in Adana and from there spread in all directions, wiping out "whole Christian villages most of them Armenians," and sending "a wave of terror over the whole Christian population of the country."[90]

Abdul Hamid's counterrevolution lasted ten days. Nearly fifty Muslims were hanged in Adana and vicinity, some of them men of wealth and high rank. The Young Turks, however, could not for long afford alienating the Muslim population, faced as they were by non-Muslim foes—the Austrians at Bosnia, the Italians in Tripolitania, the Serbians and the Macedonians, with the support of Russia, in the Balkans. Writing from inner Anatolia, missionary letters reported fear that other European countries might follow the lead of Italy. "The result of such fear, coupled with a sense of impotence to prevent the partition of Turkey, is an increased rage against the Christian portion of the population.''[91] To exacerbate matters, these were years of famine in most regions of eastern Anatolia. By 1911, wrote Pastor Andrus of Mardin, things had reverted to practically what they were before the inauguration of the Young Turk regime. He spoke of prices rising, work scarce, business prostrate, lawlessness becoming bolder. "The Lord is keeping this part of the country and not the government."[92] The Balkan-Turkish war had hardly ended when the First World War started, with Turkey fighting not only Russia but England and France as well.

The ravages and brutalities of the 1878 war were repeated with greater intensity during the world conflict of 1914-18. The German allies of Turkey wanted her to attack Russia on the Caucasus front in order to draw away the Russians from East Prussia as well as the Balkans, a move that Enver himself had envisioned. Russian troops crossed the Turkish border on 1 November 1914, a move probably precipitated by a Turkish attack on Russian installations on the Black Sea. About fifty days later the Turkish Third Army, based at Erzerum and led by Enver himself, counterattacked. Unfortunately for them, after some initial successes, a Russian counteroffensive in January 1915 almost utterly destroyed them, three-fourths being lost in retreat during a severe winter.[93] The Kurds of the Hamidiyah corps[94] had soon decided that it was "no use to stand against the Russian artillery," and most of them deserted. Fear of desertion of all soldiers ended sometimes in having the recruits "handcuffed, chained together and driven to the front like slaves," wrote one missionary from Anatollia.[95]

Turkey suffered on the civilian front as much as she did on her battlelines. As soon as the outbreak of war became imminent, the military started getting ready by seizing as much foodstuff, kerosene, tea, and sugar as possible. With every male from 20 to 45 impressed into the army, many families were left with only women and children. Animals too—horses and oxen—were taken, as were the ox carts. The confiscation hit the poor as well as the rich, Christians and Muslims both. During the first year of the war typhoid and typhus were reported raging, hitting the sick and the wounded soldiers, the underfed populace as well as the doctors and nurses who cared for them, paving the way for the invasion of other diseases: pneumonia, dysentery, and an epidemic of measles among the children. Contemporary sources do speak of the "starving Mohammedans."[96]

After the winter of 1915 the Ottoman military had come to the conclusion that they had to evacuate the Armenian population from eastern Anatolia. By mid-1915 "orders were issued to evacuate the entire Armenian population from the provinces of Van, Bitlis, and Erzerum." Professor and Mrs. Shaw have allowed themselves to be convinced by Professor and Mrs. Shaw have allowed themselves to be convinced by Turkish sources that the Armenians were to be "transported" to northern Iraq; those who lived in the countryside of the Cilician region, to be sent to central Syria. Not only were the victims of these deportations to be protected against attacks but they were to be provided "with sufficient food and other supplies to meet their needs during the march and after they were settled." Moreover, according to Turkish documents, which one historian has called "preposterous" and a "fabrication,"[97] the Armenians "were to be protected and cared for until they returned to their homes after the war. The government would provide for their return once the crisis was over"![98]

In the meantime Ottoman forces in eastern Anatolia were reinforced; in the summer of 1915 they were able to force the Russians to retreat, followed by some two hundred thousand Armenians fleeing their homes, seeking refuge in the Caucasus. About forty thousand of them perished on the way, a fate of self-exile and death not related to the forced deportations which were to lead others of their brethren to either Iraq or Syria.[99]

Reporting on the Armenians who were "transported" by the Turkish government, the *Missionary Herald* referred to "absolutely reliable" sources that indicated "a systematic, authorized, and desperate effort on the part of the rulers of Turkey to wipe out the Armenians."[100] Some correspondents of the *Herald,* however, were not so certain of Turkish motives. One missionary, Mary L. Graffam, who accompanied the Armenians on their forced exile and witnessed the murder of "a great many in every city," has recorded how Ottoman officials had read to her "orders from Constantinople again and again to the effect that the lives of these exiles are to be protected, and from their actions I should judge," she wrote, "that they must have received such orders." At Sivas the vali had allowed Armenian men to go with their families and the "government gave forty-five ox carts...and eighty horses" for the deported. This was a special favor to the Sivas people," she noted, since they "had not done anything revolutionary." Missionary Graffam also noted that most of the higher officials of the Ottoman government were "at their wit's end to stop these abuses and carry out the orders which they have received." But "this is a flood," she wrote, "and it carries everything."[101]

It should be pointed out here that no matter what role the Ottoman government played in these atrocities, these horrors did not always take place unopposed by the peaceful Muslim inhabitants. In villages around Marash, Muslim neighbors had come to the aid of the Armenians, testifying that they were not guilty of anything, "possessed no weapons, lived peaceably, and were friends with them, and were, besides, their artisans and tradesmen." Often during these years of darkness, one sees gleams of humanity. Many a missionary from the Ottoman empire "insisted" that "a number of the Turks regard with horror the deeds that they had been commanded to do to their Armenian neighbors." There were times when Turks protected Christians against Kurdish and Arab attackers. There were times when Armenians helped Turks; one reads of an Armenian named Dikran getting food and water to a wounded Turkish soldier crying out for water, or of a Kurdish chief hugging and kissing the children of an Armenian friend ordered to leave, departing in tears.[102]

It was a flood and a fury that engulfed the innocent and the guilty, Muslim[103] and Christian, a war couched in religious terms,[104] the victims easily removed from the range of scruple and sympathy. According to a Kurdish historian thousands of his people were killed between 1915 and 1918 by Armenian volunteers, "avenging former massacres."[105] This time other Christian sects besides the Armenians were also engulfed. Between 1915 and 1917, some sources estimate, about a million and a half Christians were massacred in upper Mesopotamia "without distinction of confession, including Jacobite and Catholic Syrians, Chaldeans and Protestants." In the city of Mardin alone, according to one source, the Jacobites had lost ninety-six thousand souls.[106]

6

Syrians, Lebanese, and Iraqis

1

The internal conditions in the still "Ottoman Empire" were chaotic when the war ended in 1918. Food and most commodities were at famine prices. In Istanbul, sugar, an item typical of other commodities, was retailed at three hundred instead of twenty-five piasters. "Everyone was for himself;" the *Times* of London reported hundreds of thousands of brigands, some partly organized politically; others, unorganized bands of deserters and robbers, posed the most serious problem of all.[1]

Istanbul was an occupied city, the sultan not a free agent. The negotiations conducted with his government and signed by him in the Treaty of Sèvres perpetuated the rights of the Western powers to interfere in the internal affairs of Turkey and its former provinces. The many minorities of the empire were used as a pretext for intervention. Armenians, Kurds, Maronites, Jews, and Assyrians were used at the end of the war, just as the Arabs were manipulated at its beginning.

An independent Armenia, a scheme of local autonomy for the predominantly Kurdish areas—leading to independence if the Kurds so desired;[2] a Jewish national home in Palestine, a Greater Lebanon dominated by the Maronites, special privileges for the Assyrians in northern Iraq, led to an inflation of nationalist hopes and demands that severely strained minority-majority relations, leading to antagonisms from which the Middle East is still suffering.

With the collapse of tsarist Russia, the Armenians in eastern Anatolia found themselves in an especially precarious condition. Many

99

deported Armenians had begun to return to their homes soon after Turkey had signed the armistice. Their nationalists, encouraged by the outbreak of the Russian Revolution on the one hand, and the victories of the Allied armies on the other, proclaimed the Republic of Armenia in the Caucasus in May 1918. The surrender of the Ottoman Empire to the Allies five months later led to the withdrawal of the Ottoman troops from Transcaucasia and northwestern Iran, lessening the dangers faced by the infant Armenian republic. With the help of British imperial troops, the Republic was allowed to establish its full jurisdiction throughout the Kars province during the following spring (April 1919).[3] More than fifty thousand Armenian refugees, who had left the province when the Russians abandoned it, were repatriated,[4] but with strict orders not to advance into Turkish Armenia. They found it too tempting not to, and soon proceeded to extend the Republic's borders westward to include eastern Anatolia, driven by the dream of once again ploughing "the soil of Van, Bitlis, Erzerum, Diarbekir—and lands beyond."[5] Moreover, they were encouraged by the Treaty of Sèvres, which formally recognized Armenian independence in eastern Turkey.

While the Armenians were trying to take over in eastern Turkey, the Greeks were dreaming their "Great Idea." It was in May 1919 when Greece landed troops at Smyrna (Izmir) under the protection of an Allied fleet and proceeded to secure western Anatolia for itself, envisioning the restitution of the ancient Byzantine Empire with Constantinople as its capital and St. Sophia as its cathedral.

The summer of 1920 brought more encouragement for the Anatolian Christians—the French occupation forces had arrived in southwestern Turkey. Armenian young men were enrolled as volunteers for service under French officers. The Christian communities of south-central Turkey were reported by the American missionaries to have declared an "Autonomous Christian Cilicia."[6]

Beaten and humiliated, the Turks struck back. Soon after the war's end, the return of the Armenians on Turkish soil had led to a movement designed to prevent them from settling and tilling their fields. "Bands styled brigands," wrote the *Times*, were sent by the provincial notables, leading to warfare "with all its hideous accompaniments."[7] When Smyrna was occupied, news was spread of a massacre of the Muslims by Greeks. Unarmed Muslim Turkish villages had been pillaged by the Greeks, reducing their inhabitants to starvation. Were the English now bringing in the Armenians? Many Kurds, wrote Gertrude Bell, "dreaded an enquiry by British and Armenians into their misdeeds against the Armenians in 1915."[8]

Mustafa Kemal started to round up nationalist forces in the spring of 1919 to save Turkey proper from dismemberment. We need not be detained by details of the next few years except to mention that by the second half of 1920, after the Greek danger had been contained, Turkish forces had overrun the greater part of the territory claimed by the Armenian Republic, including Kars and Ardahan.[9]

On the Cilician front American missionary reports spoke of burning and bloodshed. At Marash (Mar'ash), after three weeks of fighting, the French troops, helped by the Armenians, were forced to withdraw, the latter left behind, falling into the hands of the Turks now "inspired by an intensified hate." By the beginning of 1922 the French forces had arranged an armistice with the Turks. That summer the Turko-French agreement provided for French withdrawal from Cilicia, coupled with Kemalist recognition of French authority in Syria. The Armenians, as Turkish subjects, had to submit themselves to Turkish rule and accept Turkish guarantees for their safety. Those who wanted to leave for French-occupied Syria would be allowed to do so.[10] Armenian "disheartenment," wrote Dr. John E. Merrill, president of Central Turkey College at Aintab, exceeded that during any of the previous massacres and deportations, for added to the bitterness of the event was "the consciousness of betrayal."

In 1922 the Turks granted "permission . . . to all Christians" to leave Turkey, creating yet another flight of refugees in panic.[11] Jacobite and Chaldean Christians as well as Armenians became victims of Turkish vengeance. Large numbers of the two non-Armenian communities fled in 1921 and 1922, bringing to an end their centuries-old residence in Adana and especially Urfa.[12] The vast majority of them were helpless victims of the forces unleashed by the events that we have described, innocent of all political ambition. A Jacobite author speaks of the misdeeds of some agitated youth of his community during the French occupation, that displeased Turkish officials.[13]

Like other minorities, encouraged by the new freedoms proclaimed by the American president, the Jacobites wanted to be heard at the peace conference in Paris. Some of their leaders, especially those who had immigrated to the United States, joined the delegation of the "Assyrian National Association of America," with its ambitious claims.[14] The future patriarch of the Jacobites, Ignatius Afrām I. Brsoum, then bishop of Syria, joined the delegation in Paris even though he was soon disillusioned by what he saw there; at one session at the peace conference he found himself defending Arab rights instead of championing the cause of his community. He was cheered by the Arab delegates present, called bishop of Arabism—Muṭrān al-'Urūba—and priest of all time—"Qass al-Zamān."[15]

Outside Cilicia, large numbers of Chaldeans, Jacobites, and Syrian Catholics had remained in their own villages and towns after the Armenian deportations, and they were on the Turkish side when the Armistice was signed. They had often become objects of Turkish retaliation,[16] but it was not until the Kurdish revolt in 1925 that they again suffered massacre and deportation, long after the Turks had settled their problem with their non-Muslim subjects.

The motive of the Kurdish uprising, notes a Kurdish writer, "was the endeavor to create an independent Kurdish state and secure the national rights of the Kurdish people." The chief slogan of the revolt was "the creation of independent Kurdistan under Turkish protectorate and restoration of the Sultanate."[17] But the Turkish nationalists were determined to crush the rebellion. If the Kurds were not "taught a lesson" very early, then the eastern vilayets of the country would continue to be a source of great danger, forcing the young republic to keep a large army there at a cost that it could ill afford. The Turkish republicans were also convinced that the Kurds were encouraged by the British government in Iraq, where the mandatory administration showed great partiality to them.[18] Moreover, the Ankara government saw in the Kurds an ideological enemy; they represented a counterrevolution, the old Turkey fighting the new. When Kurdish forces temporarily occupied Diyarbakr and Kharput, they were reported to have proclaimed Muhammad Salim, the oldest son of Abdul Hamid II, as "King of Kurdistan." The insurgents demanded the restoration of the religious laws and institutions that "the atheist government of Ankara" had abolished; they called upon all Turkish Muslims to join them in a holy war (*jihād*) against the new republic.[19]

It did not take long before the heavy hand of the Ankara government had broken the Kurdish uprising and captured its leaders. By April 1925 the rebels had been driven into the mountains which Ismet Pasha, speaking before the Grand National Assembly, said "would prove to be their tomb."[20] A Turkish court martial set up at Diyarbakr condemned to death and executed in August 1925 Shayk Sa'īd and forty-seven other Kurdish leaders. "Altogether," writes Ghassemlou, "206 villages were destroyed, 8,758 houses burnt and 15,200 people killed." About a thousand of the Kurdish notable families were transferred to the western parts of Anatolia.[21]

The Jacobites who were spared during the Armenian atrocities became victims during the suppression of the Kurdish revolt. Some Syrian Christians had collaborated with the Kurds or had given them protection either from fear or conviction.[22] Consequently, a number of Jacobites and Chaldeans were surrounded and deported from that part of the Turkish territory that the British government claimed for Iraq to the north of the "Brussels Line."[23] People who conducted inquiries on the spot have also ascribed these deportations to the desire of the Turkish military authorities to seize the cattle and grain of the Christian villagers in order to feed their hungry and angry troops. Politically, the authorities also feared that the Christians' loyalties might be with the

British and Iraqi authorities across the border. General Laidoner, commissioned by the League of Nations to investigate these deportations, had "satisfied himself beyond doubt" that Turkish officers had first commanded the occupation and search of the villagers for arms. "Afterwards they pillaged the houses and subjected the inhabitants to atrocious and murderous acts of violence. The deportations were made *en masse*."[24] The Jacobite patriarch, Mar Ignatius Elias III, was expelled from Dayr Za'farān, which was turned into a Turkish barrack.[25]

Not all the Christian inhabitants of Anatolia had left their homes during and after the first World War. Some who had crossed into Syria or Iraq returned to their villages. During the conflicts, the people of Tur Abdin held on to their mountain fastnesses and, as in the past, found refuge in their churches and monasteries. Kullith,[26] Middu, Basabrina, Idil, and Hakh were among the approximately sixty villages still exclusively Christian as late as the mid-1970s. One of the churches of Hakh (Church of the Virgin), dating back to the apostolic times, its magnificent Byzantine mosaic still largely intact, may be the oldest church still in use in the world. Gertrude Bell, describing its exquisite lacework of ornaments, called it the jewel of Tur Abdin.[27]

An American student of Middle Eastern Christian churches who visited the Tur in 1974 wrote that what distinguishes the churches and monasteries of the region from other ancient Christian monuments of Asia Minor is the phrase "still in use."[28] During his visit he observed the faithful gathering at the various churches every evening for vesper prayers. The village of Kullith had a Syrian Protestant church with a membership of twenty families, remnant of the once-flourishing Protestant missionary effort there.[29]

The focal point of the Tur region remained the convent of al-Za'farān with its cathedral, the Church of the Forty Martyrs.[30] In the 1970s there were only four monks at the Dayr, which for centuries had served as the summer residence of Jacobite patriarchs of nearby Mardin, and home of sometimes up to sixty monks.[31] About ten other monks serve in other monastic centers—Mār Jibrā'īl (Gabriel) and Mār Ya'qūb (Jacob)—their time spent on maintaining them, cultivating their gardens and orchards, as well as on meditating, teaching, and entertaining guests, visitors, and villagers who come from long distances to attend Sunday services. The monastery of Mar Jibrā'il, in the village of Qarṭamin, some twenty miles east of Midyat, has been renovated, and some new buildings have been added in recent years to the old structure. In the middle ages this convent, sometimes called Dayr 'Umar, was the most famous and the richest of the Jacobite monasteries. Tradition says that its bishop, Mār Gabriel, had obtained from the caliph, 'Umar Ibn al-Khaṭṭāb, rights of jurisdiction over all the Christians in the Tur Abdin when the caliph's forces had driven the Byzantines out.[32]

These venerated structures have been maintained and expanded by the generous donations of Jacobites everywhere, especially those who have immigrated to the Americas. To the Syrian Orthodox these lands and landmarks, where in Tur Abdin alone the "Suryan" had seventy monastic centers,[33] are "hallowed by the blood of martyrs and by miraculous interventions of the Holy Spirit" throughout the centuries.[34] Today, two of the monasteries serve as seminaries. In 1974 the convents of al-Za'farān and Mar Gabriel had about fifty students, some of whom would enter priesthood.[35] One of the more distinguished graduates of al-Za'farān was Patriarch Ignatius Afrām I. Barsoum, the predecessor of the late prelate, who was a graduate of the seminary at Mār Matta, in northern Iraq.[36]

The capital center of Tur Abdin continues to be the town of Midyat, the residence of one of the two Jacobite bishops of Turkey, with a diocese of about twenty thousand faithful living in it and its nearby villages, served by forty priests. The city has five churches, each with its priest. The town is divided into two sections, separated from each other by about two kilometers, one predominantly Muslim, the other Christian.[37]

All the historic Christian communities of the eastern half of Anatolia were present in Mardin after the maelstrom of 1914-18 had swept over that part of Turkey.[38] The Jacobites were the most important group among the city's Christians, having taken the place of the Armenians. The Syrian Orthodox still had "numerous communities" in the surrounding countryside in the 1960s, some of them with their own churches and parish priests.

For a while it seemed that things were going back to the normalcy of the pre-World-War-I days. The Eastern Turkey mission of the American board was able to open its schools in Mardin in late 1924. During the Kurdish disturbances of the late 1920s and early 1930s the missionaries reported that the Turkish officials of the city were very friendly, providing the mission compound with a special guard.[39]

Although Mardin was still an Arabic-speaking city during the post-World-War-II period, all its inhabitants also spoke Turkish. In the 1960s, part of the religious services of the Syro-Jacobites, such as the sermon and the readings from the Gospels, while still in Arabic, were translated into Turkish. The liturgical books were still written in either Syriac or Arabic.[40] The city had a bishop in charge of all Syrian Orthodox Christians of Turkey until his death in the late 1960s; since then it has been under the jurisdiction of the bishopric of the Jazirah in Syria.

Outside the Tur Abdin and Mardin districts, the largest concentration of Syro-Jacobites was in Istanbul and its suburbs. There a community of about seven thousand built and consecrated a new church-school complex in 1963 called Suryāni Qadīm Maryam Ana Kilisesi, Mother

Mary's Church of the Old Syrians.[41]

As elsewhere in the Middle East, the Christian inhabitants of Turkey find more security and comfort, as well as better economic opportunities and more cordial interpersonal relations, in the large cosmopolitan urban centers. But the future of the small Christian population of Turkey seems to be dim. Unlike the Arab world, where the Christian presence is stronger and the Christians (such as the Copts of Egypt and the Greek Orthodox of Syria—original inhabitants of these countries) have thrown in their lot with the Arabs and have very largely identified themselves as a community with the national aspirations of their Muslim compatriots, the Turkish experience has resulted in estrangement. Even the future of Tur Abdin seems to be uncertain.

A well-informed visitor to the Tur noticed some obviously genuine friendship there between some Christians and Muslims, and was touched by the friendship "between a priest and a mullah." He had seen a Muslim woman with a seriously ill child, asking a Jacobite priest to bless her young with prayer; but the visitor also found the overall inter-religious relationship strained and the situation at a "deplorable stalemate." The solidly Christian villages, he wrote, "seem obsessed with the fear that Muslims will acquire property among them."[42] A whole Christian village after World War II had become Muslim in order to save the village. Indeed, there are several Muslim villages whose elders remember when they were Christian. The young, writes Horner, see little future for themselves and move steadily away from Tur—to Istanbul, into Syria and Lebanon, some to Europe, Australia, and the Americas.[43]

2

The refugees from Anatolia found new homes and villages in Syria, Lebanon, and Iraq where they were helped to settle by members of their community who had long lived in these former Ottoman territories. They also received sympathetic support from the Allied powers who during these crucial years were in occupation of these territories.

Syrian lands situated just south of Turkey attracted the majority of the Jacobites and Syrian Catholics, as well as large numbers of Chaldeans, Armenians, Kurds, and a few Jews.[44] They found refuge here thanks to the public security established by the French occupation. Many of the victims of the events of the early 1920s in the provinces of Cilicia and Turkish Kurdistan came to settle in Aleppo, Hims, Hama, and Damascus, but the majority of them found new homes and villages in the Jazirah district of Syria, a "no-man's land" which before 1927 had practically no settled population except for about forty-five Kurdish villages.[45]

As a result of the Kurdish revolts of the mid-1920s and 1930s in Turkey referred to above,[46] about twenty thousand Kurds came and settled in northern Jazirah along the Turko-Syrian frontier, most of them coming with their flocks and herds, settling down as cultivators either in villages of their own or on the estates of Kurdish landowners.[47] During the interwar years (1919-39) the population of the Jazirah increased, bringing the number of villages and settlements to about 700. In the year 1935 alone, 150 villages sprang up in the region, some of them inhabited by the latest wave of emigrants, the Assyrian tribesmen from Iraq, following the clash that they had with the Iraqi government.[48]

The Jazirah was a potentially fertile corner of Syria, its soil watered by the tributaries of the Euphrates river, the major one being the river Khābūr, which flowed through the region from its source at Rās al-'Ayn (head of the spring) on the Turkish border, down to the Euphrates south of Dayr al-Zūr. Gradually, this northeastern part of Syria was transformed into a potentially explosive region alongside the other politically volatile regions of the country such as Jabal al-Durūz (Druze) and al-Lādhiqīyah (Latakia). In one sense the Jazirah became more difficult to govern; it lacked the homogeneity that the Druze and Alawite districts had. In the late 1930s, the population of al-Jazirah was estimated as follows:[49]

Syrian Orthodox and Catholics	35,000
Armenians	25,000
Assyrians (on the Khābūr)	9,000
Kurds	20,000
Jews	1,500
Miscellaneous (including Arabs)	9,500

Made up of a population that had recently fled from fire and famine, these former refugees dreaded the prospect of another exodus after the departure of the French, a prospect which seemed to be approaching in the mid-1930s when France in Syria and Lebanon, and England in Egypt and Iraq, were willing to bring their special relationships with these countries to an end.[50] All the Christian communities in the Middle East, with the possible exception of the Greek Orthodox Arabs[51] and the Coptic Christians of Egypt, feared an untried Muslim-Arab regime taking over from the European occupying powers.[52] If the French were to leave Syria then at least the province of al-Jazirah should be granted some measure of local autonomy, with a special status such as that of Alexandretta. "The overwhelming majority of the population—Christian, Arab, and Kurdish," wrote John Hope Simpson, "is united in the demand for local autonomy."[53]

Anxiety in al-Jazirah, as in Jabal Druze and the 'Alawi districts, came to a head when the Franco-Syrian treaty was signed in 1936. The treaty provided for the replacement of the French by Syrian officials.

The minimum demand of the Kurds and Christians of the Jazirah had been that their administrators should come from the local population. The central government rejected this condition, insisting that al-Jazirah was an integral part of Syria. The officials from Damascus, unfortunately, often proved insensitive to the fears and forebodings of the local population even though the central government was counciliatory.[54]

Tensions erupted into an open conflict early in the summer of 1937 when the Kurds expressed their opposition to the Syrian nationalist officials appointed to the district. The revolt started in the Kurdish town of Ḥasaka (French Hasetche) and spread to Qāmishli and elsewhere, supported by the Christian inhabitants. Encouraged by some local French officials, the insurgents demanded autonomy. In August 1937 the village of ʿĀmūda, an important wheat-producing village of some three hundred Christian families, was raided and destroyed by Shammar Arabs and "Kurdish partisans of the Government." The Christians of ʿĀmūda were forced to take refuge at the towns of Qāmishli and Ḥasaka.[55]

French motorized infantry units and squadrons of planes were able to bring the disturbances to an end by mid-August 1937.[56] At the end of that year, the patriarch of the Syrian Catholics, Cardinal Tabbūni, representing the Christian minorities opposed to direct Syrian rule over the Jazirah, approached the French Ministry of Foreign Affairs, pointing out in a memorandum addressed to it the possible danger of a massacre of Christians in northeast Syria and elsewhere. He proposed that complete equality in religious and personal matters be granted to all the communities of the Jazirah; that an equitable number of Christian officials be appointed; that adequate means of protection be made available in areas where Christian security might be jeopardized; and that the interests of the minorities be safeguarded through the decentralization of government.[57]

There were occasional riots in the district against the Syrian officials, one of whom, the governor of the Jazirah, a Greek Orthodox Christian from Damascus, Tawfīq Shamiyah, was kidnapped in December 1937 by people from Ḥasaka.[58] He was soon released, but the kidnappers were arrested; demands for their release from prison were the cause of agitation and demonstration in the district as late as 1939.[59] The hopes of the Jazirah inhabitants were raised high that year when the Treaty of 1936 was not ratified by the French Chamber of Deputies. The Syrian president and his cabinet resigned and the French high commissioner suspended the Syrian constitution and dissolved the Chamber, appointing a nonpolitical council of directors to govern by decree under his direction.[60] The mandatory government at this late hour turned the hands of the clock back to 1920 when the French regime started its rule. Jebel Druze and Latakia, which had been separated from Syria in 1922 but which, according to the 1936 treaty, were to be incorporated into

Syria, were reestablished as separate administrations. The sanjak of Alexandretta, which had been officially a part of Syria even though enjoying its own semiautonomous administration, was handed over to Turkey, which annexed it in 1939.[61] The high commissioner's decree also removed al-Jazira from the direct control of the Syrian government and placed it under the immediate rule of his delegate at Ḥasaka. Within six months, however, with World War II raging at France's door, the functions of governor were once more transferred to a Syrian official; calm was restored as the result of an agreement reached between France and the Syrian government.[62]

The political tensions of the Jazirah did not hinder progress. The region's emigrant, refugee populations understandably felt unsafe and suspicious, but they were also a hardworking and frugal people; they very soon proved to be a very valuable element, serving their neighbors as craftsmen, mechanics, electricians, shopkeepers, and entrepreneurs. Many Christians, Jacobites as well as Armenians, especially the "Protestants" among them, were relatively well educated, having attended American mission schools in Anatolia.[63] Thanks largely to them, by the eve of World War II the district had been turned into a productive area with many prosperous villages and two large flourishing towns—Qāmishli with a population of twenty-three thousand of whom twenty thousand were Christians, and Ḥasaka, with a population of twelve thousand. In 1936 and 1937 the district, traversed by the Istanbul-Baghdad railway, exported by rail alone a hundred thousand tons of wheat in addition to what was transported to the rest of Syria by road.[64]

The war years brought in even greater prosperity to al-Jazirah as the Allies encouraged the production of foodstuffs in the Middle East. An official agency was formed during the war to help the Jazirah become a center for grain production. The high prices encouraged local enterprise; the number of tractors and harvesting machinery increased from 30 in 1942 to 930 by 1950. The acreage under cultivation multiplied from fifty thousand in 1942 to over a million acres by 1950.[65]

The wealth accumulated during the war was invested in more intensive cultivation, the expansion in cotton financed entirely from commercial as opposed to state capital. By the early 1960s, Doreen Warriner could write that the Jazirah was as fully mechanized as any other country in the world. She noted that the pioneers who changed these nomadic grazing lands to a highly mechanized agricultural region were for the most part Christian emigrants from Turkey—Armenians, Jacobites, and Syrian Catholics. There were Muslim farmer-entrepreneurs, but it was members of the Christian minorities who had taken the lead. One of the leading agricultural firms in the 1960s was owned by a former Jacobite family from Diyarbakr—Aṣfar and Najjār Brothers—with branches in Damascus, Aleppo, and Qāmishli. The firm cultivated some hundred thousand hectares of land, half of which was rented, the rest purchased. In the late fifties one of the Najjār brothers represented Qāmishli in the Syrian parliament, where he urged the government to devote more funds for the building of roads in his district.[66]

Mutual appreciation gradually took the place of mutual suspicion between the Bedouin natives and the new inhabitants. The Bedouin tribal shaykhs were the large landlords from whom the merchant-farmers rented the land and sometimes bought it, especially where, through pumped water, they irrigated it.[67] The landlords' rent amounted from 10 to 15 percent of the gross produce.[68] With the agricultural boom, the tribesmen soon developed interest in farming; the shaykhs started to count their wealth in terms of bales of cotton and tons of wheat as well as in numbers of camels and goats.[69]

The political tensions of the Jazirah gradually subsided when the French finally left Syria in 1946. Their departure made possible the realization by the minorities that they could no longer rely on French backing and intervention.[70] This realization in turn reassured the Syrian government that the minorities would and could no longer be manipulated by a foreign power as in the past in order to retain their control over the country. President Shukri al-Qūwatli's visit to the Jazirah was greeted with great jubilation in 1945.[71]

A Jacobite writer touring the Jazirah has noted the dramatic progress that the members of his community made in the district after independence. The community had two secondary schools in Syria, one in Qāmishli and one in Sadad; five preparatory (junior high) schools, in Ḥasaka, Malkiyah, Fairūzah, Zaydal, and Aleppo; and elementary schools in the various towns and villages.[72]

Independent Syria began to build on the foundations that the former refugees and emigres had laid. The government, which, according to Doreen Warriner, had "done almost nothing to promote agricultural development," began to introduce irrigation improvements during the 1960s. A "new Jazirah" was envisioned when the building of the massive Euphrates Dam was started with Soviet aid in 1964. The project, opened in 1973, is at present the second largest electricity and irrigation facility in the Middle East after Egypt's Aswan High Dam. It is estimated that the harnessed waters of the Euphrates will eventually irrigate enough land to double the farmed areas of the country and make the Jazirah "one of the most attractive and prosperous provinces of the Arab world."[73] The economic potential of this northeast corner of Syria was further enhanced after independence when oil and natural gas were discovered, thus encouraging the central government to pay greater attention to this once neglected "no-man's land."

At the time of writing, the Jazirah, where both the Syrian Orthodox and Catholics have had episcopal Sees since the late 1930s, is the most populous diocese of the twin communities.[74] After World War II, when the Christian population of Syria was either remaining stable or declining as a result of emigration, the province of al-Jazirah showed a dramatic increase even though the Muslim growth was much larger. The district remains highly heterogeneous, the proportion of its non-Arab population much greater than in any other region of Syria.[75]

Outside the Jazirah, Jacobites and Syrian Catholics settled in Hims, Hama, Aleppo, and Damascus. The Catholic branch of the community predominated in these urban centers, especially in Aleppo, long a Catholic stronghold.[76] In the 1960s major Catholic churches of the Middle East were represented in Aleppo. The Malkites or "Greek Catholics"—the most important and influential Catholic community in Syria—had seven parishes with fifteen secular and three religious priests and a population of 17,500 faithful in this archbishopric; Syrian Catholics had six parishes, with six priests and about 7,500 members; the Maronites, three parishes, with seven priests serving 2,500 people; the Armenian Catholics, seven parishes, with twelve priests, and 15,500 faithful; the Chaldeans (Catholic ex-Nestorians), six parishes, eight priests, and about 6,000 faithful. Of the almost half a million people who lived in Aleppo in 1962, the Christians were estimated to be 30 percent.[77] Most of the Syrian Orthodox in and around Aleppo had settled there after the First World War.[78]

There are few Jacobites in the Syrian capital, even though their Patriarch has resided there since 1957.[79] Most of the Jacobites of Damascus have settled there since World War I; almost all those who were there before then had embraced Catholicism.[80] In the 1960s the Syrian Catholics were estimated at about 4,250 in number, with five churches, seven priests and two elementary schools.[81]

Other important Jacobite-Syrian Catholic centers in Syria are Hums, where the Jacobite patriarch resided before moving to Damascus, Hama,[82] Sadad, and Hafar, the last two being exclusively Christian. Syrian Catholic and Orthodox population throughout Syria was estimated in the mid-1970s at just over 100,000—82,000 Jacobites, 21,000 Syrian Catholics.[83]

3

Jacobite roots in the Lebanon go back to the late Middle Ages when, after the Mongol invasions, considerable numbers of them sought refuge among the Maronites in the secluded district of Bsharri.[84] During the fourteenth and fifteenth centuries they were even successful in converting some Maronites to the Jacobite communion. The Jacobite patriarch Ignatius Nūḥ (Noah) al-Bāqūfāwi al-Lubnāni (1494-1509), who resided in Hums, was, as his name indicates, originally from the Lebanon.[85] Eventually, however, the Jacobites were either dispersed or absorbed by the more preponderant and native Maronites, who, indeed, were able to attract and assimilate even Shi'ite Muslims. Assemani has noted that "Many Maronite families both at Mount Lebanon as well as in the cities . . . of Syria are of Jacobite origin."[86] A Jacobite community in Tripoli was strong enough in the seventeenth century to have taken possession of the Crusader convent known as Dayr al-Balamand.[87]

The Maronites were instrumental, as we have seen, in the creation of the Catholic patriarchate among the Jacobites.[88] Thanks to the Maronite connection, the Jacobites who embraced Catholicism were able to establish themselves at al-Sharfah in Lebanon, a weak presence which was gradually reinforced by those who were attracted by the economic opportunities that this part of the Ottoman empire afforded and also by refugees from Anatolia after the atrocities of the 1890s and later.[89] Others came after the first World War to join their brethren. They came and settled in Beirut, Zahle, and Tripoli.[90]

It was during the post-World-War-I period that the patriarch of the Syrian Catholics established his residence permanently in Beirut, just as the first prelate of his sect had done more than 250 years before him.[91] As early as 1898 the Syrian Catholic patriarch Mār Afrām Raḥmāni had, with the consent of the pope, moved to Beirut from Mardin where the opposition of the Orthodox party and the unsettled conditions in Anatolia made the transfer advisable. The decision to stay permanently in Lebanon was made soon after the world war was over. A return to Mardin seemed impossible.[92]

Located in the center of Middle Eastern Catholicism, the Syrian Catholic (ex-Jacobite) community acquired prestige and influence far beyond its numbers, especially when its patriarch, Ignatius Jibrā'il (Gabriel) Tabbūni, elected to office in 1929, was made a cardinal of the Roman Catholic church. Tabbūni avoided the domestic politics of Lebanon and devoted his energies to his scattered community.[93] From his patriarchal diocese in Beirut, he oversaw the religious growth and well-being of his people throughout the Middle East and beyond. Today the Syrian Catholic church has four archbishoprics, two in Iraq (Mosul and Baghdad) and two in Syria (Aleppo and Damascus). In Syria there also are two bishoprics, that of Hims and Hama and that of al-Jazirah and the Euphrates. All the Syrian Catholics living outside these areas come under the jurisdiction of the patriarch, who appoints vicars for the supervision of their religious affairs. In the 1960s there were six patriarchal vicarates, usually administered by a titular bishop: four of them in the Middle East—and two in Europe—in Rome and Paris.[94]

Known as "cardinal builder," Ignatius Tabbūni launched a program to build churches and rectories, which culminated in the construction of a new cathedral in the Musaylah district of Beirut where the community had a parish church.[95] By the 1960s the Syrian Catholic community in Lebanon had grown to twenty thousand, with eight churches, two chapels, fourteen priests, two secondary schools, seven elementary schools, and three charitable institutions.[96]

The Syrian Orthodox community also found refuge in Lebanon, although they did not feel as much at home there as their Catholic brethren.[97] In their comparative loneliness as newcomers, some of the Jacobites were attracted to the more prestigious church of the Catholics, they joined it just as their ancestors had done.[98] The majority of the Orthodox settled in Beirut and Zahle, an important Christian, mostly Catholic, town on the plains of Biqā'. In both places they found members of their own community who had settled there before them, some of them settlers of the pre-World-War-I days. The refugees were welcomed and settled, encouraging others to follow them. The community built a church in Zahle in 1927, which in 1934 was expanded to serve as a school and a community center.[99] In 1939 Patriarch Afrām Barsoum established the Mār Afrām Seminary there, an institution which in 1945 was moved to Mosul because of that city's importance as a Jacobite center. The seminary was returned to Zahle after the Second World War, then transferred to its present location in 1968, to the village of 'Aṭshāna, near Bakfayya in Lebanon, where the community had acquired a property of just over ten acres.[100]

The civil war of the 1970s has brought anguish and sorrow to all the inhabitants of this once peaceful and prosperous land. To the members of the older generation, whether Syrian or Greek Orthodox, Maronite, Shi'ite, or Sunnite, it has brought back memories of the violence and death of an earlier day.

The conflict has already done its harm, "putting us back centuries," in the words of the Maronite patriarchal vicar-general, Bishop Aboujaoude.[101] As in all such eruptions new seeds for protracted intercommunity strife are sown, raising to the surface latent hostilities and mutual suspicions.[102]

This is not the place to delve into the complexities of the war in Lebanon.[103] That conflict was certainly not a religious war fought over religious doctrine. There were Christians on both sides of the warring factions and the Maronites themselves have not been united in their goals or war efforts,[104] and neither are they alone in certain of their demands.[105] The Muslims of the country as a whole, however, have been united in their challenge to the status quo, which to them is characterized by Maronite privilege and supremacy. The Druze,[106] many Christians,[107] as well as leftists from all groups, and the Palestinians,[108] have joined the Muslim majority in their challenge of the old order.

Because of the intense religious communalism of the country, it was perhaps inevitable that the conflict would have a "religious" dimension—religious, again, not in the sense of a deep spiritual faith but an intense loyalty to the religious community.[109] While the religious leaders on both sides, together with the Lebanese government, pleaded at the beginning of the war for unity and preached interfaith harmony, some among the guerilla groups started the first year of the conflict with kidnappings and roadblocks in which scores of Christians and Muslims alike were killed in cold blood merely on the basis of the religious affiliation noted on their identification cards.[110] These bloody confrontations soon deteriorated into religious hostility, and churches and mosques were desecrated, creating a situation that was easily exploited by the reactionaries of both sides, inside and outside Lebanon. In Damascus, the Muslim clergy, in their Friday sermons, spoke of the travails of their Lebanese fellow Muslims, adding to the reverberations of communal tensions to which the Syrian government has been especially sensitive.[111] The conflict started to inflame sectarian feelings in Egypt. The publication of a photograph in the newspapers of Cairo, showing a Phalangist guerilla, with a huge cross hanging from his neck, guarding Muslim prisoners lined against a wall, led within two days of its publication to disturbances between Muslims and Coptic Christians.[112]

The cry of Christian persecution in Lebanon was taken up officially by the Israel leadership.[113] The then foreign minister Yigal Allon referred to persecution of Christians "by a fanatical Moslem majority" and expressed surprise at the silence of "the Christian world."[114] With Lebanon as the major base of Palestinian operations against Israel after the liquidation of the Palestinian forces in Jordan in 1970-71, on the one hand, and the massive Israel retaliatory attacks against both the commando bases and the Lebanese villages in the south on the other hand, the road was paved for a close alliance between Israel and some Maronite factions. They received arms and military training from Israel, thus encouraging them in the hope that the Jewish state would intervene to assure their survival as a potent separatist element.[115]

In their long history of securing foreign protection, the Maronites in our time may have picked in Israel the wrong patron. Even the institution in "the Christian world" historically most sympathetic with the Maronites—the Roman Catholic church—was unhappy with the militancy of some of the Maronites and lamented their close relationship with Israel if outside the context of a comprehensive peace. At the peak of the fighting, the militant Christian leaders were reportedly warned by the Vatican that if they tried to secede from Lebanon, they would be jeopardizing the status of fifteen million Christians in the Arab world, since a secessionist Christian enclave could be another alien body like Israel.[116] There was widespread fear among Christians throughout the Middle East that the alliance of a Maronite faction with Israel might lead to guilt by association and to hostility against all of them. This in spite of the fact that on the Arab-Israeli issue, the majority of the Christians, including those of Lebanon itself, "deplore Zionism with as much vigor as do the Muslims."[117]

Some of the basic demands of Maronites are shared by both Christians and some Lebanese Muslims. A "unitary Lebanon," democratic and pluralistic, will meet the desire of all the Christians of the country for the maintenance of the freedoms that they cherish. The old confessional formula, which on the whole pleased the Christians but alienated the Muslims, can be replaced by a new one, supported by the moderates within the Christian community as well as by the Arab and international communities.[118] The non-Maronite Christian communities of Lebanon, while not united in their views and conceptions of themselves, have not been averse to seeing the Phalangists "cut down to size."[119] The Jacobite Christians, like the Armenians, have found a refuge in "Christian Lebanon" and the country has been hospitable to them. Mindful of their recent past and acutely aware of their minority status, they have preferred to stand aloof from political issues.[120]

They have not supported the Phalangists, however, and "have no appetite," observes one who knows them well, "for Maronite domination," even though they are equally unwilling to see the country fall "into Muslim hands."[121] The Christian communities that have sympathized most with the Muslim challenge of the status quo in Lebanon are the Greek Orthodox and Catholic Christians, even though they too have supported the Maronites in "Maronite-dominated districts east of Beirut,"[122] and would welcome a secular and democratic Lebanon.

Perhaps more than anything else, what the majority of the Lebanese Christians want is for their country to remain sovereign and independent, unabsorbed by the largely Muslim Arab world where, they fear, their status as a non-Muslim minority would be tainted with discrimination. It is not so much a dominant status that they seek as a position of equality. "In spite of the good relations which the Maronites have with prominent Lebanese Sunni leaders and with Jordan and Saudi Arabia," writes Elie Salem, "they continue to dread the possibility of falling into a *dhimmi* status (protected but second class religious minority under Islam)." What they see happening in their region is not in keeping with the spirit of the time and with the ideologies that stress human rights and equality regardless of creed or ethnic background.[123]

4

Eager to have the province of Mosul ceded to Iraq when Turkey seriously claimed it after the Armistice, England began to exploit the presence of Christian and Kurdish minorities there, and used them as a reason why Iraq should have Mosul.[124] Most of the Jacobites, the Syrian Catholics, and the Chaldeans who had fled Anatolia, had found refuge in the city of Mosul and its surrounding villages.[125] Mosul, seat of a

Jacobite bishop since the seventh century, had, as we have noted, become a Catholic stronghold like the other urban centers of the empire.[126]

In Baghdad, the Jacobites date back only to the post-World-War-I period, even though their ancestors had long flourished there as Catholics.[127] Outside the two cities, Basrah on the Persian Gulf has more recently become another Jacobite-Syrian Catholic center. In time, Basrah might replace Mosul as the second most important Christian city in Iraq, because of both the sensitive political situation in the north and the economic opportunities that the port on the Persian Gulf presents.

While the Jacobites did not enjoy the support that the Catholics did from the Latin missionaries and institutions, they were nevertheless able to adjust to their new country, where the national language was their own mother tongue, Arabic.[128] Unlike the Nestorians, who did not speak Arabic during the first generation of their stay in Iraq (which led to a great deal of misunderstanding and mistrust), the majority of the Jacobites spoke it well; some of their leaders, among them their patriarch, were Arabic scholars, known throughout the Arab world for their knowledge of Arabic literature and for the facility with which they used the language. One of the leading journalists of the country during the interwar period was a Syrian Catholic, Rufā'il Buṭṭi.[129] The Jacobite patriarch Ignatius Afrām I. Barsoum was a member of the Arab academy at Damascus, highly respected for his learning in both Syriac and Arabic.[130] Most of the learned and influential Syrians in the capital were Catholics and this attracted many of the Jacobites to the Syrian Catholic church, which, during this period, was under the energetic leadership of Patriarch Ignatius Afrām II Rahmāni.[131]

The leaders of both of these two sects very early realized that they could not depend on the good will of European "Christians."[132] Unlike the Assyrian leadership in Iraq, the Arabic-speaking Jacobite, Syrian Catholic, and Chaldean leaders proclaimed their unity and loyalty with the Iraqi government, emphasizing that they claimed no temporal power for themselves.[133] When the provisional constitution of Iraq provided for the representation of non-Muslim minorities in the Chamber of Deputies, the "Syro-Chaldean" hierarchy opposed it, maintaining that they sought no special "rights." They preferred to place trust in the good will of their Muslim compatriots. Mindful of the history of the last few decades of the Ottoman empire, they attributed the special rights for Christians to European designs, seeking, "as in Turkey, to drive a wedge . . . between local Christians and Muslims." One of their newspapers warned "not to forget the fate of the Armenians and Assyrians, who put their trust in the Christian powers of Europe and were practically exterminated in consequence."[134]

The Iraqi government, in turn, did not find it difficult to come to an understanding with minorities that had no political ambitions. On the eve of Iraqi independence, relations with all these communities were placed upon a satisfactory footing. In the spring of 1931 the minister of the interior, Muzāhim al-'Amīn al-Pāchachi, addressed a group of leaders of the various religious and ethnic communities in Mosul following the uneasiness among them which began with the publication of the Anglo-Iraqi Treaty of 1930. He tried to allay their fears, promising to make "our non-Moslem fellow countrymen partners with us without distinction or privilege between us as regards religion or sect." He reminded his audience of the "wise policy" that the Copts of Egypt had followed: They had rejected the inclusion in the Egyptian constitution of special provisions concerning them. The minister exhorted the Chaldean patriarch to give the help and support that he had always readily given to the Iraqi government, influencing the Vatican in its satisfaction with the policy that the Iraqi government was pursuing.[135] Al-Pāchachi warned those "certain persons" who endeavored to destroy the country's unity "at a time when Iraq is on the threshold of a new era, about to be freed from the hated Mandate," and exhorted the leaders present to "strive as brothers in unity." They were impressed and so was the Vatican apostolic delegate in "Mesopotamia."[136]

Unfortunately for the Jacobites and the Chaldeans, the political problems facing them after the war had, as in the past, a great deal to do with the neighbors among whom they lived, the Kurds. As we have seen, Christians lived on friendly terms with the Kurds—they spoke their language and lived in villages close to theirs; sometimes they were neighbors in the same villages and towns.[137] The Christians either freely identified with the Kurds or had no other choice but to throw their lot with them from fear of reprisals if they did not join them. When the conflict intensified between the Kurds and the Iraqi government, especially after the royal family was overthrown, thousands of Christians fled the war zone in the north and settled in the more secure and cosmopolitan Baghdad, where many of their community are employed in private enterprises or are self-employed craftsmen, such as goldsmiths, jewellers, electricians, and repairmen of machines and electronic equipment.[138] Many serve as shopkeepers in the bazaars or own main-street shops specializing in the sale of cloth, trinkets, carpets, and haberdashery. The educational opportunities available to the young attract them to graduate schools, where they work hard to achieve self-employment in the various professions. Many have graduated from colleges and universities in Baghdad as well as in Beirut, Damascus, Europe, and the United States.[139]

After World War II there have been instances when Christians were appointed to offices previously closed to them, including isolated cabinet positions. Rufā'īl Buṭṭi, referred to above, was made minister of state in two successive cabinets in 1953 and 1954. After the overthrow of the

monarchy, Dāwud Farhān Sarsam was appointed minister of munici-
palities and public works in Nāji Ṭālib's cabinet in August 1966, Nāji
Ṭālib himself being the first Shi'a premier. The first time that an am-
bassadorial post was entrusted to an Iraqi Christian was under 'Abd al-
Karīm Qāsim, when Najīb Sā'igh represented Iraq in Lebanon.[140]

In 1972 the Iraqi government officially recognized Syriac as one of
the languages of the country that had to be used as the medium of instruction in the elementary schools, where the majority of the students
were from the Syriac-speaking communities. In high schools wherein the
majority of the student body belonged to these communities, Syriac
would be taught as a language, with Arabic as the medium of instruction.

In 1974 the ministry of higher education sponsored in cooperation
with the recently formed academy of Syriac language a conference in
honor of a leading Jacobite, Mār Afrām, and the well-known Nestorian
physician Hunayn ibn Ishāq.[141]

Continued political instability both within Iraq and throughout the
region would also give rise to uneasiness and anxiety, especially among
the Christian minorities, a subject that will be discussed in the chapter
that follows.

5

The Jacobites have for centuries maintained a presence in Jerusalem
even though a precarious one at times.[142] From the beginning of the
Christian church but especially after Constantine's conversion, the land
where Jesus was born continued to attract devout Christians from all
denominations either as individuals or in monastic communities; they
wanted to live and worship in the shadow of the Christ's Holy Sepulchre,
also known as Church of the Resurrection.

Jacobite history in the Holy Land during the early Middle Ages is
obscure, but their presence there and especially in Jerusalem is noted by
pilgrims throughout the centuries. At the beginning, when Palestine was
dominated by the Greco-Roman Empire, the Middle Eastern Christians
who were not in communion with Byzantium or Rome were small in
number; the Jacobites had two bishoprical centers there, in Acre and
Jerusalem. Their numbers began to increase with the advent of Islam,
and thanks to the fact that the Christians of Egypt were, like the
Jacobites, of Monophysite persuasion, their interests in the Church of
the Holy Sepulchre were usually protected. After the first four centuries
of Muslim rule, the Monophysite population of Jerusalem was large
enough to occupy "about one-fourth of the Holy City." By the eleventh
century the Jacobites had a metropolitan in Jerusalem as well as in
Tiberius. Outside the city, their communities resided in Nāblus until
almost the end of the twelfth century and had their own villages in the
countryside.[143]

In the Church of the Holy Sepulchre Jacobite Syrians worshipped along with the Christians of several other sects, that shrine being the only structure under whose roof rival Christian sects worshipped. Even during the Latin Kingdom of the Crusaders, most of the Eastern churches celebrated their services there although the Europeans predominated. A twelfth-century Latin monk has noted that the Syrians held their services in one of the apses of the church at an "altar of no small size, there they sang their hymns after the daily Latin services were over." Other Eastern communities had "several small altars in the church, arranged and devoted to their own peculiar use." Those who celebrated divine services there included "the Latins, Syrians, Armenians, Greeks, Jacobite and Nubians."[144]

The favorable status that the Jacobites enjoyed in Jerusalem under the Mamluks changed with the Ottoman conquests of the early sixteenth century. Once again the Greek Orthodox church, with its center in the Ottoman capital, gained influence, not only at the expense of the Latins but also of those Middle Eastern churches which in the Greek Orthodox view were heretical. The Turks started collecting tribute from the Monophysites, a tax at times forgiven them by the sultans of Egypt. Some Christian sects, such as the Nestorians and Gregorians, were forced to "forsake their quarter," wrote the chaplain of English Levant Company at Aleppo who visited Jerusalem in the late seventeenth century, because of the "severe rents and extortions" which the Turks imposed upon them. By the end of the nineteenth century Coptic and Abyssinian Christians in Jerusalem were "purely exotic communities, having no native adherents," according to a British consular report of 1899.[145]

Visiting Palestine about fifty years after the Ottoman conquest of the country, the Dutch traveller-scholar Leonhart Rauwolff noted in his careful account of the Holy Sepulchre the presence of the following communities: Latins, Abyssinians, Greeks, Armenians, Georgians, Nestorians,[146] Syrians, and Jacobites "or Golti."[147] The fact that more than one Christian denomination shared the Church of the Holy Sepulchre meant that through most of its history, claims and counterclaims have been made over the custodianship of its various altars and shrines which, as a result, have changed hands depending on the fortunes of the claimants' political allies. The centers of worship have become sources of endless intrigues and angry disputes which have continued all the way to the present.[148] It was due largely to the historic Egyptian connections, referred to above, that the Jacobites, a comparatively small and weak community, its homegrounds in faraway southeastern Anatolia, managed to hold on to at least a small corner of this holiest ground in Christendom. The Armenians, with an influential presence in Istanbul, have also fought for the rights of their fellow

Monophysites, the Armenian patriarch claiming to be "the head of the Jacobite, Coptic and Abyssinian religious communities in Jerusalem.[149]

Jacobite rights today are limited to the Chapel of St. Nicodemus, a small dark room with one altar on the westernmost end of the rotunda of the church. During the Holy Week celebrations, their prerogatives extend to other parts of the church, where they conduct services in cooperation with their fellow Monophysites, the Armenians and the Copts.[150]

Elsewhere in Jerusalem the Jacobites have for almost the past five hundred years maintained an archbishoprical see in the city at the monastery of St. Mark.[151] It was their eighty-fourth "Archbishop of Jerusalem" who in the fifteenth century took up residence at the House of St. Mark, which according to tradition marks the site of the house where the Last Supper was first celebrated (Matthew 26:17 ff.) and where the disciples remained in hiding following the Passion and death of Christ, and later experienced his miraculous appearance (John 20:19). It was there also where St. Peter went when freed from prison by the angels (Acts 12:3 ff.).[152] At the time of writing the Jacobite bishop of Jerusalem resides in the Monastery of St. Mark and exercises jurisdiction over all the Syrian Orthodox residents of Jordan and Israel.[153]

The tiny Jacobite population of the holy cities of Palestine was enlarged after the First World War when some refugees made their way to Jerusalem and Bethlehem, where a few of them had been before the war as pilgrims. A number of them—some fifty families in all—moved to the Jewish sector of West Jerusalem and lived there until 1948, when they became refugees again, forced to seek security and shelter elsewhere. The majority of them moved to Bethlehem, a city whose population almost doubled in size because of the influx of mostly Palestinian Christian Arabs.[154] Most of the Syrian Orthodox youth left the Holy Land after the Israeli occupation of the West Bank in 1967. Many sought employment in the Persian Gulf emirates or emigrated with their families to Europe and the Americas.[155]

7

The Foreground and Conclusion

1

Ever since the beginning of Islam, the Christians of the Middle East have found themselves in the uncomfortable position of being the co-religionists of peoples and nations who were considered to be the rivals, if not the enemies, of the Muslim state. They have suffered from that position in the past[1] and continue to feel ill at ease from it at the present. A recent report on the Christians of the Muslim world noted that "from the Tigris and Euphrates to the Upper Nile" the members of this religious minority were concerned over their future in this era of major upheavals. They felt imperiled by the tide of events: the warfare in Lebanon, the antagonism among Muslims against the West, and the accompanying rise in fundamentalist and sectarian movements.[2]

In modern times, the hostility of the Arabs against the West started soon after World War I, when France and England began their colonial rule over them. Their antagonism became especially bitter, ironically, after the Franco-British rule came to an end soon after the conclusion of World War II, when, with the moral and material help of the West, Israel was created in the former British mandate of Palestine. The establishment of a Jewish national state in the heartlands of the Arab world, in a country predominantly Arab in 1918, engendered a hostile reaction that has overshadowed the outlook of all the Arabs and many non-Arab Muslims ever since.

Although most of the indigenous Christians of the region shared the views of their Muslim compatriots on the return of the Jews to Palestine, they remained the objects of mistrust, a legacy of the past century when they had identified themselves with the West and more recently had welcomed its rule during the mandate period.[3]

When the First World War ended, the majority of the Eastern Christians suspected that Arab nationalism was being used as a subtle means to revive Islam. The Christians' suspicion was not entirely imaginary; the political identification of Arab nationalism with Islam was and would continue to be strong. Arab nationalists often found that it was only under the banner of Islam that they could unite. The nineteenth century military, economic, cultural, and religious invasion of the Middle East by Western powers and institutions had now, early in the twentieth century, culminated in the political domination of the area by the European powers. That this situation intensified religious hostility is not surprising; the "Christian" West had raised its own religious banner.

In the Middle East, England and France interpreted the Allied victory as a Christian triumph. Forgetting that the Muslim Arabs had fought their own sultan-caliph in alliance with England and France, the *Times* of London pointed out that what was taking place in the region in 1918 was reminiscent of past French and English participation in the historic Crusades. "Saladin entered Jerusalem in triumph," commented the *Times*, "as Allenby enters it today." This "deliverence of Jerusalem" was looked upon as "a most memorable event in the history of Christendom." To General Allenby himself is attributed the boast that "today ended the Crusades." "Small wonder," comments A. L. Tibawi, "that the Sharif [of Mecca] offered no congratulations on the fall of Jerusalem," a fact which had caused some disappointment in London.[4]

It was not long, however, before the colonial powers alienated even the Christian Arabs. As Arab nationalism evolved and the horrors of the world war receded into memory, Christian-Muslim cooperation increased in the nationalist effort. A number of Christian leaders, always predominantly Greek Orthodox and Protestants, felt that in the long run the security of the Arab Christians depended upon their ability to cooperate with the Muslim majority.[5] Many in Syria, led by Fāris al-Khūri, worked actively for complete independence, while others, such as Qustantin Zurayq, Nabih Fāris, 'Antūn Sa'ādah, and Michel Aflaq, played important roles as the theoreticians and political philosophers of the Arab nationalist movement.[6]

The termination of the controversial mandate system, which ended soon after World War II, deprived the indigenous Christians of the false security which they had welcomed a generation earlier. Now they saw even more clearly the necessity of cooperation with their Muslim neighbors. Leaders of thought on both sides realized that European presence during the interwar years had hindered that interfaith collaboration which alone could ensure security for the region. This transitional postwar period, therefore, even though marked by great anxiety on the part of the Christians, saw also the growth among them of a movement for identification with the Arab world. While religion continued to be a barrier between the minorities and the majorities, there were at the same time other barriers that were removed as a more secular nationalism was introduced, and the foundation and structure of the government were modified and rebuilt, emphasizing a new social order, a different national allegiance. The Christians tended to reconcile themselves psychologically to their new "citizenship," be it Syrian, Iraqi, Iranian, or Egyptian. Cooperation with the Muslims became the theme emphasized most by both lay and clerical leadership everywhere as the Christians tried to reevaluate their role in a predominantly Muslim society. Christians were told that they could not keep to themselves; they had to work toward the solution of economic and social problems facing the new nation and to gain the trust of their Muslim compatriots.

The Christians' new image of themselves was received with enthusiasm by the Muslims, particularly the rapidly growing intellectual elite, who especially appreciated the contributions that their Christian compatriots were willing and able to make in the cause of Arab nationalism.[7] In their position as intermediaries, the Christian Arabs in an important sense had reversed their role by the end of World War II. They now started to make greater efforts to introduce to the West an East with which they wanted to identify themselves, instead of transmitting to the East the ideals and ideas of their Western mentors and coreligionists.[8]

In their new role, Eastern Christian leaders have worked vigorously to achieve a mutual understanding between Western Christendom and Islam. Within the Roman Catholic Church, Middle Eastern Christians such as the late patriarchs Maximos IV and Tabbūni,[9] Monsignors Medawar, Edelby, and others, in collaboration with a host of European priests and scholars who have lived and labored in the Muslim world, were effective in fostering cordial relations between the two faiths. In the 1960s their efforts bore fruit in the Second Vatican Council, where they were instrumental not only in "exonerating" Islam but also in drawing special attention to it in the historic "Declaration on the Relationship of the Church to Non-Christians." Many Western Catholics for the first time found out through the teachings of their church in 1965 that they held a number of beliefs in common with the Muslims. "Many Christians," wrote the editors of the Vatican II Documents, "have thought of Moslems as fanatical followers of a religion of power and ignorance, and sexually excessive . . . "[10] Now the faithful were told that Muslims too, "adore one God, living and enduring, merciful and all powerful . . . " Although Muslims do not "acknowledge Jesus as God, they revere Him as a prophet." They also "honor Mary, His Virgin mother; at all times they call on her . . . with devotion . . . they prize the moral life, and give worship to God especially prayer, almsgiving and fasting.''[11]

Muslims, as holders of "the faith of Abraham" were included now in "the plan of salvation."[12] The special commission formed in the summer of 1964 to study relations between the church and Islam, which consists of representatives from the congregations for the Eastern churches, was to be a separate department of the Vatican administrative system, unconnected with the secretariat for non-Christians, which included the religions of Africa and Asia. This historic recognition of Islam has removed one of the major causes of estrangement between the two religions. Muslims have for centuries resented the fact that while they acknowledged Christianity as a divinely inspired religion, Christianity has persistently refused to acknowledge the divine origin of their faith.[13]

Only a few months after the passage of the declaration, a Muslim theologian for the first time visited the Roman pontiff at the Vatican,[14] while a Roman Catholic cardinal, Franziskus Koenig of Vienna, for the first time visited al-Azhar University, where he delivered a lecture on the monotheistic religions. Introducing the cardinal, the rector of al-Azhar had asked Muslims to be "as charitable as the Christians are and let us unite with them to work for the good of humanity."[15] Still another historic departure from tradition took place when the Dutch cardinal Alfrink allowed Turkish migrant laborers in 1965 to hold their prayer service in a Roman Catholic church, explaining that "Moslems and Christians essentially adore the same God . . . only the approach is different."[16]

In their efforts to achieve a mutual understanding between Western Christianity and Islam, Orthodox and Protestant Arab Christians, as members of the World Council of Churches, have been as active in Geneva as Arab Catholics have been at the Vatican. Instead of serving Protestant missionaries as evangelists to Islam, Eastern Christians now argued, with the support of liberal Western Protestants,[17] that Western Churches should come to an understanding with Islam. A Protestant church representative who visited the Middle East in 1968 found Christian Arabs, familiar with the cordial relations that exist between American Protestants and Jews, arguing that if there are good reasons for establishing a relationship with the Jews, there are additional reasons for coming to an understanding with Islam, which "has accepted the prophetic character of Jesus Christ, as well as other distinctly Christian emphases, whereas Judaism has not." "In other words," concluded the Protestant church official, "the Arab Christians are asking us to take them more seriously by taking the world of Islam more seriously," for "they feel themselves very much at one with Muslims" in the problems facing them.[18]

On the question of Israel, Christian and Muslim Arabs have often united in their opposition to a Zionist-inspired Jewish state. Both have opposed it on theological as well as political grounds. From a theological point of view, the Muslims have found themselves in total disagreement with the Jewish settlers of the West Bank who, since the Israeli occupation of 1967, have tried to enforce their "right" to settle the land that "God promised Abraham,"[19] whom the Muslims venerate as the first faithful who embraced Islam. In Jerusalem the Muslim believer has found Israel ready to fight its own crusade for the retention of the city of David and Solomon, both of whom Islam regards "as noble and infallible prophets."[20]

The Muslim's answer to those who invoke the Old Testament as a justification for the establishment of modern Israel is that Zionism—as a joint Muslim-Coptic statement put it in 1967 "is a racial faction which is unconnected with religion."[21] The present government of Israel, argue the Arabs, does not represent the people of the Old Testament.[22]

Muslim scholars do not see a divine hand in all Hebrew history. "The Old Testament is, after all," writes Ismā'īl R. al-Fārūqi, "a Hebrew scripture written in Hebrew by the Hebrews and for the Hebrews."[23] Muslim nationalists who have sought Christian spiritual support have carefully referred to the New Testament (Injīl) in their slogans, avoiding the Arabic term for the Bible (Tawrāt) lest it be confused with the Jewish Torah and hence with sympathy for the Jews. The religion of the ancient Hebrews was their nationalism and it was "this nationalism of the ancestors that became—with its literature, its laws and customs—the religion of later times, of the Exile and post-Exile Jews down to the present day."[24]

Contrasting the Muslim with the Christian approach to the Hebrew Scripture, al-Fārūqi argues that the former is not dogmatic like the latter, but ethical. While the Christian is compelled by his dogma to rationalize the Old Testament and resorts to an allegorical interpretation of unequivocal texts, "glossing over accounts and narratives of human conduct which no morality can accept," the Muslim "is compelled to separate the ethically valid from the perverse in Hebrew Scripture, for only the former he can call the word of God." Al-Fārūqi defends this Quranic principle as being in harmony with the discipline of Old Testament criticism "which has saved Hebrew Scripture from the slow but sure process of repudiation by Christians of the last two centuries . . . "[25]

The Christian Arab, on the other hand, reads in his Old Testament that God encouraged the ancient Hebrews to drive out their neighbors from Palestine, promising that He would help in their destruction. What is especially baffling to the Christian Arab is that there are Christians in the West, whose numbers "comprise many millions,"[26] who would agree with the believing Jews that the fall of Palestine into Israel hands is a fulfillment of Biblical prophecy.[27]

This kind of theology is not only unacceptable but also offensive to the Christian Arabs. To them even the Biblical terms "Israel' and "Zion" have become hateful words, and certain verses from Deuteronomy and Joshua outrage their sense of morality and justice. Indeed, since 1948 Arab "Anglicans" have exorcised every reference to Israel in their translation of the book of Common Prayer. (As early as the 1920s, there were many among the Palestinian Christians who were beginning to question the relevance in Christian worship of the Old Testament to which the advancing claims of Zionism were being tied, and had requested that Old Testament readings be omitted from Church service.[28])

The identification of ancient Israel with the modern Jewish state led the Christian bishops and patriarchs representing Arab lands at the Second Vatican Council to vote against the schema concerning Jews. Western persecution of Jews not weighing heavily on their consciences, and well familiar with the injustices that their fellow Palestinian Christians had suffered as a result of Jewish nationalist aspirations, Christian Arab delegations opposed the Declaration, "not because they disagreed with what it said," explained Cardinal Tabbūni of the Catholic Jacobite church, speaking for himself and four other patriarchs of the Arab world, "but because its adoption would impede the pastoral work of the Church."[29]

The Catholic patriarchs were perhaps afraid of anti-Catholic feelings among both Muslim and non-Catholic Christians. Judging from the strong outburst of protest in the Arab and Islamic world that the schema on Jews provoked, it would seem that the fears of the Catholic prelates were well founded. But it would be wrong to attribute their stand on this issue merely to fear of Arab reaction. The majority of the Arabs, Christians and Muslims alike, opposed the schema because of the political benefits that they thought Israel might reap from the new Christian-Jewish relationship that the Declaration wanted to develop. It was especially feared that the Declaration, once passed, would lead to the recognition of the State of Israel by the Vatican, whose official policy of nonrecognition has emphasized to the Arabs that morally as well as legally they are in the right.[30] Jewish leaders, on the other hand, did tie the schema to the state of Israel. Long before its passage by the council, Rabbi Arthur Gilbert thought that it would be "a climactic and symbolic act of reconciliation" if the pope at this point were also "to recognize the State of Israel and to call upon Church theologians to re-define the role of the people of Israel in God's eternal purpose."[31]

There were also religious reasons for the opposition of the schema. The various non-Catholic prelates condemned the Declaration as "the greatest of sins;" it undermined "the basic principles of Christianity," and was "inconsistent with Holy Scriptures" whose inspired and holy word no one had the authority to change.[32] The Holy Synod of the Coptic Church condemned the Vatican statement and quoted liberally from the scriptures. "The Holy Bible gives a clear testimony that the Jews have crucified the Lord Jesus Christ and bore the responsibility of His crucifixion as they repeatedly said to Pontius Pilate . . . " The statement noted, however, that "the confirmation of this historical and doctrinal fact does not contradict the Christian teachings of charity, fraternity, and tolerance towards all human beings . . . " The Arab Evangelical Episcopal Church Council, which covers congregations in Jordan, Lebanon, and Syria, endorsed a statement before the declaration was voted upon, opposing attempts by the "Christian head in the west" to absolve Jews of responsibility for the crucifixion of Christ. The council expressed its "firm adherence to the clear teachings of the Gospel as dictated by divine revelation" and its belief that "any teaching contrary would constitute a departure from the Gospel."[33] The Jacobite journal, *al-Majallah al-Baṭaryarkīyah*, recently concluded a series of articles on "Zionist distortions" of the Bible.[34]

2

While the Palestinian problem brought the leadership of the Christians and Muslims together it also helped, in a very indirect manner, to pull the two communities apart—by severely straining relations between the Middle East and the "Christian" West. More than any other single issue, Palestinian homelessness symbolizes the powerlessness and the humiliation of millions of Arabs and non-Arab Muslims.[35] Combined with other factors and grievances of the region, the festering Palestinian problem has helped the rise there of a self-confident, anti-Western and revivalist Islamic sentiment, which at times has been "wrenching" for the Christian minorities.

Religion, as we have seen in this study, has always been an important idiom for political expression. Often Islamic religious movements have articulated radical social discontent, bringing together diffuse sentiments and groups through a common religious bond. Indeed even in Christendom religious movements have often mobilized populations under the banners of eschatological movements whose goal was the realization of social equality.[36] In the twentieth century the roots of the Islamic protest grew stronger and deeper after World War I.[37] The collapse of the Ottoman Empire after that war put an end to any Islamic threat, and Allied victory paved the way for Western power and presence in the heartlands of the Muslim world. With the British and French rule came Western ideas, values, and life styles, producing a whole generation of Arab elites eager to worship at the alters of these Western idols. But the alien gods soon proved to be decadent and oppressive. With the departure of the West from the scene (the only physical reminder that the West had been there was Israel), Islam started to come out of the alien shadow. Its most dramatic manifestation so far has been in Iran, where for over a half century an undeclared war between the Westernizing Pahlavi dynasty and the religious establishment has created a deep split between the popular culture of the masses and the establishment culture imposed by the shahs.[38]

Perhaps the most important difference between the present situation and the revolts and protests of the past is the mass support that the forces of religion and tradition have been able to mobilize, ironically enough, through modern technology. In countries where more than half of the population is illiterate, television, radio, and tape cassettes of political speeches have become powerful forces, stimulating the Middle Easterner's irresistible attraction to eloquent words, and at times serving as dangerous weapons, spreading alarm and violence from one end of the Muslim world to the other.

What is more, the youth and the educated classes have been attracted to the forces of religion and tradition. As leaders of the next generation, who have to find some solution to the immense number of problems facing them, the young are disillusioned with the various ideologies and strategies that have failed to work out a solution for their parents.[39] They long for something different, but familiar, with native roots. And to unite them they have found a common enemy in the West. They are able to muster some valid reasons for considering the American government especially as their enemy, granted that the United States sometimes becomes the scapegoat for their frustrations and inability to face up to their own reality. For while it is true that some of the Arab-Islamic grievances are directed against the crass materialism imported from the West, their rebellion is also aimed against the too little material welfare available for the majority of their impoverished countrymen. One of the major appeals of the Ayatollah Khomeini among the populace was certainly his image as an ascetic distributing Iran's billions in oil revenue equitably among the oppressed faithful.[40]

It is perhaps not a coincidence that the resurgence we are witnessing takes place at a time when oil wealth has generated power which, in turn, has helped generate Islam as a rallying point for a people seeking not only a greater appreciation of their own values, but also demanding their rightful share of the bounty that Allah has bestowed on their otherwise impoverished lands. To a large extent the frustrations of the Middle Easterners stem from the illusion that their countries' vast wealth would overnight bring about vast improvements in their lot. Nevertheless, it is also true that the West has failed to live up to its democratic ideals in its dealings with the non-European and the non-Christian. The Muslims are convinced—and recent history affords ample ground for that conviction—that they have shown more trust in Western governments and have had greater good will toward the West than the West has shown toward Islam. They are also convinced that England and France after World War I, and the United States after World War II, have often violated Arab-Islamic sovereignty and honor, exploited the Middle East economically, and perverted its cultural values.

Under these circumstances Arab governments and many secular liberals have come to realize that their power base should not be too narrow, like the shah's was in Iran.[41] They realize that they have to join hands with "the people" and their youthful supporters. They have approached them through Islam, which continues to predominate in popular life, defining, determining, and directing it in almost every aspect.[42] In Jordan, the Hashemite regime has given the fundamentalist Muslim Brotherhood great freedom of action, while the monarchy in Saudi Arabia has lent them encouragement and support, thus associating the most powerful Islamic party in the Arab East with two of the most politically conservative regimes in the area. In Egypt, where the Muslim Brotherhood was born as a party in the 1920s and was suppressed under Nasser, the brotherhood gradually became the largest, most important, and most vocal opposition group under President Sadat. The party violated with impudence a tacit agreement with the government that it operate as a religious society and keep out of matters political. The government, perhaps realizing that the organization had widespread appeal, especially among the students,[43] at first avoided confrontation with the brotherhood. In his effort to defuse fundamentalist Muslim dissatisfaction with his policies, including his peace initiative with Israel, President Sadat amended the Egyptian constitution through a referendum. The provision made Islamic law the principal source of legislation and not merely "a principal source," as the constitution originally specified. Unable to appease fundamentalist opposition, Sadat launched his "September 5th (1981) Revolution," when the Muslim Brotherhood was declared illegitimate, the Egyptian government announcing that it would gradually take over the supervision of about forty thousand mosques in order to assure that they were used solely for religious purposes. These moves, discussed further later in this chapter, led to the President's assassination a month after they were launched—on 6 October, 1981.

In the more radical Libya, widely publicized slogans proclaim that "the Koran is the law of our new socialist society." Even in communist Afghanistan expediency and public sentiment seem to have dictated that the government pay its respects to the devout Muslim population. The Soviet-supported leader Babrak Karmal pledged to wage "a holy war for genuine democratic justice and for the respect for the sacred Islamic religion."[44] In Syria the secularist Ba'th party, an archenemy of the

Muslim Brotherhood, emphasizes that it is "with the Islamic tide" if it serves "the Arab liberation movement and the Palestinian cause . . . We are against it if it is to the contrary."[45] Reports at the time of writing speak of a growing nationalism among Russia's Muslim intellectuals, and their desire to reestablish more autonomy for the ethnic cultures of the Muslim population.[46]

3

The position of the Middle Eastern Christians and, indeed, of the many ethnic minorities in the region,[47] becomes more and more untenable when the leadership in the government becomes more "religious," emphasizing that the state, society, and religion are one.[48] When the Egyptian government amended the constitution making Islamic law the principal source of legislation, the hierarchy of the Coptic Christian Orthodox church criticized the move, objecting that it would subject their lives to Islamic constraints and place them legally outside the country's society at large.[49]

Emphasis on Islam and its traditions tends to make non-Muslims much more visible and consequently much more uncomfortable before the suspicious eyes of their Muslim compatriots. The tension also leads to a crisis of identity.[50] "We're afraid of being suffocated," a Jordanian Christian was recently quoted in the press, referring to the flood of revivalist Islamic sentiment.[51] Perhaps the real complaint of the Jordanian Christian was the sociopsychological fact that he and his coreligionists could not participate in the important and invigorating movements that surrounded them. They simply cannot immerse themselves in the full appreciation of tradition, hence their sense of discomfort. Secular Muslims who shun tradition, on the other hand, feel no such tension, for they are still Muslims.[52]

Thus alienated, the native Christians feel as strangers in their own land and have consequently become engaged in a serious reappraisal of their identity and direction. They seem to have three basic choices: (1) reject the religious nationalism that is sweeping the region and withdraw into their own sectarianism, an alternative that is all but impossible; (2) leave their lands, immigrate to Western countries where pluralistic societies would accept them; or (3) seek a more active coexistence with their Muslim compatriots.

Religious nationalism has encouraged sectarian loyalties among the Christians as well as among other minorities. Indeed, there are extremists who have already called for the redrawing of boundaries along religious lines, creating Druze, Alawite, Maronite, Sunni, Shi'a, and Greek Orthodox states.[53] For the non-Islamic minorities to go back to the old order that prevailed prior to World War I, when, as a well-entrenched corporate group, the Christian sects were organized around the prin

ciples of a common religion, locality, and ethnicity, would be psychologically as well as politically impossible. Their autonomy and communal
organization have long been destroyed, the political base upon which
their local autonomy had been established, eroded by the establishment
of centralized power. This is especially true of such Christian minorities
as the Jacobites, granted that they are still held together by religion,
which throughout the region continues to be the core of communal identity. But their community, as we have seen, is scattered, its cohesion
weakened, its geographical base destroyed. Furthermore, these changes
have eroded the cohesion of the Christian minorities, and threatened
their ethnic identities,[54] at the same time that they have strengthened the
self-consciousness of the Muslim majorities. While it is possible for the
Muslim element to embrace religious nationalism, the Christians—with
the exception of the Maronites, whose cohesion and geographical base
were augmented rather than destroyed after World War I—cannot
return to the old millet system and the communal consciousness that it
encouraged. It is not surprising, therefore, that many Christians, faced
with this impossible alternative, find it easier to immigrate to foreign
lands.

A recent report found many Christians emigrating even from countries such as Jordan, where King Hussein has gone out of his way to
reassure his Christian subjects that they have a place in his kingdom.[55]
Many emigrate, nevertheless, because they feel there is no role for them
in a predominantly Muslim society beset by acute internal and external
conflicts and contradictions, its future likely to be more violent and more
threatening before "the irreversible forces" of history bring about a better day.[56] More often, however, Christians leave because their motiva-
tion and education drive them to the West, where a higher standard of
living, better employment and housing and greater opportunities for professional advancement have resulted in a "brain-drain" pattern experienced throughout the developing countries.[57] The Greek Orthodox
mayor of the Jordanian town of Madāba, an ancient Christian center
that is fast becoming Muslim, explained that the Christians "go mostly
out of ambition. It has nothing to do with religion . . . [They wish] to
find a better life."[58] The departure of the members of a class that usually
is well educated and well-to-do leads to a general decline in the level of
the community's education, and to an absence of committed leadership
among those who remain. Yet it is the "ponderous obligation" of those
who remain, as Richard Hovanissian has put it, to serve as the guardians
of an uprooted heritage.[59]

The majority of the Christians opt for the third, and only, alternative: to seek coexistence with their Muslim compatriots. Thanks to the
increased oil wealth, free education and gainful employment—and other
benefits offered the public—entice the Christians to remain in the

ancestral lands. Economic expansion has opened up in most parts of the Middle East new opportunities which help mitigate the strains felt by the minority groups.[60] They serve in the growing trade and industrial centers where a growing population, and a government committed more and more to serving the population's needs, create demands for skills and services that the resourceful Christian population can continue to meet: as technicians, engineers, professionals, as well as carpenters, craftsmen, mechanics, and shopkeepers.

From all the communities of the Middle East, Christians in recent years have found gainful employment in the Persian/Arabian Gulf states, where the total influx exceeds the native population of many of them, especially of Kuwait, Qatar, Abu Dhabi, and Dubai.[61] Thus oil production is attracting the native Christians to the Gulf coast of the Arabian peninsula, where their ancestors flourished centuries ago when they were gradually absorbed or driven away under the impact of Islam. One of the largest Christian groups in the area is that of the Syrian Orthodox, their numbers swelled by the presence there of Indian Christians from that church.[62] The majority of the Middle Eastern Christians go to Kuwait, the United Arab Emirates, and Bahrain, Indian Christians predominating in the other states.[63] The rulers of all the Gulf states, writes Horner, "give considerable encouragement to Christian activities through personal friendship and generosity."[64]

But in the Gulf states the Christians—like all other foreigners, including Muslim Arabs—are temporary residents. How successful they will be in their search for coexistence with their Muslim compatriots will depend a great deal on how successful Arab leaders and politicians are in their home countries in their efforts to build a more stable and coherent political order. Greater efforts have to be made to integrate not only the Christians, but all the various elements of the population. Centuries of a political tradition that has encouraged decentralization have fostered great diversity and group consciousness. Instead of emphasizing national exclusivity and political homogeneity, attention has to be paid to pluralism and diversity. Arab leaders and rulers have also to pursue what Michael Hudson calls "coalition-building strategies," as they attempt to construct a more coherent political order, without which they cannot achieve true independence.[65] They will then find their Christian compatriots willing to do their share to be an integral part of the society around them. As Karekin II, head of the Armenian Apostolic church expressed it, "If Christians keep in close contact with Moslems and show they are committed to the Middle East, they will have a greater chance of mutual understanding, growth, and survival."[66] Another church leader, Bishop N. Edelby of the Greek Catholic community, put it differently: The future of Christianity in Arab countries, he said, depended on its sharing the fate of those countries, whether this be happy or not.

"Everybody else may despair of Islam," said the bishop in the idiom of his predecessors, "but not we Eastern Christians whom the Lord has so clearly preserved, to allow us to watch by the side of Islam, suffering through it and for it."[67]

APPENDIXES

APPENDIX A. *Ottomon Edict Confirming Akhijan Patriarch of the Jacobites*
Edict of the Great Turk Granted in Favor of Monsignor Andrew Chosen
Patriarch of the Soriani[1] in Aleppo.[2]

To the greatest judges of judges, origin and source of the virtues, true decree over all the people, heirs of the knowledge of the prophets and of the Apostles, that is, judges of Aleppo and Diarbecher[3] (may their virtues multiply), the glory of judges, sources of the virtues and words, the judge of Merdin and other judges of his dependences.

When this noble edict arrives among you, you are to know that the Jacobites, those who dwell in Aleppo, Diarbecher, Merdin, and in their dependences, that Andrew, son of Abdelgial, is their Patriarch in accord with our noble edict having first sent to us an exhibition through which he made known to us that the cities of Merdin, of Aleppo, and of Diarbecher, and their dependences are under his patriarchy, and that all the Jacobites, priests, clerics, and laymen are under his power, and he is their patriarch according to their laws and customs and that when he is obliged to go to the cities, towns, and villages to visit his flock according to their ways, requesting to this purpose that the Chief of the nobles, the leaders and chiefs of our military captains and soldiers, that they are to do nothing against him contrary to our edict, and [that] they are not to injure him in any manner within the jurisdiction of his patriarchy, and that also the Sorian priests and clerics are not to deprive him of ordinary kindnesses, and that the officials of our finances are to take no bequests or legacies in accordance with our first edicts, and that his subject priests are not to marry his subject priests [sic] to the Armenians without his permission, and for all this Andrew asks of us an edict to prevent it. We have granted him and we have commanded and do command that each time the mentioned religious Patriarch departs with this noble written edict, that you are to act in accordance with its tenor and contents without disobeying it in any way in accordance with its tenor and contents regarding the things of the patriarchy and that all who are under your jurisdiction, priests, clerics, and lay Jacobites are to know with certainty that they have no other patriarch nor head but Andrew, and that they must heed him in everything and give him that which suits him according to their ways, whether little or much, and when he shall make a trip to collect some offerings for the buildings or for the poor and that the chiefs of the nobles and the officials of our finances, soldiers, and other officials are not to act against our edict and he would impede them, and if he should be obliged to change his clothes in order to travel with less danger, that no one on account of this bother him, nor take money from him, nor allow this in any manner, and do protect him, and that all who are under his government are to give him that which suits him according to the custom, and that the officials of the revenues are not to be opposed to him. And when he shall arrive that he shall raise someone of his own because of his merit, and shall demote others because of his failings, that no one shall contradict him, and that no priest or cleric dare to marry with other sects without his first knowing it, and do not ever allow this to them. And when he shall be on a trip with his cortege and horses, defend him from our couriers so that they do not take their equestrian equipment, and observe all the injunctions contained in this and do not force us to repeat it another time. And when you shall have read this edict leave it in the hands of him who brings it, and rely upon yourselves and trust this imperial seal.

Written and dated on the 14th day of the month of Alead[4] in the year 1062.

APPENDIX B. Ottoman Charters Declaring Protestants as Separate Community
First Protestant Charter, Issued in 1847 by the Grand Vizier Reshid Pasha[1]

To His Excellency The Pasha Comptroller of the City Revenue:

Whereas, The Christian subjects of the Ottoman Government professing Protestantism have experienced difficulty and embarrassments from not being hitherto under a special and separate jurisdiction, and naturally the Patriarch and the Heads of the sects from which they have separated not being able to superintend their affairs; and

Whereas, It is in contravention to the supreme will of his Imperial Majesty, our Gracious Lord and Benefactor (may God increase him in years and power), animated, as he is, with feelings of deep interest and clemency towards all classes of his subjects, that any of them should be subjected to grievance; and

Whereas, The aforesaid Protestants, in conformity with the creed professed by them, do form a separate community:

It is his Imperial Majesty's supreme will and command, that, for the sole purpose of facilitating their affairs and of securing the welfare of said Protestants, the administration thereof should be henceforward confided to Your Excellency, together with the allotment of the taxes to which they are subjected by law; that you do keep a separate register of their births and deaths in the bureau of your department, according to the system observed with regard to the Latin subjects; that you do issue passports and permits of marriage, and that any person of established character and good conduct chosen by them to appear as their Agent at the Porte for the transaction and settlement of their current affairs, be duly appointed for that purpose.

Such are the Imperial Commands, which you are to obey to the letter.

But although passports and the allotment of taxes are placed under special regulations which cannot be infringed upon, you will be careful that, in pursuance of his Majesty's desire, no taxes be exacted from the Protestants for permits of marriage and registration; that any necessary assistance and facility be afforded to them in their current affairs; that no interference whatever be permitted in their temporal or spiritual concerns on the part of the Patriarch, monks, or priests of other sects; but that they be enabled to exercise the profession of their creed in security, and that they be not molested one iota, either in that respect, or in any other way whatever.

Reshid, Grand Vizier

15 November, 1847

A new charter was granted to the Protestants by the Sultan, 'Abd al-Majid, in November 1850. Unlike the decree by the Grand Vizier, the Sultan's Charter was not liable to repeal.[2]

To my Vizier, Mohammed Pasha, Prefect of the Police in Constantinople, the honorable Minister and glorious Councillor, the model of the world, and regulator of the affairs of the community; who, directing the public interests with sublime prudence, consolidating the structure of the empire with wisdom, and strengthening the columns of its prosperity and glory, is the recipient of every grace from the Most High. May God prolong his glory!

When this sublime and august mandate reaches you, let it be known, that hitherto those of my Christian subjects who have embraced the Protestant faith, in consequence of their not being under any specially appointed superintendence, and in consequence of the patriarchs and primates of their former sects, which they have renounced, naturally not being able to attend to their affairs, have suffered much inconvenience and distress. But in necessary accordance with my imperial compassion, which is the support of all, and which is manifested to all classes of my subjects, it is contrary to my imperial pleasure that any one class of them should be exposed to suffering.

As, therefore, by reason of their faith, the above mentioned are already a separate community, it is my royal compassionate will, that, for the facilitating [of] the conducting of their affairs, and that they may obtain ease and quiet and safety, a faithful and trustworthy person from among themselves, and by their own selection, should be appointed, with the title of "Agent of the Protestants," and that he should be in relations with the Prefecture of the Police.

It shall be the duty of the Agent to have in charge the register of the male members of the community, which shall be kept at the police; and the Agent shall cause to be registered therein all births and deaths in the community. And all applications for passports and marriage licenses, and all petitions on affairs concerning the community that are to be presented to the Sublime Porte, or to any other department, must be given in under the official seal of the Agent.

For the execution of my will, this my imperial sublime mandate and august command has been especially issued and given from my sublime chancery.

Hence thou, who art the minister above named, according as it has been explained above, wilt execute to the letter the proceeding ordinance; only, as the collection of the capitation tax and the delivery of passports are subject to particular regulations, you will not do anything contrary to those regulations. You will not permit anything to be required of them, in the name of fee, or on other pretences, for marriage licenses, or registration. You will see to it that, like the other communities of the empire, in all their affairs, such as procuring cemeteries and places of worship, they should have every facility and every needed assistance. You will not permit that any of the other communities shall in any way interfere with their edifices, or with their worldly matters or concerns, or, in short, with any of their affairs, either secular or religious, that thus they may be free to exercise the usages of their faith.

And it is enjoined upon you not to allow them to be molested an iota in these particulars, or in any others; and that all attention and perseverance be put in requisition to maintain them in quiet and security. And, in case of necessity, they shall be free to make representations regarding their affairs through their Agent to the Sublime Porte.

When this my imperial will shall be brought to your knowledge and appreciation, you will have this august decree registered in the necessary departments, and then give it over to remain in the hands of these my subjects. And see you to it, that its requirements be always in future performed in their full import.

Thus know thou, and respect my sacred signet! Written in the holy month of Moharrem, 1267 [November 1850].

Given in the well guarded city Constantiniyeh.

APPENDIX C. *Jacobites in India*

Alarmed by their losses during the first half of the nineteenth century, the Jacobite hierarchy looked more and more toward India for prestige and funds. There on the coast of Malabar, over a million souls acknowledged the supremacy of the Jacobite patriarch. Most of them Indian by race, they were often referred to as "Syrian Christians" because Syriac was the ecclesiastical language of their "Syrian"[1] mother churches in the Middle East. They were also known as St. Thomas Christians and their church as the Church of Malankara, after the location where St. Thomas is believed to have landed when he reached the southwestern shores of the subcontinent.[2] Very few of these Christians of India have Middle Eastern origins, but traditions of the Malabar church record at least two early Christian immigrations to South Asia from there, one from Baghdad, Nineveh (Mosul) and Jerusalem, in 745, and another from Persia in the century following (822).[3] The early Middle Eastern immigrants were Nestorians, and so were the missionaries who transplanted Christianity across Persia and the Arabian Sea.[4]

Even though much influenced by its pagan and polytheistic environment, the St. Thomas church remained Nestorian for almost a thousand years—from at least the seventh century until the very beginnings of the seventeenth. At the synod of Diamper in 1599, however, almost the entire Christian community of Malabar was forcibly brought under the control of Portugal and of the Roman Catholic church.[5]

The break from Roman Catholicism and the gradual return to the Middle Eastern mother churches began in the seventeenth century, a move made possible after 1663, when the "Romo-Syrians" came under the more tolerant rule of the Dutch.[6] In less than two years after Holland had taken over, a Jacobite bishop, Mar Ghrīghūrīyus (Gregory), bishop of Jerusalem, was sent to Malabar by the Jacobite patriarch. While conforming to the local Indian custom, he insisted on anathematizing not only the pope but also Nestorius. Monophysitism was thus introduced without anybody knowing or caring what doctrinal changes were taking place.[7] From this time on, the first group of Indian Christians that broke away from Catholicism began to look to the Jacobites and not the Nestorians for legitimacy and guidance.

It was not long before the Nestorian patriarchs of the Ottoman Empire also tried to restore their ancient authority over the Malabar church. They sent bishops in 1700 and 1705 but, unfortunately for them, the majority of the "Syrians" of India remained loyal to the Jacobite prelate, who had been the first to deliver them.[8]

Contacts between Mardin and Malabar increased under British rule.[9] English consular agents and missionaries became especially sympathetic toward the historic Christian community that they found in "heathen" India. The first two consuls were especially anxious to help the Jacobites.[10] In 1808 a trust fund was set up by the British consul "for the expenses of benevolence" in the Syrian Orthodox Church.[11]

The Indian Christians valued their autonomy even as they cherished their historic connections with an ancient apostolic church in lands where Christianity was born. They had rebelled against Latin domination and now many of them resisted the persistent claims made upon them by the foreign patriarch of their own church. Indeed, the modern history of relations between these mother-daughter churches is a depressing one; fortunately it has already been documented in detail elsewhere[12] and concerns us only indirectly since its impact on the Syrian Orthodox community in the Middle East is not consequential.

The familial quarrels began during the first half of the last century when in 1825 the Jacobite patriarch sent one of his emissaries, Mār Athanāsiyus (Athanasius), to India. Immediately upon his arrival in Travancore, the bishop made it known that he was the legitimate mutran (metropolitan) of Malabar and demanded that he be recognized as such. He refused to recognize as legitimate some of the local bishops and condemned as invalid the appointment of the previous four mutrans, since it was not the Jacobite patriarch who had appointed them.[13] Mār Athanā siyus was deported soon after he tried forcibly to take possession of the college that the British resident and Church Missionary Society had helped build for the Syrians.[14]

Other bishops arrived from Turkey in the 1840s and 1850s. One of them, Mār Sṭīfānus (Stephen), sent in 1846, claimed all the money due from the St. Thomas church to the patriarch and wanted it handed over to him "at once."[15] He was told that the patriarch had no claim to any funds of the Indian church, a position backed by the courts of India.

Unfortunately for the patriarch, he was often drawn into the Indian controversies that arose between rival Indian parties. The legitimate bishop of Malabar was he who had the blessings of the patriarch, and legitimacy had its material as well as spiritual rewards. The legally appointed bishop could lay claim to the properties of the church and the income that they produced and, since 1808, to the interest from the trust fund set up by the British resident. Thus we find throughout the century and all the way to the present, one party or another backing, or claiming the authority of, the patriarch in faraway Dayr al-Za'faran and, later, Damascus. When the Jacobite patriarch was too distracted by developments in Anatolia to be able to send a representative to India, the Indians went to him. In 1841 deacon Matthew, nephew of a reform leader of the Malabar community, arrived at Mardin, where he stayed for two years with the patriarch. He was consecrated bishop and returned to his homeland as Mār Athanāsiyus. His supporters, writes L.W. Brown, created a precedent, claiming that the *statikon* ("letter of appointment") of the patriarch was essential to the exercise of any lawful jurisdiction in the church.[16] A few years later (1865), another Indian cleric travelled to Mardin to be consecrated at the hands of the patriarch. He returned to Malabar as Mār Dionysios and began to claim, unsuccessfully, the accumulated interest from the trust fund and an additional 14,000 rupees that had been allotted to his rival in 1840.[17]

While the St. Thomas Christians were reestablishing their contacts with the Jacobite patriarch in the nineteenth century, a faction of the "Syrians" who had remained Catholic started to communicate with the Catholic patriarchs of the Middle East. Interestingly, their contacts were with the prelate of the Chaldean church, former Nestorian, and not of the Syrian Catholic Church, former Jacobite.[18] Their communication with Mār Yusuf VI Audo, the Chaldean patriarch, spanned a period of almost thirty years (1849-78), but, ironically, resulted in the return of "Nestorianism" to Malabar, referred to earlier.[19]

The arbitrary consecration of Indian bishops by the Jacobite patriarch without consultation and approval of the Indian congregations was often cause for challenging the authority of such bishops, thus exacerbating the domestic controversies in Christian Malabar.[20] These unseemly bickerings often led to litigation. The courts of British India supported the claim that the legitimate head of the Syrian church of India was the patriarch of the Syrian Orthodox church residing in Turkey, but the courts emphasized that the patriarch's was a spiritual and not temporal authority. The British-India authorities showed no desire to interfere in the internal rivalries of the Indian congregations, but they reaffirmed the tradition or precedent that the metropolitan of Malabar had to be consecrated either by the Jacobite patriarch or by one who had his authority.[21]

In 1874 the Jacobite patriarch himself decided to visit India. He prepared the way by first going to London; there he was twice received by Queen Victoria, and at a reception in his honor at the India office, he met several ministers and celebrities. Upon his arrival in India he met the governor of Madras—all a very impressive entree to Malabar, where he was received with great joy by most of the faithful.

In an effort to bring the church of Malankara under his closer supervision, Patriarch Ighnātiyus Butrus (Peter) III[22] summoned an Indian synod (1876).[23] One of the resolutions of the conclave stipulated that in its relation to the patriarchal See, the church of Malabar would be considered just as another diocese of the Syrian Orthodox church. Each parish was to declare complete submission to the patriarch; the Malabar region was to be divided into seven dioceses, each headed by a bishop—some of the bishops he had already consecrated, without consultation of the church as a whole—all independent of each other. Regulations were enacted for an annual tax that would be levied on each church and any ecclesiastical property, for the benefit of the patriarch.

The prelate left India in 1877, leaving behind a masterful plan of divide and rule which was sure to create greater rivalries and more litigations.[24]

The second Patriarch to go to India was Ighnāṭiyūs 'Abd-Allah Saṭṭūf, who arrived in 1909 and like his predecessor, thirty-two years earlier, called a synod at Kottayam (1910) where he tried to implement the decisions of the preceding synod. Unfortunately for the patriarch, this was not a rubber-stamp synod; the bishops confirmed the authority of the See of Antioch over their church but emphasized that it was only a spiritual authority. Unhappy with the results, 'Abd-Allah excommunicated the metropolitan in the summer of 1911, charging him with insubordination and misconduct,[25] and appointed another in his place, dividing the church into two parties which later (1978) became two separate branches of the church: one of them, calling itself the Jacobite Orthodox church of India, centered at Mooratupuzha, is headed by a "catholicos" appointed by the Jacobite patriarch in Damascus; the other, named the Syrian Orthodox church of India, its center at Kottayam, is under the leadership of a catholicos elected by the local synod and backed, according to Father Hambye, by about two-thirds of the faithful.[26] The origin of what may be a permanent division needs clarification and will be briefly outlined here.[27]

When Patriarch 'Abd-Allah Saṭṭūf excommunicated the metropolitan, the latter and his party, faced with the problem of legitimacy, had the metropolitan consecrated "catholicos" by the predecessor of Saṭṭūf, the deposed Ighanāṭiyūs 'Abd al-Masīḥ II, referred to earlier.[28] Although 'Abd al-Masīḥ was deposed in the eyes of the Syrian Orthodox church, he was accepted by the rival Indian party; the latter argued that the former patriarch's deposition was brought about not because of lunacy, as charged, but because of the intrigues of none other than 'Abd-Allah Saṭṭūf, who had succeeded 'Abd al-Masīḥ as patriarch. Moreover, 'Abd-Allah had been himself excommunicated before his consecration and had embraced Catholicism before returning to his own church and heading it in 1906. The fact that the Ottoman government had also withdrawn its recognition from 'Abd al-Masīḥ, argued the aggrieved Indian party, did not mean that the former patriarch had lost his spiritual power.[29]

The Ottoman government had warned the British ministry of foreign affairs that 'Abd al-Masīḥ had no authority in the Jacobite church and when the ex-patriarch had arrived in India in 1912 the maharaja of Travancore had refused to see him. But this did not deter 'Abd al-Masīḥ or his supporters in India, where the sultan had no power. The ex-patriarch proceeded to consecrate three other bishops besides the catholicos and in order to be able to perpetrate their authority it was agreed through a signed document that the bishops had the power to consecrate a new catholicos without the approval of the Jacobite patriarch, whose spiritual supremacy was still recognized.[30]

It is of interest to note that the Jacobite churches of the Middle East and Malabar were reconciled in 1958 through the efforts of the late patriarch, Ighnāṭīyūs Yaʿqūb III, who accepted the Indian catholicosate.[31] Also in 1958 the Supreme Court of India ruled that the rightful owner of the common properties of the church was the catholicos. The reconciliation, however, did not last long; in 1972 the patriarch in Damascus denied the catholicos the claim that he was "sitting on the Throne of St. Thomas."[32] Two years later the patriarch consecrated an Indian monk as metropolitan and appointed him patriarchal delegate in India, a move made without the consent of the India synod, let alone of the catholicos. Indeed, in 1975 the catholicos was suspended from his functions. An episcopal synod called by the catholicos, in turn, suspended the bishops who sided with the patriarch. Whether the division will be temporary or permanent remains to be seen.[33]

D. *Churches of the Middle East*

The Church Also known as		Patriarchal title	Patriarchal Seat	Liturgical Language	Vernacular Language	Offshoot of (after 1500)
Independent Churches—with no outside affiliation						
Coptic Orthodox Church	Coptic Orthodox Church of Alexandria	Patriarch of Alexandria	Cairo	Coptic, Arabic	Arabic	
Armenian Orthodox Church of Cilicia	Armenian Georgian Church	Catholicos of the Armenian Orthodox Church of Cilicia	Antilyas (Lebanon)	Armenian	Armenian	
Syrian Orthodox Church	Jacobite Church, Syrian Orthodox Church of Antioch and all the East, Syrian Jacobite Church, West Syrian Church	Patriarch of Antioch and all the East	Damascus	Syriac, Arabic	Arabic, Syriac	
Ethiopian Orthodox Church	Ethiopian Church	Patriarch of the Ethiopian Orthodox Church	Addis Ababa	Geez	Amharic	
Church of the East	Nestorian Church, East Syrian Church, Assyrian Church, The Ancient Apostolic Church of the East	Catholicos of the East	Officially Baghdad	Syriac	Syriac	

Churches Affiliated with the Patriarchate of Constantinople						
Orthodox Patriarchate of Constantinople	Greek Orthodox Church of Constantinople, The Great Church	Oecumenical Patriarch of Constantinople	Constantinople (Istanbul)	Greek	Greek	
Greek Orthodox Church of Antioch	Antiochian Orthodox Church, Syrian Antiochian Orthodox Church, Rūm Orthodox	Patriarch of Antioch	Damascus	Arabic	Arabic	
Greek Orthodox Church of Alexandria	Chruch of Alexandria	Patriarch of Alexandria	Alexandria	Greek, Arabic	Greek, Arabic	
Greek Orthodox Church of Jerusalem	Church of Jerusalem	Patriarch of Jerusalem	Jerusalem	Arabic, Greek	Arabic, Greek	
For other churches in this group, see Chapter 1, note 1						

Churches United with the Roman Catholic Church						
Coptic Catholic Church		Coptic Catholic Patriarch of Alexandria	Cairo	Coptic, Arabic	Arabic	Coptic Orthodox Church
Maronite Church		Maronite Patriarch of Antioch	Bkirki	Syriac, Arabic	Arabic	
Syrian Catholic Church		Patriarch of Antioch	Beirut	Syriac, Arabic	Arabic, Syriac	Syrian Orthodox Church (Jacobite)

Armenian Catholic Church	Armenian Catholic Church of Cilicia	Armenian	Bzummār (Lebanon)	Armenian	Armenian	Armenian Orthodox Church
Chaldean Catholic Church	Chaldean Church	Chaldean Patriarch of Babylon	Baghdad	Syriac, Arabic	Arabic, Syriac	Church of the East (Nestorian)
Melchite Church	Rūm Catholic, Greek Catholic Church of Antioch	Melchite Patriarch of Antioch	Damascus	Arabic	Arabic	Greek Orthodox Church of Antioch (Rūm Orthodox)

Churches of India Affiliated with
Middle Eastern Churches

See Appendix C

Evangelical Churches

Organized since the nineteenth century as a result of West-European and American missionary effort, various Protestant churches and synods are found in the region; among them are: the Diocese of Jerusalem, Jordan, Syria, and Lebanon; the Episcopal Church in Jerusalem and the Middle East; the Protestant Church of Algeria; Evangelical Presbyterian Church in Iran; National Evangelical Church in Kuwait; National Evangelical Union of Lebanon, Coptic Evangelical Church of Egypt; etc. Most of these bodies are members of the Middle East Council of Churches

4. The first Catholic patriarch of this church, eventually known as "patriarch of Antioch, Alexandria, Jerusalem and all the East," was elected in 1724. He has residences at Cairo, Beirut, and Damascus. In the United States the group is called Melkite.

5. See p. 6.

6. John Joseph, *The Nestorians and Their Muslim Neighbors: a Study of Western Influence on Their Relations* (Princeton, N.J.: 1961), pp. 71-76; Steven Runciman, *The Christian Arabs of Palestine* (London: University of Essex, 1968-69), pp. 9, 19; cf. Edward Every, "The Christian Arabs of Palestine," *E. C. R.* 3 (1970-71): 354. To compound the confusion, the Middle Eastern Greek Orthodox church is also known today as the Syrian Antiochian Orthodox church, a usage introduced in the United States in order to distinguish between the Arab (Syrian) and the Greek communities that make up the Greek Orthodox communion here.

7. Runciman, *Christian Arabs of Palestine*, pp.3-4.

8. The Nicene formula emphasized the belief "in one God . . .and in one Lord Jesus Christ, the Son of God, the only begotten of the Father, that is, of the substance of the Father; God from God, light from light, true God from true God."

9. Theodore had carried the views of Diodorus even further, emphasizing that Christ was human in person as well as in nature; that he was troubled by passions and was peccable. See Glanville Downey, *A History of Antioch in Syria from Seleucus to the Arab Conquest* (Princeton: 1961), p. 462; Alphonse Mingana, ed. and trans., *Theodorus, bp. of Mopsuestia, d. ca. 428* (Cambridge: 1932-33).

10. Downey, ibid., p. 416; see also Carl E. Braaten, "Modern Interpretations of Nestorius," *Church History* 32 (Sept. 1963): 251-67.

11. Paul Bedjan, *Acta martyrum sanctorum* (Leipzig: 1890), vol. 2, p. 136; cf. De Lacy O'Leary, *Arabia before Muhammad* (New York: 1927), p. 129; A. Mingana, "The Early Spread of Christianity in Central Asia and the Far East: a New Document," *Bulletin of John Rylands Library* 9 (1925): 300.

12. The substance or essential nature of an individual. For a discussion of the doctrine by two present-day bishops of the "Monophysite" Syrian Orthodox church, see Mar Severius Zakka Iwas, "The Doctrine of the Union of the Two Natures of Christ," *Greek Orthodox Theological Review* 10 (Winter 1964-65): 151-53; V. C. Samuel, "The Real Point in Brief of the Fifth Century Christological Controversies," *M. B.* 2 (March 1964): 387; (April): 443; (May): 500.

13. Karl Bihlmeyer, *Church History* (Westminster, Md.: 1958), vol. 1, pp. 278-279; V. C. Samuel, "Were the Non-Chalcedonian Churches Monophysite?" *M.B.* 2 (December 1963): 204-5; O'Leary, *Arabia*, p. 138.

14. Salo W. Baron, *A Social and Religious History of the Jews* (New York: 1952), vol. 3, p. 268, n. 17; Adrian Fortescue, *The Lesser Eastern Churches* (London: 1913), p. 342.

15. Downey, *History of Antioch*, pp. 508-9; Francois N. Nau, ed. and trans., *Histoires d'Ahoudemmeh et de Marouta, metropolitains jacobites de Tagrit et de l'Orient (VI' et VII' siecles)*, in *Patrologia orientalis*, III, fasc. I (1909), p. 19, where a Jacobite writer is quoted speaking of Nestorians as "infidels."

Notes

1. The Background

1. The "Greek Orthodox" church today is divided into a group of self-governing churches, each with its own patriarch. The patriarchates of Constantinople, Alexandria, Antioch, and Jerusalem have the first place of honor because of their historic importance. Four other patriarchates were created in the succeeding centuries: the Bulgarian (formed in 917), Servian (1346), Russian (1589), and Rumanian (1925). The Georgian church is ruled by a Catholicos and the church is a catholicate and not a patriarchate, which is more exalted. Six orthodox churches, fully independent but not headed by a patriarch or catholicos, are the autocephalous churches of Cyprus (formed in 431), Sinai (1575), Greece (1830), Poland (1924), Albania (1937), and Czechoslovakia (1951). Of these, the church of Sinai (also known as Mount Sinai) is the smallest independent orthodox church. Its membership of about 100 is ruled by the superior of the monastery of St. Catherine, who is an archbishop. Until the 16th century it was part of the patriarchate of Jerusalem.

2. See Robert Mitchell Haddad, "The Orthodox Patriarchate of Antioch and the Origins of the Melkite Schism" (Ph.D. diss., Harvard University, 1965); Steven Runciman, *The Great Church in Captivity: A Study of the Patriarchate of Constantinople from the Eve of the Turkish Conquest to the Greek War of Independence* (London: 1968); Adrian Fortescue *The Orthodox Eastern Church under the Turk* (London: 1911).

3. The Muslim historian al-Birūni, writing in the 11th century, explained that the Malkites are "so called because the Greek King is of their persuasion." See his *al-Āthār al-Bāqiyah 'an al-Qurūn al-Khāliyah,* ed. and trans. E. Sachau (London: 1879), p. 282.

16. Text in *Patrologia graeca*, 86:2620-5.
17. The decree is known as Henoticon.
18. M. A. Bashir, "The Syrian Church, the Jacobites," *Word*, No. 2 (February 1957): 32; Filib di Ṭarrāzi, *Aṣdaq mā-Kān 'an Ta'rīkh Lubnān, wa-Safhat 'an Akhbār al-Suryān*, vol. 3, chap. 13. Theodora was not against the punishment of the extremists among the Monophysites; she collaborated with her husband in spite of pro-Chalcedonian policies.
19. *N.C.E.*, vol. 7, p. 796; O. H. Parry, *Six Months in a Syrian Monastery* (London: 1895), p. 292.
20. Also known as al-Barda'i, al-Bardaani, Baradai, the name said to come from the Arabic word *barda*, a species of fabric similar to felt, of which the Monophysite missionary's ragged garment was made. Others consider the name to be derived from Bardaa, the city in Armenia of which he is said to be a native. See Georg Graf, *Geschichte der christlichen arabischen Literatur* (Vatican City: 1944), vol. 1, p. 70; J. W. Etheridge, *The Syrian Churches, Their History, Liturgies, and Literature* (London: 1846), pp. 140-41: Fortescue, *Lesser Eastern Churches*, p. 324; Parry, *Six Months, p. 291;* Otto F. A. Meinardus, "The Syrian Jacobites in the Holy City," *Orientalia Seucana* (Upsala) 12 (1963), pp. 60-61; H.G. Kleyn, *Jacobus Baradaues, de Stichter der syrische monophysitische Kirk* (Leiden: 1882), pp. 164-94; Charles Frazee, "The Maronite Middle Ges," *E.C.R.* 10, nos. 1-2 (1978) p. 92.
21. See Tarrāzi *Aṣdaq mā-Kān*, vol. 2, pp. 5 seq.; vol. 3, chap. 21; Ishāq Armalah, "Naṣāra Ghassān wa-al-Suryān," *al-Mashriq*, 58 (1964): 377-96; Afrām Barsūm, "Naṣrānīyat al-'Arab," *M.B.* 7 (April 1969): 297-99; O'Leary, *Arabia*, chap. 7. For more on the Arabian origin of these Christians see also Ismā'il R Khālidi, "The Arab Kingdom of Ghassan: Its Origins, Rise and Fall," *M.W.* 46 (July 1956): 197-99, where he points out that in the Greek and Syriac sources the Ghassanids are often called "Greek Arabs," while the pro-Persian Lakhmids, most of them Nestorians, are referred to as the "Arabs of Mesopotamia"; Salāh al-Dīn Munajjid, "Manāzil al-Qabā'il al-'Arabīyah Ḥawl Damashq," *Majallat Majma' al-'Ilmi al-'Arabi* 30 (1955).
22. Graf, *Geschichte*, vol. 1, p. 70, where he also notes the letter of a 9th-century Jacobite bishop of Takrit addressed to members of his community in Bahrayn.
23. Irfan Shahid, "Ghassanids," in *E.I.* vol. 2, p. 1020; Runciman, *Christian Arabs*, p. 7; Daniel J. Sahas, *John of Damascus on Islam, the "Heresy of the Ishmaelites"* (Leiden: 1972), pp. 22 seq. For the passionate hatred that existed between the Chalcedonians and the Monophysites during the Muslim conquest, see Bar Hebraeus (Ibn al-'Ibri), *The Chronography of Gregory Abu l Faraj*, trans. E. A. Wallis Budge (London 1932), vol. 2, pp. 93-94; vol. 2, p. 100.
24. One student of Monophysite history has noted that the name Jacobite is first found in a synodical decree of A.D. 787. See Meinardus, "Syrian Jacobites," p. 61. Consult also Ṭarrāzi, *Aṣdaq mā-Kān*, vol. 3, chap. 12; Ni'mat-Allah Dannu, "al-Ya'qūbīyah Na't Dakhil 'ala Kanīsatina al-Suryānīyah, *M.B.* 2 (Dec. 1963), 83-90

25. Joseph Wolff, *Missionary Journals* (London: 1828), vol. 2, p. 245. For more on the Jewish background of the Jacobites, see Asahel Grant in *M.H.* 38 (1842): 262; Etheridge, *Syrian Churches*, p. 145. Some authors, among them Jacobites, trace the ethnicity of the community to the Aramaens. See Sykes, "Kurdish Tribes of the Ottoman Empire," pp. 453,473-74. Sykes speaks of some Jacobites as being "pure Aramaens," while others were formerly Kurds, just as many among the Kurds were originally Jacobite or Nestorian. See also Tarrāzi, *Aṣdaq mā-Kān*, vol. 1, pp. 1-5.

Because "Syria" and "Assyria" may be traced to the same root, it has been argued that people calling themselves Syrians are ethnically Assyrians. Herodotus has been often cited as a source for this equation. Researches of Randolph Helm show, however, that Herodotus "conscientiously" and "consistently" distinguished the two names and used them independently of each other. To Herodotus "Syrians" were "the inhabitants of the coastal Levant, including North Syria, Phoenicia, and Philistia." Herodotus, writes Helm, "*never* [emphasis Helm's] uses the name 'Syria' to apply to Mesopotamia. This region is always called 'Assyria' . . .[and its] inhabitants as 'Assyrians'." This distinction was "lost upon later Classical authors," concludes Helm, "some of whom interpreted [Herodotus'] *Histories VII.63* as a mandate to refer to Phoenicians, Jews, and any other Levantines as 'Assyrians'." See his "Herodotus *Histories VII.63* and the Georgraphical Connotations of the Toponym 'Assyria' in the Achaemenid Period" (paper presented at the 190th meeting of the American Oriental Society, at San Francisco, April 1980). See also his " 'Greeks' in the Neo-Assyrian Levant and 'Assyria' in Early Greek Writers" (Ph.D. diss., University of Pennsylvania, 1980), pp. 27-41. Cf. R. Lapointe, "Etymologie sémitique de Syrie," *Vetus Testamentum* 20 (1970): 233-36. Lapointe argues that Syria and Assyria are not etymologically related. For details of this discussion consult my *Nestorians*, pp. 11 seq., where, even though I have misread Herodotus, I too have upheld his geographical and ethnic distinctions between "Syria" and "Syrian" and "Syrians" on the one hand, "Assyria" and "Assyrians" on the other.

26. *al-Āthār al-Bāqiyah*, p. 282. The heads of all these Monophysite churches were in ideological union with one another. They exchanged regular "synodicon letters" in which they announced their elevation and made a confession of faith. See Graf, *Geschichte,* vol. 1, p. 71; Fortescue, *Lesser Eastern Churches,* 333-34.

27. Parry, *Six Months,* p. 314; F.J. Bliss, *The Religions of Modern Syria and Palestine* (New York: 1912), p. 75; Fortescue, *Lesser Eastern Churches*, p. 237; H. Rassam, *Asshur and the Land of Nimrod* (New York: 1897), p. 167; Etheridge, *Syrian Churches*, p. 148; Donald Attwater, *The Christian Churches of the East* (Milwaukee: 1948), vol. 2, p. 206; Isidor Silbernagl, *Verfassung und gegenwartiger Bestand samtlicher Kirchen des Orients* (Regensburg: 1904), p. 307; George P. Badger, *The Nestorians and Their Rituals* (London: 1852), vol. 1, p. 60; Horatio Southgate, Jr., *Narrative of a Visit to the Syrian (Jacobite) Church of Mesopotamia* (New York: 1856), pp. 225-26. See also Ishāq Armalah, *al-Qaṣāra fi Nakabāt al-Naṣāra* (n.p., n.d.), p. 420.

28. *Narrative of a Visit,* pp. 221-222. The present Syrian Orthodox prelate counts himself as the "122nd in the line of the legitimate patriarchs of Antioch." Consult *M.B.* 19 (April 1981): 226.

29. See article by the patriarch himself, "The Syrian Orthodox Church of Antioch at a Glance," in *M.B.* 19 (April 1981): 226. See also ibid. 2 (Sept. 1964): 51, where the patriarchal title is simply "Syrian Orthodox Patriarch of Antioch and All the East." Since the 9th century the patriarchs have assumed the name Ignatius (Ighnāṭiyūs), after St. Ignatius of Antioch, martyred in Rome early in the 2nd century.

30. Alexandria was the first patriarchate to be formed in the early church. At the Council of Constantinople in the 4th century, the patriarch of Alexandria was granted the second place of honor after the bishop of Rome.

31. For the episcopacy of St. Peter at Antioch, see Etheridge, *Syrian Churches,* pp. 22-25; Downey, *History of Antioch,* pp. 272-87, 583-86, where he emphasizes that in local opinion St. Peter had become a principal figure in the early history of the community whether or not he could be said to be literally the founder of the church at Antioch and its first "bishop."

32. The rule of the patriarchs of Antioch covered the church in the provinces of Syria, Cilicia, Arabia, and Mesopotamia. At the council of Nicaea (A.D. 325) almost half of the church fathers assembled there—150 out of 318—were from the patriarchate of Antioch.

33. Runciman, *Christian Arabs,* p. 6; Baron, *Social History,* vol. 3, p. 87. A Hellenic hierarchy would continue to dominate the Orthodox church in Palestine until the 20th century, thus sharpening the Arab nationalist feelings of the Palestinian laity and their priests in modern times.

34. See *N.C.E.,* vol. 8, p. 912.

35. *Lesser Eastern Churches,* pp. 345-46.

36. For scholarly studies on Syriac literature, see R. Duval, La Littérature syriaque (Paris: 1900); A Baumstark, *Geschichte der syrischen literatur* (Bonn: 1922); J. B. Chabot, Littérature syriaque (Paris: 1935).

37. Fortescue, *Lesser Eastern Churches,* pp. 345-46.

38. O'Leary, *Arabia,* p. 126.

39. Runciman, *Christian Arabs,* p. 14.

40. Under the Arabian dynasty of Umayyads, a Jacobite patriarch was able through the intervention of Walid to enter Antioch, where he remained for only a short time. See Parry, *Six Months,* pp. 299, 314-15.

41. See p. 110.

42. Herbert Birks, *The Life and Correspondence of Thomas Valpy French, First Bishop of Lahore* (London: 1895), p. 249.

43. For an account on Antioch in modern times, see William H. Hall, "Antioch the Glorious," *National Geographic Magazine* 38 (Aug. 1920): 81-103. For an excellent engraving of the city as it was in 1840, see *M.H.*76 (1880): 245. Toward the end of the 19th century the *qaḍā'* of Antioch, according to Vital Cuinet, had a population of 2500 Orthodox Jacobites, and 2000 Catholic Syrians (formerly Jacobites) in addition to 7000 Christians of other sects, including Nestorians and Chaldeans. See his *La Turquie d'Asie* vol. 2, p. 192.

44. Quoted by T. W. Arnold, *The Preaching of Islam* (New York: 1913), p. 51.

45. Addai Scher, ed., "Chronique de Seert," in *Patrologia orientalis* (Paris: 1907-18), vol. 2, p. 261. See also L. E. Browne, *The Eclipse of Christianity in Asia: From the Time of Mohammed till the Fourteenth Century* (New York: 1967), pp. 40-41. Cf. M. G. Morony, "Religious Communities in Umayyad Iraq" (paper presented at the Middle East Studies Association Conference, Binghampton, N.Y. 3 Nov. 1972), p.3.

46. *The Churches and Monasteries of Egypt*, ed. and trans. B. T. A. Evetts and Alfred J. Butler (London: 1970), pp. 230-31.

47. See his Chronicle quoted in Browne, *Eclipse of Christianity,* pp. 39-40; Jacob S. Raison, *Gentile Reactions to Jewish Ideals* (New York: 1953), p. 393.

48. J. B. Segal, *Edessa: "The Blessed City"* (New York: 1970), p. 192.

49. Charles K. von Euw, "The Union of the Syro-Jacobites with Rome in the Mid-Seventeenth Century" (Ph. D. diss., Papal Institute of Oriental Studies, Rome, 1959), pp. xii-xiii; Tarrazi, *Aṣdaq mā-Kān,* vol. 3, chap.51; Filib di Tarrāzi, *'Aṣr al-Suryan al-Dhahabi, bahth 'Ilmi Ta'rikhi Athari* (Beirut: 1946), pp. 50-81; Suhayl Qāsha, "Aḥwāl Naṣāra al-'Irāq fi al-'Aṣr al-'Abbāsi," *M.B.* 7 (Sept. 1969): 472-79.

50. Morony, "Religious Communities in Umayyad Iraq," G. LeStrange, *Baghdad during the Abbasid Caliphate* (London: 1924), pp. xxv-xxviii, 207-14; Parry, *Six Months*, p. 317; Browne, *Eclipse of Christianity*, pp. 50-51, where the powers of the Nestorian Catholicos over the Jacobite and Melkite bishops is discussed; A. S. Tritton, "Non-Muslim Subjects of the Muslim State," *Journal of the Royal Asiatic Society* (1942): 36-40; A. S. Tritton, *The Caliphs and Their Non-Moslem Subjects* Oxford: 1930); Antoine Fattal, *Le statute légale des non-musulmans en pays d'Islam* (Beirut: 1958); G. Najda, "Ahl al-Kitāb," *E. I. (2nd ed.)* pp. 264-66; Claude Cahen, "Dhimma," in ibid., pp. 227-31; Sahas, John of Damascus on Islam p. 25; Rūfā'il Bābu Ishāq, "Mahallat al-Shammāsiyah bi-Baghdād fi 'Ahd al-Khilāfat al-'Abbāsiyah," *Sumer* 9 (1953): 132-54.

51. Segal *Edessa*, p. 212. For details on the Nestorian influence see J. Labourt, "Le Patriarche Timothee et les Nestorians sous les Abbasids," *Révue d'histoire et littérature religieuses* 10 (1905): 384-402.

52. Consult his *History of the Arabs,* p. 315. See also O'Leary, *Arabia*, p. 141; Segal, *Edessa*, p. 210; Rūfā'il Bābu Ishāq, *Ahwāl al-Naṣāra Baghdad fi 'Ahd al-Khilāfat al-'Abbāsiyah* (Baghdad: 1960), *passim*. See also Graf, *Geschichte*, vol. 1, pp. 71-72. Cf. Brian E. Colless, "The Place of Syrian Christian Mysticism in Religious History," *Journal of Religious History* 5 (June 1968): 8-10; G. Cardahi, *Bar Hebraeus's Book of the Dove*, trans. A. Wensinck (Leyden: 1919), pp. cxi-cxxxvi, where Bar Hebraeus, writes Wensinck, closely imitates the *Ihya* of al-Ghazzāli, who in turn was greatly indebted to the Christian mystics.

53. Modern scholarship has shown that the Prophet Mohammad himself had learned a great deal from Syriac Christianity and that his monotheism is greatly influenced by the Monophysite doctrine. See John Bowman, "The Debt of Islam to Monophysite Syrian Christianity," *Nederlands Theologisch Tydschrift* (February 1965): 178; H. Gregoire, "Mahomet et le Monophysisme," *Mélanges Charles Diehl* 1 (1930): 107-119. For the in-

fluences of Monophysite Christianity on Muslim teachings in general, se Tūma al-Khūri, "Dawr al-Lughat al-Suryāniyah fi al-Adab, wa-al Falsafah,
wa-al Dīn," *M.B.* 1 (1962): 485-62; Ighnāṭiyūs Yaʻqūb III, "al-Kindi wa-
al-Suryāniyah," ibid., pp. 255-67; Fuʼād Afrām, "al-Kindi wa-al-Suryāniyah," *ibid.*, 2 (1963), 91-95; Ighnāṭiyūs Afrām III, "Āthār as-Suryāniyah
fi al-Thaqāfat al-ʻArabiyah," ibid., 1 (1962): 403-13; Ahmad Shawkat al-
Shaṭṭi, "Al-Suryān wa-Atharuhum fi al-Hadārat al- ʻArabiyah al-
Islāmiyah," ibid., 3 (1965): 550-54.

54. Yūsuf al-Shammās, *Al-Qaddis Yūhanna al-Damashqi wa-al-Kanā-'is al-
Malakiyah fi al-Qurūn al-Wusṭa, 634-1724* (Sidon: 1949).
55. Runciman, *The Great Church in Captivity,* pp. 78-79, where he speaks of
the Fatimid caliph Hākim burning down the church of the Holy Sepulchre.
Hakim's successor had apologized to the Byzantine emperor, allowing him
to rebuild the shrine and keep his officials there.
56. See below, pp. 121. See also N.H. Baynes and H. St. L.B. Moss, eds.,
Byzantium: an Introduction to East Roman Civilization (Oxford: 1948),
pp. 314-19, 323; Francesco Gabrielli, "Greeks and Arabs in the Central
Mediterranean Area," *Dumbarton Oaks Papers* 18 (1964): 64.
57. Browne, *Eclipse of Christianity,* pp. 57-58.
58. Ibid, pp. 53-54; Segal, *Edessu,* pp. 208-48.
59. When the Christians had complained to one of their governors of his con-
fiscatory taxes and policies, he had answered: "What have you to complain
of, Christians? From the time of the Romans you have devoured this land
while our ancestors wandered in the arid desert, in the cold and heat that
dries and burns . . . Now that we have conquered this land from the
Romans with our sword, why do you make trouble instead of leaving it to
us and removing yourselves from it . . . Pay the tribute and remain in
peace!" (Segal, *Edessa,* p. 198.) For restrictive measures by Muslim rulers
imposed on their Christian subjects, see ibid., pp. 196-197, 201; Philip K.
Hitti, *History of Syria, Including Lebanon and Palestine* (Londn: 1951),
pp. 487-88, 543-44, 587-88.
60. Segal, *Edessa,* p. 196. See also pp. 24,27.
61. Ibid., p. 201. See also M. Perlmann, "Notes on Anti-Christian Propaganda in the Mamluk Empire," *Bulletin of the School of Oriental and African
Studies* 10 (1940-42): 843-61.
62. Le Strange, *Baghdad,* p. 212.
63. Runciman, *Great Church,* p. 78.
64. Browne, *Eclipse of Christianity,* pp. 48-49.
65. *N.C.E.,* vol. 7, p. 796; Graf, *Geschichte,* vol. 1, pp. 70-71.
66. Mingana, "Early Spread," p. 347.
67. Fortescue, *Lesser Eastern Churches,* pp. 329-33.
68. Matthew Spinka, "The Effect of the Crusades upon Eastern Christianity,"
in John T. McNeil et al., eds., *Environmental Factors in Christian History*
(Chicago: 1939), pp. 254-55; Gibb and Bowen, *Islamic Society and the
West* (London, 1957), pt. 2, p. 229, where the authors speak of "a considerable emigration of Jacobites from Syria to Egypt," as a result of the
first crusade. For an interesting study of the emigration of the Muslim
population to Egypt, see Hadia Dajani-Shakeel, "Displacement of the

Palestinians during the Crusades," *M. W.* 68 (1978): 157-75.

69. Spinka, "Effect of the Crusades," p. 256. See also P. Martin, "Les premiers princes croises et les Syriens jacobits de Jerusalem," *Journal asiatique* 8 (1888): 471-90.

70. Spinka, ibid., p. 256; cf. Gibb and Bowen, *Islamic Society,* p. 229, where the authors speak of the eagerness of the Crusaders as missionaries for Rome, who were "even worse disposed towards dissidents from Orthodoxy than towards the Orthodox themselves." For details on relations between the Franks and the Jacobites during this period, see Isḥāq Armalah, *Athar Faransa wa-Ma'āthiruha fi al-Lubnān wa-fi-Suñya* (Beirut: 1946), p.77 et seq.

71. Spinka, "Effect of the Crusades," pp. 258-59; Tarrāzi, *Aṣdaq mā-Kān,* vol. 1, pp. 64-67. Cf. Runciman, *Christian Arabs,* p. 12. A Syriac chronicler found that Western Christians had no mercy "but only cruelty, callousness, hardness of heart, and wickedness of thought— especially among the priests, monks, and bishops." Matthew of Edessa did not spare the temporal leadership; he thought that Baldwin du Bourg "had more hatred for Christians than for the Turks." See Segal, *Edessa,* pp. 226-29, 254.

72. Claude Cahen, *Pre-Ottoman Turkey: A General Survey of the Material and Spiritual Culture and History 1071-1330* (New York: 1968), pp. 213-14; Tarrāzi, *Aṣdaq mā-Kān,* vol. 1, chap. 15.

73. Segal, *Edessa,* pp. 246-49.

74. A. Neame., "Religion in the Lebanon," *Tablet,* 212 (19 July 1958): 52, quoting William of Tyre. Researches of Kamal S. Salibi have shown that the Maronites of the mountain fastnesses were against Frankish rule and opposed to the thought of union with Rome. See his "The Maronite Church in the Middle Ages and Its Union with Rome," *Oriens christianus* 6 (1958): 93.

75. See Bernard Hamilton, "The Armenian Church and the Papacy at the Time of the Crusades," *E. C. R.*10, nos. 1-2 (1978): 61-87; Avedis K. Sanjian, *The Armenian Communities in Syria under Ottoman Dominion* (Cambridge: 1965), pp. 16, 25-26, 98; Vardges Takhtadzhian, "The Separation of the Armenian Catholics from the Armenian Apostolic Church in the 18th Century" (Masters thesis, American University of Beirut, 1972), pp. 15-21. See also Dana C. Munro, "Christian and Infidel in the Holy Land," *International Monthly* 4 (Nov. 1901): 696.

76. Segal, *Edessa,* pp. 235, 238-39, 243; R. C. Hovannisian, *Armenia on the Road to Independence* (Berkeley: 1967), p. 4.

77. Ibn al-'Ibri, *Chronography,* vol. 1, p. 430; vol. 2, pp. 504-5; Steven Runciman, *A History of the Crusades* (Cambridge: 1954), vol. 3, pp. 302-4; Gaston Wiet, *Baghdad: Metropolis of the Abbasid Caliphate,* trans. Seymour Feiler (Normal, Okla.: 1971), p. 52.

78. C. Dawson, ed. and trans., *The Mongol Mission: Narratives and Letters of the Franciscan Missionaries in Mongolia and China in the 13th and 14th Centuries* (New York: 1955), pp. 161-62; *N.C.E.,* vol. 9, p. 1060.

79. Runciman, *History,* vol. 3, pp. 302-4. For the good relations between the Nestorians and Mongols, see also Abu al-Fida, *Taqwim al-Buldān,* ed. J.

T. Reinaud and de Slane (Paris: 1840), pp. 136-37; Ibn al-'Ibri, *Chronography*, vol. 1, pp. 429-31. Cf. *N.C.E.*, vol. 2, p. 81.

80. Runciman, *History*, vol. 3, p. 304.
81. Peter Kawerau, *Die jakobitische Kirche im Zeitalter der syrischen Renaissance, Idee und Wirklichkeit* (Berlin: 1955), p. 101.
82. Browne, *Eclipse of the Chruch*, p. 150.
83. Runciman, *History*, vol. 3, pp. 311-12.
84. Ibid., pp. 305-26; 347-440; idem, *Christian Arabs*, pp. 12-13; Ibn al-'Ibri, *Chronography*, vol. 1, pp. 440-42; vol. 2, pp. 515-18.
85. Browne, *Eclipse of the Church*, pp. 154-155.
86. Philip K. Hitti, *Lebanon in History* (London: 1957), p. 33. For details on the Muslim vengeance on the Christians, see Kamal S. Salibi, "The Maronites of Lebanon under Frankish and Mamluk Rule (1099-1516)," *Arabica* 4 (1957): 294 et seq.
87. Browne, *Eclipse of the Church*, p. 172.
88. Berthold Spuler, "Die west-syrische (monophysitische) Kirche unter der Islam," *Saeculum* 9 (1958): 337. In 1964 this article was published as a chapter in Spuler's *Die morgentañdischen Kirchen*. My references are to the pages of the article.

2. Among Arabs, Turks, and Kurds

1. Suhayl Qāsha, "Al-Lughat al-'Arabīyah lada Naṣāra al-'Irāq," *M.B.* 7 (1969): 356-64.
2. See John Joseph, *The Nestorians and Their Muslim Neighbours: A Study of Western Influence on Their Relations,* (Princeton, N.J.:, 1961), pp. 33-36.
3. For an archeological study of churches and monasteries of this region, see Ugo Monneret de Villard, "Le chiese della Mesopotamia," *Orientalia chris tiana analecta* (Rome, the Pontifical Institute of Oriental Studies), no. 128 (1940): 45-65.
4. Albert Socin, "Zur Georgraphie des Tur Abdin," *Zeitschrift der deutschen morgenländischen Gesellschaft* 35 (1881): 239.
5. *M.H.* 48 (April 1852): 109; Gertrude L. Bell, *Amurath to Amurath* (London: 1911), pp. 303-5; D. G. Hogarth, *The Nearer East* (New York: 1902), p. 62
6. Bell, *Amurath*, p. 301, where she translates the name to "The Mount of the Servants of God." Cf. Horatio Southgate, Tr., *Narrative of a Visit to the Syrian (Jacobite) Church of Mesopotamia* (New York: 1856), p. 202. For a detailed discussion of the physical features of this region, see Socin, pp. 237-69.
7. The Rev. Joseph Wolff listed 103 villages of Syrian Jacobites in Jabal Tur; see his *Missionary Journals* (London., 1828), vol. 2, pp. 257-58. Southgate estimated the Tur population at 30,000; see his *Visit*, p. 278.
8. At the very beginning of this century the quickest way of reaching Mosul from Europe was by steamer to Alexandretta and from there by caravan to Aleppo and Diyarbakr and by raft from there to Mosul. See Church Missionary Society, *Proceedings 1901-1902* (London), pp. 170-171.
9. *M.H.* 49 (1853): 273-74. Travel by land often meant that traders would go

in armed caravans, sometimes of as many as a thousand persons or more. In these cases they would escape pillage but not the payment of tax, collected by the Arab shaykhs, most of them of the Shammar tribe, through whose "tents" the caravans had to pass. See E. A. Wallis Budge, *By Nile and Tigris (1886-1913)* (London: 1920), pp. 447-49; Edward B. B. Barker, *Syria and Egypt under the Last Five Sultans of Turkey; Being the Experiences, during Fifty Years, of Mr. Consul-General Barker* (London: 1876), vol. 2, p. 82; M. Niebuhr, *Travels through Arabia, and Other Countries in the East* (Edinburgh: 1792), vol. 1, pp. 174-75. For a history of the tribes that had settled around Mosul, see Sulaymān Sā'igh, *Ta'rīkh al-Mawsil* (Cairo: 1923) vol. 1, pp. 53-55. Consult also Albert H. Hourani, "The Fertile Crescent in the Eighteenth Century," in his *A Vision of History; Near Eastern and Other Essays* (Beirut: 1961), pp. 35-70.

10. Writing at the end of the 19th century, Vital Cuinet estimated the city's population at 6,000, of whom fully one-third were "Greek Orthodox," obviously meaning Syrian Orthodox or Jacobites. See his *La Turquie d'Asie* (Paris: 1891), vol. 2, p. 515.

11. Xavier Jacob, "The Christians of South-East Turkey," *E.C.R.* 1 (1967-1968): 401; Sykes, *The Caliphs' Last Heritage*, p. 356. For more on Midyat see below, pp. 103-104.

12. Parry, *Six Months in a Syrian Monastery*, pp. 299-300; Silbernagl, p. 307; Graf, *Geschichte*, vol. 1, p. 70; Spuler, "Die west-syrische Kirche," p. 329. In 1555 the patriarch would temporarily return to Diyarbakr. Consult W. De Vries, "Dreihundert Jahre syrisch-Katholische Hierarchie," *Ostkirchliche Studien* 5 (1956): 138-139; *N.C.E.*, vol. 9, p. 196; Spuler, ibid., pp. 336-37. Cf. W. Wright, *Catalogue of Syriac Manuscripts in the British Museum* (London: 1870), vol. 1, p. 16, col. 1.

13. According to a 1753 report of the Carmelite bishop of Baghdad, Mardin had a population of 620 Syrian families, only 20 of them Catholic. See Herbert Chick, *A Chronicle of the Carmelites in Persia and the Papal Mission of the XVIIth and XVIIIth Centuries* (London: 1939), vol. 2, p. 1264.

14. Southgate, *Visit*, p. 287; *M.H.* 71 (Oct. 1875): 291.

15. *M.H.* 48 (April 1852): 108: Budge, *By Nile and Tigris, vol. 1, pp. 431-32.*

16. *James S. Buckingham, Travels in Mesopotamia* (London: 1827), pp. 177-392. For a print of the city illustrating its picturesque location, see *M.H.* 71 (Oct. 1875): 19, 289.

17. J. P. Fletcher, *Notes from Ninevah* (Philadelphia: 1850), pp. 87-88. For a more favorable impression of the site and surroundings of the monastery, see William F. Ainsworth, *A Personal Narrative of the Euphrates Expedition*, 2 vols. (London: 1888), 2: 342-44.

18. W. A. Wigram and T. A. Wigram, *Cradle of Mankind: Life in Eastern Kurdistan* (London: 1914), p. 44; "Lamhat Khaṭifah 'an Dayr al-Za'farān wa-Mār Kabri'il," *M.B.* 4 (Jan. 1965): 138; Badger, *The Nestorians and Their Rituals,* vol. 1, pp. 50-51; Parry, *Six Months,* pp. 105 ff.

19. Southgate, *Visit,* pp. 196-97; for an excellent photograph of the interior and exterior of Dayr al-Za'farān, see A. Gabriel, *Voyages archéologiques dans la Turquie orientale* (Paris: 1950), plates 11 and 24; see also Conrad Preusser, *Nordmesopotamische Baudenkmäler Altchristlicher und*

islamischer Zeit (Leipzig: 1911), pp. 49-53 and plates 62-65, which have reproductions illustrating the most striking features of the monastery.

20. *N.C.E.*, vol. 4, p. 851.
21. See p. 5.
22. See Joseph, *The Nestorians.*
23. J. Labourt, *Le christianisme dans l'empire Perse sous la dynastie Sassanide (A.D. 224-632)* (Paris: 1904), pp. 217-21; Browne, *The Eclipse of Christianity*, p. 11; Sahas, *John of Damascus*, p. 25; Theodor Noldeke, *Sketches from Eastern History*, trans. J. S. Black (London: 1892), p. 244.
24. Chick, *A Chronicle of the Carmelites in Persia*, vol. 1, p. 158, n.1, p. 375; vol. 2, p. 1067. For more on the Catholic missions in Iran, see pp. 38,52.
25. The total Christian population of Mosul was estimated at about 9,000 early in this century. Of these, about 2,500 were Syrian Catholics, formerly Jacobites. See Young, "Mosul," pp. 233-34.
26. Filib Ṭarrāzi, *Khazā'in al-Kutub al-'Arabiyah fi al-Khāfiqin* (Beirut: n.d.), vol. 2, p. 768; Ibn al-'Ibri, *Chronography*, vl. 1, pp. 474-75. For a description of the region where the village lies, at the turn of this centruy, see Mark Sykes, *The Caliphs' Last Heritage* (London: 1915), p. 340.
27. For a detailed and scholarly historical study of Qaraqūsh and other Jacobite and Syrian Catholic towns and villages and their churches on the plains of Mosul, Consult J. M. Fiey, *Assyrie chrétienne* (Beirut: 1967-68), vol. 2, pp. 416-69); for details on Barṭalla, see Suhayl Qāsha, "Bartalla," *M.B.* 11, no. 101 (1973): 17-20; 12, no. 116 (1974): 326-28, and issues in between.
28. For a discussion of the non-Chalcedonian Christians, see pp. 5-6.
29. *N.C.E.*, vol. 1, p. 286, where in 1964 Aleppo is reported as the See of five Catholic and three non-Catholic bishops.
30. De Vries, "Dreihundert Jahre . . . ," pp. 138-39. See also Antoine Rabbath, *Documents inédits pour servir a l'histoire du christianisme en Orient* (Paris: 1910), vol. 1, p. 451, where Aleppo is noted as the fourth largest and richest in the Sultan's realm. Buckingham in the 1820s reported this city larger in population than both Baghdad and Damascus; consult his *Travels*, pp. 380-81.
31. See p. 39.
32. Albert H. Hourani, "Christians of Lebanon," *E. C. Q.* 12 (Spring 1957): 144. See also Horace K. Mann, *The Lives of the Popes in the Middle Ages* (St. Louis, Mo.: 1928), vol. 14, p. 211.
33. For the letter to Urban VIII, see p.
34. Badger, vol. 1, p. 43. See also Frederic von den Steen de Jehay, *De la situation légale des sujets Ottomans non-muslmans* (Brussels: 1906), p. 242; Qasha, "al-Lughat al'Arabiyah," *M R* 7 (May 1969), 356-64; Mār Ighnāṭiyūs Afrām I, "Al-Alfaẓ al-Suryāniyah fi al-Ma'ājim al-'Arabiyah," *Revue de l'Academie de Damas* 23 (1948): 161-82, 321-46, 481-506; 24 (1949): 3-21, 161-81, 321-42, 481-99; 25 (1950): 2-22, 161-78, 364-98; Yūsuf Hubayqah al-Lubnāni, "al-Dawāthir al-Suryāniyah fi Lubnān wa-Sūriyah," *al-Mashriq* 37 (1939): 290-412.
35. Parry, *Six Months*, 343.
36. At the beginning of the 19th century Buckingham found that in some towns

the turban was the only part of the dress in which particular colors were not to be used—green being prohibited even to Muslims unless they were the descendants of the Prophet Muḥammad.

37. See his *Journey in the Caucasus, Persia, and Turkey in Asia*, trans. Charles Heneage (London: 1875), vol. 2, p. 158.

38. Great Britain, F.O. 97/425 (1867). See also Buckingham, 185.

39. This qualification the Englishman could have made regarding Catholic-Anglican relations in his native England, substituting Anglicans for "Mahometans."

40. Most probably referring to the defence of Mosul about a hundred years earlier when Nadir Shah had besieged the city. See R. W. Olson, "The Siege of Mosul, War and Revolution" (Ph. D. diss., Indiana University, Bloomington, 1973), pp. 313-14; Carsten Niebuhr, *Reisebeschreibung nach Arabien und andern Umliegende Landern* (Graz: reprint, 1968), vol. 2, p. 367. Niebuhr remarks that according to the Muslim population, the defence of the city was successful because of the Christian effort.

41. Southgate, *Tour*, p. 253; Badger, vol. 1, pp. 73-74. Claudius Rich had in the 1830s visited the burial place of 'Abd al-Jalili, ancestor of the then "Mahometan governor of Mosul," at the Church of Mār Sham'ūn Sawa. See his *Narrative of a Residence in Koordistan and on the Site of Ancient Ninevah* (London: 1836), vol. 2, p. 120. For more on the Jalili family, see Olson, "Siege of Mosul."

42. The theologian-mystic Al-Ghazzāli recommended that the non-Muslim should never be greeted first. His greeting may be returned, but it is best to avoid him socially or professionally. See his *Ihya 'Ulūm al-Din* (Būlaq: 1872), vol. 2, p. 157.

43. *M.H.* 53 (1857): p. 269.

44. *Visit*, p. 240.

45. Ibid., p. 269. For more on the Christian ancestral background of Muslims, see pp. 14, p. 150 note 25.

46. *M.H.* 53 (1857): 56; *Visit*, 267. For Muslims' veneration and fear of Christian shrines in folk Islam, see F. W. Hasluck, *Christianity and Islam under the Sultans* (Oxford: 1919), vol. 1, pp. 42, 75-82. *See also* E. A. W. Budge, *The Histories of Rabban Hormizd the Persian and Rabban Bar-Idta* (London: 1902), vol. 2, pt. 1, pp. XVII, XX, and passim. The present-day Turkish author Yashar Kemal in his book *Iron Earth, Copper Sky*, writes of the naive world of the Anatolian villagers drawing on the atmosphere of superstition, fear, and wild fancies of ignorance that possess the Anatolian villagers of our day; to them, specters, saints, devils, witches, and jinns seem to be as real as they were in the past century. See Anthony Thwaite, "Turkish Delights,' *New York Times Book Review,* 19 Aug. 1979, pp. 13, 21.

47. *Report*, 1862, p. 97; H. E. Wilkie Young, "Mosul in 1909," *Middle Eastern Studies* 7 (1971): 234.

48. See his *Nestorians*, vol. 1, p. 57.

49. See his communication in *S.M.* 5 (1840): 59. A British consular report described the Jacobite peasantry as a "a fine, manly, handsome race." See F.O. 78/3132 (1880), "Confidential," sec. no. 68. Consult also Bertram

Dickson, "Journeys in Kurdistan," *Geographical Journal* 35 (1910): 278. Speaking of the Jacobites of Tur Abdin, Dickson described them as "a brave, tall, handsome race, physically superior...to any other that I have come across in Asia Minor."

50. C. H. Wheeler, *Ten Years on the Euphrates* (Boston: 1868), p. 46; B. Dickson, ibid., 361; Mark Sykes, "The Kurdish Tribes of the Ottoman Empire," *Royal Anthropological Institute of Great Britain and Ireland Journal* 38 (1908): 475, where he describes one tribal confederation as "partly complete nomads, partly completely sedentary, and partly semi-nomadic." See also Shākir Khasbak, *al-Akrād, Dirāsah Jughrāfīyah Ithnughrāfīyah* (Baghdad: 1972), p. 272; Derk Kinnane, *The Kurds and Kurdistan* (London: 1964), pp. 8-20.

51. Sykes, ibid., p. 454. See also Blanche W. Stead, "Kurdistan for Christ," *M.W.* 10 (1920): 248.

52. As in most of the other provinces of the Ottoman empire the Kurdish regions were inhabited by peoples of varying nationalities and religious sects. Each separate village maintained its own characteristics and identity, setting it apart from its neighboring villages.

53. Stead, "Kurdistan for Christ," 243; Khasbak, *al-Akrad*, pp. 335-44.

54. In Kurdish society men and women often work together, women holding property with equal rights and enjoying considerably more freedom than their Turkish, Arab, and Persian sisters. See Stead, ibid., p. 248; Kinnane, *The Kurds and Kurdistan*, p. 13. For a detailed discussion of the Kurdish women, see Khasbak, *al-Akrād* pp. 426-53, and Henry H. Hansen, *The Kurdish Woman's Life: Field Research in a Muslim Society, Iraq* (Copenhagen: 1961); H. R. al-Jawashli, *al-Ḥayāt al-Ijtimā'iyah fi Kurdistān* (Baghdad: 1970).

55. Wheeler, *Ten Years on the Euphrates*, p. 46; Sykes, "Kurdish Tribes," p. 468.

56. See Stead, "Kurdistan for Christ," p. 241.

57. Hogarth, p. 193; Leon Dominian, "The Peoples of Northern and Central Asiatic Turkey," *Bulletin of the American Geographical Society* (New York) 47 (1915): 857.

58. Stead, "Kurdistam for Christ," 242, 244.

59. Ibid., 244; see also Dickson, "Journeys in Kurdistan," p. 365; Sykes describes some semi-nomadic tribes as "wealthy shepherds"—see his "Kurdish Tribes," pp. 453-55.

60. Speaking of the Hamawand nomands, a Kurdish tribe "of some 2,000 rifles," between Kirkuk and Sulaimaniyah early in this century, a British consul describes them as "the terror of all the other Kurds and the surrounding country." See Dickson, pp. 361, 370, 376.

61. See W. Clark, "The Kurdish Tribes of Western Asia," *New Englander and Yale Review* 23 (1864): 36, 38. Sykes praised some semi nomadic Kurdish tribes for their chivalry, valor, "and thieving proclivities." See his *"Kurdish Tribes,"* pp. 454, 456.

62. Ibid., 36; see also Stead, p. 245; F.O. 424/132, inclosure 2 in no. 103 (Diarbekir, 30, April 1882), p. 139, on the Turkish government's method of "treating a whole tribe as rebels on account of some black sheep." Consul

Chermside wrote of "wholesale retaliation in sacking and destroying villages." Ibid.

63. Hogarth, *The Nearer East,* pp. 198-199, 249, where he explains that the cold temperature of the highlands made it impossible to keep the more delicate stock, especially the horses, in the hills throughout the winter. At the same time the summer heat of the plains was hardly less severe and prompted the nomads' speedy return to the higher ground.

64. Ibid. The same would apply to the Bedouin Arabs, whose camel breeding supplied the empire with an essential means of transportation.

65. In Turkey the law forbade people from carrying arms, but only in the case of the rayah Christians was it enforced. This left them under the mercy and protection of the Kurds, to whom they paid tribute usually in money and kind and free labor, a state of complete subordination to a military, dominant caste.

66. Rabbi Israel Joseph Benjamin, who visited Kurdistan in mid 19th century, described these arrangements as "a state of most oppressive slavery." See his *Eight Years in Asia and Africa,* pp. 96, 102—3. It is important to bear in mind that even in France, the feudal lords imposed corvé on the peasants on their lands as late as the end of the 18th century, when the French Revolution abolished them; these charges, imposed on all over 12 years of age, constituted a very heavy burden at times.

67. British Government, inclosure 4 in no. 103 (Diarbekir, 20, April 1882), p. 146.

68. See Lynch, *Armenia Travels and Studies* vol. 2, p. 418; Sykes, *Caliphs' Last Heritage,* p.321; Lord Warkworth, *Notes from a Diary in Asiatic Turkey* (London: 1898), p. 226; F.O. 78/3132 (1880), "Confidential," scct. no. 68. Rabbi Benjamin noted that the Christian and Jewish peasantry were "sometimes powerfully protected" from outside attacks but this was not from "love of justice"; it served the personal interest of the "selfish Kurdish masters." See his *Eight Years,* pp. 96, 102-3.

69. C. Dauphin, "The Rediscovery of the Nestorian Churches of the Hakkari (South Eastern Turkey), *E. C. R.* 8 (1976): 66, n. 27. As late as the beginning of this century Mark Sykes passed through a Christian village where the only Muslims were the servants of the Christian families. See his *Caliphs' Last Heritage,* p. 406; idem, "Kurdish Tribes," pp. 454-55; Dickson, *"Journeys in Kurdistan, "* p. 378.

70. The Christians always spoke fluently the language of their Muslim neighbors. In some cases that was their own mother tongue. See *M.H.* 68 (1871): 110; 86 (1890): 346; 97 (1901): 115; 99 (1903): 352.

71. Fletcher, *Notes from Nineveh,* p. 193.

72. Parry, *Six Months,* p. 324.

73. *Travels in Mesopotamia,* p. 184.

74. Southgate, *Visit,* p. 203; Buckingham, ibid., pp. 183-85.

75. Southgate, ibid., p. 207; Silbernagl, *Verfassung,* p. 308. Cf. Afrâm Barsūm, *Nuzhat al-Adhhān fi Ta'rīkh Dayr al-Za'farān* (Mardin: 1917), pp. 149-51. For a study of Jacobite convents and monasteries, see Bahija F. Lovejoy, "Christian Monasteries in Mesopotamia" (Ph.D. diss., Radcliffe College, *Cambridge, Mass.,* 1957); R. Bābu Ishāq, *Ahwāl al-Naṣāra*

Baghdad, pp. 75-134; al-Shabushti, *Kitāb al-Diyārāt,* ed. Kurkis 'Awwād (Baghdad: 1951); *M.B.* 6 (1968): 475-79; T.G.J. Joynboll, ed., *Yaqūt's Marāṣid al-Itlā' 'Ala Asmā' al-Amkinah wa-al-Baqā'* (Leyden: 1853), vol. 1, pp. 426, 429-32, 436, 440; Luke, *Mosul,* pp. 104-21.

76. When the Uniat churches were being reorganized in the 19th century, difficulties arose with the Apostolic See over its attempt to regulate the election of the patriarch and bishops, especially to restrain the traditional participation of the laity in the elections.
77. Silbernagl, *Verfassung* pp. 305-6.
78. Parry, *Six Months,* pp. 316-17; Euw, p. 45.
79. See Badger, commenting on the Jacobites, vol. 1, pp. 44. Horatio Southgate in the 1840s claimed that he knew every Jacobite who was considered a learned man among them, yet he could enumerate "only three or four who are good scholars in Syriac." See his *Visit,* pp. 138-39.
80. For the recognition of the Catholic Armenian patriarch, see pp. 49-50.
81. De Jehay, p. 37; Parry, *Six Months,* pp. 314-15; Badger, *The Nestorians and Their Rituals,* Spuler, "West-syrische Kirche, " p. 339; Silbernagl, p. 308. Silbernagl gives 1882 as the date when the community attained autonomy.
82. Ibid., p. 315. See also de Jehay, *De la situation légale,* pp. 37, 239.
83. H. F. Tozer, *Turkish Armenia and Eastern Asia Minor* (London: 1881), pp. 225-26; W. St. Clair Tisdall, *The Conversion of Armenia to the Christian Faith* (London: 1897), pp. 156-57; 181-82; Malachia Ormanian (formerly Armenian patriarch of Constantinople). *The Church of Armenia—Her History, Doctrine, Rule, Discipline, Liturgy, Literature, and Existing Conditions,* 2d ed. (London: 1955), p. 16; Graf, *Geschichte,* vol. 2, p. 267. For details on the close relations that at times have existed between the Armenians and Jacobites, see Sanjian, *Armenian Communities in Syria* p. 9; Segal, *Edessa,* p. 208. Cf. Fortescue, *The Lesser Eastern Churches,* p. 432, n. 3. Fortescue notes that the Armenian church is not strictly in communion with the other Monophysite churches, "and never has been."

3. Catholics, Consuls, and Conversion

1. Mār Ighnāṭiyūs Afrām I Barsūm, *Ta'rikh Tūr 'Abdin,* trans. from Syriac, G. B. Bahnām (Junieh, Lebanon: 1963), pp. 327-34.
2. Georg Graf, *Geschichte de christlichen arabrichen Literature,* 4 vols., 3: 52—54; Berthold Suler, "Die west syrische (monophysitische) Kirche unter der Islam," pp. 336-37.
3. George Every, "Syrian Christians in Jerusalem, 1183-1283, 7 (Jan.-Mar. 1947): 47, 51.
4. Kamel S. Salibi, "The Maronite Church in the Middle Ages and Its Union with Rome," pp. 92-104.
5. The terms of the union were negotiated later when Ignatius Dāwud formally submitted his profession in a letter to Pope Innocent IV, in 1247. See Ishāq Armalah al-Suryāni, *al-Hurūb al-Salibiyah fi al-Athār al-Suryāniyah* (Beirut: 1929), pp. 72-77, 219-20; Matthew Spinka, "The Effect of the Crusades upon Eastern Christianity," pp. 260-61. See also Graf, *Geschichte,* 1:71.

6. *N.C.E.,* 13: 900; Horace K. Mann, *The Lives of the Popes in the Middle Ages,* 14: 211, 215-16; 13: 415-16.

7. Steven Runciman, *A History of the Crusades,* 3 vols., 3:232.

8. Also by the 1340s the Franciscans had already reestablished themselves in Beirut, turning their monastery, attached to the Church of the Saviors—the Serail Mosque of today—into one of the largest establishments of their order in Syria. See Salibi, "Maronite Church," p. 100.

9. That same year the Maronite church was officially recognized as having reaccepted union with Rome; Maronite union with Rome since the last crusading kindom was considered nominal. Ibid., pp 99-100.

10. Armalah, "Fi al-Baṭaryarkyah al-Anṭākiyah," p. 597; cf. *N.C.E.,* 5:17; 13:901

11. Cf. Stephen, Rahhal, "Some Notes on the West Syrians," pp. 376-77. See also J. W. Etheridge, *The Syrian Churches,* p. 149, where he incorrectly states that the first Jacobite patriarch who entered into communion with the See of Rome did so in 1552.

12. See Joseph, pp. 40-41.

13. These papal concessions issued in letters dated respectively 3 and 4 May, 1493, are often referred to as Alexandrine bulls.

14. The feast of the Most Holy Rosary in the Catholic Church, originally known as the feast of our Lady of Victory, commemorates the victory at Lepanto.

15. "Sacred Congregation de Propaganda Fide (1662-1922)." *Catholic Historical Review* 6 (Jan 1921):480.

16. Consult Charles K. von Euw, "The Union of the Syros-Jacobites with Rome in the Mid-Seventeenth Century," pp. 48-49. Cf. Etheridge *Syrian Churches,* p. 149; Leonard Abel, *Une mission religieuse en Orient au seizième,* trans. and annot. by Adolphe d'Avril (Paris: 1865).

17. Euw, "Union," pp. 50-51; A. Hayek, "Le relazioni della chiese siro-giacobita con la Santa Sede dal 1143 al 1656" (Ph.D. diss., Papal Institute of Oriental Studies, Rome, 1936), pp. 109-88.See also Graf, *Geschichte,* 4:12-13; Levi della Vida, "Il soggiorno a Roma del patriarca siro Ignazio Naʿmatallah," in his *Documenti intorno alle relazioni delle chiese orientali con la S. Sede durante il pontificato di Gregorio XIII* (Vatican City: Studi e Testi, 1948), pp. 1-113.

18. Graf, *Geschichte,* 4:13.

19. Euw, "Union," p. 55; Hayek, "Relazioni della chiesa siro-giacobita," pp. 189-93. It is of interest to point out here that papal efforts toward reunion with the Middle Eastern churches in the 16th century were more successful among the Nestorians than the Jacobites since the former were more independent of Ottoman control. The position of the Jacobites was "more securely guaranteed by the Turks" and their patriarch had closer relations with the central government than the patriarch of the Nestorians. See Joseph, *Nestorians,* pp 33-7; Parry, *Six Months,* p. 302; Samuel Giamil, *Genuinae relationes inter sedem Apostolicam et Assyriorum Orientalium seu Chaldaeorum ecclesiam* (Rome: 1902).

20. *N.C.E.,* 10:963. Leopold von Ranke was of the opinion that Pope Urban favored France during the Thirty Years' War in order to humiliate the Hapsburgs. See ibid., 14:482. See also Antonio da Silva Rego, *Le*

patronage Portugais de l'Orient apercu historique, trans. from Portuguese by Jean Haupt (Lisbon: 1957); Georges Goyau, *La condition internationale des missions catholiques* (Paris: 1929), pp. 25-46.

21. *N.C.E.,* 9:932. The Jacobite church in India was indirectly involved in this conflict between the papacy and Portugal. See C. M. Agur, *Church History of Travancore* (Madras: 1903), pp. 331-32; T. Whitehouse, *Lingerings of Light in a Dark Land* (Loudon, 1873), p. 287; Eugene Cardinal Tisserant, *Eastern Christianity in India* (London: 1957), p. 105. See also pp. .

22. Euw, "Union," p. 67.

23. Chick, *A Chronicle of the Carmelites,* 2 vols., 1:683; 2:1254-56. See also Maria-Joseph, A. S. Corde Jesu, C. D., "La mission des Carmes á Baghdad et l'influence francaise en Orient," *E. C.* 3 (1913): 293-317.

24. Writing from Isfahan, the papal vicar general, an Italian, wrote that the bishop of Baghdad, a Frenchman, was "most terribly antagonistic to Italians . . . , a partisan of France beyond all moderation." See Chick, *Chronicle,* 2:1210-11; 1:682-83.

25. F.O. 97/425, Consul J. H. Skene to Sir H. Bulver, inclosure in no. 12 (20 August, 1860);see also Robert M. Haddad, *Syrian Christians in Muslim Society: An Interpretation* (Princeton: 1970), pp. 31-43.

26. Chick, *Chronicle,* 1:xxx; P. Joseph Kiera, "Baghdad und die Kapuzinermission," *Seraphisches Weltapostolat des Hl. Franz v. Assist* 9 (Feb. 1933): 36.

27. P. Sabatier, *Life of St. Francis of Assisi,* trans. L. S. Houghton (New York: 1894), p. 171; M. Roncaglia, *St. Francis of Assisi and the Middle East* (Cairo: Franciscan Center of Oriental Studies, n.d.). See also J. Spencer Trimingham, *The Christian Approach to Islam in the Sudan* (Oxford: 1948), p. 43.

28. Chick, *Chronicle,* 1:3; E. Dhunes, "Les congrégations françaises en Palestine," E.O. 8 (1905): 90-99, 166-74; Karl Bihlmeyer, *Church History,* 3 vols., 2:285; 3:431-32.

29. For details on the 17th century Catholic missions in Aleppo, see Ignazio da Seggiano, "Documenti Inediti Sull Apostolato dei Minori Cappuccini nel Vicino Oriente (1623-1683)", *Collectania franciscana* (Rome) 18 (1948): 118-244; 22 (1952): 339-86; 23 (1953): 297-338; idem "L'Opera dei Cappuccini per l'Unione dei Cristiani nel Vicino Oriente durante il Secolo XVII," *Orientalia christiana analecta,* no. 163 (Rome: Pontifical Institute for Oriental Studies, 1962); G. Goyau, "Une Capitale Missionaire du Lavant: Alep, dans la premiere moltee du XVII siècle no. 2 (June 1934): 161-86; Rocco da Cesinale, *Storia delle missioni del Capuccini* (Rome: 1873), vol. 3; Francois Tournebize, "Le catholicisme à Alep au XVII siècle (1623-1703)," *E.C.* 3 (1913): 351-70.

30. Officially known as Brothers of the Blessed Virgin Mary of Mount Carmel—from Mount Carmel in Palestine where a group of hermits had settled—they received in 1209 a strict monastic rule from the Latin patriarch of Jerusalem, approved by the papacy in 1226.

31. M. John Eldred, *The Voyage of M. John Eldred to Tripolis in Syria by Sea, and from Thence by Land and River to Babylon and Balsara, Anno*

1583 (New York: Hakluyt Voyages, 1927), vol. 3, p. 325.

32. Cited in Euw, "Union," pp. 76-77.

33. Ibid., p. 37; Alexander Russell, "A Description of Aleppo" (vol. 13 of *The World Displayed,* p. 75), where he estimates the Jacobites ('Syrians") to be the most numerous next to the "Greeks" and Armenians.

34. De Vries, "Dreihundert Jahre," p. 139.

35. Israel Joseph Benjamin, *Eight Years in Asia and Africa, from 1846-1855* (Hanover: 1859), p. 46.

36. Great Britain, Foreign Office papers, Consul J. H. Skene to Sir H. Bulivar, no. 9 (Aleppo, 4 Aug. 1860). See also E. R. Hambye, "The 'Syrian' Quadrilateral Today," *E.C.Q.,* no. 4 (1964): p. 330.

37. Chick, *Chronicle,* 1:375-76, 493, 505-6, 715; 2:1081.

38. Ibid.

39. Euw, "Union," p. 56.

40. See *fatwa* given on this subject in Eli Smith, *Toleration in the Turkish Empire* (Boston: 1846), pp. 245, 251. See also H. Rassam, *Asshur and the Land of Nimrod,* p. 160; H.A.R. Gibb and Harold Bowen, *Islamic Society and the West* pp. 245, 251.

41. The Protestant missionaries among the Middle Eastern Christians in the 19th century also found it difficult to work within the established structure of these churches even though not for precisely the same reasons as the Catholics.

42. De Vries, "Dreihundert Jahre," pp. 140-41.

43. Graf, *Geschichte,* 4:44; cf. P. P. Raphael, *The Role of the Maronites in the Return of the Oriental Churches,* trans. P. A. Eid (Youngstown, O.: 1946), p. 100, where Mardin is given as the birthplace of Andrew; De Vries gives Aleppo as his birthplace—see his "Dreihundert Jahre," p. 41.

44. It is said that the Maronite patriarch Joseph al-'Āqūri (1644-48) received Akhijan into his church at Qannūbin where he had gone to study the Catholic doctrine at the recommendation of a Carmelite father to whom Andrew had made his profession of faith.

45. Antoine Rabbath, *Documents inédits pour servir a l'histoire du christianisme en Orient,* 2 vols., 1:452.

46. The story of Akhijan is told at length in Father Euw's doctoral dissertation, already noted. In my presentation I have depended chiefly on Father Euw's scholarly work, conducted at the rich archives of the Catholic church in Rome. For other sources on the history of Akhijan, see Tarrāzi, *Asdaq mā -Kān,* 1: 306-10; idem, *Al-Salāsil al-Ta'rīkhiyah* (Beirut: 1910), pp. 178-99; Afrām Naqqāshah, *Kitāb 'Ināyat al-Rahmān fi Hidāyat al-Suryān* (Beirut: 1910), pp. 35-69; De Vries, "Dreihundret Jahre," pp. 137 seq.

47. De Vries, "Dreihundret Jahre," pp. 142-43.

48. See Euw, "Union," pp. 86-87; De Vries, ibid.; Yūsūf Ilyās al-Dibs, *Ta'rīkh Sūriyah* (Beirut: 1900), 4:713-14.

49. Among the reasons given for the issuance of the decree was the testimony of the Qadi of Aleppo that "the monk Andrā'ūs was elected bishop because of his ability and merits," and because "conforming to the ancient custom, he has paid 1,000 Misriyat as bakhshish." See Tarrāzi, *al-Salāsil,* pp. 180-81.

50. See Ṭarrāzi, ibid.

51. The Propaganda did not see this situation as fitting and suggested that the bishop be provided some subsidy for his maintenance. See Euw, "Union," p. 181.

52. Rabbath, *Documents in édits* 2:76; Euw, ibid., p. 104. Consult also De Vries, "Dreihundret Jahre," pp. 144-45, where he notes that there was a time when Akhijan had proceeded with caution; he quotes P. Sylvester von St. Aignan's report of 1 April, 1658 to the Congregation Fide in Rome that Akhijan still commemorated Dioscorus in solemn mass. On Dioscorus, see p. 5

53. Rabbath, ibid., 1:458.

54. Interestingly, when Andrew asked Rome to pass judgement over his juridical status, the Catholic hierarchy took the position that Andrew had no legitimate right to the Jacobite See of Aleppo and possessed no true jurisdiction in the Jacobite community.

55. Euw, "Union," p. 129.

56. Ibid., p. 130. Cf. De Vries, "Dreihundret Jahre," pp. 144-45, where he attributes Andrew's refusal to return to his perception that the priests did not mean what they said.

57. Rabbath *Documents inédits* 1:454; 2:287; Ewu, ibid.; De Vries, ibid.

58. Rabbath, ibid., 1:455.

59. Ibid.

60. Euw, "Union," p. 256.

61. Armalah, *Athar Faransa*, pp. 111-13; idem, "Fi Baṭaryarkiyah al'Anṭākiyah," p. 599; Buṭrus Naṣri al-Kaldāni, *Kitāb Dhakhirat . . .* (Mosul: 1913), pp. 280-85. Cf. *N.C.E.*, 13:901.

62. Archives of the Sacred Congregation of Propaganda Fide, *Scritture riferite nelle congregazioni generali*, vol. 241, fogl. 288v, and *Acta*, vol. 31, fogl. 217v, quoted by Euw, "Union," pp. 270, n. 80; 271, n. 83.

63. For the text of the *barā'ah*, see Appendix A. Consult also Ṭarrāzi, *Salāsil*, pp. 187-88.

64. See Graf, *Geschichte*, 4:45.

65. Rabbath, *Documents inédits*, 1:466; De Vries, "Dreihundret Jahre," p. 151.

66. Euw, "Union," pp. 279-80.

67. Text in Ṭarrāzi, *Salāsil*, pp. 187-88.

68. Documents of Propaganda Fide quoted by Euw, "Union," pp. 286-87; De Vries, "Driehundret Jahre," p. 151.

69. See pp. 4-5.

70. *N.C.E.*, 13:901.

71. Ibid.; Graf, *Geschichte*, 3:57.

72. Rabbath, *Documents Inédits* 1.105; Ṭarrāzi, *Asdaq mā-Kān, pp. 310-15;* Armalah, *Athar Faransa*, pp. 113-19; al-Kaldani, *Dhakhirat al-Adhhān*, pp. 185-92.

73. Armalah, ibid., pp. 110-17; *N.C.E.*, 13:901.

74. Wilhelm De Vries, *Rom und die Patriarchate des Ostens* (Munich: 1963), p. 96; Berthold Spuler, "Die west-syrische (monophysitische) Kirche," p. 337; Ignatius Mansourati, "Kurze Darstellung der syrischen katholischen

Kirche," trans. H. E. Klemens, *Der christliche Osten* 18 (1963): 117-18.
75. Raphael, *The Role of the Maronites,* pp. 107, 111; Rabbath, *Documents inédits,* 1:121-22; cf. Gibb and Bowen *Islamic Society,* vol. l, pt. 2, p. 248, n. 1; Graf, *Geschichte,* 3:57; Naqqāshah, p. 166, Ṭarrāzi, *Aṣdaq mā-Kān,* pp. 316-19.
76. Quoted by De Vries, "Driehundert Jahre, " pp. 156-57.
77. Raphael, *The Role of the Maronites* pp. 111-13.
78. For more on the Malabar union, see Appendix C.
79. See map, p. ii.
80. Chick, *Chronicle,* 1:623; P. Giambattista da Castrogiovanni et al., "Sunto Storico e Descrittivo della Missione Apostolica dei Minori Cappuccini nella Mesopotamia," *Analecta ordinis minorum Cappuccinorum* (Rome) 15 (1899): 199-208, 231-41, 263-71, 306-9, 340-45; Sā'igh, *Ta'rikh al-Mawṣil,* 1:323.
81. For a discussion of their present-day situation see pp. 111-12.
82. Graf, *Geschichte,* 4:31-32; al-Dibs, 3:714.
83. Graf, ibid., 4:60-61.
84. Ibid., 4:31-32. See Armalah, "Fi al-Baṭaryarkiyah al-Anṭākiyah," pp. 664-65. Before the patriarch's death, writes Armalah, he had expressed his wish to the bishops that Michael Jarwah be elected to succeed him.
85. Graf, *Geschichte,* 4:61; Armalah, ibid.
86. Armalah, ibid., gives January 1782 as the year of his enthronement.
87. Ibid., 3:58.
88. Ibid., 3:53; 4:34-35; 61, where Matthew is referred to as the patriarch of Tur Abdin.
89. See Pierre Chalfoun, "Le patriarche Michel Giarve" (Ph.D. diss., Papal Institute of Oriental Studies. (Rome, 1961), pp. 133 et seq.; De Vries, *Rom und die Patriarchate,* pp. 96-97; Graf, *Geschichte,* 4:31-32. See also Frédéric von den Steen de Jehay, *De la situation légale des sujets Ottomans non-muslmans,* p. 239.
90. Mount Lebanon served as a refuge for other Catholic proselytes persecuted by their Orthodox "brethren." For the case of the Armenian Catholics in Lebanon, see Panos S. Jeranian, "Catholic Armenian and Maronite Relations in Mt. Lebanon, 1720-1840" (Masters thesis, American University of Beirut, 1971).
91. al-Khūri Afrām Aḥmardiqnuh, "Nabdhah Ta'rikhiyah fi Ahwāl al-Millah al-Ya'qūbiyah" (unpaginated ms. at the library of the Sharfeh monastery). See also Chalfoun "Patriarche," pp. 55-58, 169 et seq.; for a translation of Jarwah's works, see Naqqāshah, "'Ināyat al-Rahmān," pp. 186-382; L. Cheikho, "Autobiographie du patriarche Ignace-Michel Djarwe, *R.O.C.* 6 (1901): 382-401; see also ms. entitled "Qissah Mukhtaṣarah fi māJara lil-Sayyid Ignāfiyus Mikhā'il Jarwah..." in the Sharfeh monastery, ms. no. 167 in collection marked 'Atāiq Ta'rikhiyah Suryāniyah; al-Dibs, Ta'rikh Suriyah 4:714.
92. See pp. 35-6.
93. See pp. 44-45.
94. De Vries, *Rom und die Patriarchate,* p. 97; Graf, *Geschichte,* 4:61; al-Kaldāni, *Dhakhirat al-Adhhān,* pp. 303-5; Armalah, *Athar Faransa, pp. 123-28.*

95. See Jean Chahin, "*Les patriarches de l'*église syrienne catholique," *E.O.* (Paris 1897-1898), pp. 202 et seq.; Zananiri, *Pape et patriarchs,* p. 197; al-Kaldāni, ibid., pp. 447 et seq.

96. F. Mourret, *A History of the Catholic Church,* trans. Newton Thompson (London: 1955), 7:509-510.

97. Pauline Jaricot at the age of 21 formed in 1820 the Association to Aid the Society of Foreign Missions in Paris. In 1922, on its centenary, the society was raised by Pope Pius XI to papal status and its headquarters transferred from Lyons to Rome, where it was placed under the Congregation for the Propagation of the Faith. See Katherine Burton, *Difficult Star-The Life of Pauline Jaricot* (New York: 1947), p. 59; George Gorfee, *Pauline Jaricot, une laïque engágee* (Paris: 1962), pp. 36-45, 111-18.

98. The French government, no longer "Catholic," would often manifest hostility to the French church. At times the revolutionary ardor erupted into violence, as in 1828-30, which led to the expulsion of the Jesuits, but in international and not domestic politics were to help the church in its missions.

99. About 57 Ottoman-Egyptian ships were destroyed and 8,000 soldiers and sailors were killed within three hours. See Shaw and Shaw, 2:30.

100. For details on this Russo-Turkish conflict, see pp. 83-84.

101. See C. E. Frazee, "The Formation of the Armenian Catholic Community in the Ottoman Empire," *E.O.R.* 7 (1975): 149-63; Leon Arpee, *A History of Armenian Christianity* (New York: 1946) pp. 57-58, 262; Mourret *History,* 7:530-31. For the text of the *barā'at,* in French, officially recognizing the Catholic Armenians as a millet, see George Young, *Corps de droit Ottoman* (Oxford: 1905), 2:103-4.

102. The question of Latinization would continue to pose a problem. Later in the century, in 1885, the Congregation repealed the ruling and toward the very end of the century, in 1898, Pope Leo permitted Middle Eastern non-Catholic Christians to enter the Latin rite if the individual made this transfer a condition of becoming Catholic. Vatican Council II in the mid-1960s forbade all transfers from one rite to another, enabling the churches united with Rome (Uniats) to preserve many of the forms and practices of their non-Catholic ancestral church, making Catholicism in Muslim lands more familiar and acceptable to the Christians themselves as well as to their governments.

103. Mansourati, "*Kurze Darstellung,*" 118 Cf. de Jehay, *De la situation legale,* p. 239, where 1830 is given as the date of this recognition, an improbable date since the Armenian Catholics, the first Catholic millet to be so acknowledged, were not officially recognized until January 1831. Spuler also gives the date of the Syrian Catholic recognition as 1830. See his "West-syrische Kirche," p. 338.

104. Mourret, *History,* 8:737-38.

105. Ibid.

106. Vital Cuinet toward the end of the century gave the population of the valayet of Aleppo as 26,812 Orthodox Jacobites and 20,913 Catholic Jacobites. Half of the *qadā'* of Aleppo itself was estimated to be Syrian Catholic (3704) out of a total of 7814 "Syrians." For the *qadā* of 'Ayntāb,

in the *sanjak* of Aleppo, his figures are 3,000 Orthodox and 3,000 Catholic Jacobites. See his *La Turquie d'Asie,* 4 vols., 2:114.

107. As early as 1830 he was emboldened by the new freedoms granted the Catholics, mentioned above, to come out of his mountain retreat in Lebanon and establish his See in Aleppo.

108. De Jehay, *De la situation légale,* p. 240. Cf.Spuler, "West-syrische Kirche," p. 338. Spuler gives the year 1850 as the date of the move to Mardin; before that he has the Syrian patriarch in "Antiochien" instead of Aleppo.

109. See pp. 35-36.

110. C. E. Frazee, The Formation of the Armenian Catholic Community in the Ottoman Empire," p. 162.

111. *N.C.E.,* 7:18,24

112. See John Joseph, *The Nestorians, and Their Muslim Neighbors,* pp. 29-33.

113. Kiera, "Baghdad," p. 34.

114. Ibid., pp. 36-38. For the law of apostasy as it affected the Jews, see Laurence D. Loeb, *Outcaste, Jewish Life in Southern Iran* (New York: 1977), p. 17. Loeb writes that the law remained in effect officially until 1881, but it was not until Reza Shah days that the practice ended. A Jewish "emissary" to Shiraz in 1903 wrote that there was not a single Jewish family without a convert waiting for a relative to die so that he might inherit his estate.

115. Franciscan document cited by De Vries, "Dreihundert Jahre," p. 152; Euw, "Union," p. 287. On Andrew Akhijan, see pp. 40-6.

116. See p. 37.

117. Chick, *Chronicle,* 1:342, 392, n. 1; Agathangelus of St. Teresa et al., *Chronicle of Events between the Years 1623 and 1733 Relating to the Settlement of the Order of Carmelites in Mesopotamia,* ed. and trans. Herman Gollancz (London: 1927); "Apercu historique sur la mission des Carmes Dechausses a Baghdad (Orient)," *Chroniques du Carmél* (1889-90): 140-43; Polycarpe de Marie-Joseph, C. D., "Missions des Carmes Déchausses en Mésopotamie, " ibid., 2 (1890-91): 267-72, 305-10, 333-38.

118. Steven Runciman, *The Great Church in Captivity,* p. 203.

119. Chick, *Chronicle,* 1:10, passim. Pope Clement VIII had received Shāh 'Abbās's embassy to Europe, headed by Anthony Shirley, at the very beginning of the century (1600). Venice refused to receive the embassy because the Italian city-state was more interested in improving its relations with the Sublime Porte, one of whose delegations was in Venice when Shah 'Abbās's mission was in Rome.

120. Chick, *Chronicle,* 1:641; Louis de Gonzague, "Quelques Apercus de la Vie des Capucins a Baghdad au Debut du XVIII Siécle," *Collectanea Franciscana* (Rome) 4 (1934): 564-77; Philbert de Saint-Didier, "En Syrie et Mesopotamia. La Mission Capucine hier et aujourd'hui" *Missionnaires Capucins* (Paris) 29, no. 133 (1949), 1-14. See also P.P. Raphael, *The Role of the Maronites in the Return of the Oriental Churches,* p. 109, where he refers to a "commandment" from the Sultan which the Greek Orthodox patriarch had obtained in 1725, forbidding the following of the Catholic doctrine and associations with the Latin missionaries. Naqqāshah (p. 120)

speaks of a similar decree, forbidding the reception of Catholic missionaries in non-Catholic homes, issued in 1702.

121. Chick, ibid., and 2:1251.

122. Chick, 1:622. Cf. *Nashrat al-Ahhad,* I (1922): 200, where the Catholic population is estimated at 86 families by mid-18th century.

123. Consult "Apercu historique sur la mission,"

124. *Nashrat al-Ahhad,* 10 (1931): 591-92. See also American Board of Commissioners for Foreign Missions document ABC: 16.9.7., vol. 3, no. 103, "Present Conditions for Evangelistic and Educational Efforts in Baghdad and Mosul." (The correspondence of missionaries of the American Board of Commissioners is deposited at the Houghton Library of Harvard College; it will be referred to as ABC.) (1880).

125. Known as al-Madrasat al-Suryāniyat al-Afrāmiyat al-Ahliyah. See *Nashrat al-Ahhad,* 13 (1934): pp. 182, 187.

126. See his *Through Turkish Arabia* (London: 1894), pp. 270, 275. Less than thirty years before Cowper, a British Foreign Office report from Baghdad broke down the city's Christian inhabitants as follows: Chaldeans (former Nestorians), 180 families; Syrians (Jacobites), 85; Armenian Catholics, 45; Armenian Orthodox, 110; Latins, 30; a Christian population of approximately 2,5000—as compared, interestingly, to a Jewish population of about 20,000. See F. O., 97/425, 24 April, 1867.

127. Horatio Southgate, Jr., *Narrative of a Tour through Armenia,* pp. 279-80.

128. Ibid., where Southgate remarks that the governor's mercy "was at length moved by a large sum of money."

129. *Narrative of a Visit to the Syrian (Jacobite) Church of Mesopotamia,* 137; *Narrative of a Tour,* pp. 279-80. S.M. 6 (1841): 176-77.

130. See also G. P. Badger, *The Nestorians and Their Rituals,* 1:2, where he speaks of the "venality of the Turkish ministers" who had "over and over again been bribed by the two contending parties to annul their preceding decrees."

131. The other two monasteries were those of Mār Mūsa, north of Damascus, on the road to Hims, referred to above, and the Mār Afrām of al-Rughm, near Hammāna in the Lebanon. During most of the 18th century, when the status of the newly formed Catholic Syrian community was still questionable, a vicar patriarchal of that community resided at the convent of al-Rughm. The building was destroyed and its monks massacred by the Druze during the 1860 revolts in the Lebanon. See Tarrāzi, "Dayr Mār Afrām al-Rughm fi Lubnān," in his *Asdaq mā-Kān,* 1:319, et seq.

132. For a detailed account of this tradition, see Southgate, *Narrative of a Visit,* pp. 216-17.

133. Badger, *Nestorians,* 1:94-95; H. C. Luke, *Mosul and Its Minorities,* p. 118.

134. See Tarrāzi, *Asdaq mā-Kān,* 1:328.

135. *M.H.* 55 (1859): 175.

136. See his *Missionary Journal* (1824).

137. *Narrative of a Visit,* p. 284.

138. Almost all the learned theologians and men of letters among the Syriac-speaking Christians at the turn of this century were Catholics, scholars such as Paul Bedjan, Louis Cheikho, Mār Tūma Audo, Mār Afrām Rahmāni,

Ishāq Armalah.

139. The prosperous Jacobite town of Midyat had "not a single school" during the first half of the 19th century when Badger visited it. See his *Nestorians,* 1:54-55.

140. ABC: 16.9.7 vol. 3, no 180; *M.H.* 70 (1874): 176-77; Spuler, "West-syrische Kirche," p. 339.

141. When the author visited the seminary in 1967, it had 26 students: 16 Chaldean, 10 Syrian Catholics. Fourteen seminarians were enrolled in the "theology" program, the rest in "philosophy." The promising among them would continue their studies in Rome.

142. ABC: 16.9.7 vol. 10, no. 38, 55 ("Report of Mosul, 1891-92"), 56; H.E.W. Young, "Mosul in 1909," p. 234.

143. ABC: 16.9.7, vol. 3, no. 103.

4. Protestants, Piety and Politics

1. It is important to bear in mind that the decade of the 1830s marks the period when the Middle Eastern Catholics united with Rome were being formally recognized by the Ottoman government as sects distinct from their mother churches.

2. *The Syrian Churches,* p. 149. By "Syrian" Etheridge meant "Jacobite"; the two appellations will be used interchangeably here. See p. 7.

3. P. E. Shaw, *American Contacts with the Eastern Churches, 1820-1870* (Chicago: 1937), pp. 35-36. Throughout the 19th century the evangelization of the native Christians was considered a necessary antecedent to the successful prosecution of the missionary work for the Muslim population. See resolution passed by the Mardin mission in the summer of 1887, in ABC: 16.9.7, vol. 8, no 157 (Eastern Turkey Mission).

4. Observers on the scene had found the political situation very unstable just before the war's end. Missionaries of the American Board of Commissioners for Foreign Missions (predominantly of the Congregational church) who were in Mosul and Mardin in the summer of 1839 found the Muslim population in a "riotous state." The defeat of the sultan's army had resulted in the return to Diyarbakr and Mardin area of hundreds of soldiers fleeing the battlefield, stripped by highwaymen of their apparel and all that they possessed. The defeat of the Ottoman army was ascribed by the mass of the people to the sultan's reforms, especially to the European uniform that had been introduced during the reigns of Salim III and Maḥmūd II.

5. *Spirit of Missions* 6 (1841): 80. This journal was issued by the Domestic and Foreign Missionary Society of the Protestant Episcopal church of the United States.

6. *S.M.* 1 (1836): 21.

7. It was in 1818 when the American board appointed Levi Parsons and Pliny Fisk to go to Palestine and from there start to survey the entire Middle East. They reached Jerusalem in 1821, starting the first American Protestant mission in Palestine, and from there they set forth to the other provinces of the Ottoman Empire and Persia.

8. Rufus Anderson, *History of the Missions of the American Board of Commissioners for Foreign Missions to the Oriental Churches,* 2 vols. (Boston: 1872), 2:80-81.

9. *Vindication of the Rev. Horatio Southgate: A Letter to the Members of the Protestant Episcopal Church in the United States, from the Rev. Horatio Southgate, Their Missionary at Constantinople* (New York: 1844), p. 7.

10. *S.M.* 6 (1841): 310.

11. Ibid., p. 369.

12. *M.H.* (Dec. 1842): 497.

13. Horatio Southgate, Jr., *Narrative of a Visit to the Syrian (Jacobite) Church*, p. 236. One of the major ambitions of young Southgate soon became "the rescue of the Syrian Church from Popery." See *S.M.* 12 ˙ (1847): 452.

14. See pp. 51-2.

15. *S.M.* 7 (1842): 211.

16. *S.M.* 6 (1841): 308-9.

17. For details, see his *Narrative of a Visit*.

18. *S.M.* 7 (1842): 115.

19. Ibid., p. 284.

20. Ibid., pp. 371-72.

21. Ibid., p. 210.

22. Ibid., 8 (1843): 284.

23. Ibid., p. 289.

24. Ibid., p. 204.

25. Ibid., 9 (1844): 158.

26. Ibid., pp. 321-22. For a discussion of the prominent position of the Armenians as an Ottman millet, see pp. 29-30.

27. Ibid., 12 (1847): 446.

28. Ibid., 9 (1844): 264; 11 (1846): 267.

29. Ibid., 9 (1844): 356.

30. Ibid., p. 264.

31. Southgate served at the Embassy chapel for "several months" in 1844, the year when the question of the Armenians was raised with his church's foreign committee. See *S.M.* 9 (1844): 357.

32. Ibid., p. 356.

33. Ibid., 6 (1841): 281.

34. Ibid., p. 281.

35. Ibid., pp. 248-49.

36. Ibid., 9 (1844): 358.

37. See John Joseph, *The Nestorians and Their Muslim Neighbors*, pp. 81-83.

38. "Chaldeans" and "Syrians" are used in the original. See pp. 7-8, and *S.M.* 7 (1842): 213.

39. Ibid., 6 (1841): 281.

40. Ibid., 11 (1846): 294.

41. Ibid., 12 (1847): 442.

42. In 1849 Southgate published a work in modern Greek, which he entitled, "A Treatise on the Antiquity, Doctrine, Ministry, and Worship of the Anglican Church." See *S.M.* 12 (1847): 452, where missionary Miles mentions a tract by the missionary bishop on "The 'Anglican Church'," single quotes by the Rev. Mr. Miles.

43. Ibid., 9 (1844): 263; 11 (1846): 267.

44. The bishop of Mosul, Bahnām, was sent, followed two years later by the bishop of Jerusalem, Ya'qūb. After a stay of about three years, Ya'qūb left Istanbul, in 1847, for Mardin as the patriarch of his church.

45. *S.M.* 7 (1842): 284.

46. Ibid., 13 (1848): 262.

47. The Jacobite patriarch, after his visit to Istanbul in 1838, had returned and "established everywhere schools for instruction of the children, and appointed teachers." *S.M.* 7 (1842): 167; 6 (1841): 177.

48. Ibid., 7 (1842): 211.

49. Ibid., p. 212.

50. Ibid., 12 (1847): 428, 448, 457; 13 (1848): 406.

51. Ibid., 12 (1847): 414, 418, 428.

52. Ibid., 11 (1846): 267.

53. Ibid., 9 (1844): 430; 11 (1846): 267.

54. For a detailed account of the strained relations between Bishop Southgate and the foreign committee, see P. E. Shaw, *American Contact with the Eastern Churches,* 1820-1870, pp. 35-49, 71-108, where Southgate's contacts and relations with the Jacobites are not studied because that aspect of his mission is deemed to represent an episode of "little importance" (p. 45).

55. *S.M.* 12 (1847): 440-41.

56. Ibid.

57. The Rev. Samuel A. Taylor had returned to his home in Maryland in 1847 because of ill health.

58. For his full report, see ibid., pp. 451—52.

59. Mr. Southgate was much criticized for not doing enough old fashioned preaching. In his 1847 report he wrote that he had given himself "very much to personal intercourse, discussion and correspondence." Ibid., pp. 415-16.

60. Ibid., p. 428.

61. Ibid., 13 (1848): 269.

62. Ibid., p. 266.

63. Ibid., 14 (1849): 278. These were schools opened after 1847 with the encouragement of Bishop Southgate, who was being made aware that the Jacobites should be his prime concern. The bishop of Mosul had started a school in 1847 with 110 students, and the word had spread to Jazirah and Jabal Tur, wherefrom the "most earnest invitations have been pouring," asking the Muṭrān Bahnām for schools. Ibid., 13 (1848): 263.

64. Ibid., 12 (1847): 457-58; 13 (1848): 262, 264-65; 14 (1849): 277-78; 15 (1850): 254.

65. Ibid., pp. 275-76.

66. Ibid., p. 294.

67. Ibid., 15 (1850): 254-55, 280-81. See also James T. Addison, *The Episcopal Church in the United States, 1789-1931* (New York: 1951), p. 148; Shaw, *American Contact,* p. 44.

68. *S.M.* 17 (1852): 365, 384-96. See also Shaw, ibid., p. 63.

69. For details, see Joseph, *Nestorians,* pp. 42 et. seq.

70. For more on Dr. Grant, see ibid., pp. 54 et. seq.

71. See pp. 55-6.
72. See *M.H.* 35 (1839): 398; 36 (1840): 129.
73. Letter written in the fall of 1839 in *M.H.* 36 (1840): 218. See also ibid., 37 (1841): 6.
74. Ibid., 37 (1841): 432; 36 (1840): 218.
75. The revolutionary government of Iraq renamed the province of Mosul officially as Naynawah (Ninevah) after the overthrow of the Hashimite monarcy in 1958.
76. W.I. Chamberlain, *Fifty Years in Foreign Fields* (New York: 1925):,p. 275.
77. Thomas Laurie, *Dr. Grant and the Mountain Nestorians* (Boston: 1874), p. 279.
78. See pp. 56-7.
79. Shaw, *American Contact,* p. 60.
80. The Congregational periodical, *M.H.,* spoke of the French representative in Mosul as a "bigoted papist" who acknowledged that the great object of his coming to that city was "to protect the papists and the cause of the Romish church." It was clear to the New England missionaries that "our papal enemies" were making every possible attempt to have the Americans ordered out of Mosul. See *M.H.* 38 (1842): 497.
81. *M.H.* 38 (1842): 44, 90, 253, 262—63; 46 (1850): 50. Two missionaries and their wives were sent to Mosul in 1842; one of the two couples died on their way.
82. See pp. 59-60.
83. *S.M.* 6 (1841): 174-75. See also pp. 60-1.
84. For details, see Joseph, Nestorians, pp. 46-67.
85. *M.H.* 40 (1844): 5, 165-66; 41 (1845): 116.
86. The secretary of the American Board of Commissioners for Foreign Missions, Rufus Anderson, in his *History of the Missions of the American Board of Commissioners for Foreign Mission to the Oriental Churches,* 2 vols., 2:80 81. Cf. *M H* 46 (1850): 33, 248, where the withdrawal of the mission is mistakenly attributed to Dr. Grant's death.
87. See pp. 65-6.
88. Julius Richter is in error when he writes that this mission was to work among the Nestorians. He confuses it with the earlier one started by Dr. Grant. See his *A History of Protestant Missions in the Near East* (New York: 1910), p. 117. Consult also Anderson, *History,* 2:81; *M.H.* 46 (1850): 53.
89. See p. 66.
90. Letter from Aleppo, written on 5 Dec., 1849, in *M.H.* 46 (1850): 133.
91. *M.H.* 45 (1849): 97.
92. Ibid., 46 (1850): 133.
93. For details on Mr. Perkins and the mission that he headed, See Joseph, *Nestorians,* pp. 44-6.
94. *M.H.* 46 (1850): 33.
95. Mr. Marsh reached Mosul in the spring of 1850 by way of Beirut, Aleppo, Aintab, Urfa, and Diyarbakr. From Diyarbakr he had floated down the Tigris on a raft supported by inflated goatskins, a trip that took him "less than four days." See Anderson, *History,* 2: 81-82; *M.H.* 47 (1851): 189.
96. *M.H.* 49 (1853): 53. For details on the board's Mosul mission, the "Assyrian Mission," at midcentury, see ABC: 16.8.4, vol. 1 (1850-59), nos. 82, 88, 94.
97. See p. 63.
98. *M.H.* 45 (1849): 310-11, 393-96.

99. Ibid., p. 187.
100. Ibid., 46 (1850): 56-60.
101. Ibid., p. 60.
102. Ibid., 46 (1850): 204, 314.
103. Ibid., pp. 57, 133; 54 (1858): 289.
104. Ibid., 46 (1850): 315; 54 (1858): 289.
105. *S.M.* 5 (1840): 58; 6 (1841): 247. See also pp. 57-8.
106. *M.H.* 33 (1837): 33; Justin Perkins, *A Residence of Eight Years in Persia, among the Nestorian Christians with Notices of the Muhammedans* (New York: 1843), p. 253.
107. See "Objects of the Missions to the Oriental Churches, and the Means of Prosecuting Them, " *M.H.* 35 (1839): 40.
108. Ibid., p. 41.
109. Ibid.
110. *M.H.* 48 (1852): 112.
111. O. H. Parry, *Six Months in a Syrian Monastery,* p. 308.
112. *M.H.* 51 (1855): 206.
113. Ibid., 49 (1855): 206.
114. Dr. Lobdell, worn out by the physical and emotional strain of his calling, died in 1856, after four years of service, at the age of 28. See *M.H.* 50 (1854): 352, and William E. Strong, *The Story of the American Board* (Boston: 1910), pp. 210 et. seq.
115. *M.H.* 51 (1855): 114.
116. Ibid., 48 (1852): 77. Early in this century, the conservatism of the Eastern Church and their passive resistance to evangelical influences were considered more difficult to overcome than active opposition. See comments on Jacobite conservatism in ABC: 16.9.7, vol. 17, no. 202.
117. See p. 62.
118. *M.H.* 48 (1852): 112.
119. E. A. W. Budge, *By Nile and Tigris, (1816—1913),* p. 70.
120. *M.H.* 48 (1852): 110
121. Ibid., 47 (1851): 190.
122. Ibid., 50 (1854): 20.
123. Anderson, *History,* 2: 92—93.
124. *M.H.* 49 (1853): 207; 53 (1857): 270.
125. Ibid., pp. 206-7.
126. Ibid., p. 204.
127. Ibid., 48 (1852): 75-76.
128. See pp. 49-50.
129. *M.H.* 46 (1850): 205;49 (1853): 202;55 (1859): 188, 364-65; 50 (1854): 18;51 (1855): 207; Anderson, *History,* 1:386 et seq.
130. In 1830-31 those Armenians who had embraced Catholicism were officially recognized by the government; as a distinct legal entity. For details, see pp. 49-50.
131. For a translation of the decree, see Appendix B. Consult also H. G. O. Dwight, *Christianity Revived in the East* (New York: 1850), pp. 285—86; James L. Barton, *Daybreak in Turkey* (Boston: 1908), p. 168; E. D. G. Prime, *Forty Years in the Turkish Empire, or Memoirs of Rev. William*

Goodell, D.D. (New York: 1876), pp. 352-53.

132. *M.H.* 46 (1850): 270.

133. Ibid., p. 318. For the text of the *farman,* see Appendix B, and George Young, *Corps de droit Ottoman,* 2:108-9.

134. Kenneth E. Latourette, *Christianity in a Revolutionary Age: a History of Christianity in the Nineteenth and Twentieth Centuries,* 5 vols. (New York: 1958—62). 3:48.

135. *M.H.* 51 (1855): 207.

136. Ibid., 55 (1859): 6.

137. Ibid., 54 (1858): 255.

138. In 1870 the territories of the Ottoman Empire and of Qājār Persia were divided among the Congregationalists and the Presbyterians respectively. The work in Syria and Persia was left to the Presbyterians; the Congregationalists retained the missions in Macedonia, Asia Minor, Armenia, and Kurdistan. Until 1870 the two denominations had cooperated with each other within the American Board of Commissioners for Foreign Missions, a Congregational body.

139. ABC: 16.8.4, vol. 1 (Assyrian Mission), nos. 82, 88, 94; *M.H.* 48 (1852): 59, 111; 55 (1859): 174; Strong, *Story of the American Board,* pp. 209-11.

140. For a discussion of the half-hearted mission work in Mosul and the difficulties encountered there, see ABC: 16.9.7, vol. 1, no. 499; vol. 6, nos. 193, 200, 202, 205, 210; vol. 8, nos 237-97.

141. See pp. 62-3.

142. See Church Missionary Society, *Proceedings of the Church Missionary Society for Africa and the East, 1900-1901,* p. 178; *1901-1902,* p. 171.

143. See pp. 62-3.

144. See ABC: 16.9.7, vol. 2, no. 598. See also p. 18.

145. The Catholic Armenian Church as always been much smaller than the Orthodox mother church. See *M.H.* 71 (1875): 291.

146. See pp. 81-2. Looking forward to the convening of the Congress of Berlin in 1878, an editorial of the *Missionary Herald* anticipated "a grand reconstruction of the [Ottoman] empire, developing its intellectual and its natural resources, and above all securing the early triumph of the kingdom of our Lord in regions once blessed by his personal presence."

147. Ibid. Consult *M.H.* 74 (1879): 394-95. See also ibid., 75 (1879): 380; 77 (1881): 228; 87 (1891): 427. As early as the 1850s, the missionaries reported that a number of the Jacobites had become Protestants "for political reasons." See ibid., 53 (1857): 55, and ABC: 16.9.7, vol. 1 (1860-71), no. 171. See letter in Arabic and its translation in ABC: 16.9.7, vol. 1 (1860-71), no. 109, in which the evangelical community in Mosul as early as 1862 pleaded for the return of the missions to Mosul. None of the reasons given for their request was political.

148. For an account of missionary expansion in "the southern portion of the Mardin field," see report entitled "Present Conditions for Evangelistic and Educational Efforts in Baghdad and Mosul," in ABC: 16.9.7, vol. 3, no. 103; and ibid., vol. 1, no. 171; vol. 6, no. 294; vol. 8, nos. 161, 177.

149. ABC: 16.9.7, vol. 18, no. 148; *M.H.* 81 (1885): 269; 83 (1887): 149; 84 (1888): 504-5; 94 (1898): 276; 96 (1900): 202; 99 (1903): 306. Even some Ottoman officials sent their children to these Midyat schools.

5. Russia, Rebellion and Refuge

1. Stanford J. Shaw, *History of the Ottoman Empire* (Cambridge: 1976) 1:255.
2. Richard C. Hovannisian, *Armenia on the Road to Independence* (Berkeley, Cal.: 1967), p. 8. Under the Safavids, the Armenians seem to have favored Iran over Turkey during the frequent battles between the two Muslim nations that took place on Armenian homegrounds. As early as the 1740s the Porte was worried about the role that the Kurds, Nestorian Christians, and Armenians would play in the event of an all out war with Iran. Robert W. Olson, *the Siege of Mosul,"* p. 279. See also L. Nalbandian, *The Armenian Revolutionary Movement* (Berkeley, Cal.: 1963), p. 24. During Shah 'Abbās's reign especially, the Armenians thrived as middlemen and business agents of the shah or as merchants in small enterprises of their own. See Paul G. Forand, "Accounts of Western Travelers Concerning the Role of Armenians and Georgians in 16th-Century Iran," *M.W.* 65 (1975): 278. Cf. Gaston Gallard, *Les Turcs et l'Europe* (London: 1921), p. 266. Gallard writes that the Armenians enjoyed more tranquility under the Turks than under any of the many other nationalities that have ruled Armenia in the course of her history, including the Persians.
3. Eli Smith and H. G. O. Dwight had seen these refugees fleeing to the Caucasus and had conversed with them. See Eli Smith, *Researches of the Reverend E. Smith and Reverend H. G. O. Dwight in Armenia* 2 vols. (Boston: 1833), 1:140-44. The Turks had told the American missionary-explorers that the Armenians had fled because when the Russians were in Anatolia the Armenians had "conducted themselves haughtily, worn armor, cursed the Turks and their religion, and now fled to avoid the consequences they had reason to apprehend." The Turkish informers had also noted that upon Russian withdrawal a crier had passed through the streets of Erzerum "proclaiming by order of the Pasha and Sultan, that if any should injure an Armenian, his goods would be confiscated and his life be in danger."
4. Shaw, *History,* 1:254.
5. See *Edinburgh Review* 146 (1877): 264. A meeting of Turkish military leaders, soon after the Crimean War, had planned the defense of the empire in detail in case of another Russian attack; the conference, held in 1858-60, had concluded that Armenia and Asia Minor were the "body" of the Ottoman state, the other provinces, its members. Document in Public Record Office F.O. 78/1521, pp. 12-13, entitled in French "Résumé de différents mémoires spéciaux concernant notre arrangement défensif au theatre de la guerre armenienne." quoted in Mesrob Krikorian, *Armenians in the Service of the Ottoman Empire 1860-1908,* pp. 6-7.
6. See pp. 28-29.
7. For a brief discussion of the wealthy Armenian bankers and bureaucrats of the Ottoman government, known as the "Amiras"—many of whom displaced, after the Greek war of independence, the Phanariote Greeks from the predominant position that they had held in the trade of the empire—see C. E. Frazee, "The Formation of the Armenian Catholic Community," p. 160, and Robert F. Zeidner, "Britain and the Launching of

the Armenian Question." *International Journal of Middle East Studies* 7 (1976): 472.

8. H. J. Sarkiss, "The Armenian Renaissance, 1500-1863," *Journal of Modern History* 9 (1937): 445 et seq.; James Etmekjian, *The French Influence on the Western Armenian Renaissance, 1843-1915* (New York: 1964).

9. Krikorian, *Armenians,* pp. 108-9.

10. Ibid., p. 115, n.4; Sarkiss, "Armenian Renaissance," p. 447. For the text of the document in English, see H. F. B. Lynch, *Armenia: Travels and Studies,* 2 vols., 2:445-67.

11. See *M.H.* 112 (1916): 499.

12. For details see pp. 59-60.

13. *M.H.* 102 (1906): 423.

14. Ibid., 99 (1903) 297-98; J. C. McCoan, *Our New Portectorate—Turkey in Asia,* 2 vols., 2:69. For a brief evaluation of the accomplishments of the American missions before the atrocities of the 1890s, see Henry H. Jessup, "American Missions in the Turkish Empire," *M.H.* 90 (1894): 479-83. For details on the missionary secondary school curriculum, see ABC: 16.5, vol. 6, no. 58. Reading and writing Turkish language, history, geography, arithmetic, bookkeeping, English, nature study, agriculture, and drawing were among the subjects emphasized.

15. Cited in Stephen Duguid, "The Politics of Unity," pp. 147-48.

16. "History of the Armenian Question to 1885," *University of Illinois Bulletin* 35 (1938): 132, 138.

17. James L. Barton, "The Gospel for All Turkey," *M.H.* 119 (1923): 235, where the secretary noted that the conditions which he had described gave "the false impression" that the chief mission of the American board in Turkey was "to the Armenians alone." After the First World War, Turks are reported to have told the American board, "You have devoted all these years to aiding and instructing the Armenians." See *M.H.* 118 (1922): 406, where it is acknowledged that "the main bulk of our missionary activities in Turkey for the past century has been among the Armenians and Greek people."

18. Krikorian *Armenians,* p. 116, n. 7; Sarkissian, *Armenian Question,* pp. 53-54.

19. Sarkissian, ibid., p. 52.

20. The Russians eventually had introduced a comparative order of law and stability, which benefited the many ethnic groups in the Caucasus whose lives had for centuries been disrupted by tribal or Turko-Persian antagonisms.

21. S. I Shaw and E. K. Shaw, *History of the Ottoman Empire and Modern Turkey,* 2:183-84.

22. For details on the Kurdo-Christian relations, see pp. 23-4.

23. For a text of the treaty, see Shaw and Shaw, *History,* 2:188.

24. Text in Krikorian, *Armenians,* p. 8.

25. Scholar travelers such as Lynch took the position that the interests of Great Britain and British India were "most intimately bound up with the Asiatic provinces of the Ottoman Empire." See his *Armenia,* 2:437. Consult also

D. E. Lee, *Great Britain and the Cypus Convention of 1878* (Cambridge, Mass.: 1934), pp. 63 et. seq.

26. H. M. Havelock, "Constantinople and Our Road to India," *Fortnightly* 27 (1877): 126. As early as 1829 the government of India had submitted a memorandum to the Duke of Wellington emphasizing the defenseless condition of the Euphrates Valley. The whole country from the Black Sea to the Pursian Gulf, it warned, would be Russia's if she chose to take it. See *Edinburgh Review,* 146 (1877): 271-72.

27. Grattan Geary, *Through Asiatic Turkey,* 2 vols. (London: 1878), 2:67-77. For an interesting study of British interests and policies in Mesopotamia, see Zaki Saleh, *Mesopotamia (Iraq) 1600-1914: A Study in British Foreign Affairs* (Baghdad: 1957).

28. Lynch, *Armenia,* 2:437. See also *British and Foreign State Papers, 1877-1878,* 69 (1885): 812-13.

29. McCoan, *Protectorate,* 2:100-1, 107; Lynch, *Armenia,* 2:437-41.

30. During the 1877-78 war Disraeli and Layard had envisioned "a possible British expedition into eastern Anatolia to drive the Russians back, perhaps encouraged by the 'mob' demand for a war with Russia to save India as well as the Middle East from [Russian] imperialism." Shaw and Shaw, *History,* 2:184.

31. *Through Asiatic Turkey* (London: 1878), 2: 67-77. Berthold Spuler's researches show that the Jacobites repeatedly turned to Russia with appeals for help (1843-44, 1851, 1858-71) and hinted at an "Anschluss" with the Orthodox. See his *De morgenländischen Kirchen,* p. 339.

32. For a text of the ultimatum, see A. J. Toynbee, *Survey of International Affairs, 1931* (London: 1932), pp. 355-56.

33. Lynch, *Armenia,* 2: 410-11.

34. J. Carlile McCoan (London: 1878).

35. Cited in *M.H.* 76 (1880): 68.

36. See Shaw and Shaw, *History,* 2:157; Roderic H. Davison, "Turkish Attitudes Concerning Christian-Muslim Equality in the Nineteenth Century," *American Historical Review* 59 (1954): 864.

37. *M.H.* 78 (1882): 11-13, 371; 83 (1887): 305-9. For a study of anti-Islamic bias among scholars and religious leaders of the West, see the article by an associate director of a missionary organization, John D. C. Anderson, "The Missionary Approach to Islam: Christian or 'Cultic,'" *Missiology* 4 (1976): 286-87; Normal Daniel, "Islam: Some Recent Developments in the Attitude of Christians towards Islam," *E.C.Q.* 13 (1959-60): 154-66; Christian W. Troll, "A New Spirit in the Muslim-Christian Relations," *Month* 6 (1973): 296-99. One of the very few leaders of thought in the early 19th century who was aware of the strength of this Western Christian prejudice and who spoke out strongly against it was Thomas Carlyle.

38. *M.H.* 91 (1895): 366-67; 92 (1896): 56. As early as 1844 a missionary letter from Mosul reported that"every dog of a Frank" could go to the Porte and secure a firman where their own mullahs were utterly disregarded when they complained of grinding oppression. See *M.H.* 44 (1844): 369.

39. Lord Warkworth, *Notes from a Diary in Asiatic Turkey*; pp. 247-49.

40. R. H. Davison, "Turkish Attitudes Concerning Christian-Muslim Equality," pp. 862-63. See also McCoan, *Protectorate,* 1: 248; J. P. Fletcher, *Notes from Ninevah,* p. 157, where he quotes a mullah praising the local pasha for being a just man, for he "robs Jews, Christians, and Moslems alike."

41. *M.H.* 80 (1884): 25; 82 (1886): 47-50. See also B. N. Barnum, "The Turkish Government and Mission Schools," *M.H.* 84 (1888): 62-63.
42. For the translation of the circular, see ibid., 85 (1889): 323-24.
43. Ibid., 88 (1892): 139.
44. They adopted "new refinement of cruelty toward the Christians," according to one source. See an Eastern Statesman, "Contemporary Life and Thought in Turkey," *Contemporary Review* 37 (1880): 342.
45. *M.H.* 77 (1881): 264; F.O. 424, no. 122, Confidential 4562, part IV., "Further Correspondence Respecting Administrative Reforms in the Asiatic Provinces of Turkey, December 1881," pp. 202-4. See also F. X. Clark, *The Purpose of Missions*, p. 49. At the beginning of this century a Lutheran mission from America and Germany was organized to serve the Kurds of Persia. From 1911 to 1916 the mission established a Kurdish congregation, an orphanage, and a dispensary. See N. J. Lohre, "The Highlanders of Kurdistan," *M.W.* 10 (1920): 284.
46. Church Missionary Society, *Report, 1901-1902*, p. 172.
47. During the 1860s Damascus had suffered from the civil war in Mount Lebanon and the massacres in the city itself. This was followed by a second blow, in 1869, when the opening of the Suez Canal virtually extinguished the old overland routes between the Syrian capital and Iraq and the Persian Gulf, let alone the competition that the opening of the Canal made possible from India and China for such Damascene products as silk and sesame seed.
48. Steam navigation sometimes competed directly with Ottoman goods. In the 1870s the bedouins of Iraq—whose wool was the best and dearest, exported through the merchants of Baghdad—especially felt the impact of imported wool from Australia. For one season this competition nearly suspended altogether the export of bedouin wool, when the tribesmen refused to believe the sudden fall in prices and did not offer more favorable prices See McCoan, *Protectorate*, 2: 105-106.
49. For some statistics see ibid., 2: 95-96, 100.
50. *M.H.* 76 (1880): 211.
51. *M.H.* 83 (1887): 508-9. See also "The Famine in Turkey—Increasing Distress," Ibid., 84 (1888): 98-99, 194-95; 85 (1889): 152-53, where the Jacobite country in and around Tur Abdin is specifically noted. For earthquakes, some of which were reported as "Disastrous in several villages," see *ibid*, 70 (1874): 244; 85 (1889): 27; 87 (1891): 228. It should be noted that during these disasters the American missionaries were the only ones who organized relief for the sufferers.
52. S. R. Harlow, "Community Life and Ceremonies of the Peasant Turk," *M.W.* 12 (1922): 258-59; Fredrick Barth, *Principles of Social Organization in Southern Kurdistan* (Oslo: 1953), p. 116.
53. *The Peoples of Northern and Central Asiatic Turkey*, p. 857. See also Blanche Stead, "Kurdistan for Christ," p. 245; Derk Kinnane, *The Kurds and Kurdistan*, pp. 13-14.
54. For an excellent study of conditions that led to the formation of the Hamidiyah and the role that it played as a tool of the Ottoman government to supervise and control the eastern frontier, see Duguid, "Politics of Unity," pp. 139-55. See also Hassan Arfa, *The Kurds*, pp. 24-25.

55. See his *The Caliphs' Last Heritage*, p. 406. At times, according to a British consular report, the persecuted Kurdish tribes and villagers were those who refused to attack Christians, because it was "contrary to common practice." For a précis and translation of statements made by Kurds against the Hamidiyah, see F.O. 424, no. 187, pp. 149-50. See also Sykes, Ibid., p. 321, where he notes that in the case of some tribes, the protection of Christians was considered one of the "traditional customs of the tribe."

56. F.O. 424, no. 175, Confidential 6447, March 1894 for the year 1893, p. 178.

57. "Kurdistan History," in *Encyclopedia Britannica*, 14th ed.

58. See article by Gwynne Dyer, "Turkish 'Falsifiers' and Armenian 'Deceivers': Historiography and the Armenian Massacres," *Middle Eastern Studies* 12 (Jan. 1976): 99-107. See also "Forum: The Armenian Question," in *International Journal of Middle East Studies* 9 (1978): 379-400, where Professors Richard G. Hovannisian and Stanford J. and Ezel K. Shaw, colleagues at the University of California at Los Angeles, call into question each other's scholarship on this subject. (Hovannisian on the Shaws: "turns revisionism into falsification"; "an unfortunate example of nonscholarly selectivity and deceptive presentation." Shaws: "Does Dr. Hovannisian really wish to perpetuate the biased image of the 'Terrible Turk' that has its roots in the age of the Crusades?" For a good publication on the Armenians, see Christopher J. Walker, *Armenia: The Survial of a Nation* (London: 1980).

59. See Robert F. Zeidner, "Britain and the Launching of the Armenian Question," pp. 465-66. Zeidner writes that among the Armenians, the massacres were directed against the Gregorian Armenians, care being taken to spare Catholic and Protestant Armenians and the Greek Orthodox Christians. The latter two Armenian "millets" were comparatively small, but they enjoyed the protection of foreign powers.

60. Quoted in *M.H.* 92 (1896): 55.

61. Barsūm, *Ta'rīkh Ṭūr 'Abdin,* p. 366; Armalah, *al-Qaṣāra, p. 43.*

62. Armalah, ibid., pp. 61-62; Barsūm, ibid., pp. 367, passim; F.O. 424, no. 187, pp. 23-24.

63. Barsūm, ibid., p. 366.

64. Ibid.

65. Lord Warkworth, pp. xii, 251. See also p. 227, where he writes of "rioters" pillaging the monastery of Dayr al-Za'farān "at the time of the massacres."

66. Ibid., p. 226. See also C. Shattuck, "The Massacre at Urfa," in F. D. Greene, *Armenian Massacres, or the Sword of Mohammed* (n.p., 1896), pp. 340-41, where similar observations are made. See also Armalah, *al-Qaṣāra*, pp. 53-54, where he testifies that only one non-Armenian was killed at Urfa, a "Greek Malkite."

67. See his *In the Shadow of the Crescent* (London: 1906[?]), p. 184.

68. Ibid., pp. 165-66.

69. W. A. Wigram and E. T. A. Wigram, *The Cradle of Mankind*, pp. 34-35. See also *M.H.* 94 (1898): 516-17.

70. Translated in F.O. 424, no. 187.

71. F.O. 424, 188, p. 123; no. 186, Confidential 6823, p. 40.

72. See also Armalah, *al-Qaṣāra,* pp. 64-65, where the Syrian Catholic author notes that the spiritual leaders of his people were made to sign a certified document (maẓbaṭah) drawn up by the authorities, testifying that they (the Christians) were enjoying comfort and security and that only two of their villages had been burned. Armalah also notes that government inspectors had asked the leaders to go and assure their flocks that Muslims and Christians are equal in the eyes of the government and that the Armenian revolution and England were to be blamed for the atrocities.

73. When the old patriarch died on 7 October, 1894, there began a rivalry among the bishops in a race for his vacant chair. The government interfered and, according to the American missionaries, intimated which of the bishops were acceptable, while in the meantime it held "the office before the remaining eligible candidates subject to the highest bidder." 'Abd al-Masīh II was elected in 1895; his chief rival, 'Abd Allah Saṭṭūf, embraced Catholicism the year following the election. Saṭṭūf, however, was enthroned as Jacobite patriarch in 1906 when he renounced his Catholicism. This time 'Abd al-Masīh himself became a Catholic, in 1913. For a discussion of these unseemly squabbles among the rival candidates, each with his coterie of followers during these difficult times, see Armalah, "Fi al-Baṭaryarkiyah al-Anṭākiyah," pp. 668-69. See also *M.H.* 91 (1895): 367. See also pp.   .

74. F.O. 424, no. 188, p. 123; ibid., no. 186, Confidential 6823, p. 40; no. 184, Confidential 6820, pp. 525-27.

75. The 59th Annual Report (May 1896), pp. 199-200.

76. *Turkey and the Armenian Atrocities* (n.p., 1896), p. 476. See also an 1895 letter speaking of the "vigilance of the Government troops" thwarting Kurdish attempts to attack Midyat, in ABC:16.9.7, vol. 12, no. 162. See also "Report of Mardin Station for 1896," in ibid., vol. 10, no. 125.

77. *M.H.* 97 (1901); 450.

78. See p. 85. For the various points of the reform program, see Krikorian, *Armenians,* p. 10. Articles 20 and 22 provided that in eastern vilayets the number of Muslim and non-Muslim policemen would be in proportion to the number of the Muslim and Christian inhabitants.

79. Ibid., pp. 3, 31.

80. *M.H.* 96 (1900): 276-78. Consult also P. Schoenberg, "The Evolution of Transport in Turkey (Eastern Thrace and Asia Minor) under Ottoman Rule, 1856-1918," *Middle Eastern Studies* 13, no. 3 (Oct. 1977): 359-72.

81. Cited in *M.H.* 100 (1904): 312. See also ibid., 101 (1905): 1, where the American consul is quoted estimating 5,000 dead in the Sassoun district, many of them dying "by their own hand, and some by starvation and exposure."

82. Ibid., 100 (1904): 433-35.

83. After the war's end a great "wave of Atheism" was reported sweeping over the Soviet Socialist Republic of Armenia, the long-suffering people having "lost faith in God" when their ardent and simple prayers brought no answer of protection. See *M.H.* 109 (1913): 348-50; *International Review of Missions* 12 (1923): 12-13.

84. *M.H.* 101 (1905): 1, 435.

85. *M.H.* 104 (1908): 456-57.
86. *M.H.* 105 (1909): 108, 234.
87. F.O. 424, no. 237, 20 Feb. 1913, Confidential 10339, pp. 123-25; *M.H.* 107 (1911): 228-29.
88. Large segments of the Muslim population were not happy with the constitution that the Young Turk revolution had reinstated in 1908. The London-based Church Missionary Society *Proceedings* speak of the Muslim population of Mosul as openly declaring that they "preferred bloodshed and martyrdom to the new state of affairs." *Proceedings, 1908-1909,* p. 92. See also Gertrude L. Bell, *Amurath to Amurath,* pp. 250-52.
89. Some of the sultan's Kurdish supporters, the Milli tribes, under the leadership of Ibrahim Pasha, had marched and occupied Damascus on behalf of their padishah. After the sultan was deposed, the Young Turk government, with help from the Arab tribes of the Shammar, had forced the Kurds to withdraw, killing Ibrahim Pasha. See Arfa, *Kurds,* p. 25.
90. *M.H.* 105 (1909): 244-48, 350-51; Fridtjof Nansen, *Armenia and the Near East* (London: 1928), pp. 295-96.
91. ABC:16.9.7, vol. 25b, no. 19.
92. ABC:16.9.7, vol. 25b, no. 19. See also *M.H.* 104 (1908): 130; 106 (1910): 126. For details on the political and military problems facing the Young Turks during this period, see R. W. Seton-Watson, *The Rise of Nationality in the Balkans* (London: 1917); L. P. M. Leger, *Serbes, Croates et Bulgares* (Paris: 1913); Jacques Ancel, *Peuples et Nations des Balkans* (Paris: 1926); A. J. Toynbee, *The Western Question in Greece and Turkey* (London: 1923).
93. Shaw and Shaw, *History,* 2:314-15.
94. After the Young Turk revolution, the name Hamidiyah was replaced by "Ashirat Alaylāri" (tribal regiments).
95. Ibid., 111 (1915): 78.
96. Ibid., 110 (1914): 191, 573; 111 (1915): 331-32, 416.
97. Professor Richard N. Hovannisian in note to the author.
98. Shaw and Shaw, *History,* 2:314-15.
99. Ibid., 2:316-17.
100. *M.H.* 111(Sept. 1915): 401.
101. Mary L. Graffam, "On the Road with Exiled Armenians," *M.H.* 111 (1915): 565-68.
102. See *M.H.* 111 (1915): 236, 464; 112 (1916): 70-73, 266, 446-49, 461. See also A. J. Toynbee, *Survey of International Affairs 1925,* 1:517, n.4; Frederick G. Coan, *Yeserdays in Persia and Kurdistan* (Claremont, Cal.: 1929), p. 134. The Reverend Mr. Coan, for years with the Nestorian mission, writes of the many Turks whom he met who "deeply regretted" what had happened to their Christian neighbors: "Several times Turks have said to me 'there is a righteous God in heaven who has seen the great crime committed against these offenseless people, and while you, their fellow Christians have done nothing to prevent it, God some day is going to punish us for it all.' " See also Lord Warkworth, *Notes from a Diary,* p. xii, Parry, *Six Months.* p. 162. Cf. *M.H.* 111 (1915): 43-44.

103. The "worst massacre of the war," write the Shaws, took place when the Russian troops started their advance westward into eastern Anatolia in the winter of 1916. It gave the Armenians an opportunity for revenge; thousands of Muslims were "cut down" as they followed the retreating Turkish forces. *History*, 2:322-23.

104. While the English were called "infidel," the Germans were referred to as a faithful ally. See the *London Times*, 20 March 1915, where Muslim dignitaries in Damascus are quoted writing of "our [German] ally that has adopted our religion."

105. Arfa, *Kurds*, p. 26. For widespread destruction and death among the Kurds during World War I, see also Jweideh, "The Kurdish, Nationalist Movement" (Ph.D. diss.), pp. 360-64.

106. *N.C.E.*, vol. 13, pp. 903-4. These figures are by their nature highly unreliable. A serious student of Syrian Christians estimates the total number of Jacobites who perished during the war at about 95,000 and probably about half that number more of Syrian Catholics. See *E.C.Q.*, vol. 14, nos. 6-7, p. 351. A Jacobite writer estimates a total of 100,000 Jacobites, Orthodox, and Catholics killed. See "Ibn al-'Ibri" (pen-name), "Lamhah Ta'rikhiyah: al-Tā'ifah al-Suryāniyah fī 'Ashr Sanawāt," *al-Hikmah* (Jerusalem), 3 (Feb. 1929): 68. See also Eugene Griselle, *Syriens et Chaldeens, leur martyrs, leur expérances* (Paris: 1918).

6. Syrians, Lebanese, and Iraqis

1. *Times*, 20 Nov. 1918. See also A. Attrep, " 'A State of Wretchedness and Impotence': A British View of Istanbul and Turkey, 1919," *International Journal of Middle East Studies*, (Feb. 1978): 1-9.

2. Article 64 of the Treaty provided for Kurdish "independence from Turkey," it a majority of the Kurds desired it within one year from the coming into force of the Treaty, and if the League of Nations Council considered the Kurds capable of such independence. See text in J. C. Hurewitz, *Diplomacy in the Near and Middle East; A Documentary Record* (Princeton, N. J.: 1956), 2:82.

3. As early as April 1918, the Kars province, ceded by Russia in 1878, was abandoned to the Ottoman troops. The Mudros Armistice allowed the Turkish troops to stay in the region of Kars unless it were decided that it too should be evacuated.

4. For details, see Richard G. Hovannisian, "The Armenian Occupation of Kars, 1919," in *Recent Studies in Modern Armenian History* (Cambridge, Mass.: National Association for Armenian Studies and Research, Inc., 1972), pp. 23-44.

5. Ibid., p. 38.

6. *M.H.* 116 (1920): 558; 118 (1922): 89; *New York Times*, 25 Feb., 29 March, 13 April, 1921.

7. 22 Nov. 1919; 2 Dec. 1919.

8. *Review of the Civil Administration of Mesopotamia* (London: Cmd. 1061, 1920), pp. 67-70. The Kurds were assured, wrote Bell, that the British had no intention of pursuing a vindictive policy towards them.

9. A Turco-Armenian treaty was signed in December 1920 which was

superseded by the Turkish-Russian Treaty of 1921, when the Republic of
Armenia was taken by the Soviets. See S. J. Shaw and E. K. Shaw, *History
of the Ottoman Empire and Modern Turkey*, 2:356-57.

10. *New York Times* 14 Nov. 1921; 23 Dec. 1921; *M.H.* 116 (1920): 540.

11. *M.H.* 118 (1922): 8-9, 89, 148 477-78. For a sympathetic account of these
events by one who participated in relief work among the refugees, see
Stanley E. Kerr, *The Lions of Marash* (Albany, N. Y.: 1973).

12. Urfa, ancient Edessa, is the site of the Jacobite monastery of Mār Afrām,
which stood conspicuously at the head of the bay. Urfa was reported to
have had only "Three or four Syro-Jacobite" families in the 1960s. See
Xavier Jacob, "The Christians of South-East Turkey," p. 399.

13. "Ibn al-'Ibri," "al-Tā'ifah al-Suryāniyah," pp. 70, 115. See also Norman
A. Horner, "Tur Abdin: A Christian Minority Struggles To Preserve Its
Identity," *Occasional Bulletin of Missionary Research* 2 (Oct. 1978): 134,
where the author merely mentions the Syrian Orthodox as having "their
own nationalistic ambitions."

14. For a photograph of the delegation that attended the Peace Conference see
Assyrian Star (Chicago), May-June, 1971, p. 8. For Jacobite petitions to
the peace conference, see F.O. 608, no. 85, files 3472 and 3481 (1919). Cf.
Ibn al-'Ibri, "al-Tā'ifah al-Suryāniyah," p. 71, emphasizing that the
leaders of the Jacobite community were convinced that only their own
government could restore their denied rights; those who had immigrated to
America, he adds, thought differently.

15. Ghrighūriyus Būlus Bahnām, *Nafaḥāt al-Khizām Aw Hayāt al-Batrak
Afrām* (Mosul: 1959), pp. 25-27, 193-94. See also Matti I. Moosa, "Kitāb
al-lu'lu' al-Manthūr, by Ignatius Aphram Barsoum, Syrian Patriarch of
Antioch and all the East" (Ph.D. diss., Columbia University, 1965), p. vii.

16. *Times*, 14 Jan. 1920.

17. Abdul Rahman Ghassemlou, *Kurdistan and the Kurds* (Prague: 1965), p.
50.

18. For a detailed discussion of the role of the Kurds in the border settlement
controversy between Turkey and Iraq—the so-called Mosul question—see
Joseph *The Nestorians and Their Muslim Neighbors*, pp. 167-94. Cf. A. R.
Ghassemlou, *Kurdistan and the Kurds*, pp. 60-61. See also *Times* 22 March
1926.

19. *New York Times*, 26 Feb. 1925; 19 April 1925; X, p. 12. For a discussion of
Kurdish opposition to the new regime, see Jweideh, pp. 302 et seq.; Arfa,
The Kurds, pp. 33-38, 107-108; Derk Kinnane, *The Kurds and Kurdistan*,
pp. 16-17; W. G. Elphinston, "Kurds and the Kurdish Question," *Journal
of the Royal Central Asian Society* 35 (1948): 43.

20. *New York Times*, 9 April 1925.

21. In 1932 a law passed by the Ankara government enabled it to deport "hundreds of thousands" of Kurds into areas where they would "constitute 5%
of the population." Most probably the Turkish government was infuriated
by the fact that the Kurdish nationalist organization, the *khoybun,* which
organized the 1930 revolt, was under the "direct influence" of the Armenian extreme nationalist party of the Dashnak. See Ghassemlou, *Kurdistan*, pp. 53-55; Kinnane, *Kurds*, p. 30-31; W. G. Elphinston, "The Kur-

dish Question," *International Affairs* 22 (1946): 96. Cf. Arfa, *The Kurds* p. 31. (According to a *New York Times* report, Armenian and Kurdish representatives of the "Armenian Secret Army for the Liberation of Armenia" and the "Kurdish Workers Party," respectively, told a news conference on 7 April 1980 that Turkish Kurds and Armenians had for the first time formed an alliance to fight against the government of Turkey. See *times,* 8 April 1980, p. A42).

22. "Ibn al-'Ibri," "al-Ṭā'ifah al-Suryāniyah," p. 116. For the proximity of the Jacobites and Kurdish tribes and villages to each other, see Mark Sykes, "The Kurdish Tribes of the Ottoman Empire," pp. 473-74.

23. The Brussels Line eventually became the recognized boundary line between Turkey and Iraq.

24. For details on these events, see League of Nations, "Report to the Council of the League of Nations by General F. Laidoner on the Situation in the Locality of the Provisional Line of the Frontier between Turkey and Irak fixed at Brussels on October 29, 1924, Mosul, November 23, 1925," in Great Britain, Cmd. 2560 (1925); League of Nations, Turko-Irak Frontier, Memorandum on the Enquiry conducted . . . into the Deportation of Christians in the Neighbourhood of the Brussels Line, Mosul, November 12, 1925," in Great Britain, Cmd. 2563 (1925); A. J. Toynbee, *Survey of International Affairs, 1925,* 1:19, 507-11, 516 et seq. See also *Times,* 11 Dec., 15 Dec., 1925.

25. Harry Charles Luke, *Mosul and Its Minorities* (London: 1925), p. 113. Luke gives the date of expulsion as "spring of 1924." For a discussion of Turkey's policy toward its Kurdish population after the 1930s, see Kinnane, *Kurds,* pp. 31-34.

26. Turkish Dereici, a village of some two hundred families, between Mardin and Midyat.

27. See her *Amurath to Amurath,* pp. 317-18. For photographs of the church, see Abrohom Nouro, *My Tour in the Parishes of the Syrian Church in Syria and Lebanon,* p. 60/321.

28. Norman A. Horner, "Tur 'Abdin: A Christian Minority Struggles To Preserve Its Identity," p. 134.

29. Ibid.

30. Named after the forty Roman legionnaires who, according to the legend, were thrown into an ice-cold lake early in the fourth century when they would not renounce Christianity.

31. Horner, "Tur 'Abdin", p. 136. Cf. Jacob, "The Christians of South-East Turkey," p. 401.

32. See Horner, "Tur 'Abdin," p. 134; Bell, *Amurath to Amurath,* p. 314; C. Dauphin, "Situation actuelle des communautes chrétien nes du Tur 'Abdin (Turquie Orientale)," *Proche-Orient Chrétien*(1972): 326; Nouro, *My Tour,* p. 36/297.

33. Adrian Fortescue, *The Lesser Eastern Churches,* p. 341; Gertrude L. Bell, "Churches and Monasteries of the Tur Abdin and the Neighbouring Districts," *Zeitschrift fur Geschichte der Architectur* 9 (1913): 5-6. Several of these monasteries, according to Bell, were scanty structures which most probably were intended for one or two persons. They were devoid of any

decorative features, rudely built of undressed stones. Consult her *Amurath to Amurath*, pp. 301-14, for a description of some of these convents "garrisoned by a single monk."

34. Horner, "Tur Abdin," p. 137; Nuoro, *My tour*,p. 21/282;Ibn al-'Ibri, "al-Tā'ifah al-Suryāniyah," p. 125. For details on these and other monasteries as they were in the 1970s, see Claudine Dauphin, "The Rediscovery of the Nestorian Churches of the Hakkari (South Eastern Turkey)," p. 326.

35. See "al-Madrasah al-Iklirikiyah fi Dayr al-Za'farān," *M.B.* 1 (1962): 485; ibid., 4 (1965): 138.

36. See Nouro, *My Tour*, pp. 35-36/286-97. See also pp. 20-1.

37. Dauphin, "Rediscovery," p. 325; Horner, "Tur Abdin." For more on Midyat, see p. 104.

38. Only Armenian Catholics are mentioned by Father Xavier Jacob, who visited Mardin in the 1960s. See his "Christians of South-East Turkey," pp. 399-401; see also Dauphin, ibid., p. 325.

39. *M.H.* 121 (1925): 105; 122 (1926): 338; 127 (1931): 489.

40. See pp. 17-8; Jacob, "Christians," p. 325.

41. See *M.B.* 2 (1963): 210-11; 6 (1967): 54; 11 (1973): 567-71, including photographs showing the Jacobite patriarch Ighnāṭiyūs Ya'qub III visiting the "vali" of Istanbul and other Turkish dignitaries.

42. Horner, "Tur Abdin," pp. 134-35; Dauphin, "Rediscover," p. 327. Claudine Dauphin, also a recent and well-informed visitor to Tur Abdin, found no trace of hostility between the two communities but confirms the fact that as a result of constant emigration, the Christians are "surrounded" more and more by Muslims.

43. Ibid., 135. See also Dauphin, *ibid.*, John Krajcar, "Turkey: A Graveyard of Christianity," *World Mission* 15 (Spring 1964): 64-72. Starting in the 1960s, large numbers of Jacobites, mostly from the Tur Abdin region, have settled in southern Sweden, especially in the city of Södertallje. Their number was estimated at over 15,000 in the summer of 1980. (Information in letter to the author from Dr. Yusof Matti, dated 29 July 1980, from Järfälla, Sweden.) For details on Christian workers, including the Syrian Orthodox, and refugees from Turkey in Europe, see *Christian Minorities of Turkey*, report produced by the Churches Committee on Migrant Workers in Europe (Brussels: 1979), pp. 11-30 and passim.

44. John Hope Simpson, *The Refugee Problem: Report of a Survey* (London: 1939), p. 556.

45. For a detailed account of the refugee and emigrant beginnings in the district, see ibid., pp. 458 et seq.; Ibn al-'Ibri, "al-Tā'ifah al-Suryāniyah," pp. 119-120. See also Robert Montagne, "Quelques Aspects du Peuplement de la Haute-Djezireh," *Bulletin d'Études Orientales* (Damascus) 2 (1932): 53-66. The majority of the Jazirah's Arab population was nomadic, often clashing with the Kurds, especially during the seasons when they brought their flocks close to Kurdish areas for grazing.

46. See pp. 101-2.

47. Some of the Kurdish aghas lived on the Turkish side of the border; after the French occupation of Syria, a few of them had moved to the Syrian side. See Simpson, *Refugee Problem*, pp. 458, 555; Elphinston, "Kurdish Ques-

tion," p. 100; Andre Gilbert and Maurice Fevret, "La Djezireh syrienne et son Réveil économique," *Révue de géographie de Lyon* 5 (1953): 9-10; cf. Ghassemlou, *Kurdistan*, p. 82.

48. By 1940 close to 9,000 Assyrians from Iraq had been settled on the River Khabur in 32 different villages. They were transferred to Syria and settled there under the agency of the League of Nations with backing from England, France, and Iraq. Turkey had objected in 1936 to their settlement on the Khabur on the Turko-Syrian frontier. See *New York Times*, 15 Nov. 1936; *Times*, 25 March 1940; 10 April 1940; Gibert and Fevret, ibid., p. 10; Bayard Dodge, "The Settlement of the Assyrians on the Khabur," *R. C. A. S. J.* 27 (1940): 301-320. By mid-1970 the Assyrian population of Syria, most of them in the Jazirah, was given by one informed source as 30,000, their Catholic brethren (the Chaldeans), as 9,000. See Xavier Jacob, "Die Christen im heutigen Syrien," *Stimmen der Zeit; Katholische monatschrift fur das geistesleben der gegenwart* 196 (1978): 345

49. Simpson, *Refugee Problem*, p. 556. Hourani gives another estimate for 1937, as follows: Arab Moslems, 41,900; Kurds, 81,450; Christians, 31,050; Assyrians, 8,000; others, 4,150. See his *Syria and Lebanon: A Political Essay* (London: 1946), p. 141 n.

50. Iraq received its independence in 1932; the Franco-Syrian treaty negotiated in 1936 provided for Syrian independence in 1939.

51. See pp. 9-10.

52. See Betts, "Christian Communities" pp. 70-71. Betts notes that this pro-Western sentiment continued "to dominate the outlook of a majority of Christian Arabs;" see also Hourani, *Syria and Lebanon*, p. 63.

53. *Refugee Problem*, pp. 556-57.

54. Ibid., p. 556; Hourani, *Syria and Lebanon*, p. 215.

55. Simpson, ibid., 556; Doreen Warriner, *Land Reform and Development in the Middle East: A Study of Egypt, Syria, and Iraq* (London 1962), p. 87. Robert B. Betts speaks of a "massacre of Christians" at 'Amūda which "initiated a strong movement for local autonomy . . . " *Christians in the Arab East*, pp. 36-37, using Hourani's *Syria and Lebanon* as his source. Hourani, however, rightly attributed the autonomy movement to the fears of both the Kurds and Christians of Arab rule, and speaks of the Kurds starting the revolt of 1937, and of an "altercation" at 'Amūda, "when a number of Christians were killed." Ibid., p. 216; and pp. 141, 215. Consult also *New York Times*, 13 Aug. 1937, which speaks of pillaging of Christian shops and homes in 'Amūda, attributing the revolt to Kurds "fighting for autonomy."

56. See *New York Times*, 12 Aug., 13 Aug., 1937; Simpson, *Refugee Problem*, p. 556.

57. Hourani, *Syria and Lebanon*, p. 216.

58. Almost half of the Christians in Syria belong to the native church of Syria originally affiliated with Byzantium—the Greek Orthodox church and its offshoot, the Greek Catholic church. In the early 1970s, there were almost twice as many Greek Orthodox Arabs (202,000) as there were Greek Catholic Arabs (112,000). See Jacob, "Christen im heutigen Syrien," p. 344; for statistics on Syrian Christians, consult Betts, "Christian Communities," pp. 102-3.

59. *New York Times*, 24 April 1938; Hourani, *Syria and Lebanon*, p. 216.

60. For a discussion of the reasons why the French government rejected the treaty and the deadlock that followed, see Hourani, ibid., pp. 217-29. See also *Times*, 4 July, 1939.

61. Thousands of Armenian refugees were reported "pouring" into Syria and Lebanon on 25 July 1939 from the Sanjaq when Turkish troops took over from the withdrawing French. *New York Times*, 26 July 1939. For a detailed discussion of the cession to Turkey of the Sanjaq of Alexandretta, see Toynbee, *Survey, 1938*, 1:479-92.

62. Hourani, *Syria and Lebanon,* p. 229; for the text of the decree setting up the administrative regime in al-Jazirah, see ibid., p. 356.

63. For a discussion of the American mission schools and colleges in Anatolia, see pp. 81-2. See also Jacob, "Christen im heutigen Syrien," p. 345, where he speaks of a community of about 19,000 Protestants in Syria, made up largely of Armenians and Jacobites.

64. Simpson, *Refugee Problem*, p. 556. See also Armalah, *Athar Faransa*, pp. 210-12.

65. Norman N. Lewis, "The Frontier of Settlement in Syria," *International Affairs* 31 (1955): 59-60; George Kirk, *Survey of International Affairs 1939-1946* (Oxford: 1952), pp. 88-89, 122-23, 178-82, 299; Martin W. Wilmington, *The Middle East Supply Center* (London: 1971), pp. 119-22.

66. Doreen Warriner, *Land Reform and Development in the Middle East: A Study of Egypt, Syria, and Iraq*, pp. 74, 90-92.

67. As in the case of the British in Iraq, the French mandatory authorities assigned the ownership of tribal lands—usually state lands which the tribes traditionally occupied and used for their flocks—to the tribal shaykhs. The latter became the legal owners of large tracts of uncultivated land, their tribesmen receiving nothing, even losing their rights to graze on lands which were rented or sold. During the mandatory period, the French authorities were often accused by the Syrian nationalists of willfully strengthening the bedouins as a force against the nationalist movement. Ibid., p. 88; A. R. George, "The Nomands of Syria: End of a Culture?" *Middle East International*, April 1973, p. 21. For tribal land policies in Iraq, consult Philip W. Ireland, *Iraq: A Study in Political Development* (New York: 1938), pp. 93-95.

68. The merchant-farmers received from 45 to 60 percent of the crop on lands where they supplied the water; as owners of tractors and combines as well as pumps, they commanded up to 85 percent of the output. See International Bank for Reconstruction and Development, *The Economic Development of Syria* (Baltimore, Md.: 1955), p. 37. Gilbert and Fevret, "Djezireh syrienne," pp. 93-97.

69. It should be noted that traditionally the bedouins of Syria and Iraq have produced a large part of these countries' wool as well as their meat and dairy products. See Norman N. Lewis, "The Frontier of Settlement in Syria, 1800-1950," pp. 59-60; George, "Nomads," p. 22; Warriner, *Land Reform,* pp. 92-93; International Bank for Reconstruction and Development, *Economic Development, p. 292.*

70. As late as the early 1960s foreigners were barred from entering the Jazirah

without special government permission. See Gordon H. Torrey, *Syrian Politics and the Military, 1945-1958* (Columbus, O. 1964), p. 32; Warriner, *Land Reform*, pp. 86, 88.

71. See Armalah, *Athar Faransa*, pp. 212-13.
72. See Nouro, *My Tour,* pp. 31-32/292-93, where the Jacobite author lists the major centers of his community in the Jazirah. Cf. "Ibn al-'Ibri," "al-Tā'ifah al-Suryāniyah," p. 38.
73. David Nicolle, "The New Jazira," *Middle East International* 28 (Oct. 1973): pp. 26-28. See also *Daily Star* (Beirut), 6 July 1973.
74. Called the Diocese of Jazirah and Euphrates, the Syrian Catholics numbered approximately 7,000 in the 1960s and had seven churches, five chapels, nine priests, one secondary school, and five elementary schools. See *N.C.E.*, vol. 13, p. 904; Simpson, *Refugee Problem*, p. 557, Horner, "Tur Abdin," p. 134; Armalah, *Athar Faransa*, pp. 208-9.
75. See Betts, *Christians in the Arab East,* pp. 97-101. The prosperity of the region has attracted Muslim settlers from the other parts of the country, thus reducing the numerical importance of the Christian population. In the early sixties the government itself was helping farmers to move from the congested Hama region to the sparsely populated Jazirah where new villages were constructed for them. Warriner, *Land Reform*, p. 226; Eva Garzouzi, "Land Reform in Syria," *Middle East Journal*, 17 (1963): 83, 90; George, "Nomads," p. 22. Kinnane *Kurds*, p. 44, speaks of the Syrian government's intensified effort to Arabise the Jazira under the Ba'th.
76. See pp. 37-8.
77. *N.C.E.,* vol. 1, p. 286; vol. 13, p. 904. See also Jacob, "Christen im heutigen Syrien," p. 343.
78. The Ottoman provincial yearbook of 1908 gave the Jacobite and Syrian Catholic populations of the province of Aleppo as 1852 and 3130, respectively. Cited in Krikorian, *Armenians* p. 82.
79. In 1974 a new Syrian Orthodox church, dedicated to "The Virgin," was consecrated in Damascus. See *M.B.* 12 (1974): 240-42.
80. Damascus too has always been an important center of the Catholics of the Middle East, its most important community being the Greek Catholics (Malkites), with a population divided into fourteen parishes in the 1960s, amounting to 14,000 people. Other Catholic sects during that decade included Maronites (2,000) and a small congregation of Armenian Catholics. See Hambye, "The 'Syrian' Quadrilateral," p. 334; Jacob, "Christen im heutigen Syrien," p. 344.
81. *N.C.E.*, vol. 13, p. 904.
82. Hims and Hama together form a diocese of both sister churches. Dependent on this Syrian Catholic bishopric are two well-known monasteries, one dedicated to Mār Mūsa (Saint Moses) the Ethiopian, whose original building, with frescoes of exquisite beauty, may go back to the seventh century or earlier; the other is named after Mār Yūlayān (Julian). See Armalah, *Athar Faransa,* pp. 134-36; Stephen Rahhal, "Some Notes on the West Syrians," *E.C.Q.* 6 (1946): 379.
83. Jacob, "Christen im heutigen Syrien." pp. 343-46. For a statistical account

of these communities during the 1960s, consult Betts, *Christians in the Arab East*, pp. 100-3.

84. Kamal S. Salibi, "The Maronite Church in the Middle Ages and Its Union with Rome," *Oriens Christianus*, 4th Series, 6 (1958): 102-3.

85. Armalah, "Fi al-Baṭaryarkiyah al-Anṭākiyah," p. 597.

86. Cited in Charles K. von Euw, "The Union of the Syro-Jacobites with Rome in the Mid-Seventeenth Century," p. 12. See also Tannūs al-Shidyāq *Akhbār al-'A'yān fi Jabal Lubnān* (Beirut: 1859), 1:210; Tarrāzi, *Aṣdaq mā-Kān*, 1:40-42, 101-4; 2:2-4, 102-19, 135 et seq.; Joseph Schmidlin, *Catholic Mission History*, trans. and ed. Matthias Braun (Techny, Ill.: 1933), p. 272; John Green, *A journey from Aleppo to Damascus* (London: 1736), pp. 132-89; E.R. Hambye, "The 'Syrian' Quadrilateral Today," *E.C.Q.*, 14(1962): pp. 349,356.

87. Built in the twelfth century for the monks of the Cestercian order, the monastery fell into the hands of the Greek Orthodox about a century later. See Philip K. Hitti, *Lebanon in History* (London: 1957), pp. 314-15; H. Lammens, *Taṣrih al-Absār fi mā Yaḥtawi Lubnān min al-'Athār* Beirut: 1913), 1:155.

88. See pp. 40-1. Cf. De Vries, *Rom und die Patriarchate des Ostens*, p. 96.

89. The old schoolhouse given to Michael Jarwah at al-Sharfah was eventually enlarged to become the magnificent monastery and theological seminary that it is today. Known as Dayr al-Sharfah, it was the Syrian Catholics' own first monastery, their other convents having been originally Jacobite. In 1843 the dayr was transformed into a seminary and named "Sayyidat al-Najāt" by Peter Jarwah, who believed that the Virgin had led him from danger to safety. See Graf, *Geschichte* 4:64; Tarrāzi, *Aṣdaq mā-Kān*, 1:329-33; 2:323-27; Armalah, Ishāq, *Tarfah fi Akhbār Dayr al-Sharfah* (Beirut: 1920); *Idem*, *Ta'rikh Dayr Sayyidat al-Najāt ayy Dayr al-Sharfah, 1787-1946* (Beirut: 1946); Rahhal, "Some Notes on the West Syrians," pp. 380-81; Hambye,"The 'Syrian' Quadrilateral," pp. 352-53.

90. A Catholic bishop administered to the needs of a formerly Jacobite community in Tripoli between 1886 and 1898. The Jacobites there had a church as late as the seventeenth and eighteenth centuries. See Hambye, ibid. For details on their settlement in Lebanon, see Tarrāzi, *Aṣdaq mā-Kān* 1:424-29.

91. See pp. 47-8.

92. See Rahhal, "Notes," pp. 377-78; Hambye, ibid p. 357.

93. Cf. Pierre Rondot, *Les institutions politiques du Liban* (Paris: 1947), p. 38. See also Tarrāzi, *Aṣdaq mā-Kān*, 1:419-20.

94. The patriarchal vicarate of Egypt had about 5,000 Syrian Catholics in the 1960s, four churches, five priests, one secondary school, two elementary schools and two charitable institutions. In Jordan, 1,500 faithful had two churches, one priest and one elementary school. Turkey had 9,000 Syrian Catholics, with five churches and three priests. The patriarchal vicarate of Rome, administered by a titular archbishop, had 370 faithful and one church; Paris, with 3,500 Syrians, had a church and two priests. See *N.C.E.*, vol. 13, p. 904; Ignatius Mansourati, "Kurze Darstellung der syrischen katholischen Kirche," pp. 118-19. For an interesting account on

the Syrian Catholic church in Paris, see Armalah, *Athar Faransa,* pp. 137-40. On Syrian Catholics in Turkey, see Dauphin, "Situation actuelle des communautés chrétiennes du Tur 'Abdin,'" p. 324.

95. When he died in 1968, Tabbūni was succeeded by Dionysius Hayek, who, after graduating from the Sharfah Seminary, pursued his studies in philosophy and theology at the Pontifical College of the Propaganda of the Faith in Rome. See *N.C.E.* 2 (1969): 96.

96. Cf. *N.C.E.*, vol. 2, p. 233, and vol. 13, p. 904, where these statistics slightly differ.

97. According to a 1932 census, the Syrian Orthodox and Catholic communities were almost equal in number: 2,723 and 2,803, respectively. Cited in Rondot, "Les institutions politiques," pp. 28-29.

98. See Hambye, p. 356. In an interview with the writer the Syrian Catholic archbishop of Baghdad expected his ancestral community, the Jacobites, eventually to join the prestigious Catholic church. "Five hundred million will not follow fifty thousand," referring to the world-wide Catholic population.

99. In the mid-1960s the school had 415 pupils.

100. *M.B.* 7 (1968): 47; Tarrāzi, *Aṣdaq mā-Kān,* pp. 440-41.

101. Quoted in the *New York Times,* 11 Sept. 1979.

102. Paul D. Starr, "Ethnic Categories and Identification in Lebanon," *Urban Life* 7 (April 1978): 139-40.

103. The Lebanese confessional structure has been studied by a large number of scholars, among them Kamal Salibi, *Crossroads to Civil War: Lebanon, 1958-1976* (New York: 1976); Michael W. Suleiman, *The Political Parties in Lebanon: The Challenge of a Fragmented Culture* (Ithaca, N. Y.: 1967); Halim Barakat, *Lebanon in Strife: Student Preludes to the Civil War* (Austin, Tex.: 1977); Enver M. Koury, *The Crisis in the Lebanese System: Confessionalism and Chaos* (Washington, D. C.: 1976). Elie A. Salem, "Lebanon's Political Maze: The Search for Peace in a Turbulent Land," *Middle East Journal* 33 (Autumn 1979): 444-63; Ralph E. Crow, "Religious Sectarianism in the Lebanese Political System," *Journal of Politics* 24 (1962): 489-520; Iliya F. Harik, "The Ethnic Revolution and Political Integration in the Middle East," *International Journal of Middle East Studies* 3 (1972): 303-23; Michael C. Hudson, "The Ethnoreligious Dimension of the Lebanese Civil War," *Journal of South Asian and Middle Eastern Studies* (Spring 1978): 34-45. For a brief but excellent study that takes into consideration the position of the various Christian sects, see Norman A. Horner, "The Churches and the Crisis in Lebanon," *Occasional Bulletin of Missionary Research* 1 (Jan. 1977): 8-12.

104. Maronite disunity may be illustrated by the blood feud between the phalangists and the Sulayman Franjiyah faction from Zgharta. See *New York Times,* 4 July, 9 July, 1978; 11 Sept. 1979. In a lightning attack in the summer of 1980, the phalangist forces smashed the militia of their allies under Camille Sham'ūn. For the ferocity and savagery of that fighting see *New York Times,* 11 July 1980.

105. There is a small Muslim elite that would share a number of the views espoused by the Maronites, especially their position that Lebanon should

not lose its independence. See Salem, "Lebanon's Political Maze," p. 460.

106. In 1976 the Druze leader Kamāl Janbalāṭ vowed that the military campaign that he was launching was against the phalangists, and the "National Liberals," the party of Camille Sham'ūn (Chamoun). "Our brothers of all faiths," said Janbalāṭ, "and particularly the Christians, must understand that they must reject the Phalangists and the Chamounians like the plague. We must seize their arms and impose ourselves by force." See New York Times, 22 March 1976. The Phalange party, a paramilitary organization founded by Pierre Jumayyil in 1936, has as its major goal the defense of Christian supremacy in Lebanon, especially the privileges of the Catholic Maronite community.

107. This is especially true of the Greek Orthodox Christians of the mountain, the Kūrah district near Tripoli, and parts of Beirut and its southern suburbs. The Greek Orthodox militia of the Parti Populaire Syrien has allied itself with the coalition of Lebanese Muslims, leftists, and Palestinians, known as the National Front. See Salem, "Lebanon's Political Maze," 450-541; *Economist*, 2 May 1981, pp. 33-34.

108. See Michael C. Hudson, "Palestinian Factor in the Lebanese Civil War," *Middle East Journal* 32 (Summer 1978): 261-78.

109. A recent study of a representative sample of Lebanon's secondary schools pointed out "the profound impact that sectarian affiliations have on the students' orientations." See Jabbra, p. 211. See also Barakat, *Lebanon in Strife*. Cf. Koury, *The Crisis in the Lebanese System*, where the author argues that the 1975-1976 hostilities were between rightists and leftists and not between Christians and Muslims. The Lebanese civil war was not "an explosion of primordial hatreds," in the words of Michael Hudson. He rightly points out that the fundamental problems that precipitated the conflict were not ethnoreligious; they were the regional pressures that drained the Lebanese government of its authority. Sectarian cleavages erupted into violence when the "circuits" of government finally became overloaded, as Hudson aptly puts it. "The Ethnoreligious Dimension," p. 34 et seq. See also Iliya Harik, "Political Integration," p. 322, where he emphasizes the impact of regional conflicts and instability on local turmoil and conflict.

110. W. Blakemore, "Religious Realities of the Lebanese War," *Christian Century* 93 (6 Oct. 1976): 836; Horner, "The Churches and the Crisis," p. 11.

111. For an excellent article on domestic Syrian politics, see A. R. Kelidar, "Religion and State in Syria," *Asian Affairs* 61 (Feb. 1974): 16-22.

112. *New York Times*, 11 March 1976; Horner, "Churches," p. 11. It should be noted that until the Lebanese civil war in the 1970s and the rise in Islamic fundamentalism at the end of the decade, encouraged by the triumph of the Khomeini revolution in Iran, communal differences in Egypt, which occasionally did break out in incidents of violence, were infrequent and on a relatively small scale, always discouraged and disapproved by the government officials. See Margaret J. Wyszomirski, "Communal Violence: The Armenians and the Copts as Case Studies," *World Politics* (April 1975): 438, 444-46. For a speech by President Sadat at the Coptic Hospital ceremonies exhorting "love, cohesion and solidarity" in Egyptian life, see *F.B.I.S.,* 5 (14 Oct. 1977): pp. D3-6. For more on communal tensions, see pp. 129-30.

113. Responsible officials at all levels in a number of Arab countries, always conscious of the ripple effects of an intercommunal war, have gone out of their way to avoid fanning latent sentiments. Middle Eastern press and radio broadcasts have not referred to the warring factions by their religious affiliation, but, depending on the source, it has called them "isolationist," "nationalist forces," "Lebanese forces," "Fascists," "Lebanese masses." See translations of Arabic newspapers and radio broadcasts in *F.B.I.S.*

114. *Jerusalem Post,* 23 September 1975.

115. New York Times 9 July 1978; 11 Sept. 1979; Salem, "Lebanon's Political Maze," p. 458. It should be pointed out that before the civil war, the phalangists strongly backed Palestinian rights. A study of the Arab press in Lebanon showed that "the Phalangists have never advocated acceptance of Israel." See William W. Haddad, "The Christian Arab Press and the Palestine Question: A Case Study of Michel Chiha of Bayrut's *Le Jour,*" *M.W.* 64 (April 1975): 128-29. For statements by Pierre Jumayyil on Palestine, see *Daily Star* (Beirut), 9 Nov. 1973; 28 May 1974; *Christian Science Monitor* 15 April 1975; *New York Times,* 16 April 1975, 26 May 1975.

116. *New York Times,* 11 March 1976.

117. A report on the Christians of the Middle East found them to feel "as strongly as the Moslems, that Mr. Sadat has betrayed the Arabs, particularly the Palestinians, weakening their cause by his peace with Israel." See *New York Times* 15 Sept. 1979; Horner, "Churches," p. 9.

118. See Salem, "Lebanon's Political Maze," pp. 460-62.

119. *Economist,* quoted in Swasia, 25 April 1975, p. 1. In a pamphlet entitled "The Crisis of Christianity in Lebanon and the Arab Orient," published by the Syrian Nationalist Social Party in 1978, "Ghetto Christianity" and the "Zionisation" of Lebanon are attacked, and any relationship of the Christians with Israel condemned. "There are millions of Christians in the Muhammadan Arab Orient," writes the president of the party, "the policy of the Maronite partisanship makes them all face fateful dangers" (pp. 16-24). Formerly known as the Syrian National Party, the S.N.S.P. has both Christians and Muslims as members; more than half are Christian, and of these the majority come from the Greek Orthodox and Greek Catholic communities.

120. The fighting factions have on the whole respected the neutrality of communities like the Armenians. See Horner, "Churches," p. 11; *The Armenian Mirror-Spectator* (Watertown, Mass.). 6 Dec. 1975, 14 Feb. 1976.

121. Horner, "Churches."

122. See Salem, p. 450.

123. Ibid., pp. 461-62; cf. Horner, "Churches," p. 11. Salem suggests that as a "symbolic recognition of the millions of Arab Christians" who live throughout the Muslim countries, as well as in recognition of the distinctive character of Lebanon in the Arab world, Christian presidency be retained in Lebanon. Others have proposed that the highest office alternate between a Christian and a Muslim, or simply declare the country secular with the strict separation of church and state.

124. For a detailed account of the Mosul question, see Joseph, *Nestorians*, pp. 175-94.
125. Chaldeans predominated among the Christians of the north in such well-known towns as al-Qūsh, with a population of approximately 5,000 in the mid-1960s, Tall Kayf (8,000), Baṭnāya (4,000), Tall Usquf (6,000), Karamlis (2,500), 'Ayn Kāwa (3,000), and Mankaysh (1,500). In the 1960s the Jacobite town of Qaraqūsh and Barṭalla had a population of approximately 7,000 and 3,000, respectively. Among towns with a mixed population in northern Iraq, where at least 20 percent of the inhabitants were Christian, were Zākhu, seat of a Chaldean bishop (approximately, in round figures, 2,000 out of 8,000), Duhuk (2,000 of 8,000), Shaqlāwa (1,500 of 4,500), Ba'shiqah (900 of 3,000), and Batas (400 of 1,000). For statistics on some of the leading Christian centers in the province of Mosul, see J. M. Fiey, *Assyrie chrétienne*, 2:354-469; Robert B. Betts, *Christians in the Arab East* (Atlanta, Ga.: 1978), pp. 232-33. See also Cecil J. Edmonds, *Kurds, Turks, and Arabs: Politics, Travel and Research in North-Eastern Iraq, 1919-1935* (Oxford: 1957), p. 427.
126. In the 1960s the Syrian Catholic archbishopric of Mosul had 24 priests, serving 17 churches with a total of 14,000 faithful. Two elementary schools and three kindergartens served the religious and educational needs of the young. See *N.C.E.*, vol. 13, p. 904.
127. For a history of the Syrian Catholics in Baghdad, see pp. 50-1. See also article in *Nashrat al-Aḥḥad* (Baghdad), 10 (20 Sept. 1931), pp. 591-600, entitled "Al-Suryān al-Kāthūlik fi Baghdād min 1801 ila Sanat 1931."
128. See pp. 17-8.
129. Editor of *al-Bilād*, Buṭṭi is described by Majid Khadduri as "the ablest newspaper man in Iraq," beyond all comparison, and "the most influential editor in Baghdad." See Khadduri's *Independent Iraq* (Oxford: 1951), p. 99, n. 2.
130. See M. I. Moosa, "Kitab al-Lu'lu' al-Manthur, by Ignatius Aphram Barsoum, Syrian Patriarch of Antioch and all the East" (Ph.D. diss., Columbia University, New York, 1965).
131. See Berthold Spuler, "Die west-syrische (Monophysitische) Kirche unter der Islam," p. 338.
132. See p. 87.
133. The Nestorian patriarch's claims to temporal as well as spiritual power for himself was a major reason for his failure to get along with the Iraqi authorities. See my *Nestorians*, pp. 197-200.
134. Richard Coke, "The Newest Constitution in an Ancient Land," *The Current History Magazine*, Nov. 1924, p. 243. See also Ḥanna Qaryu, "Al-Taqṣ al-Kaldān wa-al-Sulṭān al-Madani," *al-Najm* (Baghdad) 8 (Jan. 1936): 134-39—where the Chaldean author takes the position that the temporal authorities are God's representatives on earth and should be obeyed—and Bahnām, *Nafahat al-Khizām*, pp. 26-27.
135. For a text of the speech, see Great Britain, *Report on the Administration of Iraq for the Year 1931*, Colonial No. 74 (London: 1932), pp. 62-63.
136. For a letter from the apostolic delegate to the minister of the interior, dated 4 Aug. 1931, expressing satisfaction with the policies of the Iraqi govern-

ment towards its minorities, see ibid., pp. 63-64.

137. See p. 160 n. 70.

138. Robert B. Betts, "The Indigenous Arabic-Speaking Christian Communities of Greater Syria and Mesopotamia" (Ph.D. diss., Johns Hopkins University, 1968), p. 300. For a study of the Kurdish problem in Iraq both before and after the republic was established there in 1958, see Arfa, *The Kurds*, pp. 130-142; Mahmūd al-Durrah, *al-Qadiyah al-Kurdiyah* (Beirut, 1966); Edgar O'Ballance, *The Kurdish Revolt; 1961-1970* (London: 1973); and David G. Adamson, *The Kurdish War* (New York: 1965).

139. See Nouro, *My Tour,* pp. 17/278-18/279; cf. "Ibn al-'Ibri," "al-Ṭā'ifah al-Suryānīyah," p. 70.

140. See Betts, *Christians in the Arab East*, pp. 183-84.

141. Referred to as "Mahrajān Mār Afrām al-Suryāni wa-al-Tabib Hunayn bin Ishāq," the conference was attended by the Syrian Orthodox patriarch Ighnātiyūs Ya'qūb III as well as by other local and foreign experts, including Muslim specialists in Syriac. See *M.B.* 12 (1974): 174-75. See also A. de Halleux, "Une renaissance syriaque chez les chrétiens iraqiens," *Irenikon* (Belgium) 47 (1974): 209-18. For text of the law proclaiming Syriac as one of the languages of the country, see Decree No. 251 issued by the Iraqi Council of the Revolution on 16 April 1972.

142. For an account on the Syrian Orthodox presence in Jerusalem at the present, see "Qaddāsat Sayyidna al-Baṭaryark Yatafaqqad Shū'ūn Abrashiyat al-Quds," *M.B.* 2 (1963): 206-7.

143. W. Wright, *Catalogue of Syriac Manuscripts in the British Museum*, 3 vols., 1:265, 267; O.F.A. Meinardus, "The Syrian Jacobites in the Holy City," p. 66. Consult also Matthew Spinka, "The Effect of the Crusades upon Eastern Christianity," pp. 254-55.

144. H. C. Luke, "The Christian Communities in the Holy Sepulchre," in C. R. Ashbee, ed., *Jerusalem 1920-1922* (London: 1924), pp. 47-48, quoting the monk Theodoric's *Libellus de Locis Sanctis*, written about 1172. For other accounts, see Jacques de Vitry, *The History of Jerusalem, A.D. 1180,* trans. Aubrey Stewart, in Palestine Pilgrims' Text Society, vol. 11, no. 2, pp. 67-76.

145. Constantinople, 26 April 1899, no. 76. See also Luke, ibid., pp. 55-56; Meinardus, "Syrian Jacobites," 67-70.

146. The Nestorian presence has been noted in other sixteenth century accounts on Palestine. According to Assemani, as late as the eighteenth century the Nestorians had a church in Jerusalem which had been the seat of a Nestorian archbishop since the thirteenth century. See I. H. Hall, "On a Nestorian Liturgical Manuscript from the Last Nestorian Church and Convent in Jerusalem," *Journal of the American Oriental Society* 13 (1888): 290; H. C. Luke, "The Christian Communities in the Holy Sepulchre," p. 52.

147. By Jacobites, Rauwolff apparently means the Copts (Golti), since his "Syrians" are the Jacobites of Syria and Mesopotamia, the Syrian Orthodox. He states that they (the "Syrians") own the House of St. Mark in the southeast quarter of the city, a structure which the Jacobites occupy to this day. The term "Syrian" is sometimes used in conjunction with

Jacobites in order to distinguish them from the "Jacobite" Copts or Abyssinians, the term "Jacobite" apparently meaning Monophysite. (See p. 7.)

148. See Hieronymous, "Ancient Churches at Odds," *Jerusalem Post Magazine* (May 1970), p. 5. During the summer of 1979 Egypt asked Israel, through its Minister of State for Foreign Affairs Buṭrus Ghāli, a Coptic Christian, to return the eastern section of the Church of the Holy Sepulchre to the Coptic church. According to a report in *al-Ahram*, the Coptic church had decided that no Egyptian pilgrims would visit Jerusalem until the Copts were reinstated to their section of the Holy Sepulchre shrine. *Jerusalem Post*, intl. ed., 10-16 June 1979.

149. Meinardus, "Syrian Jacobites," p. 78. The Monophysite communities have not been without claims and counterclaims among themselves. As late as 1933, there were tensions between the Armenians and the Jacobites due to property claims the former made concerning the Chapel of St. Nicodemus.

150. They celebrate Christmas at the Church of the Nativity in Bethlehem, where they are accommodated by the Armenians, who traditionally furnish them the sacramental wine, the candles, and the incense, as well as the vessels, but not the chalice. For details on the celebration of the divine liturgy, see Meinardus, "Syrian Jacobites," pp. 79-80. Consult also *Middle East Forum* 39 (April 1963): 42-43.

151. Writing in the thirteenth century, Bar Hebraeus noted that the Syrian Jacobite archbishop of Jerusalem lived at the monastery of St. Simon. Jacques de Vitry noted that the monastery of St. Mary Magdalene was inhabited by 70 Syrian Jacobite monks. *History,* pp. 72 et seq.; Yūhanna Dū labāni, "al-Suryān fi Falastīn wa-dayr Maryam al-Majdalīyah," *Al-Ḥikmah* (July 1928): 434-43; G. Every, "Syrian Christians in Jerusalem 1183-1282," pp. 365-66.

152. See I. H. Hall, p. 290; Ghrighūriyūs Buṭrus Bahnām, *Bayt Marqus fi Awrūshalim, aw Dayr Mār Marqus li-al-Suryān* (Jerusalem: 1962); Ighnāṭiyūs Yaʿqūb III, "Bayt Yūhanna Marqus, Awwal Kanisah Masīhīyah," *M.B.* 2 (1964): 351-54; *Palestine Exploration Fund Quaterly (1895),* pp. 327-28.

153. *C.N.F.I.*, Dec. 1963, p. 7.

154. Rahhal, "Notes," 376; "Ibn al-ʿIbri," "al-Tā'ifah al-Suryāniyah," p. 123.

155. For a delightful account of the Jacobites in Jerusalem and Bethlehem, see Delia Khano, "The Assyrian Community in Palestine," *Middle East International* (Jan. 1976), pp. 26-28. For Jacobite presence in the Persian Gulf region, see pp. 130-1.

7. The Foreground and Conclusion

1. See pp. 128-9.

2. For the impact of the civil war in Lebanon on the Christians of the region, see pp. 112-3.

3. The Christians after the war reflected in their thinking the tragedy that had befallen them in 1914-18. See Betts, "Christian Communities of Greater Syria and Mesopotamia," p. 53. "Almost to a man," writes Betts, "the

Christians of Greater Syria and Mesopotamia were willing to accept a European mandate, and the majority favored it.'' In the rural areas, even the Greek Orthodox Christians, strong supporters of the Arab nationalist movement, shared with the rest of the Christians the fear of an untried Arab nationalism. For more on the anxieties of the Christian communities, see Kamal Salibi, *A Modern History of Lebanon,* p. 116

4. A. L. Tibawi, "Syria in War Time Agreements and Disagreements," *Middle East Forum* 43 (1967): 84-85.

5. For the reaction of the Jacobite community to the new regime, see pp. 9-10.

6. For an account of the Jacobite position, rejecting dependence on European "Christians," see pp. 115-16.

7. Betts, "Christian Communities," pp. 559-61.

8. In his study of Christian Arabs, Albert H. Hourani has shown that even during the Ottoman period there were those, like Farah 'Anṭūn, who were "at pains to dissociate the eastern Christians from the western missionaries and still more from the European Powers." Hourani calls 'Anṭūn "an eastern Christian consciousness," who asserted that "We are not responsible for what Western Christendom had done; our loyalty is to the East—we have always been faithful to the sultan." *Arabic Thought in the Liberal Age* p. 259. Cf. Hourani, *Minorities in the Arab World*, p. 24; Hourani, *Syria and Lebanon: A Political Essay*, p. 80.

9. Patriarch of the Syrian Catholics, the Uniat branch of the Jacobite church.

10. Walter M. Abbott and Joseph Gallagher trans. and eds., *The Documents of Vatican II* (New York: 1966), p. 663, n. 13.

11. Ibid. For a detailed study of the Vatican II deliberations see Fr. Julius Basetti-Sani, "For a Dialogue between Christians and Muslims," *M. W.* 57 (1967): 126-37; 186-96. In 1979, when Pope John Paul II visited Turkey, he called upon the Muslims to examine their common roots with Christians—their reverence for Jesus as prophet, and for the Virgin Mary, and their belief in one God—and spoke of the two faiths together embarking on a crusade against the evils of the consumer society and for "moral values, peace and liberty." See *Lancaster New Era* (Lancaster, Pa.), 4 Dec. 1979.

12. See Vatican II document on "Dogmatic Constitution of the Church," in Abbott and Gallagher, *Documents of Vatican II*, p. 35.

13. About ten years before the Declaration was passed a Lebanese Muslim had referred to this Christian refusal as "the only cause of estrangement between the two religions" and called for its removal, the "fulfillment of a duty long overdue." *Al-Diyār*, 3 April 1956, quoted by Nabih A. Fāris, "The Muslim Thinker and His Christian Relations," *M. W.*, 47 (1957): 62.

14. In the spring of 1966, Pope Paul received Dr. Mahdi Ruhāni and presented him with a medal. See *Arab News and Views*, April 1966, p. 3. For a study of diplomatic relations between the Arab states and the Vatican, see Hassan Suliak, "The Moslem States and the Vatican," *Unitas* 8 (Winter 1956): 225-30.

15. Alex Zanotelli, "Islam: Too Soon for a Dialogue?" *World mission* 17 (Fall 1966): 94; see also *Mélanges Institut Dominicain d'Études Orientales du*

Caire 8 (1964-66), 407-22.

16. *Ecumenical Press Service*, no. 12 (8 April 1965), p. 6.

17. For a change in the Protestant missionary outlook in recent times, see Joseph, *Nestorians,* pp. 226-29; G. Appleton, "Christian Encounter with Other Religions," *Frontier*, Summer 1959, pp. 134-39.

18. Epp. "Palestine in 1968," *Mennonite Central Committee News Service*, December 6, 1968. For a discussion of Eastern Christians as evangelists to Muslims, see Joseph, ibid., pp. 42-45, 230-33; Edward Wakin, *A Lonely Minority: The Modern Story of Egypt's Copts,* pp. 172-74.

19. Malka Rabinowitz, "Sharing the Patriarchs, Problems of Prayer in Hebrew," *Jerusalem Post Magazine,* 4 Oct. 1968, pp. 2, 12.

20. See Muhammad A. Ra'ūf, "What Jerusalem Means to My Faith, a Muslim View," *Mid East, A Middle East-North Africa Review*, vol. 8, no. 4 (1968): 13.

21. "Joint Statement Issued by the Grand Sheikh of al-Azhar, His Eminence Hassan Mamoun and the Pope of Alexandria and All Africa, His Holiness Kyrollos VI," *Majallat al-Azhar*, 39, pt. 2 (May-June 1967): 15-16.

22. *Middle East Newsletter* 2 (Dec. 1968): 3.

23. "History of Religions: Its Nature and Significance for Christian Education and the Muslim-Christian Dialogue," *Numen* (April 1956: 82.

24. See Elie Salem, "Nationalism and Islam," *M.W.* 52 (1962): 285, no. 36.

25. "A Comparison of the Islamic and Christian Approaches to Hebrew Scripture," *Journal of Bible and Religion*, vol. 31, no. 4 (1963): 283-84, 292.

26. *C.N.F.I.* 18 (Dec. 1967): 10.

27. See Thomas P. Anderson and Jacob Neusner, "After the Six Days War: Two Views on Jewish-Christian Dialogue," *Continuum* 5 (1968): 713-19, where a visiting professor of Old Testament from Chicago Theological Seminary is quoted, referring to present-day Israel as "a sacred nation that had a claim upon our affections as Christians above and beyond that which any other foreign country might have." He is also reported as saying, "The enemies of Israel are our enemies," and that the internationalization of Jerusalem was unthinkable; one could not internationalize a sacrament. See also Alice and Roy Eckhardt, *Encounter with Israel: A Challenge to Conscience* (New York, 1970). The Eckhardts' thesis is that the Christians are duty-bound to atone for their past offenses against the Jewish people by supporting zionist aspirations embodied in the state of Israel. For a more balanced work from the point of view of a Christian theologian sympathetic toward zionism, see James Parkes's *Whose Land? A History of the Peoples of Palestine.* For the growing literature by liberal Protestants challenging the fundamentalist Biblical interpretation of "Israel,' see William Holladay, *Zionism-Judaism, Is the Old Testament Zionist?* (Beirut: University Christian Center Forum, 1968).

28. Palestinian Christians point especially to such verses as Joshua 24:13: "I gave you a land which you had not built, to dwell in; you have eaten of vineyards and olive groves which you did not plant"; Deut. 8:6-9; 9:1-4; Joshua 11:16-23.

29. Abbott and Gallagher, *Documents of Vatican II,* p. 657.

30. From a purely Islamic point of view, the schema had no weight because ac-

cording to the Qur'ān Jesus was not crucified. Cairo's popular weekly *al-Muṣawwar* in an editorial wrote that from a moral point of view "the Vatican Council's decision, far from being objectionable, should be welcomed by the Arabs." Dr. Ḥasan Sa'ab, a Lebanese Muslim active in the Christian-Muslim dialogue, wrote that the Declaration "deserves to be imitated rather than criticized . . . It now approaches the Koran's concept of the unity . . . of the people of the Holy Scriptures . . . made up of Jews, Christians, and Muslims, who worship God." The Muslim religious leaders of Israel expressed "deep regrets" at the opposition to this historic decision voiced by Muslims, reminding them that the Christian statement confirmed the words of the Qur'ān: " . . . Yet they slew him not, neither crucified him, but he was represented by one in his likeness." Sura *Women,* verse 156; *C.N.F.I.* 15 (Dec. 1964): 7-8; *Ecumenical Press Service,* no.38 (28 Oct. 1965):7.

31. C.N.F.I. 13 (1962): 4-5.

32. Betts, "Christian Communities" (Ph.D. diss.) pp. 549-50; 'Iliya abu al-Rūs, *al-Yahudiyah al-'Alamiyah wa-Harbuha al-Mustamirrah 'Ala al-Masihiyah* (Beirut: 1964), pp. 14-15, 19-20.

33. *Ecumenical Press Service,* no. 8 (11 March 1965): 8.

34. Article by Suhayl Qāsha, "al-Sahyūniyah Tuharrif al-Kitāb al-Muqaddas," *M.B.* 16 (Nov. 1978): 527-530, (Dec. 1978): 602-5; 17 (Jan. 1979): 13-17, (Feb. 1979): 77-81; (March 1979): 135-41; (April 1979): 200-3; (May-June 1979): 267-71.

35. In their sermons Muslim theologians stress that Palestine is a Muslim "holy land," whose soil "is drenched with the blood of pious martyrs," including companions of the Prophet. "The case of Palestine is the case of all the Muslims," stated one of the recommendations of the Second Islamic Conference held at al-Azhar in 1965; the Muslim conscience will not be at peace until "the holy land returns to its inhabitants." See al-Azhar, *al-Mu'tamar al-Thāni li-Majma' al-Buhuth al-Islāmiyah,* May 1965, pp. 399-400. This position has been repeated in all the succeeding Islamic conferences. Consult also Bruce M. Borthwick, "The Islamic Sermon as a Channel of Political Communication in Syria, Jordan, and Egypt" (Ph.D. diss., University of Michigan, 1966), pp. 140-41, 154.

36. Consult Michael Walzer, *The Revolution of the Saints* (Cambridge, Mass.: 1965); Roland H. Bainton, "The Left Wing of the Reformation," *Journal of Religion* 22 (April 1951): 124-34; Karl Kautsky, *Communism in Central Europe in the Time of the Reformation* (New York: 1966); Peter J. Klassen, *The Economics of Anabaptism, 1525-1560,* (London: 1964).

37. See pp. 120-1.

38. This is not the place to discuss the Iranian revolution, symbolized by the Ayatollah Ruhollah Khomeini. Fueled as it was by various groups and classes, including the radical elements and the educated, the revolution most probably will not succeed to establish a theocracy in accordance with the clergy's millenarian, messianic concepts. That dream might prove to be as elusive as the visions of the shah to convert his country into a West Germany of the Middle East, neglecting the cultural base on which he tried to build his steel mills and assembly lines.

39. See James R. King, "The Theme of Alienation in Contemporary Middle

Eastern Literature," *M.W.* 68 (April 1978): 111-31. Professor King points out that it would be difficult to name an ideology or strategy of renewal that some Arab theoretician has not proposed during recent years. Tradition, reform, existentialism, secularism, logical positivism—all have competed for the loyalty of the young.

40. See remarks by Professor F. Ajami in *New York Times*, 15 Nov. 1978, and by Flora Lewis in ibid., 31 Dec. 1979. In the United States militant fundamentalists currently claim close to 50 million devoted listeners who turn to religious television for entertainment, conversion, healing, and positive thinking, as well as "political signal calling." See Martin E. Marty, "Fundamentalism Reborn, Faith and Fanaticism," *Saturday Review*, May 1980, pp. 37-42.

41. The Arab governments, with notable exceptions, have not befriended the Khomeini government. The monarchical regimes of the Arab world have been especially antagonized by the Tehran government's propaganda against the "un-Islamic despotic rulers" of Saudi Arabia and the Gulf Emirates. Early in 1980, President Bani-Sadr said that in his opinion "all Arab radio stations should be blown up because of all the lies they have told and are telling the people." See *F.B.I.S.* 5 (13 Feb. 1980). See also D. Price, "Kuwait: The Arab Reaction to Iran," *Washington Quarterly* 2, no. 2 (1979): 117-20. Long before the Iraq-Iran war started in the fall of 1980, the Iraqi radio was calling the Ayatollah a "turbaned Shah" and a "racist lunatic." (See *F.B.I.S.* 5 (16 Jan. 1980): E-1; see also ibid., (30 Jan. 1980): E-4-5. For anti-Iraq propaganda from the Tehran radio's international service in Arabic, broadcast before the Iraq-Iran conflict, see ibid., 5 (24 Jan. 1980), Supplement 023, pp. 31-33.

42. The Arab governments, unlke the shah's regime, whose aloof and energetically anti-Islamic policies helped ignite the Iranian revolution, have always shown considerable respect for the religious establishment. Indeed, in the Sunnite Arab world, the religious class and institutions have functioned as state bureaucracies, mobilizing support for the government and legitimizing its policies. In Iran, on the other hand, the theologians have existed as a hierarchy apart from the state, and Shi'ism has often served as a vehicle for mobilizing political resistance against both high-handed rulers, and the domination of foreign powers.

43. In the late 1970s, right-wing Muslim groups were reported to have control over student governments of most Egyptian universities. (A study of college students in Kuwait—the sample representing students from thirteen Arab countries and probably reflecting the conservative climate of Kuwait—showed that they "ranked religion first in their hierarchy of group affiliation, followed by family, citizenship, national origin (Arab), and political ideology." Only the Palestinians, South Yamanis, and Bahrainis ranked citizenship—"Palestinian citizenship" in the case of the Palestinians—and political party higher than religious affiliation. Consult T. E. Farah, "Group Affiliations of University Students in the Arab Middle East (Kuwait)," *Journal of Social Psychology* 106 (Dec. 1978): 161-65.)

44. *New York Times,* 29 Dec. 1979.

45. Syrian defense Minister Major General Muṣṭafa Talās, quoted in *F.B.I.S.*

(29 Jan. 1980): H-7. In neighboring Iraq, the Ba'th party follows a secularist policy; the party's state apparatus and educational system emphasize the Arab bond that unites the Iraqis.

46. See Richard M. Harley, "U.S.S.R. Muslims Quietly React to Afghanistan," *Christian Science Monitor*, 25 June 1980.

47. Within Iran, the Shi'ite but Arab Ayatollah Muhammad Tāhir al-Shubayr Khāghāni has charged that Khomeini's policies are against Islam. See comments by Khāghāni in *New York Times*, 2 June 1979.

48. In his writings and speeches, Ayatollah'Ruhollah Khomeini has emphasized that "imperialism" deliberately introduced the concept of the separation of church and state into the Muslim world in order to weaken it. The clerics were to be kept out of politics in order to remove from the conduct of affairs, argues Khomeini, the one group that is willing and able to resist Western imperialism. See Professor Daniel Dishon's article "Faith and Politics," *Jerusalem Post* (intl. ed.), 18-25 Nov. 1979, pp. 10-11.

49. President Sadat, associating the internal criticism by the Coptic church leadership with the attacks against his government by Egyptian emigrant groups overseas, made an unprecedented attack on 14 May 1980 on the Egyptian Coptic church leadership, accusing them of slandering the government abroad, and warned the Coptic leaders to cease recruiting Christian support abroad. On 1 July 1980 *al-Ahram* reported that the Coptic church had denounced emigrant Coptic groups in the United States for their "abuse and insults to our country" and had declared that these groups had "nothing to do with us." See *F.B.I.S.* 5 (15 July 1980): pp. D-2-3. For details on Christian-Muslim communal tensions in Egypt, see Center for the Study of the Modern Arab World (Saint Joseph's University, Beirut), "Tensions in Middle East Society," *CEMAM Reports* (1972-73): 1, no. 1, 7-55. President Sadat's tough new policy of 5 Sept. 1981, of stifling dissent and fighting "sectarian sedition," resulted in the deposition of Pope Shannūda III of the Coptic church. Among the 1536 persons arrested were 150 Copts, including 16 priests and 6 bishops. See *New York Times*, 8 Sept. 1981, and *F.B.I.S.*, 6-10 Sept. 1981.

50. In her excellent study of the Jews of Poland, Professor Celia S. Heller points out that it is only in some countries of the West, under the impact of capitalist development and democratic ideology, that the majority does not react to cultural and religious differences with suspicion and hostility. See her *On the Edge of Destruction* (New York: 1977), p. 63.

51. *New York Times,* 14-15 Sept. 1979. See also Flora Lewis, ibid., 31 Dec. 1979, where she describes these trends of an Islamic revival as "wrenching" for the region's minorities.

52. Early in 1980, the Khomeini government announced that Iranian Christians and Jews, "together with the rest of the nation, must participate in the formation of the 20 million-strong army"; toward this end, classes for military training were to be set up in churches, synagogues, and Zoroastrian temples. The country's religious minorities, the announcement said, "played an effective role during the revolution and sacrificed dozens of martyrs." See *F.B.I.S.* 5 17 Jan. 1980.

53. See *New York Times*, 11 Sept. 1979.

54. The old millet system made political rather than cultural demands on the subjects; the various millets maintained not only their own churches and schools, but also hospitals, courts, and quarters—as well as distinctive dress codes; today Christians and Muslims use the same educational, medical, and legal institutions. See Richard M. Schwartz, "The Structure of Christian-Muslim Relations in Contemporary Iran" (Ph.D. diss., Washington University, St. Louis, Mo., 1973), p. 171.

55. *New York Times*, 14-15 Sept. 1979. The king has been criticized for favoring Christians in high places; others point out that in the past, Christians were often favored because of their education, a fact no longer true. Most probably, the king's reason for choosing Christians was his confidence in their loyalty.

56. Looking into the future of the Arab world, two Arab scholars at a conference sponsored by Georgetown University's Center for Contemporary Arab Studies spoke of the eventual transformation of Arab society through a "popular movement," and of the triumph of "democratization and secularization of Arab society," to be brought about by "irreversible forces . . . grounded in an objective historical circumstance." See H. Barakat and H. Sharabi, in M. C. Hudson, ed., *The Arab Future* (Washington, D. C., 1979), pp. 79, 101, 104.

57. The number of Muslim youth who immigrate to Western countries, especially to the United States and Canada, has also greatly increased since World War II. Here many marry "Christian" wives and adapt themselves to the American pattern of life. See Walter Holsten, "The Muslim Presence in the West," *International Review of Missions* 55 (1966): 448-56; Yvonne Y. Haddad, "The Muslim Experience in the United States," *Link* 2, no. 4 (Sept.-Oct. 1979): 1-12; A. B. Zahlan, "The Arab Brain Drain," *Middle East Studies Association Bulletin* 6, no. 3 (1 Oct. 1972): 1-16.

58. *New York Times,* 14 Sept. 1979.

59. See Richard G. Hovannisian, "Ebb and Flow of the Armenian Minority in the Arab Middle East," *Middle East Journal 28* (Winter 1974): 32. See also pp. 104-5.

60. Schwartz, "Structure of Christian-Muslim Relations" pp. 175-76.

61. See Norman A. Horner, "Present-Day Christianity in the Gulf States of the Arabian Peninsula," *Occasional Bulletin of Missionary Research* 2 (April 1978): 54. (For information on the Christian presence in the Arabian and Persian Gulf states, the writer is indebted to Norman A. Horner for this excellent study.) For Kuwait, Horner gives the following figures (p. 54):

Greek Orthodox (Arab)	6,000
Greek Catholics (Arab)	2,900
Armenians	6,600
Armenian Catholics	350
Coptic Orthodox	1,300
Coptic Catholics	50
Syrian Orthodox and Church of Malabar	2,100
Syrian Catholic	200
Nestorians	400

Chaldeans	1,200
Maronites	1,800
Protestants and Anglicans, including Indians	4,700
Roman Catholics (Latin Rite)	6,500

62. Horner estimates that as many as 30 percent of the large Indian population employed in the Gulf region are of Christian background. Predominantly from South India, the majority of them are Roman Catholics, followed by large numbers from the other two important Christian bodies on the Malabar coast, the Syrian Orthodox and the Mar Tuma Christians. For an account of these historic congregations and their relations with the Syrian Orthodox of the Middle East, see Appendix C.
63. See "al-Kanisah al-Suryāniyah fi Kuwayt," *M.B.* 3 (June 1965): 522.
64. Horner, "Present-Day Christianity," pp. 55, 60.
65. Hudson, *The Arab Future,* p. 94.
66. Quoted in the *New York Times,* 15 Sept. 1979.
67. In Maximos IV Sayegh, *The Eastern Christians,* pp. 32-33.

Appendix A

1. The Jacobites refer to themselves as Suryan or Suryan Orthodox. See pp. 2, 7.
2. Translated by professor Robert J. Barnett, Jr., from the Italian version of the decree in Turkish. For the Italian original, see *Scritture riferite nelle congregazione generali* of the Sacred Congregation of the Propaganda of the Faith, vol. 241, fol. 328-29.
3. Diyarbakr.
4. Most probably al-ʿid (the feast) for the month of Shawwal of the Muslim calendar, when the feast of al-Fiṭr is celebrated.

Appendix B

1. Text in *M.H.,* 44 (1848), 98-99.
2. Text in Anderson, *Oriental Churches,* vol. 2, pp. 4-7.

Appendix C

1. For a distance of this term in reference to the Jacobites, see pp. 2, 7.
2. At the present the state of Kerala, created in 1956, embraces the land of the former state of Travancore-Cochin, of which Malabar was a part.
3. See O. H. Parry, *Six Months in a Syrian Monastery,* pp. 347-48.
4. For a detailed study of the Nestorian apostolic labors in India, see L. W. Brown, *The Indian Christians of St. Thomas* (Cambridge: 1956).
5. Consult *N.C.E.,* vol. 13, p. 899. See also Cardinal E. Tisserant, *Eastern Christianity in India,* pp. 56-68, 163-71; Brown, ibid., pp. 32-37.
6. For the unsuccessful efforts by the Syrians to free themselves from Portugese-Catholic control and their attempts to contact the churches of the Middle East, see Julius Richter, *A History of Missions in India* (London: 1908), pp. 83-85, and Brown, ibid., pp. 99-101.
7. Brown, ibid., pp. 111-112; Adrian Fortescue, *The Lesser Eastern Churches,* p. 365. Most probably the Jacobites, with better contacts with the West than the Nestorians, in such cosmopolitan centers as Aleppo and Jerusalem where they were in daily touch with European merchants and

pilgrims, were much better informed than the Nestorians of the grievances of the Christians in India and hence of their earlier presence there.

8. Another party of the Romo-Syrians rebelled and returned to the Nestorian Church at the turn of this century. In 1907 a rebel church centered in Trichur,accepted the authority of the Nestorian patriarch, Mār Sham'ūn XIX Benjamin, returning Nestorianism to India after almost 300 years of eclipse. For historical details tracing the formation of the present Nestorian Church of Trichur, see B. Jashanmal, "The Origin of the Nestorian Church of Trichur" (Master's thesis, Carleton University, Ottawa, Canada, 1966).

9. It was in 1795 that the Malabar coast was taken by the British; a resident was appointed in the region in 1800.

10. Brown, *Indian Christians*, p. 125. Eventually the Mar Thoma (St. Thomas) Syrian church would be formed by the Indian-Syrian reformers who were educated in the schools and seminaries of the London-based Church Missionary Society. For a discussion of their break from the Jacobite church, see ibid., pp. 140-48; Tisserant, *Eastern Christianity*, pp. 148-49; *N.C.E.*, vol. 5, p. 16.

11. Brown, ibid., 148. See also P. Cheriyan, *The Malabar Syrians and the Church Missionary Society*, pp. 83-104, and ibid., Appendix E (p. 384), for the deed describing the property and endowment set up for the use of the "Syrian College."

12. See Brown, ibid., G. T. MacKenzie, *State of Christianity in Travancore* (Trivandrum, India: 1901); Tisserant, *Eastern Christianity*.

13. Traditionally the patriarch or one of his bishops consecrated an Indian as metropolitan. We read that in 1751 an Indian aspirant ordered from the Dutch East India Company a "consecrating bishop" at the cost of 4,000 rupees. See Julius Richter, *A History of Missions in India*, pp. 88-89.

14. Brown, *Indian Christians*, pp. 136-37. For a detailed account of Mar Athanasiyus's mission, see Cheriyan, *Malabar Syrians*, pp. 161-74; E. R. Hambye, "A Syrian Orthodox Mission to Malabar in 1825-1826, "*Orientalia Christiana Periodica* 34, no. 1, pp. 141-44.

15. Brown, ibid., p. 142; see also Tiserant, *Eastern Christianity*, p. 149.

16. Brown, ibid., pp. 141-43.

17. Ibid., p. 144.

18. In 1930 a former Jacobite priest and his congregation made a Catholic profession of faith and after lengthy negotiations with the Vatican were recognized as a Catholic church. Known as Malankars, they follow the rite of the Syrian Catholic church. In the early 1960s they had one metropolitan province and about 130,000 faithful. See *N.C.E.*, vol. 13, p. 899; Bertold Spuler, *Die morgenländischen Kirchen*, p. 338; Stephen Rahhal, "Some Notes on the West Syrians," p. 380; Tisserant, *Eastern Christianity,* pp. 157-60.

19. See n. 8 above, and also Jashanmal, pp. 91-95; Tisserant, ibid., pp. 105-20.

20. For a scholarly and detailed account of these rivalries, see Brown, *Indian Christians*.

21. Parry, *Six Months*, pp. 349-50; Brown, ibid., p. 148.

22. Armalah, "Fi al-Baṭaryarkiyah al-Anṭākiyah," p. 668.

23. Known as the Synod of Mulanturutti, where it was held.
24. For details on the synod, see Brown, *Indian Christians*, p. 145; Tisserant, *Eastern Christianity*, pp. 151-52.
25. Brown, ibid., p. 152; *N.C.E.*, vol. 5, p. 16. Tisserant writes that the excommunication came about when the metropolitan stubbornly refused to let the patriarch "examine the finances." *Eastern Christianity*, p. 153.
26. See his enlightening communications to *E.C.R.* 6 (1974): 116; 7 (1975): 91, 196; 10 (1978): 148-49; see also ibid., 1 (1966): 56-58 183-85.
27. For details, with emphasis on the Indian scene, see Brown, *Indian Christians,* pp. 150-55; Tisserant, *Eastern Christianity*, 153-55.
28. It is curious that the Nestorian term "Catholicos" and not the Jacobite title "Maphrian" was used. Historically both titles conferred upon the holder ecclesiastical jurisdiction in distant provinces. In the case of the Nestorians, "Catholicos" signified independence from Antioch.
29. Tisserant notes that the Turkish government had deposed the patriarch, and does not mention the church doing likewise; *Eastern Christianity*, p. 153.
30. Brown, *Indian Christians,* 151-55.
31. Previous efforts at reconciliation were made by the two predecessors of Mār Ya'qūb III, Ilyās (Elias) III, and Barsūm, Ilyās dying in India in 1932 while on his peace mission. See also Spuler, *Morgenländischen Kirchen*, p. 339; Brown, ibid., 155-56.
32. Hambye, *"Syrian Orthodox Mission," 7:91.*
33. *Ibid., 6:116.*

List of Abbreviations

A.B.C.	American Board of Commissioners (for Foreign Missions)
al-M.	al-Masarrah
C.N.F.I.	Christian News from Israel
E.C.	Etudes Carmélitaines
E.C.Q.	Eastern Churches Quarterly
E.C.R.	Eastern Churches Review
E.I.	Encyclopedia of Islam
E.O.	Echos d'Orient
F.B.I.S.	Foreign Broadcast Information Service
M.B.	al-Majallat al-Baṭaryarkīyah
M.H.	Missionary Herald
M.W.	Muslim World
N.C.E.	New Catholic Encyclopedia
P.O.C.	Proche-Orient chrétien
R.C.A.S.J.	Royal Central Asian Society Journal
R.H.M.	Révue d'histoire des missions
R.O.C.	Révue de l'Orient chrétien
S.M.	Spirit of Missions

Bibliography

Unpublished Sources

Archives and Manuscripts

Archives of the American Board of Commissioners for Foreign Missions, deposited at Houghton Library of Harvard College, Cambridge, Mass.

Eastern Turkey Mission, ABC:16.9.7, vols 1-2 (1860-71), 3-5 (1871-80), 6-9 (1880-90), 10-16 (1890-99), 17-25 (1900-09), 25 a-e (1910-19), 26 (1920-22).

Miscellaneous Papers Relating to the Near East Missions, ABC:16.5, vols. 3(1830-42), 5 (1860-1900, 1919-31), 6 (1900-19), 8 (1874-1930), 10 (1920-29).

Assyrian Mission, ABC:16.8.4, vol. 1 (1850-59).

L'archivio della S. Congregazione di Propaganda Fide, Rome.

Scritture riferite nelle congregazione generali, vol. 241, fol. 42-43, 173, 328-29, 478, 485.

Curia Generale dei Frati Minori Cappuccini. Archivum Generale, Rome.

"Missio: Mesopotamia," *Documenta officialia,* nos. H72, H72A (1843-87); *communicationes ordinariae* (1845-89)

Dayr al-Sharfah, Lebanon.

Ahmardiqnuh, Afrām. *Nabdhah Ta'rıkhiyah fī Ahwāl al-Millah al-Ya'qūbiyah min hın Infiṣāliha 'an al-Kanīsah al-Kathūlikiyah Hatta al-Yawm.* Umpaginated manuscript, no. 3.

'Atā' iq Ta' rikhiyah Suryānıyah, No. 16/7.

Ministère des Affairs Etrangères: Archives diplomatiques, agence consulaire; Paris.

Correspondance commerciale, Mossoul, 1878-1907.

Public Record Office, London. Foreign Office papers on Turkey, 1840-1913, from the British Embassy in Istanbul and the Consulates in Diyarbakr, Mosul, and Aleppo, F. O. Nos. 78/2398-2702; 97/425; 195/603; 424/141, 144, 145, 187, 188, 192, 202, 206, 208, 210, 238.

Presbyterian Church in the United States of America: Board of Foreign Missions, New York, N Y

Archives, 1870-1950.

Doctoral Dissertations

Betts, Robert B. "The Indigenous Arabic-Speaking Christian Communities of Greater Syria and Mesopotamia." (Ph. D. diss., Johns Hopkins University, Baltimore, Md., 1968).

Carleton, Alford. "The Millet System" (Ph.D. diss., Hartford [Conn.] Theological Seminary, 1936).

Chalfoun, Pierre. "Le patriarche Michel Giarve" (Ph.D. diss., Papal Institute of Oriental Studies, Rome, 1961).

Euw, Charles K. von, S.E.O.L. "The Union of the Syro-Jacobites with Rome in the Mid-Seventeenth Century" (Ph.D. diss., Papal Institute of Oriental Studies, Rome, 1959).

Haddad, Robert Mitchell. "The Orthodox Patriarchate of Antioch and the Origins of the Melkite Schism" (Ph.D. diss., Harvard University, Cambridge, Mass., 1965).

Hayek, A. "Le relazioni della chiesa siro-giacobita colla Santa Sede dal 1143 al 1656" (Ph.D. diss., Papal Institute of Oriental Studies, Rome, 1936).

Hickey, Edward John. "The Society for the Propagation of the Faith—Its Foundation, Organization, and Success (1822-1922)" (Ph.D. diss., Catholic University of America, Washington, D. C., 1922).

Jwaideh, Wadie. "The Kurdish Nationalist Movement: Its Origins and Development" (Ph.D. diss., Syracuse [N. Y.] University 1960).

Lovejoy, Bahija F. "Christian Monasteries in Mesopotamia" (Ph.D. diss., Radcliffe College, Cambridge, Mass., 1958).

Moosa, Matti Isaac. "Kitāb al-Lu' lu' al-Manthūr, by Ignatius Aphram Barsoum, Syrian Patriarch of Antioch and all the East" (Ph.D. diss., Columbia University, New York, 1965).

Olson, Robert W. "The Siege of Mosul: War and Revolution in the Ottoman Empire, 1720-1743" (Ph.D. diss., Indiana University, Bloomington, 1973).

Schwartz, Richard M. "The Structure of Christian-Muslim Relations in Contemporary Iran" (Ph.D. diss., Washington University, St. Louis, Mo., 1973).

Masters Theses

Frankel, Ephraim, Jr. "The Maronite Patriarchate and Its Role in Lebanese Politics—a Case Study of the 1958 Lebanese Crisis" Masters thesis, American University of Beirut, 1971).

Jeranian, Panos S. "Catholic Armenian and Maronite Relations in Mt. Lebanon, 1720-1840" (Masters thesis, American University of Beirut, 1971).

Perry, Robert P. "European Explorations in Turkish Kurdistan, 1800-1842" (Masters thesis, American University of Beirut, 1965).

Takhtadzhian, Vardges. "The Separation of the Armenian Catholics from the Armenian Apostolic Church in the 18th Century" (Masters thesis, American University of Beirut, 1972).

Papers

Morony, M. G. "Religious Communities in Umayyad Iraq" (paper delivered at the Middle East Studies Association Conference, Binghampton, New York, 3 Nov. 1972).

Printed Documents, Contemporary Sources, and Chronicles

Abcl, Léonard. *Une mission religieuse en Orient au seizième siècle,* trans. and annotated by Adolphe d'Avril. Paris: 1865.

Agathangelus of St. Theresa, et al. *Chronicle of Events between the Years 1623 and 1733 Relating to the Settlement of the Order of Carmelites in Mesopotamia,* ed. and trans. Herman Gollancz. London: 1927.

American Board of Commissioners for Foreign Missions. *Annual Reports.* Boston, Mass., 1835-1880.

Armani, al-, Abu Ṣālih. *The Churches and Monasteries of Egypt and Some Neighboring Countries.* Oxford: 1895.

Assemani, J. S. *De Syris monophysitis dissertatio* (separate edition of vol. 2 of his *Bibliotheca Orientalis*). Rome: 1730.

Barhebraeus. See Ibn al- 'Ibri.

Bell, Gertrude L. *Review of the Civil Administration of Mesopotamia.* London: Cmd. 1061, 1920.

al-Birūni. *al-Āthār al-Bāqiyah 'an al-Qurūn al-Khāliyah*, trans. E. Sachau. London: 1879.

Chick, Herbert. *A Chronicle of the Carmelites in Persia and the Papal Mission of the 17th and 18th Centuries.* 2 vols. London: 1939.

Church Missionary Society. *Proceedings of the Church Missionary Society for Africa and the East.* London: 1890-1914.

Da Castrogiovanni, P. Giambattista, et al. "Sunto storico e descrittivo della missione apostolica dei Minori Cappuccini nella Mesopotamia,' *Analecta Ordinis Minorum Cappuccinoram* (Rome) 15 (1899), 199-208, 231-41, 263-71, 306-9, 340-45.

Dandini, Jerom. *A Voyage to Mount Libanus.* London: 1745.

Da Seggiano, Ignazio. "Documenti inediti sull apostolato dei Minori Cappuccini nel Vicino Oriente (1623-1683)," *Collectanea Franciscana* (Rome) 18 (1948), 118-244; 22 (1952), 339-86; 23 (1953), 297-338.

_____. "L'Opera dei Cappuccini per l'unione dei Cristiani nel Vicino Oriente durante il secolo XVII," *Orientalia Christiana Analecta*, No. 163. Rome: Pontifical Institute of Oriental Studies, 1962.

D'Avril, A. *Documents relatifs aux Églises de l'Orient* Paris: 1885.

De Gonzague, Louis. "Quelques aperçus de la vie des Capucins à Bagdad au début du XVIII' Siècle," *Collectanea Franciscana* (Rome) 4 (1934), 564-77.

De Vitry, Jacques (Jacobus de Vitriaco, Cardinal, d. 1240). *The History of Jerusalem A.D. 1180*, trans. from Latin by Aubrey Stewart, in Palestine Pilgrims' Text Society, vol. 11, no. 2. London: 1896.

Eldred, M John. *The Voyage of M. John Eldred to Tripolis in Syria by Sea, and from Thence by Land and River to Babylon* & Balsara, Anno. 1583, vol. 3. New York: Hakluyt Voyages, 1927.

Goodell, W., et al. *A Letter from the Missionaries at Constantinople in Reply to Charges by Rev. Horatio Southgate.* Boston: 1846.

Goormachtigh, B. M. "Histoire de la mission Dominicaine en Mésopotamie et en Kurdistan," *Analecta sacri ordinis fratrum praedicatorum* 2 (1895-96), 271, 405-19; 3 (1897-98), 79-88, 141-58, 197-214, 533-45.

Great Britain. *British and Foreign State Papers.* 1840-1930.

_____. *Parliamentary Debates.* 1850-1950.

_____. *Sessional Papers.*

   Correspondence respecting Christian Privileges, 1856.
   Reports received by H.M.'s Consuls relating to: Christians in Turkey, 1861, 1867.
   Conditions of Christian Subjects of the Porte, 1877.

Conditions of Population in Asia Minor and Syria, 1876-79, 1880, 1881, 1889.

Correspondence respecting the Asiatic Provinces of Turkey, 1905.

Green, John. *A Journey from Aleppo to Damascus—to Which Is Added an Account of the Maronites Inhabiting Mount Libanus, etc.: Collected from their own historians.* London: 1736.

Ibn al-' Ibri (Gregory Barhebraeus). *Chronicon syriacum,* ed. Paul Bedjan. Paris: 1890.

———. The Chronography of Gregory Abu 1 Faraj, trans. E. A. Wallis Budge. 2 vols. London: 1932.

'Irāq. al-Samarrā'i, Kāmil, ed. *Majmū'at al-Qawānin al-Khāṣṣah bi-al-Tawā'if al-Masihiyah wa-al-Mūsawiyah wa-al-Anẓimah wa-al-Bayānāt wa-al-Ta'limāt al-Sādirah bi-Mūjibiha.* Baghdad: 1951.

———. *Waqā'i'al-'Irāqiyah,* 1930-1954.

John of Ephesus. "Vita Baradai," in *Analecta Syriaca,* ed. J. P. N. Land, vol. 2. Leiden: 1862-75, pp. 364-83.

Lanza, Domenico. *al-Mawṣil fi al-Qarn al-Thāmin-'Ashar Hasab Mudhakkarāt Domenico Lanza,* trans. from Italian by R. Bidawid. Mosul: 1953.

League of Nations, Frontier Commission. *Question of the Frontier between Turkey and Iraq.* Document C. 400. M. 147, 1925, vii.

———. *Report to the Council of the League of Nations by General F. Laidoner on the Situation in the Locality of the Provisional Line of the Frontier between Turkey and Irak Fixed at Brussels on October 29, 1924.* Mosul: 23 Nov. 1925.

Lebanon. Ministry of Justice. *al-Majmū'at al-Ḥadīthah li-al-Qawānin al-Lubnāniyah.* Beirut: 1954.

Levi della Vida, G. *Documenti intorno alle relazioni delle chiese orientali con la S. Sede durante il pontificato di Gregorio XIII.* Rome: Studi e Testi, vol. 143, 1948.

———. *Ricerche sulla formazione del più antico fondo dei manoscritti orientali della biblioteca Vaticana.* Vatican: 1939.

Louis de Sainte-Therese. "Histoire de la mission d'Alep," in series of articles under the title "Documents sur les missions des Carmes dechausses," *Études Carmélitaines* 7 (1922), 50-74, 206-23.

Michael the Syrian. *Chronique de Michael le Syrien, patriarche jacobite d'Antioche (1166-99),* ed. J. B. Chabot. 4 vols. Paris: 1899-1910.

Mingana, Alphonse, ed. and trans. "Editions and Translations of Christian Documents in Syriac and Garshuni," *Bulletin of the John Rylands Library* 11 (1927), 10-49.

———. "The Early Spread of Christianity in Central Asia and the Far East: A New Document," in ibid. 9 (1925), 297-367.

———. *Theodorus, Bishop of Mopsuestia, d. ca. 428.* Cambridge: 1932-33.

Muqaddasi, al-. *Bibliotheca geographorum arabicorum (Ahsan al-Taqāsim fi Ma'rifat al-Aqālim),* ed. De Goeje, vol. 3. Leiden: 1877.

Nau, François N., ed. and trans. *Histoires d'Ahoudemmeh et de Marouta, metropolitains jacobites de Tagrit et de l'Orient (VI' et VII' siècles)* in *Patrologia Orientalis,* III, fasc. I. Paris: 1909.

Niebuhr, M. *Travels through Arabia, and Other Countries in the East,* trans. R.

Heron. 2 vols. Edinburgh: 1972.

Parry, O. H. *Six Months in a Syrian Monastery*. London: 1895.

Presbyterian Church in the United States of America, Board of Foreign Missions. *Annual Reports*. 1875-1958.

Protestant Episcopal Church in the U.S.A. *Proceedings of the Board of Missions,* 1842-50; *Proceedings of the General Convention,* 1847-50; *Journal of the General Convention,* 1841-50.

Rabbath, Antoine. *Documents inédits pour servir a l'histoire du christianisme en Orient*. 2 vols. Paris: 1910.

Russell, Alexander. *Natural History of Aleppo*. 2 vols. London: 1794.

St. John of Damascus. "Disputatio Saraceni et christiani," in *Patrologia Graeca,* vols. 94, 96.

Scher, Addai, ed. "Chronique de Seèrt," in *Patrologia Orientalis*, vol. 2. Paris: 1907-18).

Severius. "Vie de Sevère" (biography of the Jacobite church father Severus, written by one of his students), trans. Kugener, M.-A, in *Patrologia Orientalis* (Paris) 2 (1907), 1-115.

Southgate, Horatio, Jr. *Narrative of a Tour through Armenia, Kurdistan, Persia, and Mesopotamia with an Introduction and Occasional Observations upon the Condition of Mohamedanism and Christianity in Those Countries*. 2 vols. New York: 1840.

_____. *Narrative of a Visit to the Syrian (Jacobite) Church of Mesopotamia; with Statements and Reflections upon the Present State of Christianity in Turkey, and the Character and Prospects of the Eastern Churches*. New York, 1856.

_____. *A Letter for a Friend, In Reply to a Recent Pamphlet, from the Missionaries of the American Board of Commissioners for Foreign Missions, at Constantinople*. New York, 1845.

_____. "Proposed Mission to the Syrian Christians of Mesopotamia," *S.M.* 5 (1840), 56-63.

_____. *Vindication of the Rev. Horatio Southgate: A Letter to the Members of the Protestant Episcopal Church in the United States, from the Rev. Horatio Southgate, their Missionary at Constantinople*. New York, 1944.

Shābushti, al-. *Kitāb al-Diyārāt*, ed. *Kurkis Awwād* Baghdad: 1951.

Tritton, A. S., trans., and H. A. R. Gibb, annotator. "The First and Second Crusades from an Anonymous Syriac Chronicle," *Journal of the Royal Asiatic Society* (1933): 69-101; 273-305.

Tyler, William Seymour (1810-97). *Memoir of the Rev. Henry Lobdell, M.D., late Missionary of the American Board at Mosul; Including the Early History of the Assyrian Mission*. Boston: 1859.

Von Thielmann, Max F. G. *Journey in the Caucasus, Persia, and Turkey in Asia,* trans. Charles Heneage. 2 vols. London: 1875.

Wolff, Joseph. *Missionary Journal*. 2 vols. London: 1827-28.

Wright, W. *Catalogue of Syriac Manuscripts in the British Museum*. 3 vols. London: 1870-72.

Yāqūt. *Marāṣid al-'Iṭlā 'Ala 'Asmā' al-Amkinah wa-al-Biqā'*, ed. T. G. J. Joynboll. Vol. 1. Leyden: 1953.

Middle Eastern Sources: Books

'Abdāl, Afrām. *Kitāb al-Lu' lu' al-Nazid fi Ta' rikh Dayr Mār Bahnām al-Shahid.* Mosul, 1951.

Abu al-Fida. *Taqwim al-Buldān,* ed. J. T. Reinaud and de Slane. Paris, 1840.

Abu al-Rus, Iliya. *al-Yahūdiyah al- 'Alamiyah wa-Harbuha al-Mustamirrah 'ala al-Masihiyah.* Beirut, 1964.

Afrām, I. See Barsūm.

Afrām II, Ighnātiyūs. *al-Mabāhith al-Jaliyah fi al-Litirjiyāt al-Sharqiyah.* Dayr al-Sharfah (Lebanon), 1924.

al-'Aqqād, 'Abbās Mahmūd. *Athar al- 'Arab fi al-Hadārat al-Awrubbiyah.* Cairo, 1965.

Armalah, Ishāq. *Athar Faransa wa-Ma'āthiruha fi al-Lubnān wa-fi Sūriya.* Beirut, 1946.

_____. *al-Hurūb al-Salibiyah fi al-Athār al-Suryāniyah.* Beirut, 1929.

_____. *Kitāb al-Zahrat al-Dhakiyah fi al-Bataryarkiyah al-Suryāniyah al-Antā kiyah.* Beirut, 1909.

_____. *Lam'ah Ta'rikhiyah fi Adyār Mārdin al-Qadimah wa-Dayr Mār Afrām al-Suryāni al-Mushayyad 'Am 1884.* Beirut, 1909.

_____. *al-Qasāra fi Nakabāt al-Nasāra.* n.p., n.d.

_____. *al-Ri'āsa al-Bābawiyah fi al-Kanisat al-Suryāniyah.* Beirut, 1933.

_____. *Tarfah fi Akhbār Dayr al-Sharfah.* Beirut, 1920.

_____. *al-Tarfah fi Makhtūtāt Dayr al-Sharfah.* Junih (Lebanon), 1937.

Arsānis, Binyamin. *Ktaw-Qula d'M' alyūtih Mahammad Nwiya d'Islam.* Tehran, 1950.

Babū Ishāq, Rufā'il. *Ahwāl al-Nasāra Baghdad fi 'Ahd al-Khilāfah al-'Abbāsiyah.* Baghdad, 1960.

_____. *Ta'rikh Nasāra al-'Irāq Mudh Intishār al-Nasrāniyah fi al-aqtār al-'Irāqiyah ila Ayyāmina.* Baghdad, 1948.

Bahnām, Ghriighūriyūs Būlus. *Bayt Marqūs fi Awrushalim aw Dayr Mār Marqus lil-Suryān.* Jerusalem, 1962.

_____. *Nafahāt al-Khizām, Aw Hayāt al-Batrak Afrām.* Mosul, 1959.

Barsūm, *Nuzhat al-Adhhān fi Ta' rikh Dayr al-Za 'farān.* Mardin, 1917.

Barsūm, Mār Ighnātiyūs Afrām I. *Lam'ah fi Ta'rikh al-Ummah al-Suryāniyah fi al-'Irāq.* Jerusalem, 1936.

_____. *al-Muhadarāt allati alqāha Ghibtat al-Hibr al-'Allāmat Sayyidna Mār Ighnātiyūs Afrām Barsūm fi al-Jāmi'at al-Amirkiyah fi Bayrūt bi-Da-'wat Minha fi 1, 2, 4 Ayār Sanat 1933.* Jerusalem, 1933.

_____. *Ta'rikh Tūr 'Abdin, trans. from Syriac Ghrighūriyus Butrus Bahnām, Junih, Lebanon, 1963.*

al-Biruni. *al-Athār al-Bāqiyah 'an al-Qurūn al-Khāliyah,* ed. and trans. E. Sachau. London, 1879.

al-Dibs, Yūsuf Ilyās. *Ta' rikh Sūriyah,* vol. 4, Beirut, 1900.

al-Durrah, Mahmūd. *al-Qadiyah al-Kurdiyah.* Beirut, 1966.

al-Duwayhi, Istifān. *Ta'rikh al-Tā' ifa al-Mārūniya.* Beruit, 1870.

al-Ghazzi, Kāmil Ibn-Husayn. *Nahr al-Dhahab fi Ta' rikh Halab.* 3 vols. Aleppo, 1342-45/1923-26.

Giamil, Samuel. *Ktāwa d'Mat'aninwāti d' 'Ita d'Kaldāyi 'am Kursya Shlikhāya d'Rūmi.* Rome, 1902.

Günel, 'Aziz. *Türk Süryaniler Tārihi.* Diyarbakir, 1970.

al-Hasani, 'Abd al-Razzāq. *Ta'rikh al-'Irāq al-Siyāsi al-Hadith,* vol. 3, Sidon, 1948.

———. *Ta'rikh al-Wizārāt al-'Irāqiyah,* vol. 3 Sidon, 1953.

———. *al-'Irāq fi Dawrayy al-Ihtilāl wa-al-Intidāb.* 2 vols. Baghdad, 1935.

al-Jawashli, Hādi Rashid. *al-Hayāt al-Ijtimā 'iyah fi Kurdistān.* Baghdad, 1970.

al-Kaldāni, Butrus Nasri. *Kitāb Dhakhirat al-Adhhān fi Tawārikh al-Mashāriqah wa-al-Maghāribah al-Suryān.* Mosul, 1913.

Kāmil, Murād and Muhammad H. al-Bakri. *Ta'rikh al-Adab al-Suryāni min Nash'atihi ila al-Fath al-Islāmi.* Cairo, 1949.

Khasbāk, Shākir. *al-Akrād, Dirāsah Jughrāfiyah Ithnughrāfiyah.* Baghdad, 1972.

Lammens, Henri. *Tasrih al-Absār fi ma Yahtawi Lubnān min al-Athār.* 2 vols. Beirut, 1913-14.

Manna, Ya' qūb A. *Margi Pighyanayi d'Mardūta d'Aramayi.* Musul, 1901.

al-Mawsili, Yūsuf D. *Kitāb al-Lam'ah al-Shahiyah fi Nahu al-Lughat al-Suryāniyah 'ala Kilā Madhhabayy al-Gharbiyin wa-al-Sharqiyin,* vol. 1. Musul, 1896.

Mazlūm, Maksimūs. *Nabdhah Ta' rikhiyah fi-mā Jara li-Tā' ifat al-Rūm al-Kathūlik Mundh Sanat 1837 fa-ma ba'diha.* N.p., 1907(?).

Naqqāshah, Afrām. *Kitāb 'Ināyat al-Rahmān fi Hidāyat al-Suryān.* Beirut, 1910.

Nasri, Butrus. See al-Kaldāni.

al-Qāsim, Anis. *Nahnu wa-al-Fātikān wa-Isrā'il.* Beirut, 1966.

Sā' igh, Sulaymān. *Ta' rikh al-Mawsil.* 2 vols. Cairo, 1923, vol. 1; Beirut, 1928, vol. 2.

Sālih, Zaki. *Muqaddamah fi Dirāsat al'-Irāq al-Mu'āsir.* Baghdad, 1953.

al-Shammās, Yūsuf. *al-Qaddis Yuhanna al-Damashqi wa-al-Kanā'is al-Malakiyah fi al-Qurūn al-Wusta.* Sidon, 1949.

al-Shidyaq, Tannūs. *Akhbār fi Jabal Lubnān.* 2 vols. Beirut, 1959.

al-Suryāni, Ishāq Armalah. See Armalah.

Tarrāzi, Fikūnt Filib di. See Tarrāzi, Filib.

Tarrāzi, Filib. *Asdaq mā-Kān 'āw Ta'rikh Lubnān, wa-Safha min Akhbār al-Suryān.* 2 vols. Beirut, 1948.

———. *'Asr al-Suryān al-Dhahabi: Bahath 'Ilmi Ta' rikhi Atharī.* Beirut, 1946.

———. *Khazā'in al-Kutub al-'Arabiyah fi al-Khāfiqin.* 2 vols. Beirut, n.d.

———. *al-Salāsil al-Ta' rikhiyah.* Beirut, 1910.

Tūma, Mār Siwariyūs Ya'qūb. *Ta'rikh al-Kanisat al-Suryāniyah al-Hindiyah.* Beirut, 1951.

al-'Umari, Munyat al-'Udabā' fi Ta'rikh al-Mawsil al-Hadbā'. Mosul, 1955.

Middle-Eastern Sources: Articles

Afrām I. See Barsūm.

Afrām II, Ighnātiyūs. "Dayr Mār Matta. . . ," al-Shaykh wa-Dayr Mār Bahnam al-Shahid fi Jawār al-Mawsil," *Majallat al Athār al-Sharqiyah* 3 (1928), 11-22, 35-44.

Afram III, Ighnātiyūs. "Athar al-Suryāniyah fi al-Thaqāfat al-'Arabiyah," *M.B.* 1 (1962), 403-13.

Afrām, Fu'ād. "al-Kindi wa-al-Suryāniyah," *M.B.* 2 (December 1963), 91-95.

Allah-Wardi, Mikhā' il. "Hall Qadiyat al-Falastin," *M.B.* 7 (1969), 369-76.

Armalah,Ishāq. "Fi al-Baṭaryarkīyat al-Anṭākiyah," al-Mashriq 21 (1923), 494-507; 589-99; 660-71.

_____. "Naṣāra Ghassān wa-al-Suryān," al Mashriq 58 (1964), 377-96.

_____. "Siyāhah fi Ṭūr 'Abdin," al-Mashriq 16 (1913), 561-78, 662-75, 739-54, 835-54.

_____. 'al-Suryān fi al-Quṭr al-Maṣri," al-Mashriq 23 (1925), 741-55, 810-17.

_____. "al-Ṭā' ifah al-Suryāniyah wa-al-Qunṣuliyah al-Faransāwiyah fi Baghdad," al-Mashriq 24 (Feb. 1926), 99-113.

Ayyūb, Barṣum Yusuf. "al-'Aṣārat al-Naqiyah fi Ta' rikh al-Kanisat al-Suryāniyah al-Hindiyah," M.B. 12 (1974), 95-103.

Babū Ishāq, Rufā'il. "Mahallat al-Shammāsiyah bi-Baghdad fi 'Ahd al-Khilāfat al-'Abbāsiyah," Sumer, A Journal of Archaeology in Iraq 9 (1953), 132-54.

Barsūm, Mār Ighnāṭiyūs Afrām I. "Al-Alfāẓ al-Suryāniyah fi al-Ma'ājim al-'Arabiyah," Révue de l'Académie Arab de Damas 23 (1948), 161-82, 321-46, 481-506; 24 (1949), 3-21, 161-81, 321-42, 481-99; 25 (1950), 2-22, 161-78, 364-98.

_____. "Naṣrāniyat al-'Arab," M.B. 7 (April 1969), 297-99.

Barṣūm, Siwāriyus Afrām. "Hal Kāna Ghrighūriyus Ibn al-'Ibri min Jins Yahū di?" al-Hikmah (St. Mark, Jerusalem), January 1927.

Al-Barṭalli, Abu Naṣr. "al-Rukn al-Ta'rikhi, Baṭārikat al-Sharq," M.B. 7 (January 1969), 135-42.

Būlus, Ghrighūriyus. "Ta 'qib Ta' rikhi fi Nasab al-'Allāmah Mār Ghrighūriyus Ibn al-'Ibri," M.B. 2 (January 1963), 146-48.

Chaiko, L. See Shaykhu.

Dannu, Ni'mat-Allah. "al-Ya'qūbiyah Na'at Dakhil 'Ala Kanisatina al-Suryāniyah," M.B. 2 (1963), 83-90.

Dulabāni, Yūhanna. "al-Suryān fi Falasṭin wa-Dayr Maryam al-Majdaliyah," al-Hikmah, July 1928.

Hubayqah, Yūsuf. See al-Lubnāni, Y.H.

"Ibn al-'Ibri" (pen-name). "Lamhah Ta 'rikhiyah: al-Ṭā'ifah al-Suryāniyah fi 'Ashr Sanawāt," al-Hikmah 3 (Feb. 1929), 66-72; (April-May 1929), 113-128.

Īsa, Razzūq. "al-Kanisah al-Suryāniyah (fi Baghdād)," Majallat Nashrat al-'Ahhad (Baghdad) 4 (1925), 827-34.

_____. "Nabdhat fi Ta' rikh al-Madrasah al-Suryāniyah al-Baghdādiyah," Majallat Nashrat al-'Ahhad (Baghdad) 13 (1934), 182-92.

al-Khūri, Tūma. "Dawr al-Lughat al-Suryāniyah fi al-Adab, wa-al-Falsafah, wa-al-Din," M.B. 1 (1963), 458-62.

Lammens, Henri. "al-Rūm al-Malakiyūn-Nabdhat fi Aṣlihim wa-Jinsiyatihim," al-Mashriq 3 (1900), 267-73.

al-Lubnāni, Yūsuf Hubayqah. "al-Dawāthir al-Suryāniyah fi Lubnān wa-Sūriyah," al-Mashriq 37 (1939), 290-412.

Marhaba, Muhammad 'Abd al-Rahmān. "Jami' al-Thaqāfāt Tatalāqa," al-'Arabi (Kuwayt) 36 (1961), 20-24.

Munajjid, Ṣalāh al-Din. "Manāzil al-Qabā'il al-'Arabiyah Hawl Damashq," Majallat Majma' al-'Ilmi al-'Arabi 30 (1955).

al-Nakadi, 'Ārif. "al-Islām fi Naẓar al-Gharb," Majallat Majma' al-Lughat *al-'Arabiyah* (Damascus) 36 (1961), 299-302.

Ni'mat-Allah al-Suryāni, Ighnātiyus. "Risālat al-Baṭrak Ighnātiyūs Ni'mat-Allah al-Suryāni," trans. from Syriac by Yūhanna 'Azzu, *al-Mashriq* 31 (1933), 613-23, 730-37, 831-38.

Qāsha, Suhayl. "Ahwāl Naṣāra al-'Irāq fi al-'Aṣr al-'Abbāsi," *M.B.* 7 (1969), 472-79.

————. "al-Lughat al-'Arabiyah Lada Naṣāra al-'Irāq," *M.B.* 7 (1969), 356-64.

————. "Mawqif al-Khulafā' al-Muslimin min Naṣāra al-'Irāq," *M.B.* 13, no. 121 (1975), 21-25 to 13, no. 130 (1975), 584-86.

Shabakah, Mahmūd M. "Qarārāt Hukamā' Sahyūn," *Majallat al-Azhar* 39, no. 2 (1967), 163-66; no. 4, 252-55; no. 5, 445-48.

al-Shaṭṭi, Ahmad Shawkat. "al-Suryān wa-Atharuhum fi al-Hadārat al 'Arabiyah al-Islāmiyah," *M.B.* 3 (1965), 550-54.

Shaykhū, Luwis, "Ghrighūriyus Abu al-Faraj al-Ma' rūf bi-al-Ibn al-'Ibri," *al-Mashriq* 1 (1898), 289-95; 365-70; 413-18; 449-53; 505-10; 555-61; 605-12.

al-Suryāni, Ishāq Armalah. See Armalah.

Ya'qūb III, Ighnāṭiyūs. "al-Kindi wa-al-Suryāniyah," *M.B.* 1 (1963), 255-67.

————. "al-Rukn al-Ta'rikhi - 'Allāmatuna Ghrighūriyus Ibn al-'Ibri," *M.B.* 2 (1964), 302-10.

————. "al-Kanisat al-Suryāniyah al-Hindiyah fi al-Qarn al-'Ashrin," *M.B.* 3 (1965), 524-43.

————. "Bayt Yuhanna Marqūs, Awwal Kanisa Masihiyah," *M.B.* 2 (1964), 351-54.

Zayyāt, Habib. "al-Rūm al-Malakiyūn fi al-Islām" *al-Mashriq* 47 (1953), 273-80; 401-22; 689-725.

General Sources

Western Sources: Books

Adamson, David Grant. *The Kurdish War.* New York: 1965.

Addison, James T. *The Christian Approach to the Moslem.* New York: 1942.

————. *The Episcopal Church in the United States, 1789-1931.* New York: 1951.

Adeny, Walter F. *The Greek and Eastern Churches.* New York: 1908.

Agur, C. M. *Church History of Travancore.* Madras: 1903.

Ainsworth, William F. *A Personal Narrative of the Euphrates Expedition.* London: 1888.

Ancel, Jacques. *Peuples et nations des Balkans.* Paris: 1926.

Anderson, Rufus. *History of the Missions of the American Board of Commissioners for Foreign Missions to the Oriental Churches.* 2 vols. Boston: 1872.

————. *Mr. Southgate and the Missionaries at Constantinople: A Letter from the Missionaries at Constantinople in Reply to Charges by Reverend Horatio Southgate.* Boston: 1844.

Andrews, Charles W. *Historical Notes of Protestant Missions to Oriental Churches.* Richmond, Va.: 1866.

Arberry, A. J., ed. *Religion in the Middle East: Three Religions in Concord and Conflict.* 2 vols. London: 1969.

Arfa, Hassan. *The Kurds, an Historical and Political Study.* London: Oxford University Press, 1966.

Arnold, T. W. *The Preaching of Islam.* New York: 1913.

Arpee, Leon. *The Armenian Awakening: A History of the Armenian Church, 1820-1860.* Chicago: 1909.

———. *A History of Armenian Christianity.* New York: 1946.

Atiya, Aziz S. *History of Eastern Christianity.* South Bend, Ind.: 1968.

Attwater, Donald. *The Christian Churches of the East.* 2 vols. Milwaukee, Wis. 1947-48.

Ayrout, Henry. *Catholics in Egypt.* Cairo: 1950.

Bacon, Francis D. *Eastern Pilgrimage.* London: 1944.

Badger, G. P. *The Nestorians and Their Rituals.* 2 vols. London: 1852.

Bailey, Frank Edgar. *British Policy and the Turkish Reform Movement: A Study in Anglo-Turkish Relations, 1826-1853.* Cambridge, Mass.: 1942.

Banfield, Edward C. *The Moral Basis of a Backward Society.* Glencoe, Ill.: 1958.

Barker, Edward B. B. *Syria and Egypt under the Last Five Sultans of Turkey; Being the Experiences, during the Fifty Years, of Mr. Consul-General Barker.* London: 1876.

Baron, Salo W. *A Social and Religious History of the Jews,* vol. 3. New York: 1952.

Barth, Fredrik. *Principles of Social Organization in Southern Kurdistan.* Oslo: 1953.

Barton, James L. *Daybreak in Turkey.* Boston: 1908.

———. *The Treaty Rights of American Missionaries in Turkey.* Boston: 1893.

Batch, Georges. *Statut personnel, introduction a l'étude de la condition juridique des chrétiens de Palestine sous la domination Ottomane, 1517-1917.* Rome: 1963.

Baumstark, A. *Geschichte der Syrischen literatur.* Bonn: 1922.

Baynes, Norman J., and Miss, H. St. L. B., eds. *Byzantium; an Introduction to East Roman Civilization.* Oxford: 1948.

Bedjan, Paul. *Acta martyrum sanctorum.* 2 vols. Leipzig: 1890.

Bell, Gertrude Lowthian. *Amurath to Amurath.* London: 1911.

Benjamin, Israel Joseph. *Eight Years in Asia and Africa, from 1846-1855.* Hannover: 1859.

Benni, Cyril Behnam. *The Tradition of the Syriac Church of Antioch Concerning the Primacy and the Prerogatives of St. Peter and of His Successors the Roman Pontiffs,* trans. Rev. Joseph Gagliardi. London: 1871.

Betts, Robert B. *Christians in the Arab East.* Atlanta, Ga.: 1978.

Bihlmeyer, Karl. *Church History.* 3 vols. Westminster, Md.: 1958-66.

Birks, Herbert. *The Life and Correspondence of Thomas Valpy French, First Bishop of Lahore,* vol. 2. London: 1895.

Bliss, Edwin M. *Turkey and the Armenian Atrocities.* n.p., 1896.

Bliss, Frederick J. *The Religions of Modern Syria and Palestine.* New York: 1912.

Bridgeman, Charles T. *The Episcopal Church and the Middle East.* New York: 1958.

Brown, L. W. *The Indian Christians of St. Thomas.* Cambridge: 1956.

Browne, L. E. *The Eclipse of Christianity in Asia—from the Time of Mohammed till the Fourteenth Century.* New York: 1967.

Bruneau, André. *Traditions et politique de la France au Levant.* Paris: 1932.

Buchthal, H. *The Painting of the Syrian Jacobites in its Relation to Byzantine and Islamic Art.* Paris: 1939.

Buckingham, James Silk. *Travels in Mesopotamia.* London: 1827.

Budge, E. A. Wallis. *By Nile and Tigris (1866-1913),* vol. 1. London: 1920.

_____. ed. and trans. *The Histories of Rabban Hôrmîzd the Persian and Rabban Bar-'Idtâ.* 2 vols. London: 1902.

Burckhardt, John Lewis. *Travels in Syria and The Holy Land.* London: 1822.

Burton, Katherine. *Difficult Star, the Life of Pauline Jaricot.* New York: 1947.

Butler, Howard Crosby, ed. and completed by E. Baldwin Smith. *Early Churches in Syria, Fourth to Seventh Centuries.* Princeton: 1929.

Cahen, Claude. *Pre-Ottoman Turkey: A General Survey of the Material and Spiritual Culture and History, 1071-1330.* New York: 1968.

Campbell, J. Alston. *In the Shadow of the Crescent.* London: 1906(?).

Cardahi, G. *Bar Hebraeus's Book of The Dove Together with Some Chapters of His Ethikon,* trans. A. Wensinck. Leyden: 1919.

Carrington, P. *The Early Christian Church.* Cambridge: 1957.

Carne, J. *Syria, the Holy Land and Asia Minor.* London: 1842.

Cash, W. W. *Christendom and Islam; Their Contacts and Cultures Down the Centuries.* London: 1937.

Chabot, J. B. *Littérature Syriaque.* Paris: 1935.

Chamberlain, W. I. *Fifty Years in Foreign Fields.* New York: 1925.

Charles-Roux, F. *France et chrétiens d'Orient.* Paris: 1939.

Chopourian, Giragos H. *The Armenian Evangelical Reformation, Causes and Effects.* New York: 1972.

Cheikho, L. *La littérature Arabe au XIX' siècle.* 2 vols. Beirut: 1908.

Cheriyan, P. *The Malabar Syrians and the Church Missionary Society 1816-1840.* Kottayam, India: 1935.

Clair-Tisdall, W. St. *The Conversion of Armenia to the Christian Faith.* London: 1897.

Clark, Francis X. *The Purpose of Missions; A Study of Mission Documents of the Holy See, 1909 1946.* New York: 1948.

Coan, Frederick G. *Yesterdays in Persia and Kurdistan.* Claremont, Cal.: 1939.

Colbi, S. *Short History of Christianity—the Holy Land.* Jerusalem: 1965.

Connolly, R. H., and Codrington, H. W. *Two Commentaries on the Jacobite Liturgie.* London: 1913.

Coptic Orthodox Patriarchate. *St. Mark and the Coptic Church.* Cairo: 1968.

Cowper, H. Swainson. *Through Turkish Arabia.* London: 1894.

Cuinet, Vital. *La Turquie d'Asie. Géographie administrative statistique déscriptive et raisonnée de chaque province de l'Asie-mineure.* 4 vols. Paris, 1890-1900.

Curzon, Robert. *Visits to Monasteries in the Levant.* Ithaca, N.Y.: 1955.

Cutts, E. L. *Christians Under the Crescent in Asia.* London: 187-(?).

Da Casinale, Rocco. *Storia delle missioni dei Cappuccini,* vol. 3. Rome: 1873.

Daniel, K. *A Critical Study of Primitive Liturgies, Especially That of St. James.* Tiruvalla, India: 1948.

Dann, Uriel. *Iraq Under Qassem: A Political History, 1958-1963.* Jerusalem: 1969.

Da Silva Rego, António. *Le patronage Portugais de l'Orient aperçu historique.* Trans. from Portuguese by Jean Haupt. Lisbon: 1957.

Davis, Ralph. *Aleppo and Devonshire Square: English Traders in the Levant in the Eighteenth Century.* London: 1967.

Dawson, C., ed. and trans. *The Mongol Mission: Narratives and Letters of the Franciscan Missionaries in Mongolia and China in the 13th and 14th Centuries.* New York: 1955.

De Jehay, Frédérick von den Steen. *De la situation légale des sujets Ottomans non-muslmans.* Brussels: 1906.

De Vries, Wilhelm. *Rom und die Patriarchate des Ostens.* Munich: 1963.

De Baulx, Bernard. *Histoire des missions catholiques Françaises.* Paris: 1951.

Downey, Glanville. *A History of Antioch in Syria from Seleucus to the Arab Conquest.* Princeton: 1961.

Drower, E. S. *Water into Wine, A Study of Ritual Idiom in the Middle East.* London: 1956.

Duval, R. *La littérature syriaque.* Paris: 1900.

Dvornik, Francis. *The Ecumenical Councils.* New York: 1961.

Dwight, H. G. O. *Christianity in Turkey.* London: 1854.

———. *Christianity Revived in the East.* New York: 1850.

Dziob, Michael W. *The Sacred Congregation for the Oriental Churches.* Washington, D.C.: Catholic University of America Canon Law Studies, No. 214, 1945.

Edmonds, Cecil John. *Kurds, Turks, and Arabs; Politics, Travel and Research in North-eastern Iraq, 1919-1935.* Oxford: 1957.

E.S.A. *Eastern Churches, Containing Sketches of the Nestorian, Armenian, Jacobite, Coptic, and Abyssinian Communities.* London: 1850.

Etheridge, J. W. *The Syrian Churches.* London: 1846.

Etteldorf, Raymond. *The Catholic Church in the Middle East.* New York: 1959.

Evetts, B. T. A., and Butler, Alfred J., eds. *The Churches and Monasteries of Egypt: And Some Neighbouring Countries: Attributed to Abu Salih, the Armenian.* London: 1970.

Faris, Nabih A., and Hussein, M. T. *The Crescent in Crisis.* Lawrence, Kan.: 1955.

Fattal, Antoine. *Le statute légale des non-musulmans en pays d'Islam.* Beirut: 1958.

Fiey, J. M. Assyrie chrétienne. 3 vols. Beirut: 1967-68.

———. *Mossoul chrétienne.* Beirut: 1959.

Fletcher, J. P. *Notes from Nineveh.* Philadelphia: 1850.

Fortescue, Adrian. *The Lesser Eastern Churches.* London: 1913.

———. *The Orthodox Eastern Church.* London: 1911.

Fowler, George. *Three Years in Persia; Traveling adventures in Koordistan.* 2 vols. London: 1841.

Frend, W. H. C. *The Rise of the Monophysite Movement—Chapters in the History of the Church in the Fifth and Sixth Centuries.* Cambridge: 1972.

Gabriel, A. *Voyages archéologiques dans la Turquie orientale.* Paris: 1940.

Garbe, R. *India and Christendom: The Historical Connections between Their Religions.* La Salle, Ill.: 1959.

Garnett, Lucy M. J. *Turkey of the Ottomans.* London: 1911.

George, Munduvel V. *New Life in an Old Church.* Calcutta: 1963.

George, V. K. *The Holy Apostolic and Catholic Church of the East and Mar Nestorius.* Ernakulam, India: 1961.

Ghassemlou, Abdul Rahman. *Kurdistan and the Kurds.* Prague: Publishing House of the Czechoslovak Academy of Science, 1965.

Giamil, Samuel. *Genuinae relationes inter Sedem Aspostolicam et Assyriorum orientalium seu Chaldaeorum ecclesiam.* Rome: 1902.

Gibb, H. A. R., and Bowen, Harold. *Islamic Society and the West,* vol. 1, part II. London: 1957.

Gidney, J. B. *A Mandate for Armenia.* Kent, O: 1967.

Gildemeister, Joannes, ed. *Idrisii Palaestina et Syria.* Bonn: 1885.

Glazik, Josef P. *Die Islammission der russischorthodoxen Kirche.* Munster, Westf.: 1959.

Goodell, William. *Mr. Southgate and the Missionaries at Constantinople.* Boston: 1844.

Gorrée, Georges. *Pauline Jaricot, une läique engagée.* Paris: 1962.

Goyau, Georges. *La condition internationale des missions catholiques.* Paris: 1929.

_____. *Un prêcurseur: Francois Picquet, consul de Louis XIV en Alep et évêque de Babylone.* Paris: 1942.

Graf, Georg. *Geschichte der christlichen arabichen Literatur.* 4 vols. Vatican City: 1944-53.

Grant, Asahel. *The Nestorians; or, The Lost Tribes.* New York: 1845.

Grant, Christina P. *The Syrian Desert—Caravans, Travel and Exploration.* New York: 1938.

Greene, Frederick Davis. *Armenian Massacres or, The Sword of Mohammed* (n.p., 1896).

Griselle, Eugene. *Syriens et Chaldéens, leur martyrs, leur expériences.* Paris: 1918.

Grousset, R. *Histoire des croisades et du royaume Franc Jerusalem.* Paris: 1934.

Haddad, Robert M. *Syrian Christians in Muslim Society, an Interpretation.* Princeton, N. J.: 1970.

Hage, Wolfgang. *Die syrisch-Jacobitische Kirche in früh islamischer Zeit nach orientalischen Quellen.* Wiesbaden: 1966.

Hairi, Abdul Hadi. *Shi'ism and Constitutionalism in Iran.* Leiden: 1977.

Hajjar, Joseph. *Les Chrétiens uniates du Proche Orient.* Paris: 1962.

_____. *L'Europe et les destinées du Proche Orient.* Paris: 1970.

Hamlin, C. *Among the Turks.* New York: 1878.

Hansen, Henny Harald. *The Kurdish Woman's Life; Field Research in a Muslim Society, Iraq.* Copenhagen: 1961.

Hasluck, F. W. *Christianity and Islam Under the Sultans.* 2 vols. Oxford: 1929.

Hayes, E. R. *L'école d'Edesse.* Paris: 1930.

Hepworth, George H. *Through Armenia on Horseback.* New York: 1898.

Hickey, E. J. *The Society for the Propagation of the Faith.* Washington, D. C.: 1922.

Hitti, Philip K. *History of Syria, Including Lebanon and Palestine,* London: 1951.

_____. *History of the Arabs.* London: 1949.

_____. *Lebanon in History.* London: 1957.

Hogarth, D. G. *The Nearer East.* New York: 1902.

Honigmann, E. *Le couvent de Barsaumá et le patriarcat Jacobite d'Antioche et de Syrie.* Louvain: 1954.

Hourani, A. H. *Minorities in the Arab World.* London: 1947.

_____. *Syria and Lebanon: A Political Essay*. London: 1946.

_____. *A Vision of History; Near Eastern and Other Essays*. Beirut: 1961.

Hovannisian, R. D. *Armenia on the Road to Independence*. Berkeley, Cal.: 1967.

Hurewitz, Jacob C., ed. *Diplomacy in the Near and Middle East; a Documentary Record*. 2 vols. Princeton, N. J.: 1956.

International Bank for Reconstruction and Development. *The Economic Development of Syria*. Baltimore, Md.: 1955.

Ireland, Philip W. *Iraq: A Study in Political Development*. New York: 1938.

Jessup, Henry H. *Fifty-Three Years in Syria*. 2 vols. New York: 1910.

_____. *The Greek Church and Protestant Missions*. New York: 1891.

Joseph, John. *The Nestorians and Their Muslim Neighbors*. Princeton, N. J.: 1961.

Jowett, William. *Christian Researches in Syria and the Holy Land*. London: 1826.

Kane, Thomas a. *The Jurisdiction of the Patriarchs of the Major Sees in Antiquity and in the Middle Ages*. Washington, D. C.: Catholic Univeristy Canon Law Studies, No. 276, 1949.

Kawerau, Peter. *Amerika und die orientalischen Kirchen*. Berlin: 1958.

_____. *Das Christentum des Ostens*. Stuttgart: 1972.

_____. *Die jacobitische Kirche im Zeitalter der syrischen Renaissance, Idee und Wirklichkeit*. Berlin: 1955.

Kazemzadeh, Firuz. *The Struggle for Transcaucasia, 1917-1921*. New York: 1951.

Keay, F. E. *A History of the Syrian Church of India*. London: 1938.

Kerame, Oreste. *Unionisme, uniatisme, Arabisme chrétien*. Beirut: 1957.

King, Jonas. *The Oriental Church and the Latin*. New York: 1865.

Kinnane, Derk. *The Kurds and Kurdistan*. London: 1964.

Kinneir, John Madconald. *Journey through Asia Minor, Armenia, and Koordistan in the Years 1813 an 1814*. London: 1818.

Kirk, George. *Survey of International Affairs, 1939-1946*. Oxford: 1952.

Kleyn, H. G. *Jacobus Baradaeus, de Stichter der syrische monophysitische Kirk*. Leiden: 1882.

Krikorian, Mesrob K. *Armenians in the Service of the Ottoman Empire, 1860-1908*. London: 1977.

Labourt, J. *Le christianisme dans l'empire Perse sous la dynastie Sassanide (A.D. 224-632)*. Paris: 1904.

Ladas, S. P. *The Exchange of Minorities: Bulgaria, Greece,, and Turkey*. New York: 1932.

Lammens, Henri. *La Syrie*. Beirut: 1921.

Lane-Poole, Stanley. *The Life of Lord Stratford de Redcliffe, K. G.* London: 1890.

Latourette, Kenneth S. *The Nineteenth Century outside Europe*. Vol. 3 of *Christianity in a Revolutionary Age: A History of Christianity in the Nineteenth and Twentieth Centuries*. 5 vols. New York: 1958-62.

Laurie, Thomas. *Dr. Grant and the Mountain Nestorians*. Boston: 1874.

Leach, E. R. *Social and Economic Organization of the Rowanduz Kurds*. Monographs in Social Anthropology, no. 3. London School of Economics and Political Science. London: 1940.

Lee, D. E. *Great Britain and the Cyprus Convention of 1878*. Cambridge, Mass.: 1934.

Le Fur, Louis. *Le protectorat de la France sur les catholiques d'Orient.* Paris: 1914.

Leger, L. P. M. *Serbes, Croates et Bulgares.* Paris: 1913.

Leroy, Jules. *Monks and Monasteries of the Near East,* trans. Peter Collin. London: 1963.

Leslau, W. *Ethiopians Speak: Studies in Cultural Background.* Berkeley, Cal.: 1965.

Le Strange, G. *Baghdad during the Abbasid Caliphate.* London: 1924.

_____. *The Lands of the Eastern Caliphate: Mesopotamia, Persia, and Central Asia from the Moslem Conquest to the Time of Timur.* Cambridge: 1905.

Loeb, Laurence D. *Outcaste, Jewish Life in Southern Iran.* New York: 1977.

Longrigg, S. H. *Four Centuries of Modern Iraq.* Oxford: 1925.

_____. *Iraq, 1900 to 1950, a Political, Social, and Economic History.* London: 1956.

_____. *Syria and Lebanon under French Mandate.* London: 1958.

Luce, A. A. *Monophysitism Past and Present: A Study in Christology.* London: 1920.

Luke, Harry Charles. *Mosul and Its Minorities.* London: 1925.

Lynch, H. F. B. *Armenia Travels and Studies.* 2 vols. Beirut: 1965.

MacKenzie, G. T. *State of Christianity in Travancore.* Trivandrum, India: 1901.

Mann, Horace K. *The Lives of the Popes in the Middle Ages,* vol. 14. St. Louis, Mo.: 1928.

Mar Shimun, Surma d'Bait. *Assyrian Church Customs and the Murder of Mar Shimun.* London: 1923.

Marquart, J. *Südarmenien und die Tigrisquellen.* Vienna: 1930.

Mason, Alfred De Witt, and Barney, Frederick J. *History of the Arabian Mission.* New York: 1926.

McCoan, J. Carlile. *Our New Protectorate—Turkey in Asia.* 2 vols. London: 1879.

Meinardus, O. F. A. *The Copts in Jerusalem.* Cairo: Commission on Ecumenical Affairs of the See of Alexandria, 1960.

Mélia, Jean. *Chez les chrétiens d'Orient.* Paris: 1929.

Mikhail, Kyriakos. *Copts and Moslems Under British Control.* Kenikat, 1971.

Millingen, Frederick. *Wild Life Among the Koords.* London: 1870.

Mourret, F. *A History of the Catholic Church,* trans. Newton Thompson, vol. 7. London: 1955.

Mundadan, A. Mathias. *The Arrival of the Portuguese in India and the Thomas Christians under Mar Jacob, 1498-1662.* Bangalore, India: 1967.

Nalbandian, L. *The Armenian Revolutionary Movement.* Berkeley, Cal.: 1963.

Nansen, Fridtjof. *Armenia and the Near East.* London: 1928.

Nau, François N. *Les Arabes chrétiens de Mésopotamie et de Syrie du VII' au VIII' siècle.* Paris: 1935.

Neale, F. A. *Eight Years in Syria, Palestine, and Asia Minor.* 2 vols. (n.p., 1851).

Neale, John Mason. *A History of the Holy Eastern Church, the Patriarchate of Antioch.* 3 vols. London: 1847-1873.

Nöldeke, Theodor. *Sketches from Eastern History,* trans. J. S. Black. London: 1892.

Norman, C. B. *Armenia and the Campaign of 1877,* 2d ed. London: n.d.

Nouro, Abrohom. *My Tour in the Parishes of the Syrian Church in Syria and Lebanon.* Beirut: 1967.

O'Ballance, Edgar. *The Kurdish Revolt: 1961-1970.* London: 1973.

O'Hanlon, Douglas. *Features of the Abyssinian Church.* London: 1946.

O'Leary, De Lacy. *Arabia before Muhammad.* New York: 1927.

_____. *The Syriac Church and Its Fathers.* London: 1909.

Ormanian, Malachia. *The Church of Armenia—Her History, Doctrine, Rule, Discipline, Liturgy, Literature, and Existing Conditions.* London: 1955.

Palmer, Hurley Pring. *Joseph Wolff, His Romantic Life and Travels.* London: 1935.

Parkes, James. *Whose Land? A History of the Peoples of Palestine.* London: 1970.

Percy, Henry A. G. See Warkworth, Lord, M. P., under General Sources (Western Sources: Books).

Perkins, Justin. *A Residence of Eight Years in Persia, among the Nestorian Christians with Notices of the Muhammedans.* New York: 1843.

Piolet, J.B. *Les missions catholiques françaises au XIX siècle,* vol. 1. Paris: 1901.

Poladian, Terenig. *The Doctrinal Position of the Monophysite Churches.* Addis Ababa: 1963.

Pothan, Sri Sidney George. *The Syrian Christians of Kerala.* London: 1963.

Preusser, Conrad. *Nordmesopotamische Baudenkmäler altchristlicher und islamischer Zeit.* Leipzig: 1911.

Prime, E. D. G. *Forty Years in the Turkish Empire or, Memoirs of the Reverend William Goodell.* New York: 1876.

Raison, Jacob S. *Gentile Reactions to Jewish Ideals.* New York: 1953.

Raphael, P. P. *Le role des Maronites dans le retour des églises Orientales.* Beyrouth: 1935.

_____. *The Role of the Maronites in the Return of the Oriental Churches,* trans. P. A. Eid. Youngstown, Ohio: 1946.

Rassam, H. *Asshur and the Land of Nimrod.* New York: 1897.

Rhétoré, P. J. *Grammaire de la langue Soureth ou Chaldéen vulgaire selon le dialecte de la plaine de Mossoul et des pays adjacents.* Mossoul, Iraq: 1912.

Rich, Claudius James. *Narrative of a Residence in Koordistan and on the Site of Ancient Nineveh.* 2 vols. London: 1836.

Richter, Julius. *A History of Missions in India.* London: 1908(?).

_____. *A History of Protestant Missions in the Near East.* New York: 1910.

Robinson, Charles H. *History of Christian Missions.* New York: 1915.

Roncaglia, M. *St. Francis of Assisi and the Middle East.* Cairo: Franciscan Center of Oriental Studies, n.d.

Rondot, P. *Les chrétiens d'Orient.* Paris: 1955.

_____. *Les institutions politiques du Liban.* Paris: 1947.

Roux, F. Charles. *France et chrétiens d'Orient.* Paris: 1939.

Runciman, Steven. *A History of the Crusades.* 3 vols. Cambridge: 1953-54.

_____. *The Christian Arabs of Palestine.* London: 1969.

_____. *The Great Church in Captivity. A Study of the Patriarchate of Constantinople from the Eve of the Turkish Conquest to the Greek War of*

Independence. London: 1968.

Rycaut, Paul. *The Present State of the Ottoman Empire,* 2nd ed. London: 1688.

Sabatier, Paul. *Life of St. Francis of Assisi,* trans. L. S. Houghton. New York: 1894.

Sachau, Eduard. *Die Chronik von Arbela*. Berlin: 1915.

———. *Reise in Syrien und Mesopotamien*. Leipzig: 1883.

———. *Skizze des Fellichi-Dialekts von Mosul*. Berlin: 1895.

Sahas, Daniel J. *John of Damascus on Islam the "Heresy of the Ishmaelites."* Leiden: 1972.

Saleh, Zaki. *Mesopotamia (Iraq) 1600-1914, a Study in British Foreign Affairs*. Baghdad: 1957.

Sanderczki, C. *Reise nach Mosul und durch Kurdistan nach Urumia*. 3 vols. Stuttgart: 1857.

Sanjian, Avedis Krikor. *The Armenian Communities in Syria Under Ottoman Dominion*. Cambridge: 1965.

Sarkissian, Karekin. *The Council of Chalcedon and the Armenian Church*. London: 1965.

———. *The Witness of the Oriental Orthodox Churches: Recovery, Rediscovery, Renewal*. Beirut (?): 1968.

Schmidlin, Joseph. *Catholic Mission History,* trans. and ed. Matthias Braun. Techny, Ill.: 1933.

Schmidt, Dana Adams. *Journey among Brave Men*. Boston: 1964.

Scott, S. Herbert. *The Eastern Churches and the Papacy*. London: 1928.

Sédès, Jean Marie. *Histoire des missions françaises*. Paris: 1950.

Segal, J. B. *Edessa: "The Blessed City."* New York: 1970.

Seton-Watson, R. W. *The Rise of Nationality in the Balkans*. London: 1917.

Shahid, I. *The Martyrs of Najran*. Brussels: 1971.

Shaw, P. E. *American Contact with the Eastern Churches, 1820-1870*. Chicago: 1937.

Shaw, Stanford J. *History of the Ottoman Empire and Modern Turkey,* vol. 1, Cambridge: 1976.

———. Shaw, Ezel Kural. *History of the Ottoman Empire and Modern Turkey,* vol. 2. Cambridge: 1977.

Silbernagl, Isidor. *Verfassung und gegenwärtiger Bestand sämtlicher Kirchen des Orients*. Regensburg: 1904.

Simpson, John Hope. *The Refugee Problem, Report of a Survey*. London: 1939.

Smith, Eli. *Researches of the Reverend E. Smith and Reverend H. G. O. Dwight in Armenia: Including a Journey Through Asia Minor, and into Georgia and Persia, with a Visit to the Nestorian and Chaldean Christians of Oormiah and Salmas*. 2 vols. Boston: 1833.

———. *Toleration in the Turkish Empire*. Boston: 1846.

Socin, Albert, and Prym, Eugen. *Der neu-aramaeische Dialekte des Tûr 'Abdîn*. 2 vols. Gottingen: 1881.

Speer, Robert E. *Missions an Modern History: A Study of the Missionary Aspects of Some Great Movements of the Nineteenth Century*. 2 vols. New York: 1904.

———. and Carter, Russell. *Report on India and Persia: of the Deputation Sent by the Board of Foreign Missions of the Presbyterian Church in the*

U.S.A. To Visit These Fields in 1921-1922. New York: 1922.

Spuler, Bertold. *Die morgenländischen Kirchen.* Leiden: 1964.

Stanley, Arthur P. *Lectures on the History of the Eastern Church, with an Introduction on the Study of Ecclesiastical History.* New York: 1867.

Stock, Eugene. *The History of the Church Missionary Society.* 4 vols. London: 1899-1916.

Streit, Robert. *Catholic Missions in Figures and Symbols.* N.p., 1927.

Strong, William Ellworth. *The Story of the American Board: An Account of the First Hundred Years of the American Board of Commissioners for Foreign Missions.* Boston: 1910.

Suleiman, Michael W. *Political Parties in Lebanon: The Challenge of a Fragmented Political Culture.* Ithaca: 1967.

Sykes, Mark, Sr. *Dar ul-Islam, Record of a Journey through the Asiatic Provinces of Turkey.* London: 1924.

———. *The Caliphs' Last Heritage: A Short History of the Turkish Empire.* London: 1915.

Ter-Minassiantz, Edward. *Die Beziehungen der armenischen Kirche zu den syrischen bix zum ende des 6. jahrhunderts.* Leipsig: 1904.

Thomas, Navakatesh J. *Die syrisch-orthodoxe Kirche der südindischen Thomas-Christen.* Wurzburg: 1967.

Tisserant, Cardinal E. *Eastern Christianity in India.* New York: 1957.

Torrey, Gordon H. *Syrian Politics and the Military, 1945-1958.* Columbus, O.: 1964.

Toynbee, Arnold J. *Survey of International Affairs 1925,* vol. 1. London: 1927.

———. *The Western Question in Greece and Turkey.* London: 1923.

Tozer, H. F. *Turkish Armenia and Eastern Asia Minor.* London: 1881.

Tritton, A. S. *The Caliphs and Their Non-Muslim Subjects, A Critical Study of the Covenant of Umar.* London: 1970.

Tuchman, Barbara W. *Bible and Sword: England and Palestine from the Bronze Age to Balfour.* New York: 1956.

Vernier, Bernard, *L'Iraq d'aujourd'hui.* Paris: 1963.

Vööbus, A. *A History of Asceticism in the Syrian Orient: A Contribution to the History of Culture in the Near East.* 2 vols. Louvain: Corpus Scriptorum Christianorum Orientalium (Nos. 184, 197), 1958-60.

Vorgrimler, Herbert, ed. *Commentary on the Documents of Vatican II.* 2 vols. New York: 1967.

Vosté, Jacques. *Catalogue de la bibliothèque Syro-Chaldéene du couvent de notre-dame des semences près d'Alqoŝ (Iraq).* Rome: 1929.

Waddams, Herbert M. *Meeting the Orthodox Churches.* London: 1964.

Wakin, Edward. *A Lonely Minority: The Modern Story of Egypt's Copts.* New York: 1963.

Walker, Christopher J. *Armenia: The Survival of a Nation.* London: 1980.

Warkworth, Lord, M. P. (Percy, Henry A. G.). *Notes from a Diary in Asiatic Turkey.* London: 1896.

Warriner, Doreen. *Land Reform and Development in the Middle East: A Study of Egypt, Syria, and Iraq.* London: 1962.

Wensinck, Arent J., ed. *Legends of Eastern Saints, Chiefly from Syriac Sources.* Leyden: 1911.

Wheeler, C. H. *Ten Years on the Euphrates.* Boston: 1868.

Whitehouse, T. *Lingerings of Light in a Dark Land.* London: 1873.

Wilmington, Martin W. *The Middle East Supply Centre.* London: 1971.

Wiet, Gaston. *Baghdad; Metropolis of the Abbasid Caliphate,* trans. S. Feiler. Norman, Okla.: 1971.

Wigram, W. A. *The Separation of the Monophysites.* London: 1922.

_____. and Wigram, Edgar T. A. *The Cradle of Mankind: Life in Eastern Kurdistan.* London: 1914.

Williams, Gwyn. *Eastern Turkey: A Guide and History.* London: 1972.

Wismar, Adolph L. *Study in Tolerance: as Practised by Muhammad and His Immediate Successors.* New York: 1927.

Woodward, E. L. *Christianity and Nationalism in the Later Roman Empire.* London: 1916.

Wortabet, John. *Researches into the Religions of Syria or, Sketches, Historical and Doctrinal, of Its Religious Sects.* London: 1860.

Young, George. *Corps de droit Ottomun,* vol. 2. Oxford: 1905.

Zananiri, Gaston. *Pape et patriarches.* Paris: 1962.

_____. *Catholicisme oriental.* Paris: 1966.

Western Sources: Articles

Abu-Jaber, Kamel. "The Millet System in the 19th Century Ottoman Empire," *M.W.* 57 (1967), 212-23.

Ajamian, Bishop Shahe. "Brief Notes on the Armenian People and the Armenian Patriarchate of Jerusalem," *C.F.N.I.* 18 (Dec. 1967), 37-40.

Alexander, Y. "A Christian Church in search of peace in the Middle East," *International Problems* 10 (June 1971), 41-45.

Ambrose, Gwilyn. "English Traders at Aleppo (1658-1756)," *Economic Historical Review* 3 (1931-32), 246-67.

Americans for Middle East Understanding. "Church statistics for the Middle East," *Link* 4 (March-April 1971), 3.

Anawati, G. C. "The Roman Catholic Church and Churches in Communion with Rome," in A. J. Arberry, ed., *Religion in the Middle East,* vol. 1, pp. 347-422.

_____. "Vers un dialogue islamo-chrétien: Chronique d'islamologie et d'arabisme," *Révue Thomiste* 64 (1964), 280-326.

Anderson, John D. C. "The Missionary Approach to Islam: Christian or 'Cultic'," *Missiology* 4 (1976), 285-300.

Anderson, Thomas P., and Neusner, Jacob. "After the Six Days' War: Two Views on Jewish-Christian Dialogue," *Continuum* 5 (Winter 1968), 713-19.

Andrus, Alpheus N. "The Patriarch of the Jacobite Syrian Church," *M.H.* 91 (Jan. 1895), 9-11.

Antweiler, A. "Welteres zur islamisch-christlichen Zusammenarbeit," *Zeitschrift fur missions-wissenschaft* 42 (1958), 221-23.

Appleton, G. "Christian Encounter with Other Religions," *Frontier* (Summer 1959), 134-39.

Artinian, V. "The Formation of Catholic and Protestant Millets in the Ottoman Empire," *Armenian Review* 28 (1975), 3-15.

Assad, Maurice M. "The Coptic Church and Social Change in Egypt," *Interna-

tional Review of Missions 61 (1972), 117-29.

Attrep, A. " 'A State of Wretchedness and Impotence': A British View of Istanbul and Turkey, 1919," *International Journal of Middle East Studies* 9 (February 1978), 1-9.

Ayrout, H. H. "Melkites and the Mohammedans," *E.C.Q.* 4 (1940-41), 64-66.

Barnum, B. N. "The Turkish Government and Mission Schools," *M.H.* 84 (1888), 62-63.

Barnum, B. N. "The Kuzzel-Bash Koords," *M.H.* 86 (Aug. 1890), 343-46.

Bartlett, S. C. "Missions in Turkey," in his *Historical Sketches of the Missions of the American Board,* New York, 1972.

Barton, James L. "The Gospel for All Turkey," *M.H.* 119 (1923), 235-36.

Basetti-Sani, J. "For a Dialogue between Muslims and Christians," *M.W.* 57 (1967), 126-37.

Bashir, M. A. "The Syrian Church, the Jacobites," *Word* (Feb. 1957), 31-34.

Basil, Archbishop. "The Third Pan Orthodox Conference on the Island of Rhodes," *One Church* 19 (1965), 166-80.

Baumstark, A., et al. "Die literarischen Handschriften des jakobitischen Markusklosters in Jerusalem," *Oriens Christianus,* New Series 2 (1912), 120-36, 317-33; 3 (1913), 128-34, 311-27.

Bell, Gertrude L. "Churches and Monasteries of the Tur Abdin and the Neighboring Districts," *Zeitschrift fur Geschichte der Architektur* 9 (1913), 5-6.

Benz, Ernst. "Christianity and Other Religions in a Changing World Situation," *Journal of Church and State* 11 (1969), 205-19).

Bishop, E. F. F. "Jerusalem: Byways of Memory," *M.W.* 57 (1967), 33-41.

————. "Palestine or the Holy Land: Meeting Place of History, Geography and Faith," *M.W.* 59 (July, October 1969), 181-90.

————. "The Bhamdun Conference: 1954," *M.W.* 45 (1955), 37-44.

————. "What is the Place of the Old Testament in Christian Worship?" *Hibbert Journal* 52 (Jan. 1954), 134-40.

Bishop, Isabella L. "The Shadow of the Kurd," *The Contemporary Review* 59 (1891), 642-54.

Blakemore, William. "The Religious Realities of the Lebanese War," *Christian Century*, 6 Oct. 1976, pp. 832-37.

Bliss, Frederick Jones. "The Jacobite or Old Syrian Church," in his *The Religions of Modern Syria and Palestine*, pp. 74-80.

Bliss, Edwin M. "Kurdistan and the Kurds," *Andover Review* 4 (1885), 16-32.

————. "Ma' lula and its Dialect," *Palestine Exploration Fund Quarterly Statement for 1890,* pp. 74-98.

Boré, E. "Statement Addressed to the Central Councils of the Society for the Propagation of the Faith," *Annals of the Propagation of the Faith* 8 (1845), 75-85.

Bowman, John. "The Debt of Islam to Monophysite Syrian Christianity," *Nederlands Theologisch Tydschrift* (Feb. 1965), 177-201.

Braaten, Carl E. "Modern Interpetations of Nestorius," *Church History* 32 (Sept. 1963), 251-67.

Briere, M., trans. "Histoire du couvent de Rabban Hormizd de 1808 a 1832," *R.O.C.* 15 (1910), 410-24; 16 (1911), 113-27, 249-54, 346-55.

Browne, L. E. "The Patriarch Timothy and the Caliph al-Mahdi," *M.W.* 21 (Jan. 1931), 38-45.

Bruning, James. "The Catholic Apostolate to Separated Christians in the Near East," *Unitas* 8 (Autumn 1956), 158-63.

Cahen, Claude. "Dhimma," *E.I.,* pp. 227-31.

Calian, Carnegie S. "Ecumenical Shift in the Middle East—Reflections on Protestant-Orthodox Relations," *Christian Century* 83 (1966), 1140-42.

Cameron, Kenneth Walter. "The Oriental Manuscripts of Horatio Southgate," *Historical Magazine of the Protestant Episcopal Church* 10 (March 1941), 57-61.

Chabot, J. B. "Les Evêques Jacobites," *R.O.C.* 4 (1899), 444-51, 495-511.

Chahin, Jean. "Les patriarches de l'église syrienne catholique," *E.O.* 1 (1897-98), 201, 203.

Charles, H. "Le Christianisme des Arabes nomades sur le limes," Paris, Bibliothèque de l'école des hautes etudes. *Sciences religieuses,* vol. 52, 1936.

Charon, C. "L'origine ethnographique des Melkites," *E.O.* 11 (1908), 35-40, 82-91.

Chaumont, M. L. "Les Sassanides et la christianisation de l'empire Iranien au III' siecle de notre ere," *Revue de l'histoire des religions* 165 (April-June 1964), 165-202.

Cheikho, L. "Autobiographie du Patriarche Ignace-Michel Djarwe," *R.O.C.* 6 (1901), 382-401.

Chorley, E. Clowes. "The Missionary March of the American Episcopal Church 1789-1835," *Historical Magazine of the Protestant Episcopal Church* 15 (Sept. 1946), 169-208; 17 (March 1948), 3-43.

Clark, W. "The Kurdish Tribes of Western Asia," *New Englander & Yale Review* 23 (January 1864), 28-49.

Colles, B. E. "Muslim Sufism and Syrian Christian Mysticism," *Proceedings and Papers of the 11th Australian Universities Language and Literature Association* (1967), pp. 36-49.

_____. "The Place of Syrian Christian Mysticism in Religious History," *Journal of Religious History* 5 (June 1968), 1-15.

Cummins, J. S. "The Suppression of the Jesuits, 1773," *History Today* 23 (Dec. 1973), 839-48.

Dajani-Shakeel, Hadia. "Displacement of the Palestinians during the Crusades," *M.W.* 68 (1978), 157-75.

Daniel, Norman. "Islam: Some Recent Developments in the Attitude of Christians Towards Islam," *E.C.Q.* 13 (1959-1960), 154-66.

Dauphin, Claudine. "Situation actuelle des communautés chrétiennes du Tur 'Abdin (Turquie Orientale), *P.O.C.* (1972), pp. 323-27.

_____. "The Rediscovery of the Nestorian Churches of the Hakkari (South Eastern Turkey)," *E.C.R.* 8 (1976), 56-67.

Davison, Roderic H. "Turkish Attitudes Concerning Christian-Muslim Equality in the Nineteenth Century," *American Historical Review* 59 (1954), 844-64.

Delaporte, L. "Malatia," *Révue hittite et asiatique* 2 (1932-1934), 259-85.

De Villard, Ugo Monneret. "Le chiese della Mesopotamia," *Orientalia christiana analecta,* No. 128 (Rome 1940).

De Vitry, J. "A History of Early Jerusalem,' in *Extracts from Aristeas,*

Hecataeus, Origen, and Early writers, ed. and trans. A. Stewart, London, 1895, pp. 72-89.

De Vries, Wilhelm, "The Origin of the Eastern Patriarchates and Their Relationship to the Power of the Pope," trans. Rev. F. Charles Rooney, *One in Christ* 2 (1966), 50-69.

_____. "The Eastern Patriarchates and Their Relationship to the Power of the Pope," trans. Rev. F. Charles Rooney, *One in Christ* 2 (1966), 130-42.

_____. "Dreihundert jahre syrisch-katholische Hierarchie," *Ostkirchlche Studien* 5 (1956), 137-57.

_____. "Sakramententheologie bei den syrischen Monophysiten," *Orientalia Christiana analecta* (Rome), No. 125 (1940).

Dhunes, E. "Les congrégations françaises en Palestine, *E.O.* 8 (1905), 90-99, 166-74.

Dicey, Edward. "Nubar Pasha and Our Asian Protectorate," *Nineteenth Century* (Sept. 1878), 548-59.

Dickson, Bertram. "Journeys in Kurdistan," *Geographical Journal* 35 (April 1910), 357-79.

Dodge, Bayard, "The Settlement of the Assyrians on the Khabbur," *R.C.A.S.J.* 27 (1940), 301-20.

Dominian, Leon. "The Peoples of Northern Central Asiatic Turkey," *Bulletin of the American Geographical Society* (New York) 47 (1915), 832-71.

Dorman, H. G. "Churches and Missions in the Near East," *International Review of Missions* (Jan. 1962), 42-49.

Douglas, J. A. "The Survivors of a Lost Christendom," *Review of the Churches* 3 (April 1926), 221-33.

Duguid, Stephen. "The Politics of Unity: Hamidian Policy in Eastern Anatolia," *Middle Eastern Studies* 9 (May 1973), 139-55.

Duval, R. "Histoire politique, religieuse et littéraire d'Edesse jusqu'a la premiere croisade," *Journal asiatique* 8th series, 18 (1891), 87-130, 201-78, 381-447; 19 (1892), 5-102.

Dyer, Gwynne. "Turkish 'Falsifiers' and Armenian 'Deceivers': Historiography and the Armenian Massacres," *Middle Eastern Studies* 12 (Jan. 1976), 99-107.

Eastern Statesman, An. "Contemporary Life and Thought in Turkey," *Contemporary Review* 37 (1880), 334-56.

Edelby, Neophytos. "The Ecumenical Role of the Eastern Bishops in the Vatican Council," *E.C.R.* 1 (Spring 1966), 12-18.

Elisee de la Nativite, O.C.D. "Deux siècles de vie chrétienne a Bagdad, 1721-1921," *R.H.M.* 13 (1936), 357-70; 14 (1937), 91-107,, 246-57, 389j-94, 514-20; 16 (1939), 349-80.

Elphinston, W. G. "The Kurdish Question," *International Affairs* (London) 22 (1946), 91-103.

_____. "Kurds and the Kurdish Question," *R.C.A.S.J.* 35 (1948), 38-51.

Epstein, E. "Al Jezireh," *R.C.A.S.J.* 27 (1940), 68-82.

Every, Edward. "The Christian Arabs of Palestine" (book review of Steven Runciman's volume by the same title), *E.C.R.* (1970-71), 353-54.

Every, G. "Syrian Christians in Jerusalem 1183-1283," *E.C.Q.* 7 (Jan.-March 1947), 46-55.

_____. "Syrian Christians in Palestine in the Early Middle Ages," *E.C.Q.* 6 (July-Sept. 1946), 363-71.

Farah, Tawfic E. "Group Affiliations of University Students in the Arab Middle East (Kuwait)," *Journal of Social Psychology* 106 (December 1978), 161-65.

Faris, N. A. "The Muslim Thinker and His Christian Relationships," *M.W.* 47 (1957), 62-70.

Feitelson, Dina. "Aspects of the Social Life of Kurdish Jews," *Jewish Journal of Sociology* 1 (1959), 201-16.

Ferrier, R. W. "An English View of Persian Trade in 1618," *Journal of the Economic and Social History of the Orient,* 19 (1976), 182-214.

Fetter, George C. "A Comparative Study of Attitudes of Christian and of Moslim Lebanese Villagers," *Journal for the Scientific Study of Religion* 4 (Fall 1964), 48-59.

Fiey, J. M. "Tagrit, esquisse d'histoire chrétienne," *L'Orient syrien* 8 (1963), 289-342.

Forand, Paul G. "Accounts of Western Travelers Concerning the Role of Armenians and Georgians in 16th-Century Iran," *M.W.* 65 (Oct. 1975), 264-78.

Frazee, C. E. "The Formation of the Armenian Catholic Community in the Ottoman Empire," *E.C.R.* 7 (1975), 149-63.

_____. "The Maronite Middle Ages," *E.C.Q.* 10 (1978), 88-100.

Fry, E. J. B. "Melkites and Their Churches in Galilee and the Lebanon," *E.C.Q.* 3 (1938-39), 362-65.

Gabrielli, Francesco. "Greeks and Arabs in the Central Mediterranean Area," *Dumbarton Oaks Papers* 18 (1964), 64.

Garden, R. J. "Description of Diarbekr," *Journal of the Royal Geographical Society* (London) 37 (1867), 182-93.

Garzouzi, Eva. "Land Reform in Syria," *Middle East Journal* 12 (1963), 83-90.

George, A. R. "The Nomads of Syria: End of a Culture?" *Middle East International,* April 1973, pp. 21-22.

Germanos, Mgr. "The Greek Orthodox Patriarchate of Jerusalem," *C.N.F.I.* 18 (Dec. 1967), 22-26.

Gilbert, André, and Fevret, Maurice. "La Djezireh syrienne et son reveil économique," *Révue de géographie de Lyon* 5 (1953), 1-15; 83-100.

Goitein, S. D. "Jewish Society and Institutions under Islam," *Journal of World History* 11 (1968), 170-84.

Gollancz, Herman, ed. and trans. "Aperçu hilstorique sur la mission des Carmes déchausses a Baghdad (Orient)," *Chroniques du Carmél* 1 (1889-1890),, 140-43.

Gottheil, R. "An Answer to the Dhimmis," *Journal of American Oriental Society* 41 (Dec. 1921), 383-457.

Goyau, G. "Le role religieux du consul Francois Picquet dans Alep (1652-1662)," *R.H.M.* 12 (June 1935), 160-98.

_____. "Une capital missionaire du Levant: Alep, dans la premiere motié du XVII' siècle," *R.H.M.* 11 (June 1934), 161-86.

Graffam, Mary L. "On the Road with Exiled Armenians," *M.H.* 111 (1915), 565-68.

Gregoire, H. "Mahomet et le monophysisme," *Mélanges Charles Diehl* (Paris) 1 (1930), 107-19.

Guilday, P. "The Sacred Congregation de Propaganda Fide, 1622-1922," *Catholic Historical Review* 6 (1921), 478-94.

Haddad, William W. "The Christian Arab Press and the Palestine Question: A Case Study of Michel Chiha of Bayrut's *Le Jour,*" *M.W.* 64 (April 1975), 119-31.

Haim, S. "Aspects of Jewish Life in Baghdad under the Monarchy," *Middle Eastern Studies* 12 (May 1976), 188-208.

Hall, I. H. "On a Nestorian Liturgical Manuscript from the Last Nestorian Church and Convent in Jerusalem," *Journal of the American Oriental Society* 13 (1888), 1286-290.

Hall, William H. "Antioch the Glorious," *National Geographic Magazine* 38 (August 1920), 81-103.

Hamberger, J. "Les écoles Russes de Palestine et de Syrie," *E.O.* 8 (1905), 160-62.

Hambye, E. R. "The 'Syrian' Quadrilateral Today," *E.C.Q.* 14 (1962), 336-59.

_____. "A Syrian Orthodox Mission to Malabar in 1825-1826: Some Remarks," *Orientalia Christiana periodica* 34 (1968), 141-44.

Hamilton, Bernard. "The Armenian Church and Papacy at the Time of the Crusades," *E.C.R.* 10 (1978), 61-87.

Harb, Paul. "A Revival in the Lebanon of the Spiritual and Cultural Activity of the Early Syrian Churches," *E.C.R.* 1 (1966-68), 248-52.

Hardi, C. "Easter in Jerusalem in Ancient and Modern Times," *C.N.F.I.* 23, 152-57.

Harlow, S. R. "Community Life and Ceremonies of the Peasant Turk," *M.W.* 12 (1922), 248-62.

Havelock, H. N. "Constantinople and Our Road to India," *Fornightly* 27 (1877), 119-34.

Hendriks, Olaf, A. A. "L'activité apostolique du monachisme monophysite et nestorien," *P.O.C.* 10 (1960), 3-25, 97-113.

Hess, Andrew. "The Battle of Lepanto and Its Place in Mediterranean History," *Past and Present,* no. 57 (November 1972), 53-73.

Hieronymous. "Ancient Churches at Odds," *Jerusalem Post Magazine* (May 1970), 5.

Horner, Norman A. "Present-Day Christianity in the Gulf States of the Arabian Peninsula," *Occasional Bulletin of Missionary Research* 2 (April 1978), 53-60.

_____. "The Churches and the Crisis in Lebanon," *Occasional Bulletin of Missionary Research* 1 (Jan. 1977), 8-12.

_____. "Tur Abdin: A Christian Minority Struggles To Preserve Its identity," *Occasional Bulletin of Missionary Research* 2 (Oct. 1978), 134-38.

Hornus, Jean-Michel. "L'église assyrienne et la mission de l'archévêque de Cantorbery," *Le Monde non-Chrétien* 84 (1967), 3-13.

Hourani, A. H. "Christians of Lebanon," *E.C.Q.* 12 (Spring 1957), 135-44.

_____. "The Fertile Crescent in the Eighteenth Century," in his *A Vision of History; Near Eastern and Other Essays,* pp. 35-70.

Hovannisian, Richard G. "The Critic's View: Beyond Revisionism," *International Journal of Middle East Studies* 9 (1978), 379-88.

_____. "The Ebb and Flow of the Armenian Minority in the Arab Middle East," *Middle East Journal* 28 (1974), 19-32.

Iwas, Mar Severius Zakka. "The Doctrine of the Union of the Two Natures of Christ," *Greek Orthodox Theological Review* 10 (Winter 1964-65), 151-53.

Jacob, Xavier. "The Christians of South-East Turkey," *E.C.R.* 1 (Winter 1967-68), 399-401.

_____. "Die Christen im heutigen Syrien," *Stimmen der Zeit; katholische monatschrift fur das geistesleben der gegenwart* 196 (1978), 343-46.

Jensen, Peter Kincaid. "The Greco-Turkish War, 1920-1922," *International Journal of Middle East Studies* 10 (1979), 553-565.

Jessup, Henry H. "American Missions in the Turkish Empire," *M.H.* 90 (1894), 479-83.

Job, K. E. "The Homecoming of Syrian Schismatics," *Catholic World* 142 (Fall 1936), 605-8.

Karmi, H. "The Ecumenical Movement and Islam," *R.C.A.S.J. (July-Oct. 1965),* 263-66.

Karmiris, John. "The Dialogue Between the Orthodox and the Non-Chalcedonian Churches," *Go Ye* 7 Nos. 27-28 (1965).

Kedourie, Elie. "Religion and Politics: The Diaries of Khalil Sakkakini," *St. Anthony's Papers, Middle Eastern Affairs* 4 (1959), 77-94.

Keighley, D. Alan. "Israel as an Ecumenical Question," *London Quarterly and Holborn Review* 188 (Jan. 1963), 38-46.

Kelidar, A. R. "Religion and State in Syria," *Asian Affairs* 61 (Feb. 1974), 16-22.

Khalidi, Isma 'il R. "The Arab Kingdom of Ghassan: Its Origins, Rise and Fall," *M.W.* 46 (July 1956), 193-206.

Kiera, P. Joseph. "Baghdad und die Kapuzinermission," *Seraphisches Weltapostolat des Hl. Franz v. Assisi* 9 (1933), 33-42.

_____. "Mosul und die Kapuzinermission," *Seraphisches Weltapostolat des Hl. Franz v. Assisi* 9 (1933), 65-68.

_____. "Vor dem Kapuzinerkloster im Mardin," *Seraphisches Weltapostolat des Hl. Franz v. Assisi* 9 (1933), 65-68.

Klein, C. "Vatican and Zionism, 1897-1967," *Christian Attitudes on Jews and Judaism,* Nos. 36-37 (June-August 1974), 11-16.

Krajcar, J. "Turkey: A Graveyard of Christianity," *Worldmission* (Spring 1964), 64-72.

Kruger, P. "Das syrisch-monophysitische monchtum im Tur-Ab(h)din: von seinen anfangen bis zur mitte des 12 jahrhunderts," *Orientalia Christiana periodica* 4 (1938), 5-46.

Kudsi-Zadeh, A. Albert. "A Diary on Mesopotamia in 1906," *Die Welt des Islams* 13 (1971), 125-28.

Labourt, J. "Le patriarche Timothée et les Nestoriens sous les Abbasides," *Révue d'histoire et littérature religieuses* 10 (1905), 384-402.

Lammens, Henri. "A propos d'un colloque entre le Patriarche Jacobite Jean 1er et 'Amr Ibn al-'Asi," *Journal asiatique* 13 (1919), 97-110.

_____. "Notes de géographie ecclésiastique Syrienne," *R.O.C.* 8 (1903), 313-19.

Lapide, Pinchas E. "Ecumenism in Jerusalem," *Christian Century* (26 June 1968), pp. 839-42.

Laurent, J. "Des Grecs aux Croises: Études sur l'histoire d'Edesse de 1071 a 1098," *Byzantion* 1 (1924), 367-449.

Laurie, Thomas. "Khowaja Meekha, of Mosul," *M.H.* 78 (1882), 15-18.

Lewis, Norman N. "The Frontier of Settlement in Syria, 1800-1950," *International Affairs* 31 (1955), 48-60.

Lohre, N. J. "The Highlanders of Kurdistan," *M.W.* 10 (July 1920), 282-86.

Louis, T. R. P. "Mossoul, et la mission de Mésopotamie et du Kurdistan," in *Conference Proceedings of l'Apostolat Missionaire de la France,* 3rd series, sponsored by the Institut catholique de Paris par l'union missionaire du clerge (Paris, 1927), pp. 25-55.

Lowrie, Donald A., trans. "Missions and Imperialism" (from the *Great Soviet Encyclopedia*), in *Occasional Bulletin from the Missionary Research Library* 10 (15 August 1959).

Ludovicus, S. Teresia. "Histoire de la mission d'Alep," *E.C.* 6 (1921), 169-215; 7 (1922), 50-74.

Luke, H. C. "The Christian Communities in the Holy Sepulchre," in C. R. Ashbee, ed., *Jerusalem 1920-1922* (London 1924), pp. 46-56.

Maccoll, Malcolm. "The Christian Subjects of the Porte," *Contemporary Review* 28 (1876), 970-89.

Malikian, Levon, and Diab, Lutfy. "Group affiliations of university students in the Arab Middle East," *Journal of Social Psychology* 44 (1959), 145-59.

Malek, Zdenek. "Contemporary Islamic Education in the Secondary Schools of the Syrian Arab Republic," *Archiv orientalni* (Prague) 42 (1974), 1-15.

Malik, C. H. "The Orthodox Church," in A. J. Arberry, ed., *Religion in the Middle East,* vol. 1, pp. 297-346.

Malik, Gabriel. "The Spiritual Mission of Lebanon," *Worldmission* 3 (1952), 142-46.

Mansourati, Ignatius. "Kurze Darstellung der syrischen katholischen Kirche," trans. H. E. Klemens, *Der christliche Osten* 18 (1963), 117-18.

Maria-Joseph, A. S., Corde Jesu, C. D. "La mission des Carmes à Baghdad et l'influence française en Orient," *E.C.* 3 (1913), 293-317.

Martin, P. "Les premiers princes croises et les Syriens Jacobites de Jerusalem," *Journal asiatique* 8 (1888), 471-90.

Maximos IV. "Orient catholique et unite chrétienne: Notre vocation oecumenique," *P.O.C.* 10 (1960), 291-302.

_____. "Arab Countries," *E.C.Q.* 14 (1961), 58-61.

_____. "Latins, Orthodox and Eastern Catholics," *Word* 7, no. 2, 4-9.

_____. *"On the Institution of the Patriarchate,"* One in Christ 1 (1965), 74-77.

McAfee, H. "Anatolian Journey," *Yale Review* 3 (April 1914), 536-48.

McLeod, N. Bruce. "Christian-Muslim Dialogue: Toward a Wider Ecumenism," *Christian Century*, 18 Oct. 1972, pp. 1044-46.

Meinardus, O. F. A. "The Coptic Church in Egypt," in A. J. Arberry, *Religion in the Middle East,* vol. 1, pp. 423-53.

_____. "The Syrian Jacobites in the Holy City," *Orientalia Suecana* (Upsala) 12 (1963), 60-82.

Merrill, John E. "American Colleges in the Near East—a Summary," *M.H.* 117 (1921), 371-75.

Meyendorff, J. "Chalcedonians and Monophysites after Chaldecon," *Greek Or-*

thodox Theological Review 10, No. 2 (1964-65), 16-31.

Minorsky, V. "The Middle East in Western Politics in the 13th, 15th and 17th Centuries," *R.C.A.S.J.* 27 (1940), 427-61.

Montagne, M. Robert. "Quelques aspects du peuplement de la haute-Djezire," *Bulletin d'études orientales* (Damascus) 2 (1932), 53-66.

Munro, Danan Carleton. "Christian and Infidel in the Holy Land," *International Monthly* 4 (Nov.-Dec. 1901), 690-704, 726-41.

Murphy, J. J. W. "Historical Background of Christendom in the Middle East," *Studies* 47 (Summer 1958), 155-68; 47 (Autumn 1958), 269-84.

Najda, G. "Ahl al-Kitāb," *Encyclopedia of Islam.*

Nasrallah, J. *"L'église Melchite en Iraq, en Perse et dans l'Asie centrale: Les Melchites en Iraq et dans les provinces orientales, du califat Omayyade aux invasions mongoles,"* P.O.C. 26 (1976), 16-33.

Nau, F. "Dans quelle mesure les Jacobites, sont-ils monophysites," *R.O.C.* 10 (1905), 113-34.

———. "Lettre du patriarche Jacobite Jean X (1064-1105," *R.O.C.* 17 (1912), 145-98.

Neyron, Gustave. "Rome et les églises d'Orient," *Cahiers de l'est* 3 (1945), 31-40.

Nino, M. M. "The Situation of Minorities and of Christian Communities under Israeli Jurisdiction," *International Problems* 11, Nos. 3-4 (Dec. 1972),28-44.

Nicolle, David. "The New Jazira," *Middle East International* 28 (October 1973), 26-28.

Nolet, Yves. "An interview with the Syrian Orthodox Metropolitan of Baghdad." *E.C.Q.* 15, Nos. 3-4 (1963), 177-80.

Nolin, Kenneth E. "Truth: Christian—Muslim," *M.W.* 55 (July 1965), 237-45.

Norton, Thomas H. "Influence of an American College in Turkey, " *M.H.* 99 (1903), 297-98.

Panjikaran, J. C. "Christianity in Malabar with Special Reference to the St. Thomas Christians of the Syromalabar Rite," *Orientalia christiana analecta* 6 (1926), 93-136.

Parisot, R. P. Dom, "La Bibliotheque du Seminaire Syrien de Charfé, " *R.O.C.* 4 (1899), 150-74.

Pelliot, P. "Les Mongols et la papaute, " *R.O.C.* 23 (1922-23), 3-30.

Perlmann, M. "Notes on Anti-Christian Propaganda in the Mamluk Empire." *Bulletin of the London School of Oriental and African Studie* 10 (1940-42), 843-61.

Philibert de Saint-Didier, O. M. Cap. "En Syrie et Mésopotamie: La mission Capucine hier et aujourd'hui," *Missionaires Capucins* (Paris) 29, no. 133 (1949), 1-14.

Polycarpe de Marie-Joseph, C. D. "Mission des Carmes Déchausses en Mésopotamie," *Chroniques du Carmél* 1 (1889-90), 140-43; 2 (1890-91), 267-72, 305-10, 333-38.

Puyade, D. Julien. "Liturgie Jacobite et liturgie Syrienne catholique," *R. O. C.* 17 (1912), 258-67.

Rabbath, Edmond, "Esquisse sur les populations Syriennes," *Révue internationale de sociologie* 46 (Sept.-Oct. 1938), 443-525.

Rahhal, Stephen. "Some Notes on the West Syrians," *E.C.Q. 6 (July-Sept. 1946),* 372-81.

Reich, Sigismund. "Études sur les villages Arameens de l'anti-Liban," *Documents d'Études Orientales* (Paris) 7 (1938), 1-196.

Reid, Donald M. "Syrian Christians, the Rags-to-Riches Story, and Free Enterprise," *International Journal of Middle East Studies* 1 (Oct. 1970), 358-67.

Rios, Don Romanos. "Benedictine Contacts, Ancient and Modern, with the Eastern Churches, *E.C.Q.* 4 (1940-41), 244-55.

Rondot, Pierre. "The Minorities in the Arab Orient Today," *Middle Eastern Affairs* 10 (June-July 1959), 214-27.

Rowlands, J. "The Khabur Valley," *R.C.A.S.J.* 34 (1947), 144-49.

Russell, Alexander. "A Description of Aleppo, and the Adjacent Parts," in *The World Displayed* (London, 1762-90), vol. 13 (1774), 63-103.

Ryan, Arthur C. "Good Turks," *M.H.* 112 (Oct. 1916), 446-49.

Saab, Hassan, "Communication between Christianity and Islam," *Middle East Journal* 18 (1964), 41-62.

Safrastian, Arshak. "Armenian Thought and Literature Since 1828." *Asiatic Review* 26 (April 30), 331-36.

Salem, Elie A., "Lebanon's Political Maze: The Search for Peace in a Turbulent Land," *Middle East Journal* 33 (Autumn 1979), 444-63.

_____. "Nationalism and Islam," *M.W.* 52 (1962), pp. 177-87.

Salibi, Kamal S. "The Maronite Church in the Middle Ages and Its Union with Rome," *Oriens Christianus,* 4th Series, 6 (1958), 92-104.

_____. "The Maronites of Lebanon under Frankish and Mamluke Rule (1099-1516)." *Arabica* 4 (1957), 288-303.

Samuel, V. C. "The Real Point in Brief of the Fifth-Century Christological Controversy," *M.B.* 2 (March 1964), 387; (April 1964), 443; (May 1964), 500.

_____. "Were the Non Chalcedonian Churches Monophysite?" *M.B.* 2 (December 1963), 204-5.

Sandwith, Humphry. "How the Turks Rule Armenia," *Living Age* 136 (1878), 809-18.

Sarkiss, Harry J. "The Armenian Renaissance, 1500-1863." *Journal of Modern History* 9 (1937), 433-48.

Sarkissian, A. O. "Concert Diplomacy and the Armenians, 1890-1897," in A. O. Sarkissian, ed., *Studies in Diplomatic History and Historiography in Honor of G. P. Gooch (London, 1961), pp. 48-75.*

_____. "History of the Armenian Question to 1885." *University of Illinois Bulletin* 35 (1938), 11-151.

Sarkissian, Karekine. "Les églises orientales et l'unite chrétienne," *P.O.C.* 16 (1966), 105-12.

_____. "The Armenian Church," in A. J. Arberry, *Religion in the Middle East,* vol. 1, pp. 482-520.

Saunders, J. J. "The Decline and Fall of Christianity in Medieval Asia," *Journal of Religious History* 5 (Dec. 1968), 93-104.

Schwab, M. "Les non-musulmans dans le monde de l'Islam," *Revue du monde musulman* 6 (1908), 622-39.

Segal, J. B. "Mesopotamian Communities from Julian to the Rise of Islam," *Proceedings of the British Academy 41 (1955), 109-39.*

Seikaly, S. *"Coptic communal reform: 1860-114,"* *Middle Eastern Studies* 6 (Oct.

1970), 247-75.

Shattuck, Corinna. "The Massacure at Urfa," in F. D. Greene, *Armenian Massacres.*

Shahid, Irfan. "Ghassanids," *E.I.,* pp. 1020-21.

Shaw, Stanford J., and Shaw, Ezel Kural. "The Authors Respond," *International Journal of Middle East Studies* 9 (1978), 388-400.

Sherbowitz—Wetzor, Olgerd P. "The Holy See and the Oriental Churches in the Post-War Period." *Catholic History Review,* 23 (Jan. 1938), 427-45.

Shiel, J. "Notes on a Journey from Tabriz through Kurdistan to Sulaimaniyeh in July and August 1836," *Journal of the Royal Geographical Society* 8 (1838), 54-101.

Socin, Albert. "Zur Geographie des Tur-Abdin," *Zeitschrift der deutschen morgenländischen Gesellschaft* 34 (1881), 237-69.

Spiessens, C. L. "Les patriarches d'Antioche et leur succesion apostolique," *L'Orient syrien* 7 (1962), 389-434.

Spinka, Matthew. "The Effect of the Crusades upon Eastern Christianity," in John T. McNeil, et al., eds., *Environmental Factors in Christian History,* Chicago, 1939.

Spuler, Berthold. "Die west-syrische (monophysitische) Kirche unter der Islam," *Saeculum* 9 (1958), 322-44.

Stapleton, Ida J. "Shut Up in Erzroom," *M.H.* 112 (June 1916), 266-67;.

Stead, Blanche. "Kurdistan for Christ," *M.W.* 10 (1920), 241-50.

Streck, M. "Tur Abdin," *E.I.* [old edition] *Encyclopedia of Islam.*

Suliak, Hassan. "The Moslem States and the Vatican." *Unitas* 8 (Winter 1956), 225-31.

Swartz, Merlin. "The Position of Jews in Arab lands Following the Rise of Islam," *M.W.* 60 (1970), 6-24.

Sykes, Mark. "The Kurdish Tribes of the Ottoman Empire," *Royal Anthropological Institute of Great Britain and Ireland Journal* 38 (1908), 451-86.

Temperley, H. W. V. "British Policy towards Parliamentary Rule and Constitutionalism in Turkey, 1830-1914," *Cambridge Historical Journal* 4 (1933), 156-91.

Texier, Ch. "La ville et les monuments d'Edesse (aujourd'hui Orfa) en Mésopotamie," *Revue orientale et américaine* 1 (1859), 326-54.

Thwaite, Anthony. "Turkish Delights," *New York Times Book Review,* 19 August, 1979, pp. 13, 21.

Tournebize, François. "Le catholicisme a Alep au XVII siécle (1623-1703)," *E.C. E.C.* 3 (1913), 351-70.

Tritton, A. S. "Non-Muslim Subjects of the Muslim State," *Journal of the Royal Asiatic Society* (1942), 36-40.

Troll, Christian W., S. J. "A New Spirit in Muslim-Christian Relations," *Month* 6 (1973), 296-99.

Ullendorff, Edward. "Herbraic-Jewish Elements in Abyssianian Monophysite Christianity," *Journal of Semitic Studies* 1(1956), 216-56.

Vailhe, S. "Formation du patriarcat d'Antioche," *E.O.* 15 (1912), 109-14, 193-201.

Vasiliev, A. A. "Byzantium and Islam," in Norman H. Baynes and H. St. L. B.

Moss, eds., *Byzantium,* pp. 308-25.

Verghese, Paul. "The Ethiopian Orthodox Church and the Syrian Orthodox Church," in A. J. Arberry, *Religion in the Middle East,* vol. l, pp 454-8l.

———. "The Orthodox Churches-Chalcedonian and Non Chalcedonian," *E.C.R.* 1 (Autumn 1966), 136-4l.

Vidal, J. M. "La France et l'archévêche Latin De Babylone," *R.H.M.* 10 (1933), 321-71.

Villian, M. "Reflections on the Christian Communities of the Near East in Union with Rome." *E.C.Q.* 14 (1961), 119-25.

Voste, Jacques, M. "David, Clement-Joseph archévêque Syrien de Damas (23 mai 1829-4 anout 1890)," *Orientalia Christiana periodica* 14 (1948), 219-302.

Wakin, Edward. "Egypt's Christian Minority," *Christian Century* 81 (11 March, 1964), 332-34.

Warren, M. "Where Three Religions Meet,"*Frontier,* (Spring 1965), 41-44; (Summer 1965), 103-7.

White, George E. "One of the Races in Turkey, the Circissians," *M.H.* 101 (June 1905), 26-29.

Wirth, Louis, "Research in Racial and Cultural Relations," *Proceedings of the American Philosophical Society* 92 (November 1948), 381-86.

Young, H. E. Wilkie. "Mosul in 1909," *Middle Eastern Studies* 7 (May 1971), 229-35.

Zander, W. "Holy Places and Christian Presence in Jerusalem-a New Emphasis in the Attitude of the Catholic Church," *New Middle East* 34 (July 1971), 18-20.

———. "The Russian Church in the Middle East-New Developments," *New Middle East* 33 (July 1970), 36.38.

Zeidner, Robert F. "Britain and the Launching of the Armenian Question," *International Journal of Middle East Studies* 7 (1976), 465-483.

Zeitlin, Solomon, "The Ecumenical Council Vatican II and the Jews," *Jewish Quarterly* 56 (1965-66), 93-111.

INDEX

'Abbās, Shāh, 51
'Abd-Allah, Ignatius, 34
'Abd al-Majīd, Ottoman Sultan, 50
'Adb al-Masīh, 45
Acacian Schism, 6
Afghanistan, 128
Afrām I Barsoum, Ignatius, 104
Akhijān, Andrew: Patriarch of the Syrian
    Catholic Church, 40; consecrated
    Maronite bishop., 40; Ottoman edict
    confirming him patriarch of the
    Jacobites, 134-35
Aleppo, 167n.106; as a Christian
    city, 21-22; Jews in, 37; patriarchal
    residences in, 37; Catholic missions in,
    163n.29
Alexandria, Patriarchate of, 151n.30
'Ali, Muhammad, 56, 57
'Āmuda, 107
Anatolia: trade routes in, 89; exports of,
89
Antioch, 151n. 32,n.43
Antioch, Patriarch of, 7-8
Arabs: and the West after World
    War I, 120
Arabs, Christian, See Christian Arabs,
    Middle Eastern Christians
Armenian Catholics, 50

Armenians: interest in the Episcopal
    Mission, 60; favored by Missions,
    76;82; experience literary, national
    renaissance, 80; and treaties of San
    Stefan, the Congress of Berlin, 84;
    Young Turk honeymoon with, 94-5;
    Adana massacres, 1909,95; 1914-18
    evacuations and massacres, 96; Pro-
    claim Republic of Armenia, 99; and
    the Jacobites, 161n.83; and American
    Church Missions, 177n.14,17; and
    massacres of 1895-96, 91f, 180n.58;
    and post-World War I Turkey, 100; in
    post-World War I Syria, 106f
Asia Minor. See Anatolia
"Assyria, Assyrians:" origin of the name,
    150n.25
Assyrians: in Syria, 106, 187n.48
'Atshāna, 112

Badr Khan, 88
Baghdad: Syrian Catholics in, 52-3;
    Jacobites in, 115; Christian population
    of, 19th century, 169n.126
Bahnām I, Ignatius, 32
Bahnām, Mutrān: and Southgate mission,
    62f; and the Congregationalists, 70;
    anti-Protestant, 70